Course   Encounters in World History

Tom Sanders

United States Naval Academy

History

http://create.mheducation.com

This McGraw-Hill Create text may include materials submitted to
McGraw-Hill for publication by the instructor of this course.
The instructor is solely responsible for the editorial content of such
materials. Instructors retain copyright of these additional materials.

ISBN-10: 1121651151   ISBN-13: 9781121651159

Contents

Credits

CHAPTER 2

Creation–Origin Myths and the Mythic Mode of Thought

INTRODUCTION

In contemporary American usage, *myth* and *mythic* have very restricted and generally very negative connotations. For us, a "myth" is a more or less conscious lie. A candidate for political office, for example, in a campaign speech will assert that "My opponent claims that he will launch all these new programs without raising taxes. That is just a myth." The implication is that his opponent is either too dense to see the real facts or, more likely, is knowingly attempting to deceive the voters. The way that the terms *myth* and *mythic* are used by cultural anthropologists and students of comparative religions is profoundly different from this common contemporary usage. For them, myths function for human social organizations in much the same way that binary languages operate within computers: they encode a particular structure of understanding and functioning in the world and predicate and shape all social processes. The social anthropologist Bronislaw Malinowski, for instance, defined myth as a tale

> told in satisfaction of deep religious wants, moral cravings, social . . . requirements. Myth fulfills in primitive culture an indispensable function: it expresses, enhances, and codifies belief; it safeguards and enforces morality; it . . . contains practical rules for the guidance of man. Myth is thus a vital ingredient of human civilization; it is not an idle tale, but a hard-worked active force; it is not an intellectual explanation or an artistic imagery, but a pragmatic charter of primitive faith and moral wisdom[,] . . . a statement of a primeval, greater, and more relevant reality, by which the present life, fates and activities of mankind are determined. . . .[1]

Myth, then, provides a substructure of values and justifies and privileges specific types of behavior. The themes of this chapter are the mythic mode of thought and the way that myths structure and define human life.

Virtually every human society has generated myths to fill this human need to explain. In American culture, the story of George Washington and the cherry tree affirms the legitimacy of the American constitutional system by showing that its main founding father was constitutionally incapable of telling an untruth. Similarly, the myth of the frontier operates as a kind of deep background behind much of American consciousness. The frontiersman ethos lies at the base of everything from our eagerness to "be our own boss" to the names of sport utility vehicles, which all conjure up images of the "rugged individualism" of a people who "tamed the wild frontier." Understood in this way, myth is not something that is the cultural property only of humans in "primitive" civilizations, who are trying to understand the mystifying and threatening power of nature in the only ways that their limited understanding of science allows for. Rather, myth informs every human culture, from the earliest human social organisms to our present-day developed societies. In fact, it has been said that "nothing is really important until it becomes a myth."

One of the most fundamental of human desires is to explain where the world and humans came from. Human societies have used a variety of mythic forms to achieve this purpose. Tales that explain where the cosmos or the world came from are called creation myths, and those that relate how humans came into being or how a particular people came into existence are called origin myths. In addition, there are heroic tales that acquire mythic stature. The documents in this chapter represent three creation and origin myths and one mythic epic from four distinctive cultural traditions—the Mesopotamian, Hindu, Jewish, and Mayan cultures. The readings were selected from the vast array of creation and origin myths produced by different human societies, because they provide explanations not merely of how things came into existence but also why they coalesced into the particular social order and way of life that they did. As such, they are rich with significance about how different cultural traditions conceived of the proper way for humans to interact with each other, with the divine, and with the natural world.

The first document presented here comes from *The Epic of Gilgamesh,* a tale with very deep roots in the culture of Mesopotamia and the ancient Middle East. The tale in the form that we have it was transcribed as part of a general royal order by the Assyrian king Assurbanipal (668–626 BCE) to collect and record all the ancient literature of Mesopotamia. Lost for centuries, the story was rediscovered by European archaeologists in the nineteenth century, although there are still lines and sections missing. It is thought that there was in the third millennium BCE a great king of Uruk named Gilgamesh, but the main character in this tale is pure epic hero—going on quests, slaying monsters, even spurning the affections of the goddess of love. This tale is valued, however, not only for its heroic scale but also for its tragic aspect. Through that tragic dimension, it helps to explain aspects of human life, and it was undoubtedly so popular and widespread in the ancient world because of its implicit lessons.

The second texts are products of the ancient Hindu culture in India. Hinduism is a very ancient and multifaceted religious system that evolved over the course of about three millennia, starting around 2500 BCE. Because of its diversity, Hinduism has many creation stories. Roughly in the middle of that three-thousand-year process of development, a series of religious works known as Vedas ("Wisdoms") were composed. The "Purusha Hymn" included here is from the Rig-Veda, the first of the Veda texts, and it portrays the creation of the universe, the gods, and the human social order. The second Hindu text excerpted here is a later representation of the creation process in slightly different terms. It is from the *Code of Manu* from the second to third centuries CE, and it restates and reaffirms the values and structures of the "Purusha Hymn."

Our third source is the best-known creation story in the Western world. It comes from the book of Genesis, which forms the first part of both the Jewish Torah and the Christian Bible. Indeed, in English the word *genesis* means "origin" or "creation." From Genesis we have excerpted the story it contains of creation and the tale of the expulsion of Adam and Eve from the Garden of Eden. In addition, as a counterpoint to the tales of divine anger and destructive floods in the other cultural traditions presented in this chapter, the tale of Noah and the Flood is also included.[2] The tales are saturated with explanations for the human condition and with prescriptions for human behavior. Although these are familiar stories in the Western canon, reconsideration of them in this comparative context should shed new light on them.

Finally, we leave the Old World and present one of the oldest tales of pre-Columbian native culture. Popol Vuh is the sacred text of the Quiche Maya peoples. Although it is a very ancient tale, the form that has come down to us was recorded by an unknown Mayan intellectual or priest in the 1500s. It was written down, then, after the Spanish Conquest so that the old beliefs would not be lost. This was undoubtedly inspired by the vigorous Christianization of the Americas pursued by the Spanish and by the onslaught that native cultures endured as a result of Spanish political, military, and economic domination. According to the worldview of the Maya and of Popol Vuh, spiritual forces are deeply embedded in the world, and proper knowledge of them is necessary for successful life. Both the point of view and the tone of Popol Vuh differ from those of the other texts and traditions represented here. It is perhaps the most profoundly and thoroughly mythical of the four cultures.

All of these creation and origin stories explain why humans are the way we are and why we have such and such relationship with the gods, with nature, and with each other. The selections in this chapter were chosen because—in the words of Mircea Eliade—they "narrate not only the origin of the World, of animals, of plants, and of man, but also the primordial events in consequence of which man became what he is today—mortal, sexed, organized in a society, obliged to work in order to live, and working in accordance with certain rules."[3] Because of the sophistication and complexity of modern life, the significance of myths and of the mythic mode of thought is misunderstood and underappreciated. The readings in this chapter allow us to explore the diverse ways that humans have understood the basic spiritual and social structure of the universe. In addition, they are designed to deepen our understanding of the mythic orientation to reality and to enhance our appreciation of the "mythic" as a fundamental part of human existence.

CHAPTER QUESTIONS

1. What is the relationship between humans and the divine (God or gods) presented in these different religious texts? How are hierarchies of the relative authority, power, and value of the divine and human portrayed here?

2. List the aspects of human social order and existence—such as different relations between humans, how humans came to live the types of lives they lead, our relationship with nature—that you can identify in these texts. What do you think of these mythic explanations? What significant themes emerge from your list?

3. Some of these stories include destruction tales, as well as creation narratives. Identify the different reasons that the God or gods destroyed life. What do these reasons tell you about the human relationship to nature and each other?

4. In general, what can we conclude about the values attributed to gods from the stories presented here? How does a society's view of the divine affect its understanding of the human and natural worlds?

5. What common answers to the mysteries of spiritual and social life are presented in these myths? Which mythic understandings are most similar to each other and which most distinctive? Are the ideas about religious and social values and about the mythic mode of understanding presented in these texts relevant to your life?

A CREATION MYTH FROM ANCIENT MESOPOTAMIA

The first selection in this chapter is from the oldest epic poem in history, *The Epic of Gilgamesh,* a heroic tale of ancient Mesopotamia that became one of the best-known stories of the ancient Middle East. Mesopotamia formed the heart of one of the early centers of agricultural civilization. By 3000 BCE great Sumerian city-states dominated Mesopotamia, and the city-states in turn were dominated by military leaders, who ruled as kings. Gilgamesh was one of these military leaders, a *lugal,* or big man, of the city of Uruk around 2700 BCE. Although based on an actual historical figure, the character of Gilgamesh in this story assumed mythic proportions. By 2000 BCE it had become the most widespread story of the ancient world. The tale was told across the territory stretching from the headwaters of the Persian Gulf to the coast of the eastern Mediterranean. It has been found recorded in many different sites and languages, showing that it enjoyed enduring and extensive popularity.

As befits an epic figure, Gilgamesh was involved in all kinds of heroic adventures with his friend Enkidu, a wild man sent by the gods as a rival capable of absorbing Gilgamesh's excess energy. Eventually, they become too great for their station in life and become a challenge to the gods, who kill Enkidu as punishment. Beset by grief and fearful that he too must die someday, Gilgamesh sets out to get answers from Ut-napishtim, a Noah-like character, who had earned immortality himself. Ultimately, Gilgamesh's quest for immortality fails.

Gilgamesh and his story touch on many issues that are frequently present in creation and origin myths: the relationship between man and the gods, the distinction between civilized life and the wilderness, and the all-too-human subject of mortality. The selections included here contain the introduction to Gilgamesh, the creation and taming of his friend–companion Enkidu, Enkidu's dream vision of death, advice to Gilgamesh on how to live life, the Flood story, and Gilgamesh's search for immortality. Although it is not a creation myth, *The Epic of Gilgamesh* nonetheless contains complex explanations to thorny questions about aspects of human existence. As such, it both provides an encoded set of values and serves as a point of comparison with the other readings in this chapter.

QUESTIONS TO CONSIDER

1. Describe the relationship between the people of Uruk and their king, Gilgamesh. Were they proud of him and their city? What did they pray to the gods for?

2. The three modes of human existence by the time of the Gilgamesh tale were hunter–gatherer, pastoral, and agricultural. Based on the description of Uruk and of the taming of Enkidu, how were these modes of existence viewed by the Mesopotamians?

3. How does the Flood story here compare with the famous Flood story from Genesis? Compare the reasons for the Flood and the gods' reaction afterward with Yahweh's behavior in Genesis.

4. Compare the visions of life presented by Siduri and Ut-napishtim. In your opinion, which of them offers a better way of approaching life and death? Why?

5. What do you think explains the popularity of the Gilgamesh tale? What are its heroic aspects? What parts might appeal to the common man? Does any part of the story appeal to you?

THE EPIC OF GILGAMESH

Of him who found out all things, I shall tell the land,
Of him who experienced everything, I shall teach the whole.
He searched lands everywhere.

Source: From *Myths from Mesopotamia: Creation, the Flood, Gilgamesh, and Others,* trans. Stephanie Dalley, 50–56, 88–89, 95–116, 118–19, 150–51. Copyright © 1989 Oxford University Press, Inc. Used by permission of Oxford University Press, Inc.

He who experienced the whole gained complete wisdom.
He found out what was secret and uncovered what was hidden,
He brought back a tale of times before the Flood.
He had journeyed far and wide, weary and at last resigned.
He engraved all toils on a memorial monument the whole of stone. . . .
The story of that man, Gilgamesh, who went through all kinds of sufferings.
He was superior to other kings, a warrior lord of great stature,
A hero born of Uruk, a goring wild bull.
He marches at the front as leader,
He goes behind, the support of his brothers,
A strong net, the protection of his men, . . .
Son of Lugalbanda,* Gilgamesh, perfect in strength,
Son of the lofty cow, the wild cow Ninsun.†
He is Gilgamesh, perfect in splendour,
Who opened up passes in the mountains, . . .
Who crossed the ocean, the broad seas, as far as the sunrise.
Who inspected the edges of the world, kept searching for eternal life,
Who reached Ut-napishtim the far-distant, by force. . . .
There is nobody among the kings of teeming humanity
Who can compare with him,
Who can say "I am king" beside Gilgamesh.
Gilgamesh was named from birth for fame.
Two-thirds of him was divine, and one-third mortal.

Belet-ili‡ designed the shape of his body,
Made his form perfect, . . .
In Uruk the Sheepfold he would walk about,
Show himself superior, his head held high like a wild bull.
He had no rival, . . .

The young men complain to the gods, because Gilgamesh keeps them out on
    military campaigns.
The young maidens complain, because he won't leave them alone.

The gods often heard their complaints. . . .
They called upon great Aruru:§
"You, Aruru, create someone for him, to match the ardour of his energies!
Let them be regular rivals, and let Uruk be allowed peace!"
When Aruru heard this, she pinched off a piece of clay, cast it out into open country.

---

*The hero of two early Sumerian epic poems. Gilgamesh is sometimes indicated to be his son.
†Lugalbanda's wife. Also, the cow goddess.
‡Goddess of fertility.
§A Babylonian mother goddess.

She created a primitive man, Enkidu the warrior: offspring of silence, sky-bolt of
   Ninurta.*
His whole body was shaggy with hair, he was furnished with tresses like a woman,
His locks of hair grew luxuriant like grain.
He knew neither people nor country; he was dressed as cattle are.
With gazelles he eats vegetation,
With cattle he quenches his thirst at the watering place
A hunter . . . saw him . . . beside the watering place and was dumbstruck to see him. . . .
The hunter went off to see . . . Gilgamesh:
"There was a young man who came from the mountain,
On the land he was strong, he was powerful.
His strength is very hard, like a sky-bolt of Anu.† . . .
I am too frightened to approach him.
He kept filling in the pits that I dug,
He kept pulling out the traps that I laid.
He kept helping cattle, wild beasts of open country, to escape my grasp.
He did not allow me to work in the open country."
Gilgamesh spoke to him, to the hunter,
"Go, hunter, lead forth the harlot Shamhat, . . .
He will see her and go close to her.
Then his cattle, who have grown up in open country with him, will become alien
   to him."
The hunter went; he led forth the harlot Shamhat with him, . . .
And he, Enkidu, . . . satisfied his need for water with wild beasts. . . .
"Here he is, Shamhat, bare your bosom, . . .
Do for him, the primitive man, as women do. . . ."
Shamhat did for him, the primitive man, as women do.
His love-making he lavished upon her. . . .
When he was sated with her charms,
He set his face towards the open country of his cattle.
The gazelles saw Enkidu and scattered,
The cattle of open country kept away from his body.
For Enkidu had stripped; his body was too clean.
His legs, which used to keep pace with his cattle, were at a standstill.
Enkidu had been diminished, he could not run as before.
Yet he had acquired judgement, had become wiser. . . .
The harlot spoke to him, . . . "You have become profound, Enkidu, you have become
   like a god.
Why should you roam open country with wild beasts?
Come, let me take you into Uruk the Sheepfold,
To . . . Gilgamesh. . . . "

---

*God of thunderstorms and the plow. In some stories, he was the hero of climactic battles for order,
and he is sometimes equated with Marduk.

†God of heaven and chief god of their pantheon.

[After this, Enkidu encounters Gilgamesh in Uruk. They become fast friends and companions in fantastic adventures. They slay the terrifying monster Humbaba, who guards the pine forest in the north. Ishtar, the goddess of sex, is smitten with Gilgamesh and offers to marry him. Knowing that Ishtar quickly tires of her husbands and then inflicts horrible punishments on them, Gilgamesh rejects her. Insulted, Ishtar gets her father, Anu, the chief of the gods, to send the Bull of Heaven against Gilgamesh and Enkidu. But the two heroes kill the Bull of Heaven and insult Ishtar with part of its carcass. The gods decide they have gone too far and one of them must die: Enkidu. Enkidu has a dream, which foreshadows his death and which provides a picture of what happens after death.]

Then Enkidu wept, for he was sick at heart. . . .
He spoke what was in his mind to his friend.
"Listen, again, my friend! I had a dream in the night.
The sky called out, the earth replied.
I was standing in between them.
There was a young man, whose face was obscured.
His face was like that of . . . [a] bird.
He had the paws of a lion, he had the claws of an eagle.
He seized me by my locks, using great force against me. . . .
Like a wild bull he trampled on me, . . .
I cried out: "Save me, my friend, don't desert me!"
But you were afraid, and did not help me. . . .
He seized me, drove me down to the dark house, . . .
To the house which those who enter cannot leave,
On the road where traveling is one way only.
To the house where those who stay are deprived of light,
Where dust is their food, and clay their bread.
They are clothed, like birds, with feathers,
And they see no light, and they dwell in darkness.

[As Enkidu sickens and dies, Gilgamesh mourns and fears his own death. He decides to visit Ut-napishtim, who is legendary for wisdom and has attained immortality, to find the answers. To reach Ut-napishtim Gilgamesh must undertake a dangerous journey to the land beyond the realm of the living. He has various encounters along the way, one of which is with an innkeeper, who is actually Siduri, the goddess of brewing and wisdom. She advises Gilgamesh.]

The alewife spoke to him, to Gilgamesh,
"Gilgamesh, where do you roam?
You will not find the eternal life you seek.
When the gods created mankind
They appointed death for mankind,
Kept eternal life in their own hands.
So, Gilgamesh, let your stomach be full,
Day and night enjoy yourself in every way,

Every day arrange for pleasures.
Day and night, dance and play,
Wear fresh clothes.
Keep your head washed, bathe in water,
Appreciate the child who holds your hand,
Let your wife enjoy herself in your lap.
This is the work . . . [of] the living.*

[Gilgamesh perseveres and with the help of Ur-shanabi, the ferryman, he finally reaches Ut-napishtim.]

Ut-napishtim spoke to him, to Gilgamesh,
"Why are your cheeks wasted, your face dejected,
Your heart so wretched, your appearance worn out,
And grief in your innermost being? . . ."
Gilgamesh spoke to him, to Ut-napishtim,
"How would my cheeks not be wasted, nor my face dejected,
Nor my heart wretched, nor my appearance worn out, . . .
Enkidu my friend was the hunted mule, wild ass of the mountain, leopard of open
    country.
We who met and scaled the mountain,
Seized the Bull of Heaven and slew it,
Demolished Humbaba who dwelt in the Pine Forest,
Killed lions in the passes of the mountains, . . .
Enkidu my friend whom I love so much, who experienced every hardship
    with me—
The fate of mortals conquered him! For six days and seven nights I wept over him, . . .
I was frightened. I am afraid of Death, and so I roam open country. . . .
The words of Enkidu my friend weigh upon me. . . .
How, O how could I stay silent, how, O how could I keep quiet?
My friend whom I love has turned to clay:
Enkidu my friend whom I love has turned to clay.
Am I not like him? Must I lie down too,
Never to rise, ever again?" . . .
Ut-napishtim spoke to him, to Gilgamesh,
"Why do you prolong grief, Gilgamesh?
Since the gods made you from the flesh of gods and mankind,
Since the gods made you like your father and mother,
Death is inevitable at some time, both for Gilgamesh and for a fool. . . .
Why have you exerted yourself? What have you achieved?
You have made yourself weary for lack of sleep,
You only fill your flesh with grief,
You only bring the distant days of reckoning closer.
Mankind's fame is cut down like reeds in a reed-bed.

---

*This section comes from the Old Babylonian Version.

40 CHAPTER 2 ◆ Creation–Origin Myths and the Mythic Mode of Thought

A fine young man, a fine girl, . . .
Nobody sees Death,
Nobody sees the face of Death,
Nobody hears the voice of Death.
Savage Death just cuts mankind down.
Sometimes we build a house, sometimes we make a nest,
But then brothers divide it upon inheritance.
Sometimes there is hostility in the land,
But then the river rises and brings flood-water.
Dragonflies drift on the river,
Their faces look upon the face of the Sun,
But then suddenly there is nothing.
The sleeping and the dead are just like each other,
Death's picture cannot be drawn. . . .
The Anunnaki,* the great gods, . . . appointed death and life.
They did not mark out days for death,
But they did so for life."
Gilgamesh spoke to him, to Ut-napishtim the far-distant, . . .
"[Tell me] how you came to stand in the gods' assembly and sought eternal life?
Ut-napishtim spoke to him, to Gilgamesh,
"Let me reveal to you the secret of the gods. . . .
[T]he gods . . . decided [to] make a flood. . . .
Far-sighted Ea† swore the oath (of secrecy) with them,
So he repeated their speech to a reed hut,‡
"Reed hut, reed hut, brick wall, brick wall:
This is the message:
Man of Shuruppak, son of Ubara-Tutu,§
Dismantle your house, build a boat.
Leave possessions, search out living things.
Reject chattels** and save lives!
Put aboard the seed of all living things, into the boat.
The boat that you are to build
Shall have her dimensions in proportion,
Her width and length shall be in harmony,
Roof her like the Apsu."††
I realized and spoke to my master Ea,
"I have paid attention to the words that you spoke in this way,
My master, and I shall act upon them. . . .

---

*The first-born gods.

†God of fresh water, wisdom and magic; helper of mankind.

‡Ea uses the ploy of speaking to an inanimate object in a way that Ut-napishtim can overhear, in order to get around his oath that he would not reveal the coming Flood to humans.

§This is Ut-napishtim, son of Ubara-Tutu, king of the city of Shuruppak.

**Property.

††Apsu is the realm of fresh water under the earth, from which streams arise; the domain of Ea.

The Epic of Gilgamesh 41

I loaded her with everything there was,
Loaded her with all the silver,
Loaded her with all the gold
Loaded her with all the seed of living things, all of them.
I put on board the boat all my kith and kin.
Put on board cattle from open country, wild beasts from open country, all kinds of
  craftsmen. . . .
That hour arrived; . . .
I saw the shape of the storm,
The storm was terrifying to see.
I went aboard the boat and closed the door. . . .
For six days and seven nights
The wind blew, flood and tempest overwhelmed the land;
When the seventh day arrived the tempest, flood and onslaught
Which had struggled like a woman in labour, blew themselves out.
The sea became calm, the wind grew quiet, the flood held back.
[S]ilence reigned, for all mankind had returned to clay. . . .
The boat had come to rest on Mount Nimush.* . . .
When the seventh day arrived,
I put out and released a dove.
The dove went; it came back,
For no perching place was visible to it; and it turned round.
I put out and released a swallow.
The swallow went; it came back,
For no perching place was visible to it, and it turned round.
I put out and released a raven.
The raven went, and saw the waters receding.
And it ate, preened, lifted its tail and did not turn round.
Then . . . I made a sacrifice, . . .
The gods smelt the pleasant fragrance and . . . gathered like flies over the
  sacrifice. . . .
Ellil† . . . was furious,
Filled with anger at the Igigi‡ gods. . . .
"No man should have lived through the destruction!" . . .
Ea made his voice heard and spoke,
He said to the warrior Ellil,
"You are the sage of the gods, warrior,
So how, O how, could you fail to consult, and impose the flood?
Punish the sinner for his sin, punish the criminal for his crime, . . .

*[As Gilgamesh prepares to go back to the land of the living, Ut-napishtim tells him a
secret that promises eternal life. Gilgamesh gets it, but loses it again.]*

---

*A high mountain in modern-day Iraq.

†Main god of the second generation of gods (Igigi); his realm was earth.

‡The second generation of gods. Compare with Anunnaki, the first-born gods.

"Gilgamesh, . . . let me tell you the secret of the gods.
There is a plant whose . . . thorn, like a rose's, will spike your hands.
If you yourself can win that plant, you will find rejuvenation."
When Gilgamesh heard this, he . . . tied heavy stones to his feet.
They dragged him down into the Apsu,* . . .
He took the plant himself: it spiked his hands.
He cut the heavy stones from his feet.
The sea threw him up on to its shore.
Gilgamesh spoke to him, to Ur-shanabi the boatman,
"Ur-shanabi, this plant is a plant to cure a crisis!
With it a man may win the breath of life. . . .
Its name shall be: 'An old man grows into a young man.'
I too shall eat it and turn into the young man that I once was." . . .
At thirty leagues they stopped for the night. . . .
A snake smelt the fragrance of the plant.
It came up silently and carried off the plant.
As it took it away, it shed its scaly skin.
Thereupon Gilgamesh sat down and wept.
His tears flowed over his cheeks. . . .
"For what purpose, Ur-shanabi, have my arms grown weary? . . .
I did not gain an advantage for myself,
I have given the advantage to the 'lion of the ground.'"†

HINDU CREATION MYTHS

The second set of texts derives from the Hindu religious tradition. Hinduism, which developed in the Indus Valley region between 2500 BCE and 800 CE, is an extremely diverse religion that evolved from a mixture of two religious systems. One was the belief system of the pastoral, horse-based Aryans, an Indo-European people who migrated into the Indus River valley beginning around 1500 BCE. The other was the religious system of the agricultural civilization that already existed in India at the time of the Aryan in-migration.

Hinduism and the Hindu religious texts contain more contradictory, or at the very least unreconciled, elements than is true of the texts of the main mono-theistic religions (Judaism, Christianity, and Islam). An example of this is poly-theism versus monotheism in Hinduism. Hindus worship literally thousands of

---

*A primordial body of water believed to be under the earth. Ea resided there.
†The snake. This story explains why snakes shed their skins.

gods. At the same time, a basic tenet of Hinduism is that the ultimate goal of all souls is *moksha*, which is release from ego-based attachment to the material world. One who achieves *moksha* unites with Brahman, which is translated variously as the One, the World Soul, and the Ultimate Reality. Hence, because all spirit is ultimately part of Brahman, Hinduism can also be thought of as a monotheistic religion.

Two other related elements of Hindu belief influence the nature of the texts presented here. They are reincarnation and the caste system. According to Hindu beliefs, all life forms are reincarnations of spirits from previous existence. The "first end of man" is *dharma*. Although *dharma* can be defined as the religious duties associated with one's social and family position, its essence is much more fundamental than that. The meaning of the root of *dharma* is "to sustain." So the fulfilling of the "first end of man" by living according to the demands of station in life serves to sustain the order of the world. In addition, if one properly fulfills one's *dharma*, then one achieves good *karma* and moves up in the next incarnation to a higher life form. If not, then one develops bad *karma* and moves down. All life represents the constant flow of spirits along the reincarnation path, having unification with Brahman as the ultimate goal. Connected with this understanding of life and belief in reincarnation is the Hindu caste system. Caste probably originated from linguistic, social, and ethnic differences between the Aryan intruders and the preexisting population of India. Eventually, the system of castes (*varna*) developed many subcastes, called *jatis*. Different obligations, privileges, and marriage and employment possibilities exist for members of different castes and subcastes.

An enormous body of religious writings has developed in Hinduism. The selections presented here come from only two parts of that religious literature. The first text is the "Purusha Hymn," and it comes from the first of the Vedas, the Rig-Veda. The Vedas (deriving from the word *veda*, or "wisdom") are the earliest religious works in Hinduism. They are considered by Hindus to be sacred utterings and were composed orally between 1200 and 400 BCE by the Aryans. The Vedas include hymns dedicated to gods and goddesses, as well as sacrificial, mystical, and philosophical texts. The passage included here is a creation story. It differs from the Judeo–Christian creation story from Genesis because of the cosmic continuity of the relationship between divinity and humanity that is characteristic of Hinduism, in which an individual human soul can achieve unity with Brahman in a way that is inconceivable to a Christian. The "Purusha Hymn" also explains the sacred origins of the caste system.

The second text is included here to help clarify the principles of the "Purusha Hymn." The two main sources of authority in Hinduism are the *Shruti*, or divine revelation, which includes the Vedas and the "Purusha Hymn." The other type of source is *Smriti*, or human traditions. The *Smriti* were believed to be based on and consistent with the *Shruti*, so they had the authority of divine revelation. One of the most important examples of *Smriti* is the *Code of Manu*, which dates from the second to third centuries CE. The *Code of Manu* came after a period of unrest and instability, and it seeks to reaffirm *dharma*.

QUESTIONS TO CONSIDER

1. Identify the different roles that Purusha plays in the creation of the universe. How does Purusha's part in creation differ from that of Yahweh in Genesis?

2. What aspects of the natural, spiritual, and social worlds were created by Purusha? How does the "Purusha Hymn" explain the origins of castes? How do the parts of Purusha used to create different castes correspond to the social role of each group? What is the significance both of this correspondence and of the organic unity of the social body that is created?

3. Religions frequently ask their followers to act in imitation of the God or gods. What might a Hindu do to act in imitation of Purusha? How might imitation of Purusha contribute to achieving *moksha,* or release?

4. Which of the two texts do you find to be clearer in the way it presents its ideas? Which of the texts is more rigid in the way it defines castes? What explanations can you come up with to explain the differences in these texts?

5. The caste system has been interpreted as a very rigid social ordering device. What can you find in these two texts that supports that point of view? How might a Hindu argue that, on the contrary, Hinduism provides for great social flexibility and mobility?

Hindu Gods and Spiritual Characters

Purusha—Embodied spirit of Man, the Male principle

Indra—King of the Gods

Agni—God of Fire

Vayu—God of Wind

Viraj—The Female counterpart to Purusha, the Female principle

Hindu Castes

brahmans   priests

rajanya   warrior or ruling class

vaishya   merchants and landowners

shudra   servants and landless farmers

PURUSHASUKTA (PURUSHA HYMN)

1 A thousand heads hath Purusha, a thousand eyes, a thousand feet. On every side pervading earth he fills a space ten fingers wide.

2 This Purusha is all that yet hath been and all that is to be; The Lord of Immortality which waxes greater still by food.

Source: Hinduism: The Rig Veda, trans. Ralph T. H. Griffith (New York: Book-of-the-Month Club, 1992 [1896]), 602–603, from Book X, Hymn XC.

3 So mighty is his greatness; yea, greater than this is Purusha. All creatures are one-fourth of him, three-fourths eternal life in heaven.

4 With three-fourths Purusha went up: one fourth of him again was here. Thence he strode out to every side over what eats not and what eats.

5 From him Viraj was born; again Purusha from Viraj was born. As soon as he was born he spread eastward and westward o'er the earth.

6 When Gods prepared the sacrifice with Purusha as their offering, its oil was spring, the holy gift was autumn; summer was the wood.

7 They balmed as victim on the grass Purusha born in earliest time. With him the Deities and all Sadhyas and Rsis* sacrificed.

8 From that great general sacrifice the dripping fat was gathered up. He formed the creatures of the air, and animals both wild and tame.

9 From that great general sacrifice Rcas[†] and Sama-hymns[‡] were born: Therefrom were spells and charms produced; the Yajus[§] had its birth from it.

10 From it were horses born, from it all cattle with two rows of teeth: From it were generated kine,[**] from it the goats and sheep were born.

11 When they divided Purusha how many portions did they make? What do they call his mouth, his arms? What do they call his thighs and feet?

12 The Brahman was his mouth, of both his arms was the Rajanya made. His thighs became the Vaisya, from his feet the Sudra was produced.

13 The Moon was gendered from his mind, and from his eye the Sun had birth; Indra and Agni from his mouth were born, and Vayu from his breath.

14 Forth from his navel came mid-air, the sky was fashioned from his head, Earth from his feet, and from his ear the regions. Thus they formed the worlds.

15 Seven fencing-sticks had he, thrice seven layers of fuel were prepared, when the Gods, offering sacrifice, bound, as their victim, Purusha.

16 Gods, sacrificing, sacrificed the victim, these were the earliest holy ordinances. The Mighty Ones attained the height of heaven, there where the Sadhyas, Gods of old, are dwelling.

CODE OF MANU

But in the beginning he assigned their several names, actions, and conditions to all (created beings), even according to the words of the Veda.

---

*Ancient celestial beings and saints.

[†]Hymns related to sacrifice from the Rig-Veda.

[‡]Hymns related to sacrifice from the Sama-Veda.

[§]Ritual portions of the Yajur-Veda.

[**]Cattle.

Source: The Law of Manu, in *The Sacred Books of the East,* vol. XXV, trans. G. Bühler (Oxford, UK: Clarendon Press, 1886), 12–14, 24.

46   CHAPTER 2 ◆ Creation–Origin Myths and the Mythic Mode of Thought

He, the Lord, also created the class of the gods, who are endowed with life, and whose nature is action; and the subtile class of the Sadhyas,* and the eternal sacrifice.

But from fire, wind, and the sun he drew forth the threefold eternal Veda, called Rik, Yagus, and Saman,† for the due performance of the sacrifice.

Time and the divisions of time, the lunar mansions and the planets, the rivers, the oceans, the mountains, plains, and uneven ground,

Austerity, speech, pleasure, desire, and anger, this whole creation he likewise produced, as he desired to call these beings into existence. . . .

Whatever he assigned to each at the (first) creation, noxiousness or harmlessness, gentleness or ferocity, virtue or sin, truth or falsehood, that clung (afterwards) spontaneously to it.

As at the change of the seasons each season of its own accord assumes its distinctive marks, even so corporeal beings (resume in new births)‡ their (appointed) course of action.

But for the sake of the prosperity of the worlds, he created the Brahmana, the Kshatriya, the Vaishya, and the Shudra to proceed from his mouth, his arms, his thighs, and his feet. . . .

To Brahmanas he assigned teaching and studying (the Veda), sacrificing for their own benefit and for others, giving and accepting (of alms).

The Kshatriya he commanded to protect the people, to bestow gifts, to offer sacrifices, to study (the Veda), and to abstain from attaching himself to sensual pleasures;§

The Vaishya to tend cattle, to bestow gifts, to offer sacrifices, to study, to trade, to lend money, and to cultivate land.

One occupation only the lord prescribed to the Shudra, to serve meekly even these (other) three castes.

THE CREATION STORY OF THE JEWS

The third selection in this chapter encompasses some of the best-known religious passages of western civilization. The selections come from the beginning of the book of Genesis, which is the first chapter of both the Jewish Torah and the Christian Bible. These passages are included here both as a seminal text of three great religious traditions (Jewish, Christian, and Muslim) and as a point of comparison with other religious traditions. The portions of Genesis included here involve the creation of the universe and of life, as well as the expulsion from Eden and the story of the Flood.

---

*The "Gods of old."

†These are variant spellings of the Rcas, Sama, and Yajur Vedas.

‡That is, upon reincarnation.

§That is, to exercise self-discipline.

Christianity divides its books of revealed literature into the Old and New Testaments. The first five books of the Old Testament are called the Pentateuch, and the traditional Christian understanding of the Pentateuch is that it is the revealed word of God as written down by Moses. Many Christians still hold this belief. Many Biblical scholars, however, approach the material from a much different perspective. Beginning in the nineteenth century, scholars applied to the Bible the techniques of literary criticism that are commonly used on other texts. They have discerned different narrative strands in the Old Testament. The most prominent are the Elohim (E strand) or Jahweh (J strand), which identify texts depending on how God is referred to. These scholars have also called into question the early history of the Jews as it is presented in the Old Testament, the nature of their monotheism at various points in the evolution of Judaism, and the originality of many of the stories. According to this point of view, the material that makes up the Old Testament is a combination of different materials put together relatively late in the history of the Jews (by the time of the Babylonian Captivity in 586 BCE).

Of course, these are questions of enormous significance, especially concerning the authority of the biblical texts. At the same time, the texts themselves can be approached and assessed independent of the question of their origins. That is to say, they can be analyzed for the answers they provide about the origins of the universe and mankind, the nature of divinity, and man's key relationships with each other, with the divinity, and with the material world, regardless of whether one believes that they are the revealed word of God recorded directly by Moses or were produced out of a variety of different sources. Hence, the introductory passages of Genesis serve as an excellent touchstone against which to assess different visions and explanations of divinity and of the universe and the place of human and other life forms in it.

QUESTIONS TO CONSIDER

1. According to Genesis, what is the relationship between humans and the rest of creation? What does this tell us about the understanding of the relationship between humans and nature in this religious tradition?

2. What is the order and method of creation of Adam and Eve? What might this imply about the proper relationship between men and women, according to Genesis? How else does Eve figure in the Garden of Eden story, and how might it affect the way that women are viewed?

3. What are the consequences of Adam and Eve's "fall from grace" as a result of eating the forbidden fruit? List the aspects of human life that are explained by this story.

4. Why does God destroy all humans and other living things, except for Noah and those on the Ark? In your opinion, is God justified in unleashing this devastating Flood?

5. Based on the story of the expulsion from the Garden of Eden and the story of Noah and the Flood, what does God value most in humans? Does the thing most valued change between the two stories? In general, what can we tell about the nature of God from these Genesis stories?

THE BOOK OF GENESIS

In the beginning God created the heavens and the earth. The earth was without form and void, and darkness was upon the face of the deep; and the Spirit of God was moving over the face of the waters.

And God said, "Let there be light"; and there was light. And God saw that the light was good; and God separated the light from the darkness. God called the light Day, and the darkness he called Night. And there was evening and there was morning, one day. And God said, "Let there be a firmament in the midst of the waters, and let it separate the waters from the waters." And God made the firmament and separated the waters which were under the firmament from the waters which were above the firmament. And it was so. And God called the firmament Heaven. And there was evening and there was morning, a second day.

And God said, "Let the waters under the heavens be gathered together into one place, and let the dry land appear." And it was so. God called the dry land Earth, and the waters that were gathered together he called Seas. And God saw that it was good. And God said, "Let the earth put forth vegetation, plants yielding seed, and fruit trees bearing fruit in which is their seed, each according to its kind, upon the earth." And it was so. The earth brought forth vegetation, plants yielding seed according to their own kinds, and trees bearing fruit in which is their seed, each according to its kind. And God saw that it was good. And there was evening and there was morning, a third day.

And God said, "Let there be lights in the firmament of the heavens to separate the day from the night; and let them be for signs and for seasons and for days and years, and let them be lights in the firmament of the heavens to give light upon the earth." And it was so. And God made the two great lights, the greater light to rule the day, and the lesser light to rule the night; he made the stars also. And God set them in the firmament of the heavens to give light upon the earth, to rule over the day and over the night, and to separate the light from the darkness. And God saw that it was good. And there was evening and there was morning, a fourth day.

And God said, "Let the waters bring forth swarms of living creatures, and let birds fly above the earth across the firmament of the heavens." So God created the great sea monsters and every living creature that moves, with which the waters swarm, according to their kinds, and every winged bird according to its kind. And God saw that it was good. And God blessed them, saying, "Be fruitful and multiply and fill the

Source: The Holy Bible, Revised Standard Edition (New York: American Bible Society, 1952): Genesis 1; 2:1–9, 15–25; 3; 6:1–3, 5–8, 13–14, 22; 7:1–5, 11–12, 17, 22–24; 8:1, 4, 6–12, 18–22; 9:1, 9–13.

The Book of Genesis   49

waters in the seas, and let birds multiply on the earth." And there was evening and there was morning, a fifth day.

And God said, "Let the earth bring forth living creatures according to their kinds: cattle and creeping things and beasts of the earth according to their kinds." And it was so. And God made the beasts of the earth according to their kinds and the cattle according to their kinds, and everything that creeps upon the ground according to its kind. And God saw that it was good.

Then God said, "Let us make man in our image, after our likeness; and let them have dominion over the fish of the sea, and over the birds of the air, and over the cattle, and over all the earth, and over every creeping thing that creeps upon the earth."

So God created man in his own image, in the image of God he created him; male and female he created them. And God blessed them, and God said to them, "Be fruitful and multiply, and fill the earth and subdue it; and have dominion over the fish of the sea and over the birds of the air and over every living thing that moves upon the earth." And God said, "Behold, I have given you every plant yielding seed which is upon the face of all the earth, and every tree with seed in its fruit; you shall have them for food. And to every beast of the earth, and to every bird of the air, and to everything that creeps on the earth, everything that has the breath of life, I have given every green plant for food." And it was so. And God saw everything that he had made, and behold, it was very good. And there was evening and there was morning, a sixth day.

Thus the heavens and the earth were finished, and all the host of them. And on the seventh day God finished his work which he had done, and he rested on the seventh day from all his work which he had done. So God blessed the seventh day and hallowed it, because on it God rested from all his work which he had done in creation.

These are the generations of the heavens and the earth when they were created.

In the day that the Lord God made the earth and the heavens, when no plant of the field was yet in the earth and no herb of the field had yet sprung up—for the Lord God had not caused it to rain upon the earth, and there was no man to till the ground; but a mist went up from the earth and watered the whole face of the ground—then the Lord God formed man of dust from the ground, and breathed into his nostrils the breath of life; and man became a living being. And the Lord God planted a garden in Eden, in the east; and there he put the man whom he had formed. And out of the ground the Lord God made to grow every tree that is pleasant to the sight and good for food, the tree of life also in the midst of the garden, and the tree of the knowledge of good and evil. . . .

The Lord God took the man and put him in the garden of Eden to till it and keep it. And the Lord God commanded the man, saying, "You may freely eat of every tree of the garden; but of the tree of the knowledge of good and evil you shall not eat, for in the day that you eat of it you shall die."

Then the Lord God said, "It is not good that the man should be alone; I will make him a helper fit for him." So out of the ground the Lord God formed every beast of the field and every bird of the air, and brought them to the man to see what he would call them; and whatever the man called every living creature, that was its name. The man gave names to all cattle, and to the birds of the air, and to every beast of the field; but for the man there was not found a helper fit for him. So the Lord God caused a deep sleep to fall upon the man, and while he slept took one of his ribs and closed up its place with flesh; and the rib which the Lord God had taken from the man he made into a woman and brought her to the man. Then the man said, "This at last is bone of my bones and flesh of my flesh; she shall be called Woman, because she was taken out of Man."

Therefore a man leaves his father and his mother and cleaves to his wife, and they become one flesh. And the man and his wife were both naked, and were not ashamed.

Now the serpent was more subtle than any other wild creature that the Lord God had made. He said to the woman, "Did God say, 'You shall not eat of any tree of the garden'?" And the woman said to the serpent, "We may eat of the fruit of the trees of the garden; but God said, 'You shall not eat of the fruit of the tree which is in the midst of the garden, neither shall you touch it, lest you die.'" But the serpent said to the woman, "You will not die. For God knows that when you eat of it your eyes will be opened, and you will be like God, knowing good and evil." So when the woman saw that the tree was good for food, and that it was a delight to the eyes, and that the tree was to be desired to make one wise, she took of its fruit and ate; and she also gave some to her husband, and he ate. Then the eyes of both were opened, and they knew that they were naked; and they sewed fig leaves together and made themselves aprons.

And they heard the sound of the Lord God walking in the garden in the cool of the day, and the man and his wife hid themselves from the presence of the Lord God among the trees of the garden. But the Lord God called to the man, and said to him, "Where are you?" And he said, "I heard the sound of thee in the garden, and I was afraid, because I was naked; and I hid myself." He said, "Who told you that you were naked? Have you eaten of the tree of which I commanded you not to eat?" The man said, "The woman whom thou gavest to be with me, she gave me fruit of the tree, and I ate." Then the Lord God said to the woman, "What is this that you have done?" The woman said, "The serpent beguiled me, and I ate." The Lord God said to the serpent, "Because you have done this, cursed are you above all cattle, and above all wild animals; upon your belly you shall go, and dust you shall eat all the days of your life. I will put enmity between you and the woman, and between your seed and her seed; he shall bruise your head, and you shall bruise his heel."

To the woman he said, "I will greatly multiply your pain in childbearing; in pain you shall bring forth children, yet your desire shall be for your husband, and he shall rule over you."

And to Adam he said, "Because you have listened to the voice of your wife, and have eaten of the tree of which I commanded you, 'You shall not eat of it,' cursed is the ground because of you; in toil you shall eat of it all the days of your life; thorns and thistles it shall bring forth to you; and you shall eat the plants of the field. In the sweat of your face you shall eat bread till you return to the ground, for out of it you were taken; you are dust, and to dust you shall return." The man called his wife's name Eve, because she was the mother of all living. And the Lord God made for Adam and for his wife garments of skins, and clothed them.

Then the Lord God said, "Behold, the man has become like one of us, knowing good and evil; and now, lest he put forth his hand and take also of the tree of life, and

The Book of Genesis   51

eat, and live for ever"—therefore the Lord God sent him forth from the garden of Eden, to till the ground from which he was taken. He drove out the man; and at the east of the garden of Eden he placed the cherubim, and a flaming sword which turned every way, to guard the way to the tree of life. . . .

When men began to multiply on the face of the ground, and daughters were born to them, the sons of God saw that the daughters of men were fair; and they took to wife such of them as they chose. Then the Lord said, "My spirit shall not abide in man for ever, for he is flesh, but his days shall be a hundred and twenty years." . . .

The Lord saw that the wickedness of man was great in the earth, and that every imagination of the thoughts of his heart was only evil continually. And the Lord was sorry that he had made man on the earth, and it grieved him to his heart. So the Lord said, "I will blot out man whom I have created from the face of the ground, man and beast and creeping things and birds of the air, for I am sorry that I have made them." But Noah found favor in the eyes of the Lord. . . .

And God said to Noah, "I have determined to make an end of all flesh; for the earth is filled with violence through them; behold, I will destroy them with the earth. Make yourself an ark of gopher wood. . . ." Noah did this; he did all that God commanded him.

Then the Lord said to Noah, "Go into the ark, you and all your household, for I have seen that you are righteous before me in this generation. Take with you seven pairs of all clean animals, the male and his mate; and a pair of the animals that are not clean, the male and his mate; and seven pairs of the birds of the air also, male and female, to keep their kind alive upon the face of all the earth. For in seven days I will send rain upon the earth forty days and forty nights; and every living thing that I have made I will blot out from the face of the ground." And Noah did all that the Lord had commanded him. . . .

[A]nd the windows of the heavens were opened. And rain fell upon the earth forty days and forty nights . . . ; and the waters increased, and bore up the ark, and it rose high above the earth. . . . [E]verything on the dry land in whose nostrils was the breath of life died. He blotted out every living thing that was upon the face of the ground, man and animals and creeping things and birds of the air; they were blotted out from the earth. Only Noah was left, and those that were with him in the ark. And the waters prevailed upon the earth a hundred and fifty days.

But God remembered Noah and all the beasts and all the cattle that were with him in the ark. And God made a wind blow over the earth, and the waters subsided. . . . [T]he ark came to rest upon the mountains of Ar'arat.

At the end of forty days Noah opened the window of the ark which he had made, and sent forth a raven; and it went to and fro until the waters were dried up from the earth. Then he sent forth a dove from him, to see if the waters had subsided from the face of the ground; but the dove found no place to set her foot, and she returned to him to the ark, for the waters were still on the face of the whole earth. So he put forth his hand and took her and brought her into the ark with him. He waited another seven days, and again he sent forth the dove out of the ark; and the dove came back to him in the evening, and lo, in her mouth a freshly plucked olive leaf; so Noah knew that the waters had subsided from the earth. Then he waited another seven days, and sent forth the dove; and she did not return to him any more. . . .

So Noah went forth, and his sons and his wife and his sons' wives with him. And every beast, every creeping thing, and every bird, everything that moves upon the earth, went forth by families out of the ark.

Then Noah built an altar to the Lord, and took of every clean animal and of every clean bird, and offered burnt offerings on the altar. And when the Lord smelled the pleasing odor, the Lord said in his heart, "I will never again curse the ground because of man, for the imagination of man's heart is evil from his youth; neither will I ever again destroy every living creature as I have done. While the earth remains, seedtime and harvest, cold and heat, summer and winter, day and night, shall not cease."

And God blessed Noah and his sons, and said to them, "Be fruitful and multiply, and fill the earth. . . . Behold, I establish my covenant with you and your descendants after you, and with every living creature that is with you, . . . that never again shall all flesh be cut off by the waters of a flood, and never again shall there be a flood to destroy the earth." And God said, "This is the sign of the covenant which I make between me and you and every living creature that is with you, for all future generations: I set my [rain]bow in the cloud, and it shall be a sign of the covenant between me and the earth."

THE CLASSICAL CREATION STORY OF MESOAMERICA

The final mythic structure included in this chapter comes from Mesoamerican civilization, in particular from the culture of the people known as Quiche Maya. The Classical Era of Mayan history runs from around 600 to 800 CE, and the Mayan cultural zone extended across parts of what is now southern Mexico, Guatemala, and Belize. Mayan civilization seems to have been influenced by the earlier Olmec culture, and it definitely influenced in its own turn the Aztec civilization encountered by the Spanish in 1519. Theirs was a maize-based economy with traditional social classes: rulers (believed to be gods or related to the gods), priests, nobility, and peasants.

What distinguishes Mayan civilization in particular was their intricate calendar computations and their sophisticated knowledge of astronomy (although parts of their system we might consider closer to astrology). The Mayan calendar year was based on eighteen "months" of twenty days each plus five intercalendrical days. Each day was identified with a specific symbol and character, which determined what one should do on that day. Because of this fixation on matters of time and calendars, the Mayans produced calendar computations of extraordinary precision. Their calendar year was 365.2420 days long, an infinitesimal 3/10000ths off from the actual length of a year and more accurate than the calendars used in Europe.[4]

Calendar computations based on their so-called Long Count system created a cycle that would not begin to repeat for 377,440 years![5] Of most immediate impact in terms of their daily lives and their religious beliefs were their twenty-day months and intercalendrical days. Each day was identified with a specific symbol and character, and each was a propitious or inauspicious day, a good or a bad day

The Classical Creation Story of Mesoamerica   53

for certain types of activities. Hence, the Quiche assumed a deep structure of meaning and direction to the universe according to which one could and should organize one's life.

The foundation for this view of time is the sacred Mayan story known as the Popol Vuh, or the Council Book. It is of quite ancient vintage, although the version that we have was produced by a Mayan around 1560, that is, after the Spanish Conquest and the forced Christianization that accompanied it. It was discovered some two hundred years later by a priest and translated into Spanish. The extant copy of it is now in the Newberry Library in Chicago. Its anonymous recorder wanted to ensure that there was still "a place to see 'The Light That Came from Across the Sea,' . . . a place to see 'The Dawn of Life.'" The passages reproduced here present the Mayan view of creation, which the Popol Vuh calls "'the fourfold siding, fourfold cornering, measuring, fourfold staking, halving the cord, stretching the cord in the sky, on the earth, the four sides, the four corners,' as it is said, 'by the Maker, Modeler, mother–father of life, of humankind, giver of breath, giver of heart, bearer, upbringer in the light that lasts of those born in the light, begotten in the light; worrier, knower of everything, whatever there is: sky–earth, lake–sea.'"[6] The passages included here cover the gods' efforts at creating proper worshippers, a process that required some trial and error. Between the two passages included here there is a very long but still delightful narrative of the clever undertakings of two sets of twins. Their actions provide much of the material for a proper reading of the days. The passages presented here narrate and explain what was necessary to produce creatures capable of properly reading and observing the days.

QUESTIONS TO CONSIDER

1. Describe the process by which the gods created life. How does this story compare with the creation stories in Genesis and in the Hindu texts?

2. How does the destruction presented in Popol Vuh compare with the Flood stories from *Gilgamesh* and Genesis? Compare the motivation behind the destruction unleashed by Yahweh in Genesis and by the gods in Popol Vuh.

3. Compare the relationship between man and nature presented in Genesis with that implicit in Popol Vuh. Why was animals' flesh made food for others? Human possessions and domestic animals destroy the wood-carving people with the gods' approval. What does that imply about the justification for human use of the material and animals found in the world?

4. What does Popol Vuh tell us about proper human behavior? What about the relationship between men and women? What do you think of the explanations for human limitations given in Popol Vuh, Genesis, and the Gilgamesh story? In your opinion, are any of them more acceptable or convincing than others?

5. What can we discern about the nature of the divine (the gods) in the Mayan belief system from Popol Vuh? How does this compare with Yahweh's nature in Genesis and the behavior of the gods in *Gilgamesh* and in the Hindu texts?

POPOL VUH

Part One

This is the account, here it is:

Now it still ripples, now it still murmurs, ripples, it still sighs, still hums, and it is empty under the sky.

Here follow the first words, the first eloquence:

There is not yet one person, one animal, bird, fish, crab, tree, rock, hollow, canyon, meadow, forest. Only the sky alone is there; the face of the earth is not clear. Only the sea alone is pooled under all the sky; there is nothing whatever gathered together. It is at rest; not a single thing stirs. It is held back, kept at rest under the sky.

Whatever there is that might be is simply not there: only the pooled water, only the calm sea, only it alone is pooled.

Whatever might be is simply not there: only murmurs, ripples, in the dark, in the night. Only the Maker, Modeler alone, Sovereign Plumed Serpent, the Bearers, Begetters are in the water, a glittering light. They are there, they are enclosed in quetzal feathers, in blue-green.

Thus the name, "Plumed Serpent." They are great knowers, great thinkers in their very being.

And of course there is the sky, and there is also the Heart of Sky. This is the name of the god, as it is spoken.

And then came his word, he came here to the Sovereign Plumed Serpent, here in the blackness, in the early dawn. He spoke with the Sovereign Plumed Serpent, and they talked, then they thought, then they worried. They agreed with each other, they joined their words, their thoughts. Then it was clear, then they reached accord in the light, and then humanity was clear, when they conceived the growth, the generation of trees, of bushes, and the growth of life, of humankind, in the blackness, in the early dawn . . . .

So . . . Heart of Sky . . . came to the Sovereign Plumed Serpent, when the dawn of life was conceived: "How should it be sown, how should it dawn? Who is to be the provider, nurturer?"

"Let it be this way, think about it: this water should be removed, emptied out for the formation of the earth's own plate and platform, then comes the sowing, the dawning of the sky–earth. But there will be no high days and no bright praise for our work, our design, until the rise of the human work, the human design," they said.

And then the earth arose because of them, it was simply their word that brought it forth. For the forming of the earth they said "Earth." It arose suddenly, just like a cloud, like a mist, now forming, unfolding. Then the mountains were separated from the water, all at once the great mountains came forth. By their genius alone, by their cut-

Source: Reprinted with the permission of Simon & Schuster Adult Publishing Group from *Popol Vuh: The Definitive Edition of the Mayan Book of the Dawn of Life and the Glories of the Gods and Kings.* Trans. Dennis Tedlock, 72–85, 163–67. Copyright © 1985, 1996 by Dennis Tedlock.

Popol Vuh   55

ting edge alone they carried out the conception of the mountain-plain, whose face grew instant groves of cypress and pine.

And the Plumed Serpent was pleased with this: . . . .

And the earth was formed first, the mountain-plain. The channels of water were separated; their branches wound their ways among the mountains. The waters were divided when the Great mountains appeared.

Such was the formation of the earth when it was brought forth by the Heart of the Sky, Heart of Earth, as they are called, since they were the first to think of it. The sky was set apart, and the earth was set apart in the midst of the waters.

Such was their plan when they thought, when they worried about the completion of their work.

Now they planned the animals of the mountains, all the guardians of the forest, creatures of the mountains: the deer, birds, pumas, jaguars, serpents, rattlesnakes, yellow-bites,* guardians of the bushes.

A Bearer, Begetter speaks:

"Why this pointless humming? Why should there merely be rustling beneath the trees and bushes?"

"Indeed, they had better have guardians," the others replied. As soon as they thought it and said it, deer and birds came forth.

And then they gave out homes to the deer and the birds:

"You, the deer: sleep along the rivers, in the canyons. Be here in the meadows, in the thickets, in the forests, multiply yourselves. You will stand and walk on all fours," they were told.

So then they established the nests of the birds, small and great:

"You, precious birds: your nests, your houses are in the trees, in the bushes. Multiply there, scatter there, in the branches of trees, the branches of bushes," the deer and birds were told.

When this deed had been done, all of them had received a place to sleep and a place to stay. So it is that the nests of the animals are on the earth, given by the Bearer, Begetter. Now the arrangement of the deer and birds was complete.

And then the deer and birds were told by the Maker, Modeler, Bearer, Begetter:

"Talk, speak out. Don't moan, don't cry out. Please talk, each to each, within each kind, within each group," they were told—the deer, birds, puma, jaguar, serpent.

"Name now our names, praise us. We are your mother, we are your father. Speak now:

'Hurricane,
Newborn Thunderbolt, Raw Thunderbolt,
Heart of Sky, Heart of Earth,
Maker, Modeler,
Bearer, Begetter,'

---

*The poisonous snake known as fer-de-lance.

speak, pray to us, keep our days,"* they were told. But it didn't turn out that they spoke like people: they just squawked, they just chattered, they just howled. It wasn't apparent what language they spoke; each one gave a different cry. When the Maker, Modeler heard this:

"It hasn't turned out well, they haven't spoken," they said among themselves. "It hasn't turned out that our names have been named. Since we are their mason and sculptor, this will not do," the Bearers and Begetters said among themselves. So they told them:

"You will simply have to be transformed. Since it hasn't turned out well and you haven't spoken, we have changed our word:

"What you feed on, what you eat, the places where you sleep, the places where you stay, whatever is yours will remain in the canyons, the forests. Although it turned out that our days were not kept, nor did you pray to us, there may yet be strength in the keeper of days, the giver of praise whom we have yet to make. Just accept your service, just let your flesh be eaten.

"So be it, this must be your service," they were told when they were instructed—the animals, small and great, on the face of the earth.

And then they wanted to test their timing again, they wanted to experiment again, and they wanted to prepare for the keeping of days again. They had not heard their speech among the animals; it did not come to fruition and it was not complete.

And so their flesh was brought low: they served, they were eaten, they were killed—the animals on the face of the earth.

Again there comes an experiment with the human work, the human design, by the Maker, Modeler, Bearer, Begetter:

"It must simply be tried again. The time for the planting and dawning is nearing. For this we must make a provider and nurturer. How else can we be invoked and remembered on the face of the earth? We have already made our first try at our work and design, but it turned out that they didn't keep our days, nor did they glorify us.

"So now let's try to make a giver of praise, giver of respect, provider, nurturer," they said. . . . "There is yet to find, yet to discover how we are to model a person, construct a person again, a provider, nurturer, so that we are called upon and we are recognized: our recompense is in words. . . .

"It is well that there be your manikins, wood-carvings, talking, speaking, there on the face of the earth."

"So be it," they replied. The moment they spoke it was done: the manikins, wood-carvings, human in looks and human in speech.

This was the peopling of the face of the earth:

They came into being, they multiplied, they had daughters, they had sons, these manikins, wood-carvings. But there was nothing in their hearts and nothing in their minds, no memory of their mason and builder. They just went and walked wherever they wanted. Now they did not remember the Heart of Sky.

---

*That is, to prepare someone to keep track of and honor the sacred days of the calendar.

Popol Vuh   **57**

And so they fell, just an experiment and just a cutout for humankind. They were talking at first but their faces were dry. They were not yet developed in the legs and arms. They had no blood, no lymph. They had no sweat, no fat. Their complexions were dry, their faces were crusty. They flailed their legs and arms, their bodies were deformed.

And so they accomplished nothing before the Maker, Modeler who gave them birth, gave them heart. They became the first numerous people here on the face of the earth.

Again there comes a humiliation, destruction, and demolition. The manikins, wood-carvings were killed when the Heart of Sky devised a flood for them. A great flood was made; it came down on the heads of the manikins, wood-carvings. The man's body was carved from the wood of the coral tree by the Maker, Modeler. And as for the woman, the Maker, Modeler needed the pith of reeds for the woman's body. They were not competent,* nor did they speak before the builder and sculptor who made them and brought them forth, and so they were killed, done in by a flood:

There came a rain of resin from the sky.

There came the one named Gouger of Faces: he gouged out their eyeballs.

There came Sudden Bloodletter: he snapped off their heads.

There came Crunching Jaguar: he ate their flesh.

There came Tearing Jaguar: he tore them open.

They were pounded down to the bones and tendons, smashed and pulverized even to the bones. Their faces were smashed because they were incompetent before their mother and their father, the Heart of Sky, named Hurricane. The earth was blackened because of this; the black rainstorm began, rain all day and rain all night. Into their houses came the animals, small and great. Their faces were crushed by things of wood and stone. Everything spoke: their water jars, their tortilla griddles, their plates, their cooking pots, their dogs, their grinding stones, each and every thing crushed their faces. . . .

Now they run for it, helter-skelter.

They want to climb up on the houses, but they fall as the houses collapse.

They want to climb the trees; they're thrown off by the trees.

They want to get inside caves, but the caves slam shut in their faces.

Such was the scattering of the human work, the human design. The people were ground down, overthrown. The mouths and faces of all of them were destroyed and crushed. And it used to be said† that the monkeys in the forests today are a sign of this. They were left as a sign because wood alone was used for their flesh by the builder and sculptor.

So this is why monkeys look like people: they are a sign of a previous human work, human design—mere manikins, mere wood-carvings. . . .

---

*They could not offer prayer and praise to the gods nor keep track of the sacred days.

†Before the imposition of Christianity by the Spanish.

58 CHAPTER 2 ◆ Creation–Origin Myths and the Mythic Mode of Thought

Part Four

And here is the beginning of the conception of HUMANS, and of the search for the ingredients of the human body. So they spoke, the Bearer, Begetter, the Makers, Modelers named Sovereign Plumed Serpent:

"The dawn has approached, preparations have been made, and the morning has come for the provider, nurturer, born in the light, begotten in the light. Morning has come for humankind, for the people of the face of the earth," they said. It all came together as they went on thinking in the darkness, in the night, as they searched and they sifted, they thought and they wondered.

And here their thoughts came out in clear light. They sought and discovered what was needed for human flesh. . . .

And these were the ingredients for the flesh of the human work, the human design, and the water was for the blood. It became human blood, and corn was also used by the Bearer, Begetter.

And so they were happy over the provisions of the good mountain, filled with sweet things, thick with yellow corn, white corn, and thick with . . . rich foods . . . [and all] the edible fruits were there: small staples, great staples, small plants, great plants. . . .

And then the yellow corn and white corn were ground, and . . . did the grinding nine times. Corn was used, along with the water she rinsed her hands with, for the creation of grease; it became human fat when it was worked by the Bearer, Begetter, Sovereign Plumed Serpent, as they are called.

After that, they put it into words:

the making, the modeling of our first mother–father,
with yellow corn, white corn alone for the flesh,
food alone for the human legs and arms,
for our first fathers, . . .

They were simply made and modeled, it is said: they had no mother and no father. We have named the men by themselves. No woman gave birth to them, nor were they begotten by the builder, sculptor, Bearer, Begetter. By sacrifice alone, by genius alone they were made, they were modeled by the Maker, Modeler, Bearer, Begetter, Sovereign Plumed Serpent. And when they came to fruition, they came out human:

They talked and they made words.
They looked and they listened.
They walked and they worked.

They were good people, handsome, with looks of the male kind. Thoughts came into existence and they gazed; their vision came all at once. Perfectly they saw, perfectly they knew everything under the sky, whenever they looked. The moment they turned around and looked around in the sky, on the earth, everything was seen without any obstruction. They didn't have to walk around before they could see what was under the sky; they just stayed where they were.

As they looked, their knowledge became intense. Their sight passed through trees, through rocks, through lakes, through seas, through mountains, through plains. Jaguar Quitze, Jaguar Night, Mahucutah, and True Jaguar were truly gifted people.

And then they were asked by the builder and mason:

Popol Vuh   59

"What do you know about your being? Don't you look, don't you listen? Isn't your speech good, and your walk? So you must look, to see out under the sky. Don't you see the mountain-plain clearly? So try it," they were told.

And then they saw everything under the sky perfectly. After that, they thanked the Maker, Modeler:

"Truly now
double thanks, triple thanks
that we've been formed, we've been given
our mouths, our faces,
we speak, we listen,
we wonder, we move,
our knowledge is good, we've understood
what is far and near,
and we've seen what is great and small
under the sky, on the earth.
Thanks to you we've been formed,
we've come to be made and modeled,
our grandmother, our grandfather,"
they said when they gave thanks for having been made and modeled. They understood everything perfectly, they sighted the four sides, the four corners in the sky, on the earth, and this didn't sound good to the builder and sculptor:

"What our works and designs have said is no good:

"'We have understood everything, great and small,' they say." And so the Bearer, Begetter took back their knowledge:

"What should we do with them now? Their vision should at least reach nearby, they should see at least a small part of the face of the earth, but what they're saying isn't good. Aren't they merely 'works' and 'designs' in their very names? Yet they'll become as great as gods, unless they procreate, proliferate at the sowing, the dawning, unless they increase."

"Let it be this way: now we'll take them apart just a little, that's what we need. What we've found out isn't good. Their deeds would become equal to ours, just because their knowledge reaches so far. They see everything," so said the Heart of Sky,
Hurricane,
Newborn Thunderbolt, Raw Thunderbolt,
Sovereign Plumed Serpent,
Bearer, Begetter,
Xpiyacoc, Xmucane,
Maker, Modeler,
as they are called. And when they changed the nature of their works, their designs, it was enough that the eyes be marred by the Heart of Sky. They were blinded as the face of a mirror is breathed upon. Their eyes were weakened. Now it was only when they looked nearby that things were clear.

And such was the loss of means of understanding, along with the means of knowing everything, by the four humans. The root was implanted.

60   CHAPTER 2   ✦   Creation–Origin Myths and the Mythic Mode of Thought

And such was the making, modeling of our first grandfather, our father, by the Heart of Sky, Heart of Earth.

And then their wives and women came into being. Again, the same gods thought of it. It was as if they were asleep when they received them, truly beautiful women were there. . . . With their women there they became wider awake. Right away they were happy at heart again, . . .

So these are . . . their wives, who became ladies of rank, giving birth to the people of the tribes, small and great.

And this is our root. We who are the Quiche people.

NOTES

1. B. Malinowski, *Myth in Primitive Psychology* (New York: W. W. Norton & Co., 1926, 19, 30.

2. There is a Hindu tale about Manu and the Flood, but it contains no moral implications or reflections on divine anger, and so it is not included in this chapter.

3. Mircea Eliade, *Myth and Reality* (New York: Harper Torchbooks, 1963), 11.

4. Miguel Leon-Portilla, *Time and Reality in the Thought of the Maya,* 2nd ed. (Norman, OK: University of Oklahoma Press, 1988), 11.

5. Ibid., p. 6.

6. *Popol Vuh: The Definitive Edition of the Mayan Book of the Dawn of Life and the Glories of the Gods and Kings.* Trans. Dennis Tedlock (New York: Simon and Schuster, 1985), 71–72.

CHAPTER 3

Kingship and Authority in the Ancient World

INTRODUCTION

In J. R. R. Tolkien's *The Lord of the Rings,* when Aragorn healed the victims of the evil Ringwraiths, he proved himself the true king, because it was said that "the hands of the king are the hands of the healer." Tolkien did not invent this idea. As an Oxford professor and expert in early English literature, he knew of the deeply rooted belief in medieval Western Europe that "the royal touch" had sacred powers, and he transplanted that idea to Middle Earth. In Europe, belief in the healing powers of the king was intimately connected with the idea that royal power acquired legitimacy because of divine approval. This conception of royal authority stemming from divine sanction was a part of most political cultures. From Israel and Mesopotamia to India and China, from Asia to Mesoamerica, royalty was viewed as "anointed." Although this idea of ruling by "divine right" contributed at times to despotism and abuse of power, it also established very real expectations and assumptions about the purposes of royal government. Moral limitations were placed on royal power, because each culture generated its own understanding of what constituted the legitimate exercise of power. The relationship between the legitimacy of royal authority in different cultures and the proper fulfillment of the moral requirements of those cultures—and, more generally, the character and functioning of authority in human cultures—are the themes of this chapter.

The readings in this chapter show that the elevated stature of one chosen and anointed by the heavens carried with it obligations and responsibilities that qualified and limited "despotic" power. In different cultures divinity was conceived of in different ways: in one culture as a monotheistic God, in another as a group of polytheistic gods, in a third as an impersonal power of Heaven. Similarly, the ruler was viewed in various ways: as a manifestation of the divine, as a quasi-divine figure, or merely as a divinely designated human. Despite these differences, royal authority—understood as the legitimate exercise of power, as opposed to illegitimate force or mere coercion—was nested in value systems that constrained and compelled the emperor or king to live up to certain expectations. Failure to do so could and did lead to dethronement and death. More routinely, dynastic turmoil and foreign conquest were interpreted as resulting from inability or refusal to adhere to the ethical responsibilities of the office.

The issues raised here also allow us to consider the nature and working of authority in human social relations. A useful way to approach this subject might be to contrast "authority" with "power." Someone in a position of power—a parent, a teacher, a boss, a political figure—can wield that power, and within certain limits there is nothing that can be done legally to take that power away or diminish it. At the same time, the raw exercise of power by itself cannot lend legitimacy to an action. In fact, the arbitrary exercise of power actually diminishes legitimacy. The reason for this is that an action's legitimacy is a function of a social value system that the individual holder and exerciser of power can do little to affect or define. *Monarchy* literally means "one-person rule." But if authority is understood as power based on respect for and wielded in accordance with a moral value system, then it is easy to see that legitimate authority cannot be "monarchical" in the literal sense of the word. Rather, it can only be exercised in conjunction with the values of the society, and so its operation is mutually defined by the ruler and the ruled. If this is the case for royal authority, then it applies all the more to modern democratic political systems. Moreover, ethical limitations are also part of parental, educational, and other forms of authority. Hence the encounter between the structures of political authority and the society over which they rule retains its relevance to the present day.

An example of the effect of popular understanding of royal authority on other types of authority in the society is the idea of the monarch as literally or symbolically serving as the "father" of a nation or a people. By analogy, then, the behavior expected of him coincided with the ideal actions of the father in a human family. Conversely, the attributes of the ideal ruler were by extension applied to fathers in the society as a whole. The result invariably was a network of mutually reinforcing expectations, responsibilities, and ideals that served to define right action within the social and political order as a whole. This is a far cry from unlimited royal power, from one-person rule.

The first two readings come from Mesopotamia. The first document includes excerpts from one of the most famous legal documents in history, the Code of Hammurabi. Although Hammurabi's code dates from around 1750 BCE, it includes elements of previous law codes, and it was copied in turn in law codes issued after it. Most famous for its principle of *lex talionis,* or "an eye for an eye, a tooth for a tooth," Hammurabi's code also addresses the social and governmental purposes behind the law code, so it encodes an image of legitimate legal authority. The second document is from another empire in the same region a thousand years later. The Neo-Assyrian empire was noted for the ferocious violence that it used to establish and maintain power. Yet in the document "Advice to a Prince" presented here, we see the endurance of many of the ideals of legitimate authority incorporated in Hammurabi's code.

The second document comes from the Jewish and Christian traditions, and it represents the ideals of kingship in ancient Israel. The selections included here come from 1 Samuel. The Jewish interpretation of royal authority was distinctive in certain ways. An important undercurrent in the sacred literature up through Samuel was the idea that Israel did not need a king, because it received leadership and guidance directly from Yahweh. Although that principle was altered in Samuel, it continued to affect the way kingship and the legitimacy of the ruler were defined in the Jewish tradition.

Next, we turn to the Hindu culture of India and the way that political authority was comprehended there. The best and best-known representation of royal authority and legitimacy in Indian culture is their magnificent epic, *The Ramayana*. This tale existed as part of the oral tradition of India for centuries before it was written down, so it reflects deeply rooted and enduring Hindu values. Because the main character Rama is a physical incarnation of the Hindu god Vishnu, his behavior and values literally embody the Hindu ideal of kingship.

Finally, we include a foundation text of Chinese political culture. "The Mandate of Heaven," which comes from the *Shu Ching* (*The Book of History*), may have been edited by Confucius (551–479 BCE). Although it certainly reveals a Confucian understanding of the basis of legitimate political authority, "The Mandate of Heaven" also reflects earlier Chinese views of the encounter between political power and the society it governs. Because of its antiquity and because it remained a part of the political tradition of China for centuries, this text is of singular importance.

The traditions presented here, no matter how authoritarian, defined legitimate government as the fulfillment of binding social obligations. In examining the specific traditions, their distinctive characteristics, and the implications of both their social systems and their values, then, we will be, in effect, assessing the extent to which human social systems and the authority by which they are governed are ethical constructions. Thus the theme of this chapter is the exercise of legitimate political authority as a continuous encounter between leaders and the moral and religious values of their societies.

CHAPTER QUESTIONS

1. How is authority represented in these depictions? Is there a universal representation or set of characteristics for authority common to all the cultures?

2. How is authority limited? Later in European history there will be something known as "absolute monarchs." Based on what you've read here, is that a contradictory term?

3. In different societies the emperors or kings were thought of differently—human, semidivine, divine. Can you see any correlations between a society's understanding of the ruler's nature and the freedom from constraint that royal authority enjoyed?

4. Group together any readings that express similar ideas of the proper exercise of royal authority. What accounts for the similarities? Which tradition of political authority is most distinctive? Why?

64   CHAPTER 3 ❖ Kingship and Authority in the Ancient World

5. Do the depictions of royal authority in these readings and the kinds of constraints that the climate of social expectations imposed compare at all to the
way that authority operates in your world, in either private or public circumstances? How has your understanding of authority changed as a result of these
readings?

KINGSHIP IN ANCIENT MESOPOTAMIA

The first two readings come from the Babylonian and Neo-Assyrian empires, respectively, and they represent the Mesopotamian royal tradition. Because of its geography, Mesopotamia was open to the movements of different peoples, and it
was a multiethnic region from very early on in its history. Despite its ethnic diversity and the fact that it was unified under different kingdoms dominated by different peoples, there developed a common conception of the rights and responsibilities of the king. The king was thought to be a divinely designated individual.
According to an ancient text known as the "Sumerian King List," "kingship was
lowered from heaven." A document from the city-state of Lagash circa 2450 BCE
describes the king as having a divine father and being nursed and given his span of
years by a goddess.[1] Because *lugals* ("big men" or kings) were key to the organization and management of the early agriculture-based city-states, it is understandable that kings should have enjoyed such an elevated profile.

Central and fundamental to the Mesopotamian understanding of proper royal
behavior were the two Akkadian words *andurarum* (freedom) and *misharum* (equity) that expressed the public idea of royal responsibilities in the general
Mesopotamian cultural zone.[2] An important part of the process of providing freedom and equity was legal action by the monarch. A common New Year practice
of kings was rectifying some of the uncertainties of life—for example, robbers attacking a trade caravan, wolves devastating a flock, or bad weather wiping out a
crop. Kings acted to ensure that the individuals who suffered these catastrophes
would not be punished for debt. More generally, legal codes such as Hammurabi's
gave substance to these principles, so the law was seen as an agent for rectifying
injustice and for ensuring those core principles of freedom and equity. This legal
tradition views the law as a public entity, independent of and greater than any
individual.

The first document in this section comprises the Prologue, Epilogue, and certain statutes from the famous Code of Hammurabi, a king of Babylon. The dates
of the Babylonian Empire are given as 1894–1595 BCE, but Babylon was really a
regional city-state until Hammurabi became king, and it began a slow decline after
his death. Even under him, there was very little expansion until he had already
reigned for thirty years. Then in a dramatically condensed period of time
(1763–1755 BCE), he established control over most of Mesopotamia. His code is
known from a beautiful dark stone stele over seven feet tall on which it is carved.
Much of the code is made up of legal statutes based on the principle of *lex talionis,* or "an eye for an eye, a tooth for a tooth." Punishments differed according to

social class, gender, and age (noble, commoner, slave, male and female, minor and adult). These laws served to affirm public, royal authority in a society still accustomed to private "justice" by means of vendetta and blood feuds. Because of their value as sources for social history and for the functioning of the law code, we have included representative selections of those laws. Those statutes are interesting sources for social history. Preceding and following them, we present the introduction and conclusion of the law code, including Hammurabi's self-representation and the public ideal of kingship.

QUESTIONS TO CONSIDER

1. What purposes does Hammurabi cite for issuing the law code? Who is it supposed to serve? Can you think of other purposes for law codes and other groups to serve?

2. Identify the terms that Hammurabi uses to describe himself. What does he compare himself to? What do those descriptive terms and comparisons have to do with the purpose of the law code?

3. From what source does Hammurabi derive his authority? Why does he think he was given that authority (i.e., what is he supposed to do with it)?

4. How do the specific statutes compare with Hammurabi's claims in the Prologue and Epilogue? In your opinion, do the statutes achieve what he claims? Are the statutes fair? Do you think they would be effective?

5. How do the Prologue, Epilogue, and statutes embody the twin Mesopotamian legal principles of *andurarum* (freedom) and *misharum* (equity)? How does equity differ from equality and how is that reflected in the statutes?

CODE OF HAMMURABI (circa 1750 BCE)

Prologue

When the lofty Anu,* king of the Anunnaki,† and Enlil,‡ lord of heaven and earth, who determines the destinies of the land, committed the rule of all mankind to Marduk§, the first-born son of Ea, and made him great among the Igigi;** when they

---

Source: J. M. Powis Smith, *The Origin and History of Hebrew Law* (Chicago: The University of Chicago Press, 1931), 181, 183, 186, 190–91, 198–99, 209–10, 218–20, 222.

*Father and king of the gods.

†Gods of the earth.

‡God of wind.

§Patron god of Babylon.

**Gods of the heavens.

66 CHAPTER 3 ◆ Kingship and Authority in the Ancient World

pronounced the lofty name of Babylon, made it great among the quarters of the world and in its midst established for him an everlasting kingdom whose foundations were firm as heaven and earth—at that time Anu and Enlil named me, Hammurabi, the exalted prince, the worshiper of the gods, to cause righteousness to prevail in the land, to destroy the wicked and the evil, to prevent the strong from plundering the weak, to go forth like the sun over the black-headed race, to enlighten the land and to further the welfare of the people. Hammurabi, the shepherd named by Enlil am I, who increased plenty and abundance; who made everything complete. . . . The ancient seed of royalty, the powerful king, the sun of Babylon, who caused light to go forth over the lands of Sumer and Akkad; the king who caused the four quarters of the world to render obedience; the favorite of Innanna* am I. When Marduk sent me to rule the people and to bring help to the land, I established law and justice in the language of the land and promoted the welfare of the people.

Statutes

If a man accuse a man, and charge him with murder, but cannot convict him, the accuser shall be put to death. . . .

If a man practice brigandage and be captured, that man shall be put to death.

If the brigand be not captured, the man who has been robbed shall establish the amount of his loss before the god, and the city and the governor, in whose land or border the robbery was committed, shall compensate him for whatsoever was lost. . . .

If a man owe a debt and Adad† inundate the field or the flood carry the produce away, or, through lack of water, grain have not grown in the field, in that year he shall not make any return of grain to the creditor, he shall alter his contract-tablet and he need not pay the interest for that year. . . .

If a man neglect to strengthen his dike, and do not strengthen his dike, and a break be made in his dike and he let the water carry away the farmland, the man in whose dike the break has been made shall restore the grain which has been damaged.

If he be not able to restore the grain, they shall sell him and his goods, and the farmers whose grain the water has carried away shall divide [the results of the sale]. . . .

If a man give to another silver, gold, or anything else for safekeeping, whatever he gives he shall show to witnesses and he shall draw up contracts and then give it for safekeeping.

If a man give for safekeeping without witnesses or contracts, and at the place of deposits they dispute with him, that case has no penalty.

If a man give to another silver, gold, or anything else for safekeeping in the presence of witnesses and the latter dispute with him [or deny it], they shall call that man to account and he shall double whatever he has disputed and repay it.

If a man give anything of his for safekeeping and at the place of deposit either by burglary or by pillage his property along with the property of the owner of the house be carried off, the owner of the house who has been negligent and has lost whatever was

---

*The goddess of love; a different name for the goddess Ishtar in the Gilgamesh tale.

†Sumerian name of the god of rain and storms.

given to him on deposit shall make good [the loss] and restore [it] to the owner of the goods; the owner of the house may institute a search for what has been lost and take it from the thief.

If a man, nothing of whose has been carried off, say, "Something of mine has been carried off," alleging he sustained loss when nothing of his had been carried off, he shall declare his [alleged] loss in the presence of God, and he shall double and pay the amount for which he had made claim for his [alleged] loss. . . .

If a man take a wife and do not draw up a contract with her, that woman is not his wife.

If the wife of a man be taken in lying with another man, they shall bind them and throw them into the water. If the husband of the woman spare the life of his wife, the king shall spare the life of his . . . subject [the offending man]. . . .

If a man force the [betrothed] wife* of a man, who has not known a male and is living in her father's house, and lie in her bosom, and they take him, that man shall be put to death and that woman shall go free.

If a man accuse his wife and she have not been taken in lying with another man, she shall take an oath in the name of God and she shall return to her house.

If the finger have been pointed at the wife of a man because of another man, and she have not been taken in lying with another man, for her husband['s sake] she shall throw herself into the sacred river [i.e., she shall submit to the ordeal by water]. . . .

If the wife of a man bring about the death of her husband because of another man, they shall impale that woman. . . .

If a man, after [the death of] his father, lie in the bosom of his mother, they shall burn both of them. . . .

If a man strike his father, they shall cut off his hand.

If a man destroy the eye of another man, they shall destroy his eye.

If he breaks a man's bone, they shall break his bone.

If he destroy the eye of a common man or break a bone of a common man, he shall pay one mana of silver.

If he destroy the eye of a man's slave or break a bone of a man's slave, he shall pay one-half his price.

If a man knock out a tooth of a man of his own rank, they shall knock out his tooth.

If he knock out a tooth of a common man, he shall pay one-third mana of silver.

Epilogue

The righteous laws which Hammurabi the wise king established and by which he gave the land a firm support and a gracious rule. Hammurabi the perfect king am I. I was not careless nor was I neglectful of the black-headed people, whom Bel† presented to me and whose care Marduk gave to me. Regions of peace I spied out for

---

*Fiancée.

†Babylonian god of the earth.

68   CHAPTER 3 ◆ Kingship and Authority in the Ancient World

them. With the powerful weapon which Zamama* and Innanna intrusted to me, with the breadth of vision which Ea allotted to me, with the might which Marduk gave me, I expelled the enemy north and south; I made an end of their raids; I promoted the welfare of the land; I made the peoples to rest in habitations of security; I permitted no one to molest them. The great gods have named me and I am the guardian shepherd whose scepter is righteous; my beneficent shadow is spread over the city. In my bosom I have carried the peoples of the land of Sumer and Akkad, under my protection I brought their brethren into security; with my wisdom I covered them; that the strong might not oppress the weak, and that they should give justice to the orphan and the widow, in Babylon, the city whose head Anu and Enlil raised aloft, in Esagila,† the temple whose foundations stand firm as heaven and earth, to pronounce judgements for the land, to render decisions for the land, to give justice to the oppressed, my weighty words I have written upon my monument, and in the presence of the image of me, king of righteousness, have I set it up.

The king who is preeminent among kings am I. My words are precious, my wisdom is unrivaled. By the command of Shamash,‡ the great judge of heaven and earth, may I make righteousness to shine forth on the land; by the word of Marduk, my lord, may there be none to set aside my statutes; in Esagila which I love may my name be remembered with favor forever. Let any oppressed man who has a cause come before the image of me, the king of righteousness! Let him have read to him the writing on my monument! Let him give heed to my weighty words! And may my monument enlighten him as to his cause and may he understand his case! May it set his heart at ease. "Hammurabi indeed is a ruler who is like a real father to his people; he has given reverence to the word of Marduk, his lord; he has obtained Marduk's victory north and south; he has made glad the heart of Marduk, his lord; he has established prosperity for all time and has led the land aright," let him proclaim aloud and let him pray with his whole heart before Marduk, my lord, and Zarpanit,§ my lady, and may the protecting deities, the gods who enter Esagila, the walls of Esagila, make his thoughts acceptable daily before Marduk, my lord, and Zarpanit, my lady! In the days to come, for all time, let the king who arises in the land observe the words of righteousness which I have written upon my monument! Let him not alter the judgements of the land which I have pronounced, the decisions of the country which I have rendered! Let him not efface my statutes! If that man have wisdom and be able to guide his land aright, let him give attention to the words which I have written upon my monument! And may this monument enlighten him as to procedure and administration, the judgements of the land which I have pronounced, and the decisions of the land which I have rendered! And let him guide aright the black-headed people! Let him pronounce their judgements and render their decisions! Let him root out the wicked and the evildoer from his land! Let him promote the welfare of his people!

---

*A warrior god associated with Marduk.

†The temple of Marduk.

‡The god of Justice.

§Marduk's consort.

Hammurabi, the king of righteousness, to whom Shamash has presented these laws am I. . . . If that man do not give heed to my words which I have written upon my monument, . . . as for that man, . . . may the great Anu, father of the gods, . . . take from him the glory of sovereignty, may he break his scepter and curse his fate! . . . May the great lords of heaven and earth, the Anunnaki in their totality . . . curse him with powerful curses and may they [i.e., the curses] come upon speedily!

KINGSHIP IN ANCIENT ASSYRIA

The period of Mesopotamian history from 934 to 610 BCE is known as the Neo-Assyrian era, because during this time period the Assyrian kingdom was restored and its power expanded to cover most of the Middle East. Our second Mesopotamian source dates from that era. Some sense of the ebb and flow of empires in that region and of its multiethnic nature can be gauged from the different eras, empires, and sources we have already referred to. The material we include here comes from the second period of Assyrian imperial glory, which reached its peak in the last century and a half of that era, from 745 to 610. In some ways, the Assyrians took elements of Mesopotamian kingship to an extreme. They believed in the active involvement of the gods in human affairs and that the preservation of order in the world called for strict application of the divinely established requirements. A leading scholar of the ancient Middle East gave as the subheading for a section on the Neo-Assyrian empire "Loyalty, Terror, Mercy, and Vengeance." This might be said to describe Neo-Assyrian imperial policy. A carving in one of the royal palaces depicts the great Assyrian king Assurbanipal in repose in a garden and drinking wine with his queen with the severed head of his defeated enemy, the King of Elam, hanging by its nose in the background.[3]

There is an unprecedented ferocity about Neo-Assyrian political culture, and yet, as the following reading demonstrates, the royal concern with public welfare remains present in the education and moral formation of princes. The following document was intended to teach princes how they should rule. In typical Assyrian style, it presents a sort of negative ideal for a ruler: If you do not do this, here is what will happen to you.

QUESTIONS TO CONSIDER

1. According to this "Advice," what are the most important things that a ruler must do? Whose interests does this "Advice" serve (the king, the nobles, the people)?

2. On the basis of the "Advice" presented here, devise a composite picture of an unsuccessful prince. Characterize the failings of this unsuccessful prince (for example, moral, political, religious, economic, and so on).

3. If the prince fails in his duty, who will punish him? Identify the actions against him that will occur if the prince fails to do his duty. Which involve moral punishments and which involve political rebellion?

4. How are *andurarum* (freedom) and *misharum* (equity) defended in this document? How does it compare with the Code of Hammurabi?

5. The American Declaration of Independence rejected British rule on both moral and political grounds. How do the abuses warned against here compare with those that the American Founding Fathers accused the British of?

ADVICE TO A PRINCE (circa 750 BCE)

If a king does not heed justice, his people will be thrown into chaos and his land will be devastated.

If he does not heed the justice of his land, Ea, king of destinies, will alter his destiny and he will not cease from hostilely pursuing him.

If he does not heed his nobles, his life will be cut short.

If he does not heed his adviser, his land will rebel against him.

If he heeds a rogue, the status quo in his land will change.

If he heeds a trick of Ea, the great gods in unison and in their just ways will not cease from prosecuting him.

If he improperly convicts a citizen of Sippar,* but acquits a foreigner, Shamash, judge of heaven and earth, will set up a foreign justice in his land, where the princes and judges will not heed justice.

If citizens of Nippur are brought to him for judgement, but he accepts a present† and improperly convicts them, Enlil, lord of the lands, will bring a foreign army against him to slaughter his army, whose prince and chief officers will roam his streets like fighting-cocks.

If he takes silver of the citizens of Babylon and adds it to his own coffers, or if he hears a lawsuit involving men of Babylon but treats it frivolously, Marduk, lord of Heaven and earth, will set his foes upon him, and will give his property and wealth to his enemy.

If he imposes a fine on the citizens of Nippur, Sippar or Babylon, or if he puts them in prison, the city where the fine was imposed will be completely overturned, and a foreign enemy will make his way into the prison in which they were put.

If he mobilized the whole of Sippar, Nippur and Babylon, and imposed forced labor on the people, exacting from them a corvée‡ at the herald's proclamation,

---

Source: W. G. Lambert, *Babylonian Wisdom Literature*, 113, 115. Copyright © 1967 Clarendon Press. Reprinted by permission of Eisenbrauns, Inc., Winona Lake, IN. Only one version of this text, which was on a tablet in the libraries of Assurbanipal, exists.

*Another ancient Mesopotamian city. Shamash, the god of Justice, was its patron.

†Takes a bribe.

‡Forced labor for some specified period of time.

Marduk, the sage of the gods, the prince, the counsellor, will turn his land over to his enemy so that the troops of his land will do forced labour for his enemy, for Anu, Enlil and Ea, the great gods, who dwell in heaven and earth, in their assembly affirmed the freedom of those people from such obligations.

If he gives the fodder of the citizens of Sippar, Nippur and Babylon to his own steeds, the steeds who eat the fodder will be led away to the enemy´s yoke, and . . . mighty Erra,* who goes before his army, will shatter his front line and go at this enemy´s side.

If he looses the yokes of their oxen, and puts them into other fields, . . . If he seizes their . . . stock of sheep, Addu,† canal supervisor of heaven and earth, will extirpate his pasturing animals by hunger and will amass offerings for Shamash.

If the adviser or chief officer of the king´s presence denounces them‡ and so obtains bribes from them, at the command of Ea, king of the Apzu, the adviser or chief officer will die by the sword, their place will be covered over as a ruin, the wind will carry away their remains and their achievements will be given over to the storm wind.

If he declares their treaties void, or alters their inscribed treaty stele, sends them on a campaign or press-gangs them into hard labour, Nabu, scribe of Esagila, who organizes the whole of heaven and earth, who directs everything, who ordains kingship, will declare the treaties of his land void, and will decree hostility.

If either a shepherd or a temple overseer, or a chief officer of the king, who serves as a temple overseer of Sippar, Nippur or Babylon imposes forced labour on them§ in connection with the temples of the great gods, the great gods will quit their dwelling in their fury and will not enter their shrines.

KINGSHIP IN ISRAEL

Our second section is devoted to the kingship of ancient Israel as depicted in the Jewish Bible. The selection we include deals with the tribes' insistence on having a king against the objections of both the prophet/judge Samuel and what the work presents as the will of Yahweh himself. One tradition presented in the Jewish Bible up to I Samuel is that the real king of Israel was their god Yahweh, and that they did not need a mortal placeholder for him, because he made his wishes known to them via prophets and revelations. A second, opposing theme in the last chapters of Judges is that moral and political rot had set in during the period before the kingship was established. The ethical mess is summed up in the assertion that ends Judges, "In those days there was no king in Israel; every man did what was right in his own eyes."[4]

---

*God of war.

†God of storm and rain.

‡The people of Sippar, Nippur, and Babylon.

§The people of Sippar, Nippur, and Babylon.

72   CHAPTER 3 ❖ Kingship and Authority in the Ancient World

In historical terms, the Jews had been a patriarchal people organized in a clan system (tribes), but the power and challenge of the Philistines over both resources and land contributed to the emergence of kingship in Israel. Historically, the Philistines had occupied the southern coastal regions, and the Jews had been centered in the inland highlands. There was not much trouble between them until both peoples had expanded enough to come into competition over resources and land. The Philistines had advantages over the Jews in both political organization and technology, at one point even capturing the Ark of the Covenant. To muster resources and manpower to meet the Philistine challenge, the Jews came to accept, and even demand, that a king be established.

Around 1000 BCE the Jews began the transition to a monarchical government. The basic story in 1 Samuel, although different versions appear in both 2 Samuel and 1 Chronicles,[5] is as follows: The Jews insist on a king; although Samuel and the Yahweh figure object, Yahweh accedes to this and designates Saul as leader. Saul demonstrates a certain effectiveness in fighting the Philistines, but, when the great Philistine champion Goliath comes forth and calls on the Jews to send out a challenger, none comes forth except for a young man slight of build and untested in terms of combat: David. Of course, David slays Goliath, but the fame that David garners from this also earns him Saul's envy and suspicion. Eventually, Saul proves his unworthiness for kingship, and he is defeated by the Philistines and killed, to be succeeded by the much more successful David, who had been anointed by Samuel. We learn little of Saul and much more about David, which accurately reflects their political and military achievements. Here our main concern is the picture of kingship that is presented, the form of election, and the responsibilities of a good ruler.

QUESTIONS TO CONSIDER

1. According to 1 Samuel, why do the Jews want a king? Why does this seem ungrateful to the Yahweh figure in these passages, and what kind of picture does the Yahweh figure draw of kingship? Is this an accurate picture of what royal governments, especially in that age, did?

2. Examine the reason that Saul had proven unworthy to be king and what made David pleasing to Yahweh. According to this material, what does the Yahweh figure value most in a king?

3. What reasons does Saul give that David is more fit than he to be king? According to this view, what should a Jewish king be like?

4. How does the role of kingship in Jewish society, according to 1 Samuel, differ from Mesopotamian kingship?

5. In your opinion, which system is closer to what legitimate government should be? Why?

1 SAMUEL

Samuel judged Israel all the days of his life. . . .

When Samuel became old, he made his sons judges over Israel. . . . Yet his sons did not walk in his ways, but turned aside after gain; they took bribes, and perverted justice.

Then all the elders of Israel gathered together and came to Samuel at Ramah and said to him, "Behold, you are old, and your sons do not walk in your ways; now appoint for us a king to govern us like all the nations." But the thing displeased Samuel when they said, "Give us a king to govern us." And Samuel prayed to the Lord. And the Lord said to Samuel, "Hearken to the voice of the people in all that they say to you; for they have not rejected you, but they have rejected me from being king over them. According to all the deeds which they have done to me, from the day I brought them up out of Egypt even to this day, forsaking me and serving other gods, so they are also doing to you. Now then, hearken to their voice; only, you shall solemnly warn them, and show them the ways of the king who shall reign over them."

So Samuel told all the words of the Lord to the people who were asking a king from him. He said, "These will be the ways of the king who will reign over you: he will take your sons and appoint them to his chariots and to be his horsemen; and to run before his chariots; and he will appoint for himself commanders of thousands and commanders of fifties, and some to plow his ground and to reap his harvest, and to make his implements of war and the equipment of his chariots. He will take your daughters to be perfumers and cooks and bakers. He will take the best of your fields and vineyards and olive orchards and give them to his servants. He will take the tenth of your grain and of your vineyards and give to his officers and to his servants. He will take your menservants and maidservants, and the best of your cattle and your asses, and put them to his work. He will take the tenth of your flocks, and you shall be his slaves. And in that day you will cry out because of your king, whom you have chosen for yourselves; but the Lord will not answer you in that day."

But the people refused to listen to the voice of Samuel; and they said, "No! but we will have a king over us, that we also may be like all the nations; and that our king may govern us and go out before us and fight our battles." And when Samuel had heard all the words of the people, he repeated them in the ears of the Lord. And the Lord said to Samuel, "Hearken to their voice, and make them a king." . . .

[Yahweh selects Saul to be king and has Samuel anoint him. The people have what they wanted, but Yahweh is displeased at their insistence on having a king, and Saul will eventually prove his unfitness for kingship. Yahweh says that he will give Saul victory, and then Saul must destroy all the livestock of the conquered people. Saul wins the victory, but together with the Jews he keeps the best livestock, arguing

Source: The Holy Bible, Revised Standard Edition (New York: American Bible Society, 1952), 1 Samuel 7:15; 8:1, 3–22; 13:1; 15:22–28; 16:4, 6–8, 10–13; 24:6–20.

74 CHAPTER 3 ◆ Kingship and Authority in the Ancient World

to Samuel that the very best were sacrificed to Yahweh. For this Saul loses Yahweh's approval.]

And Samuel said, "Has the Lord as great delight in burnt offerings and sacrifices, as in obeying the voice of the Lord? Behold, to obey is better than sacrifice, and to hearken than the fat of rams. For rebellion is as the sin of divination, and stubbornness is as iniquity and idolatry. Because you have rejected the word of the Lord, he has also rejected you from being king."

And Saul said to Samuel, "I have sinned; for I have transgressed the commandment of the Lord, and your words, because I feared the people, and obeyed their voice. Now therefore, I pray, pardon my sin, and return with me, that I may worship the Lord." And Samuel said to Saul, "I will not return with you: for you have rejected the word of the Lord, and the Lord has rejected you from being king over Israel." As Samuel turned to go away, Saul laid hold upon the skirt of his robe, and it tore. And Samuel said to him, "The Lord has torn the kingdom of Israel from you this day, and has given it to a neighbor of yours, who is better than you. . . ."

[Yahweh directs Samuel to the place where Saul's successor will be, so that Samuel may anoint him.]

Samuel did what the Lord commanded, and came to Bethlehem. . . . When they came, he looked on Eliab and thought, "Surely the Lord's anointed is before him." But the Lord said to Samuel, "Do not look on his appearance or on the height of his stature, because I have rejected him; for the Lord sees not as man sees; man looks on the outward appearance, but the Lord looks on the heart." Then Jesse . . . made seven of his sons to pass before Samuel. And Samuel said to Jesse, "The Lord has not chosen these." And Samuel said to Jesse, "Are all your sons here?" And he said, "There remains yet the youngest, but behold, he is keeping the sheep." And Samuel said to Jesse, "Send and fetch him: for we will not sit down till he come here." And he sent, and brought him in. Now he was ruddy, and had beautiful eyes, and was handsome. And the Lord said, "Arise, anoint him; for this is he." Then Samuel took the horn of oil, and anointed him in the midst of his brothers: and the Spirit of the Lord came mightily upon David from that day forward. . . .

[The Philistine armies and their great champion Goliath challenge Saul to send out a champion to fight him. David was away when this challenge was issued, but he returns and accepts the challenge. David's faith gives him courage. Although the armor is too big and heavy for him, he goes into battle and fells Goliath with a stone from his slingshot, and then cuts off Goliath's head with the giant's own sword. The people now praise David, and Saul becomes jealous. He tries to get David killed in combat, to marry his daughter to him, and even throws a spear at him in anger. David flees, but Saul chases him to a remote spot. Though hidden, David is very close to Saul and cuts off the hem of his robe. But he could not harm the king, and he shows himself to Saul.]

He said to his men, "The Lord forbid that I should do this thing to my lord, the Lord's anointed, to put forth my hand against him, seeing he is the Lord's anointed."

So David persuaded his men with these words, and did not permit them to attack Saul. And Saul rose up and left the cave, and went upon his way.

Afterward David also arose, and went out of the cave, and called after Saul, saying, "My lord the king!" And when Saul looked behind him, David bowed with his face to the earth and did obeisance. And David said to Saul, "Why do you listen to the words of men who say, 'Behold, David seeks your hurt?' Lo, this day your eyes have seen how the Lord gave you today into my hand in the cave; and some bade me kill you, but I spared you. I said, 'I will not put forth my hand against my lord; for he is the Lord's anointed.' See, my father, see the skirt of your robe in my hand; for by the fact that I cut off the skirt of your robe, and did not kill you, you may know and see that there is no wrong or treason in my hands. I have not sinned against you, though you hunt my life to take it. May the Lord judge between me and you, may the Lord avenge me upon you; but my hand shall not be against you. As the proverb of the ancients says, 'Out of the wicked comes forth wickedness'; but my hand shall not be against you. After whom has the king of Israel come out? After whom do you pursue? After a dead dog! After a flea! May the Lord therefore be judge, and give sentence between me and you, and see to it, and plead my cause, and deliver me from your hand."

When David had finished speaking these words to Saul, Saul said, "Is this your voice, my son David?" And Saul lifted up his voice and wept. He said to David, "You are more righteous than I; for you have repaid me good, whereas I have repaid you evil. And you have declared this day how you have dealt well with me, in that you did not kill me when the Lord put me into your hands. For if a man finds his enemy, will he let him go away safe? So may the Lord reward you with good for what you have done to me this day. And now, behold, I know that you shall surely be king, and that the kingdom of Israel shall be established in your hand.

KINGSHIP IN INDIA

The Indian cultural and political traditions, to which we turn next, developed along far different lines than did those of Mesopotamia and the Jews. The model of kingship that will be presented here derives from the Hindu religious and cultural traditions. The main Hindu principle relating to kingship is *dharma*. In general, *dharma* means right actions necessary to sustain the moral, social, and political order. It encompasses the meanings of a whole range of duties and ethical obligations and ideals, such as duty, righteousness, virtue, justice, and morality. It also implies proper fulfillment of rituals.

The most important and best-known source in Hindu culture for the representation of ideal royal *dharma* is the great Indian epic, *The Ramayana*. It was probably originally composed somewhere around 400 BCE. Like *The Iliad*, *The Ramayana* was only recorded in written form hundreds of years after it had taken shape as a product of oral culture. Hence, we cannot know to what degree the modern form of it corresponds to the way it was told for any of the centuries before it was written down. Nonetheless, it is one of the great central tales of

Hinduism, and it is still a very popular story. Thus it embodies core values of Hindu culture. One of the most important Hindu feast days, the Festival of Lights, celebrates the triumph of good over evil and order over disorder, one example of which is from *The Ramayana*.

There is a fairy-tale quality about *The Ramayana* that distinguishes it both from the other sources in this section and from the other traditions. Rama is very much the ideal ruler in the Indian political culture. In the story, he is opposed by Ravana, who heads up a demon kingdom and who kidnaps Rama's wife, Sita. In the contrast between Rama and Ravana, we have the Indian representation of good and bad rulership. Although he does not know it, Rama is an incarnation of the god Vishnu. Unaware that he is a human form of a god, he undergoes various adventures and tests before he is finally crowned king. For our purposes, there are two parts of interest. The first is the scene in which Rama's human father, King Dasaratha, decides to step down from the throne and transfer power to his son. In this scene, we get a variety of indications, both direct and indirect, of what proper behavior for a king should be. The second is a brief description of Ravana, holding court in his palace. He is a photographic negative of Rama. His description shows what Hindu culture valued in rulers by sketching the traits of the worst sort of ruler by way of contrast.

QUESTIONS TO CONSIDER

1. According to his father, what are Rama's attributes that will make him an ideal king? Most of the focus of this passage is on Rama, but Dasaratha is a king too, of course. What ideals of royal behavior does he portray? Taken together, how do their attributes compare with the ideal traits of a Mesopotamian or Jewish king?

2. In the other traditions, we saw that there were certain obligations placed on the king both by the gods and by the people over whom the king ruled. Are there any such obligations expressed here?

3. What are the connections between the people and the kings (i.e., Dasaratha and Rama)? How do these compare with the linkages between monarch and people in the other readings in this section?

4. Identify Ravana's main features. Can you identify attributes of Rama that are the opposite of Ravana's traits? What does the negative image add to the ideal of kingship?

5. How does it change your perception of what this ideal means in Hindu culture to know that Rama is a manifestation of a god? Does this strengthen or weaken the obligations of human kings to act according to this model? How does it affect the representation of authority?

THE RAMAYANA

Ramayana

[One day Rama's father, King Dasaratha, realized that age had creeped up on him. He decided that it would be vanity to hold on to power any longer and that Rama was certainly capable of handling the responsibilities.]

In the loneliness of his chamber, Dasaratha told himself, "One must know when to cease, and not wait for death or dotage. While my faculties are intact, let me seek retirement and rest. There is no sense in continuing and repeating the same set of activities performed all these . . . years, as it seems to me now. Enough, I have done enough. I must now find the time to stand back and watch and lay aside the burdens of office."

He arrived at a drastic decision. He summoned his aide to the door, and told him to summon Sumanthra, his chief minister, immediately. "Send round an announcement for all our officers and public men, sages and wise men, and all our allies and kings and relations to gather at our hall of assembly. Let as many as possible arrive."

. . . Messengers were dispatched in all directions. The assembly hall filled up. Dasaratha ascended the steps to his seat and, after the routine ceremonials, gestured to all to resume their seats, and spoke: "I have performed my duties as King of this country long enough. Now I have an irresistible feeling that the burden must be shifted over to younger shoulders. What do you gentlemen think about it? Under the white umbrella of the royal state, apparently there has been no change—but actually the body under it is withering. I have lived and functioned long enough. If I still thought that I should continue thus endlessly, it would amount to avarice. The other day I realized that my signature on a document was hazy. My hand must have trembled without my knowing it. The time has come for me to sit back and rest—and anticipate the coming of grandchildren. If you will agree, I want to hand over the kingdom to Rama. He should be my successor, an embodiment of all perfection. He is perfect and will be a perfect ruler. He has compassion, a sense of justice, and courage, and he makes no distinction between human beings—old or young, prince or peasant; he has the same consideration for everyone. In courage, valour, and all the qualities—none to equal him. He will be your best protector from any hostile force, be it human or subhuman or superhuman. His asthras,* acquired from his master, . . . have never been known to miss their mark. . . . I hope I shall have your support in anointing him immediately as the Emperor of Kosala."

A joyous shout rang through the assembly. Dasaratha waited for it to subside and asked, "I note the zest with which you welcome my successor. Should I take it that you do so because you have been bearing with me silently for any reason all

Source: R. K. Narayan, *The Ramayana*, 35–38, 79. Copyright © 1977 Penguin Books. Used by permission of Penguin Putnam Group (USA) Inc.

*Any kind of weapon powered by a supernatural force.

78   CHAPTER 3   ◆   Kingship and Authority in the Ancient World

these years, although I had thought I had dedicated my life fully to the welfare of my subjects?"

A spokesman arose and explained. "Do not mistake us, Your Majesty. It is our love for Rama that makes us so happy now. We have long looked forward to this moment. To see him ride the Royal Elephant in full paraphernalia through the streets of our capital is a vision of the future that we cherish, young and old alike, for we are lost in the splendour of Rama's personality. It is that anticipation that makes us applaud your proposal so unreservedly. It is not that we do not wish for the continuance of Your Majesty."

Dasaratha said, "I agree with you. I just wanted to know without a trace of doubt that you approve of my desire to make Rama your King. I desire that tomorrow when the *Pushya* star* is in combination with the moon, and the time is auspicious, Rama be crowned."

He summoned his minister and the priest. "Let everything, every little detail be ready for the ceremony of coronation tomorrow. Let there be widespread decorations and have all items ready at the coronation hall. Let the streets be washed, cleaned, and decorated. Let people feast and play and enjoy themselves unlimitedly. Let there be arrangements to serve a feast continuously in every corner of this capital. . . ."

He sent for Rama. He watched his arrival from his balcony, received him warmly, took him aside, and said, "Tomorrow, you will be crowned my successor. I need rest from work."

Rama accepted the proposal with a natural ease. Dasaratha continued. "You know everything, but still I feel it a duty to say a few words. You will have to pursue a policy of absolute justice under all circumstances. Humility and soft speech—there could be really no limit to these virtues. There can be no place in a king's heart for lust, anger, or meanness." He went on thus for some time and terminated the meeting. . . .

Ravana

Ravana, the supreme lord of this and other worlds, sat in his . . . hall, surrounded by a vast throng of courtiers and attendants. The kings of this earth whom he had reduced to vassaldom stood about with their hands upraised in an attitude of perpetual salutation, lest at any moment Ravana should turn in their direction and think that they were not sufficiently servile. Beauties gathered from all the worlds surrounded him, singing, dancing, ministering to his wants, ever ready to give him pleasure and service, with all their eyes fixed on him watching for his slightest sign of command. Every minute vast quantities of flowers were rained on him by his admirers. . . .

KINGSHIP IN CHINA

The material in this selection relates to the principle of imperial legitimacy in China, a component of Chinese political culture that endured into the twentieth century. China differed from the other cultural zones treated in this section in

---

*An Indian astrological or birth star.

that its moral values rested on an ethical system rather than on a dominant religious foundation. Or perhaps it is more accurate to say that ethics and religion were woven together indistinguishably, and as a result China lacked a separate, powerful priestly or ecclesiastical order. From very early on in Chinese cultural development there arose an idea that the cosmos is possessed of a divine order and that humans must live in concert with that order. The dominant answer that evolved as to how one should go about living in concert with the cosmic order is called *Confucianism*. Confucianism has been called "a world view, a social ethic, a political ideology, a scholarly tradition, and a way of life."[6] Though Confucius lived from 551 to 479 BCE, the body of literature on which Confucianism is founded includes both earlier literature and later commentaries and interpretations. Confucian philosophy was optimistic and maintained that humans could live in accord with the requirements of a depersonalized divine order (Heaven), if one lived the right life and maintained properly the five key relationships (king–subject, father–son, husband–wife, brother–brother, and friend–friend).

In terms of political theory, the same idea was maintained. That is, if the emperor lived and ruled properly, carried out the proper rituals and maintained the right order, then the kingdom would know peace and prosperity. Thus, in extreme cases, the absence of domestic peace and prosperity could be used to legitimize the overthrow or replacement of one dynasty by another. This aspect of Chinese political culture is known as the "Mandate of Heaven."

The earliest expression of the theory of the Mandate of Heaven appears in one of the so-called Five Classics, which make up part of the accepted body of works in the Confucian tradition. The selection that follows is from *Shu Jing*, or the *Book of History*. Confucius himself is supposed to have edited and written commentary for this book. The passage you will read is supposed to involve advice given to a young king of the Shang dynasty by Yi Yin. Yi Yin is explaining to the young monarch why the Shang dynasty had legitimately replaced the earlier Xia dynasty. In actual fact, this text was written after the overthrow of the Shang dynasty by the Zhou dynasty. Hence the text justifies the seizure of power by the Zhou dynasty (from the Shang) by showing that the Shang dynasty itself had initially come to power by a similar process and had been legitimized by the same principle—the Mandate of Heaven. Thus the ascent to power of the Zhou dynasty could only have occurred because of the loss of the Mandate by the Shang.

QUESTIONS TO CONSIDER

1. What evidence can you find of the Confucian emphasis on proper maintenance of relations? Can you identify instances of the Chinese tradition of the correct performance of rituals?

2. What are some examples of improper or immoral behavior that will lead to the disruption of the kingdom? What happens as a result of this improper behavior?

80   CHAPTER 3 ◆ Kingship and Authority in the Ancient World

3. In some of the other texts we have read, there is an emphasis on a paternal relationship and also on justice. Do you see any signs of those in this text? If not, how do you explain their absence from this text? Do you think the Chinese were indifferent to these considerations?

4. In some of the texts you have already read, the rulers are at pains to show their concern and their intention to help and serve the people. Can you see anything in this text that reflects those same concerns?

5. How are authority and legitimate rule related in the Chinese tradition? How does the Chinese relationship between authority and legitimacy compare with the other traditions presented in this chapter?

THE INSTRUCTIONS OF YI (THE MANDATE OF HEAVEN)

In the twelfth month of the first year . . . , Yi Yin sacrificed to the former king* and presented the heir-king reverently before the shrine of his grandfather. All the princes from the domain of the nobles and the royal domain were present; all the officers also, each continuing to discharge his particular duties, were there to receive the orders of the chief minister. Yi Yin then clearly described the complete virtue of the Meritorious Ancestor for the instruction of the young king.

He said, "Oh! of old the former kings of Xia cultivated earnestly their virtue, and then there were no calamities from Heaven. The spirits of the hills and rivers alike were all in tranquility; and the birds and beasts, the fishes and tortoises, all enjoyed their existence according to their nature. But their descendant did not follow their example, and great Heaven sent down calamities, employing the agency of our ruler[†]— who was in possession of its favoring appointment. The attack on Xia may be traced to . . . [their] orgies . . . , but our rise began in Po.[‡] Our king of Shang brilliantly displayed his sagely prowess; for oppression he substituted his generous gentleness; and the millions of the people gave him their hearts. Now your Majesty is entering on the inheritance of his virtue—all depends on how you commence your reign. To set up love, it is for you to love your relations; to set up respect, it is for you to respect your elders. The commencement is in the family and the state. . . .

Oh! the former king[§] began with careful attention to the bonds that hold men together. He listened to expostulation, and did not seek to resist it; he conformed to the wisdom of the ancients; occupying the highest position, he displayed intelligence; occupying an inferior position, he displayed his loyalty; he allowed the good qualities of

---

Source: James Legge, trans., *The Sacred Books of China: The Texts of Confucianism,* in *The Sacred Books of the East,* ed. F. Max Mueller, 50 vols. (Oxford, UK: Clarendon Press, 1879–1910), vol. 3, pp. 92–95.

*That is, to the young king's recently deceased father.

†That is, the young king's grandfather and founder of the Shang dynasty.

‡The name of the home territory of the Shang dynasty.

§Again, the young king's grandfather.

the men whom he employed and did not seek that they should have every talent. . . . It was thus he arrived at the possession of the myriad regions. How painstaking was he in these things!

He extensively sought out wise men, who should be helpful to you, his descendant and heir. He laid down the punishments for officers, and warned those who were in authority, saying, "If you dare to have constant dancing in your palaces, and drunken singing in your chambers—that is called the fashion of sorcerers; if you dare to set your hearts on wealth and women, and abandon yourselves to wandering about or to the chase,*—that is called the fashion of extravagance; if you dare to despise sage words, to resist the loyal and upright, to put far from you the aged and virtuous, and to seek the company of precocious youth—that is called the fashion of disorder. Now if a high noble or officer be addicted to one of these three fashions with their ten evil ways, his family will surely come to ruin; if the prince of a country be so addicted, his state will surely come to ruin. The minister who does not try to correct such vices in the sovereign shall be punished with branding." These rules were minutely inculcated also in the son of officers and nobles in their lessons.

"Oh! do you, who now succeed to the throne, revere these warnings in your person. Think of them!—sacred counsels of vast importance, admirable words forcibly set forth! The ways of Heaven are not invariable: on the good-doer it sends down all blessings, and on the evil-doer it sends down all miseries. Do you but be virtuous, be it in small things or in large, and the myriad regions will have cause for rejoicing. If you be not virtuous, be it in large things or in small, it will bring the ruin of your ancestral temple."

NOTES

1. Amelie Kuhrt, *The Ancient Near East*, vol. 1 (New York: Routledge, 1998), 33.

2. See C. C. Lamberg-Karlovsky, "The Near Eastern 'Breakout' and the Mesopotamian Social Contract," in *The Breakout: The Origins of Civilization,* ed. M. Lamberg-Karlovsky (Cambridge, MA: Peabody Museum Monographs, 2000), 14–15, 20–21.

3. Amelie Kuhrt, *The Ancient Near East*, vol. 2 (London and New York: Routledge, 1998), 514, 517.

4. On Judges, see Howard Clark Lee, et al., *The Cambridge Companion to the Bible* (Cambridge, UK: Cambridge University Press, 1997), 118–19. The passage cited is from Judges 21:25.

5. See Cyrus H. Gordon and Gary A. Rendsburg, *The Bible and the Ancient Near East* (New York: W. W. Norton & Co., 1997 [1953]), 186–87. In 2 Samuel, a different hero named Elhanan kills Goliath. 1 Chronicles has Elhanan killing Goliath's brother.

6. Tu Wei-ming, "The Confucian Tradition in Chinese History," in *Heritage of China: Contemporary Perspectives on Chinese Civilization*, ed. P. S. Ropp (Berkeley, CA: University of California Press, 1990), 112.

---

*Hunting.

CHAPTER 4

Individual Ethics and Social Responsibility

INTRODUCTION

The Corporate and Criminal Fraud Accountability Act of 2002, signed into law on July 30, 2002, by President George W. Bush, established strong protections for corporate whistleblowers. "Without protecting the whistleblowers, corporate reform efforts would have failed," said Kris Kolesnik, Executive Director of the National Whistleblower Center.[1]

Whistleblowers—employees who report illegal (but usually profitable) behavior on the part of their employers—face a modern version of an old dilemma: the potential conflict between individual actions and the harmonious workings of the larger social group of which the individual is a member (in the case of whistleblowers, the company they work for). Is it better to obey one's leaders without question, on the premise that unless everyone does their part loyally the society will fall apart? If no one questions authority, however, will the result be a mindlessly conformist society in which, for example, six million Jews could die because everyone was "only following orders"? Is it therefore better for each individual to do as he or she thinks best? Or will chaos and social breakdown result from a lack of agreed-on leadership and norms—how, after all, does one decide what is best? Is there a middle ground where individual ethical action can contribute to the harmonious functioning of society? As the director of the National Whistleblower Center points out, whistleblowers who are disruptive troublemakers from one perspective are from another perspective social reformers serving a higher cause.

There are no easy answers to these questions. They arise in any complex society, but they become particularly acute in times of crisis and transformation, when the need for reform may be greatest. Around 600 BCE, many of the most populous and complex societies of Eurasia seemed to face just such a time of crisis. A number of factors—including growing population, increased contact with other cultures, the spread of iron-working technology, and political disruptions often associated with nomadic incursions—brought instability to older systems of political

86   CHAPTER 4   ◆   Individual Ethics and Social Responsibility

organization and so brought the intellectual systems that legitimized those political organizations into question. Mythic worldviews based in sacrifice and obedience to angry gods, although not discarded, no longer provided adequate answers to the problems of social organization and individual ethical action within society.

In this context, there arose a remarkable range of thinkers, both secular and religious, who suggested answers to these problems within their own societies. A simple list of names from the first several centuries after 600 BCE suggests the importance of the theories developed during this period and their continuing impact: Confucius, Mencius, Lao Tzu, the Buddha, Zarathustra, Isaiah, Socrates, and Plato, to name only some of the most prominent. These thinkers produced systems of philosophy and religion of such power and intellectual coherence that they have formed the foundations of social and ethical theory in many parts of the world ever since. In this sense, these are the names of a classical age, an age of the creation of great traditions. This chapter explores some of these systems of philosophy and religion and the encounter between individual ethics and social responsibility within them.

But as the list of names suggests, societies tended to produce many different answers to such complex questions, and another set of encounters this chapter examines is the philosophical encounter of thinker against thinker. In every area, there were arguments, experiments, and, usually, an ultimate synthesis that began to emerge sometime around 200 BCE. Thus, as you read different sources from any one civilization, look not just for the points of disagreement between them, which will be fairly clear, but for their bases of agreement as well. Often this agreement will reside at the level of fundamental assumptions about the topic rather than in the details of what each source says, and it is the character of these fundamental assumptions that would come to characterize the synthesis, or the Great Tradition, and the intellectual nature of the civilization that produced it. For example, Pericles, in the funeral oration Thucydides records in his *History of the Peloponnesian Wars,* outlines a conception of citizenship in which civic duty is paramount. Sophocles, on the other hand, bases the tragedy of *Antigone* on the conflict between such civic duty and a higher duty to family and the gods. The disagreement is clear. The perhaps less obvious agreement is that the *polis,* the independent city-state, was the natural and proper realm of both individual action and social organization. The question for each, in other words, is the proper functioning of the *polis* and the limits of its power over individuals. Although Confucius and Lao Tzu deal with the same big issue—the relationship of individual ethical action and social order—their unstated assumptions, or the particular way they frame the question, are different. Figuring out what those assumptions are will reveal important intellectual and cultural characteristics about each civilization.

The encounter between philosophies also brought to the fore the issue of education, for individual thinkers gained influence only insofar as they gathered followers who spread the master's teachings, creating a school of thought. And education became a topic for many of these thinkers, as well as a practical issue, because depending on where one sees the balance between social order and individual action, one will see the function of education differently. Is the purpose of education to produce free thinkers, creative minds that will question authority and accepted ways of doing things? This is a dominant modern conception of the purpose of education, embodied in the liberal arts education offered at many colleges and universities. But it has by no means eclipsed another conception: that the purpose of education is to train people in a society's accepted principles and ways of doing things, thereby producing good citizens (or subjects) and social harmony. One need only look at the arguments about national history standards in the United States today to see both sides of this argument flourishing, with one side arguing that we need a common history to hold us together, the other side arguing that the myths and exclusiveness of the usually told common story contribute to oppression and prejudice.

We look at thinkers from four Great Traditions that emerged in this age. First, Confucius, Lao Tzu, and Han Fei Tzu are three of the wellsprings of the Chinese tradition. The first two lived near the end of the Chou dynasty (771 to 464 BCE); the last lived in the middle of the subsequent Warring States era of Chinese history (464 to 221 BCE). The later Chou era saw the breakdown of the political unity established in China by the Chou, as the regional princes who owed obedience to the Chou king increasingly followed their own paths, including fighting each other for prestige and honor. The shift to the Warring States was marked by an increase in the intensity of warfare and the gradual disappearance of many of the hundreds of small states of the Chou era. The centrality of warfare and conflict in Chinese life during these centuries, as well as the lack of political unity, proved intensely troublesome to many Chinese thinkers, some of whom looked back to the early Chou era as a sort of "Golden Age" of peace and harmony in the Chinese cultural world, others of whom looked for contemporary answers to these problems.

Next, we look at Thucydides and Sophocles, mentioned previously, from the Greek tradition. Frequent warfare also characterized the world of Classical Greece (650–350 BCE), but political disunity was taken as the norm in the Greek world, which was divided into numerous small *poleis* (singular *polis*), or city-states. Each *polis* was defended by groups of its own citizens, who also participated in the fractious and competitive politics of their city-state. This participation ranged from informal, in more narrowly ruled monarchical or aristocratic cities, to completely formal and empowered in democratic Athens. In this world, and especially in Athens, where broad participation in politics raised questions of social order with special intensity and where leadership in the war against the Persians broadened the importance of the issues, questions of individual ethics and social order were debated by politicians, philosophers, and makers of culture, including playwrights.

The Greeks and Chinese approached these issues from a basically secular perspective. This does not mean that religion had no importance in these societies. But religion in both places tended to serve purposes other than answering questions of individual ethical action within the context of social order. Religion was central, however, to the next two traditions we examine, rising in both places to the level of philosophical systems that functioned in the same way the secular traditions of China and Greece did. First, we have a classic statement of social responsibility from India in the *Bhagavad-Gita*, followed by the early teachings of the Buddha. Indian religion, in particular what would come to be known as the Hindu religion, developed over a long period after the Aryan invasions of the subcontinent around 1500 BCE. By the period 700–500 BCE, the major outlines of Brahminical Hinduism, a faith shaped by the teachings of the Brahmins, the

88   CHAPTER 4   ◆   Individual Ethics and Social Responsibility

priestly class, were moving from the realm of oral traditions to texts known as *Upanishads,* which means "to sit down before [a teacher]." The Upanishads' orientation toward a priest-dominated religion reflects the movement of Indian society from a warrior-dominated system in the wake of the invasions to a society in which the Brahmins occupied the highest position in what was becoming a caste system. *Caste* refers to hierarchical social divisions determined at birth—that is, a rigid class system with no mobility between castes. The four major castes, or *varna,* were the Brahmins; the Kshatriyas, or rulers and warriors; the Vaisyas, or laborers; and the Sudras, or slaves. The caste system and the cosmological[2] assumptions that underlay it came to dominate the intellectual landscape of India. It shaped both efforts to explain and justify social order and individual responsibility within it, which is the function of the *Bhagavad-Gita,* and efforts to escape the rigidity of the caste system, which characterizes early Buddhism.

Finally, we look at two statements of ethical theism from southwest Asia: the Persian tradition, stemming from the prophet Zarathustra, and the Hebrew tradition, as stated by the prophet Isaiah. Southwest Asia, perhaps the area of the world most open to external influences because of its position as a crossroads of Afro-Eurasian trade, migration, and invasion, had already witnessed by 600 BCE the rise and fall of many kingdoms and empires and the encounters of numerous peoples. Around 600, one of these peoples, the Persians of the Iranian plateau, inherited the imperial mission in the area and created the first of the great empires of this age. It was in the context of Persian conquest of and rule over many peoples and already venerable civilizations that both the Persians and the Hebrews developed remarkably similar (and probably cross-fertilized) religious views of the cosmos, history, and their peoples' place in the social order and ethical struggles of the universe.

Though their approaches differed widely, all of these traditions addressed the problems of social order and its interaction with individual ethical decision making and action. Hence these readings involve fundamental aspects of human existence: encounters between individual ethics and systems of social values, encounters between individual thinkers within the grand ethical traditions, and encounters between the ethical systems themselves. The answers that the thinkers of these traditions arrived at continue to have relevance today.

CHAPTER QUESTIONS

1. What are the crucial issues that bring individual ethics and social order into focus for these authors? That is, what problems face the societies of this age? Are they similar across Eurasia?

2. Considering these sources as a group, where does the balance seem to lie in classical societies between individually motivated action and social constraints? Is there variation among the sources? Which seems most individualistic and which most socially oriented?

3. What appears to be the basis for underlying agreement within each tradition? That is, what would the authors from each tradition agree on that distinguishes them from the authors of the other traditions?

4. What are the vested interests in these debates? That is, does the position of a source's author within the social hierarchy seem to influence where he draws the line between individual and society (or between stability and reform)? And does that line differ for different members of society as determined by class, gender, or occupation?

5. What would each author think about whistleblowers? Would they wish to reward or punish a whistleblower's "betrayal" of his or her employer? Which of these authors might be considered a whistleblower in his own society?

THE CHINESE TRADITION

Classical Chinese systems of thought arose during the last centuries of the Chou dynasty (771 to 464 BCE) and the period known as the Warring States (464 to 221 BCE). During this time the political unity established in north China by the first dynasty for which we have substantial information, the Shang, and continued by their Chou successors after 1050 BCE broke down, and China became a land of many small states that tended to engage in constant warfare with each other. Many Chinese thinkers responded to this disorder with programs for social and political reform. We shall look at the foundational texts for what proved, in the long run, to be the most influential of these many schools of thought: Confucianism, Taoism, and Legalism. Each addresses the problem of social order, individual responsibility, and the role of the state in maintaining the balance between the two, but each puts the emphasis on a different aspect of this set of factors. Although the three schools competed with and criticized each other, their different emphases meant that in many ways they proved complementary rather than mutually exclusive.

The Confucian Tradition

In the long run the most influential of Chinese philosophers was Kung Fu Tzu (Master Kung Fu), whose name was Latinized by the Jesuits in the seventeenth century to Confucius. Born in 551 BCE in the state of Lu, Confucius traveled widely, looking for a ruler who would heed his advice on good rulership and restoring the harmony to Chinese civilization. His prescriptions for reform looked back to the age of the founders of the Chou dynasty, King Wen and King Wu— and, indeed, even farther back to the semilegendary founders of the Shang dynasty—for models of leadership, correct individual behavior, and the foundations of social order. His program of reform was, therefore, like many such programs in the traditional world, backward looking, advocating a return to the virtues of an earlier Golden Age. But Confucius was no simple imitator of old ways. His teachings—collected by his students and eventually written down in several versions, one of which is *The Analects* as we have it—stress the importance of education and the malleability of human nature, and so offered openings for further interpretation. The nature of the *Analects* themselves—fragmentary, organized apparently haphazardly, but with an underlying coherence that invites further study and thought—contributed to the vitality of Confucian philosophy.

90   CHAPTER **4** ✦ Individual Ethics and Social Responsibility

Confucius himself, however, found no real takers for his services among those in power during his lifetime. He died in 479 BCE, thinking that he had failed as a teacher and government advisor. It was only in later generations that his teachings became central to the Chinese tradition.

Key terms and concepts in *The Analects*

li: ritual, decorum, civility, rites, rules of propriety

ren: humanity, humaneness, human-heartedness, benevolence, goodness

te: virtue, moral force, power

tien ming: the biddings or mandate of Heaven, the will of Heaven

wen: culture, civilization, refinement

Confucius weaves these concepts together into a coherent account of social relationships and individual responsibility within them. As the list of terms shows, proper behavior—not just what we would call manners, but also ritual, rites, and the music that accompanied them—was central to Confucius's teaching.

QUESTIONS TO CONSIDER

1. What are the qualities of a Confucian "gentleman"? How does he differ from a "small man"?

2. What does Confucius mean by "humanity" or "being humane"? Why does he think that the wrong way to cultivate humanity is through chastisement, regulations, and law? What is the right way?

3. What are the foundations of social order for Confucius? What models of authority and obedience does he cite?

4. What sort of social order would be produced if everyone strictly followed his advice? What is the relationship for Confucius between individual behavior and social order? Would Confucian government benefit the common people, as he claims? How practical do you think his program of reform is?

5. Would Confucius encourage whistleblowers?

THE ANALECTS

Confucius

Book 1

1.1. The Master said, To learn and at due times to repeat what one has learned, is that not after all a pleasure? That friends should come to one from afar, is this not after all

Source: The translation is a version of *The Analects of Confucius,* trans. Arthur Waley, edited in part by David Blix of Wabash College. Copyright © 1989. Used by permission of Vintage Books, a division of Random House, Inc.

delightful? To remain unsoured even though one's merits are unrecognized by others, is that not after all what is expected of a gentleman?

1.2. Master Yu [a disciple of Confucius] said, Those who in private life behave well towards their parents and elder brothers, in public life seldom show a disposition to resist the authority of their superiors. And as for such men starting a revolution, no instance of it has ever occurred. It is upon the root that a gentleman works. When that is firmly planted, the Way* grows. And surely proper behavior towards parents and elder brothers is the root of humanity.

1.5. The Master said, A country of a thousand war-chariots cannot be administered unless the ruler attends strictly to business, punctually observes his promises, is economical in expenditure, shows affection towards his subjects in general, and uses the labor of the common people only at the proper times of year.

1.6. The Master said, A young man's duty is to behave well to his parents at home and to his elders abroad, to be cautious in giving promises and punctual in keeping them, to have kindly feelings towards everyone, but to associate with humane men. If, when all that is done, he has any energy to spare, then let him study the polite arts [*wen*].

Book 2

2.1. The Master said, He who rules by virtue [*te*] is like the pole-star, which remains in its place while all the lesser stars do homage to it.

2.2. The Master said, If out of the three hundred *Songs*† I had to take one phrase to cover all my teaching, I would say "Let there be no evil in your thoughts."

2.3. The Master said, Govern the people by regulations, keep order among them by chastisements, and they will flee from you, and lose all self-respect. Govern them by virtue, keep order among them by ritual, and they will keep their self-respect and come to you of their own accord.

2.4. The Master said, At fifteen I set my heart upon learning. At thirty, I had taken my stance. At forty, I no longer suffered from perplexities. At fifty, I knew what were the biddings of Heaven [*t'ien-ming*]. At sixty, I heard them with docile ear. At seventy, I could follow the dictates of my own heart; for what I desired no longer overstepped the boundaries of righteousness.

2.5. Meng Yi Tzu [a disciple] asked about the treatment of parents. The Master said, Never disobey! When Fan Ch'ih [another disciple] was driving his carriage for him, the Master said, Meng asked me about the treatment of parents and I said, Never disobey! Fan Ch'ih said, In what sense did you mean it? The Master said, While they are alive, serve them according to ritual. When they die, bury them according to ritual, and sacrifice to them according to ritual.

---

* *Tao*, meaning "The Way," is the word used by virtually every Chinese school of thought to name its teachings as a whole. Thus, there is a Confucian Way, a Legalist Way, and so forth. But later Chinese and Western scholarship have also attached *Tao* specifically to the teachings of Taoism (see next source). This is not the sense used here; this is the Way of Confucius (or the Way of the Gentleman, as Confucius might have said).

† *The Book of Songs*, a collection of poems from Chou times taken as a canonical text by Confucius. As songs, they were connected with music and rites in the realm of Confucian proper behavior.

92 CHAPTER 4 ◆ Individual Ethics and Social Responsibility

2.13. Tzu-kung [a disciple] asked about the true gentleman. The Master said, He does not preach what he practices till he has practiced what he preaches.

2.14. The Master said, A gentleman can see a question from all sides without bias. The small man is biased and can see a question only from one side.

2.15. The Master said, He who learns but does not think, is lost. He who thinks but does not learn is in great danger.

Book 3

3.3. The Master said, A man who is not humane, what can he have to do with ritual [*li*]? A man who is not humane, what can he have to do with music?

3.7. The Master said, Gentlemen never compete. You will say that in archery they do so. But even then they bow and make way for one another when they are going up to the archery-ground, when they are coming down, and at the subsequent drinking-bout. Thus even when competing, they still remain gentlemen.

Book 6

6.16. The Master said, When inborn qualities prevail over culture, you get the boorishness of the rustic. When culture prevails over inborn qualities, you get the pedantry of the scribe. Only when culture and inborn qualities are duly blended do you get the true gentleman.

Book 8

8.2. The Master said, Courtesy not bounded by the prescriptions of ritual becomes tiresome. Caution not bounded by the prescriptions of ritual becomes timidity, daring becomes turbulence, inflexibility becomes harshness. The Master said, When gentlemen deal generously with their own kin, the common people are incited to humanity. When old dependents are not discarded, the common people will not be fickle.

8.9. The Master said, The common people can be made to follow it; they cannot be made to understand it.

Book 13

13.3. Tzu-lu said, If the prince of Wei were waiting for you to come and serve in his government, what would be your first measure? The Master said, It would certainly be the rectification of names.* Tzu-lu said, Can I have heard you aright? Surely what you say has nothing to do with the matter. Why should names be rectified? The Master said, Tzu-lu! How boorish you are! With regard to things he does not understand, a gentleman should maintain an attitude of reserve. If names are not rectified, then what is said does not correspond to what is meant. If what is said does not correspond to what is meant, then what is to be done will not be accomplished. If what is to be

---

*"Rectification of names" is an important Confucian doctrine that advocated not just calling things by their proper names but also encouraging people to conform to the proper meaning of the "name" of their social position. Thus Confucius said: "Let the father be a father, let the son be a son." That is, let each rectify his behavior to match the ideal implied by the word, and let the word be used only of fathers and sons who act as true fathers and sons. The doctrine recognizes and attempts to shape the social power of language.

done cannot be accomplished, then ritual and music will not flourish. If ritual and music do not flourish, then punishments will go astray. If punishments go astray, then the common people will not know where to put hand and foot. Thus the gentleman gives to things only those names which can be used in speech, and says only what can be carried out in practice. A gentleman, in what he says, leaves nothing to mere chance.

Book 15

15.14. The Master said, To demand much from oneself and little from others is the way for a ruler to banish discontent.

15.20. The Master said, The demands that a gentleman makes are upon himself. Those that a small man makes are upon others.

15.21. The Master said, A gentleman is proud, but not quarrelsome, allies himself with individuals, but not with parties.

15.23. Tzu-kung asked, Is there any single saying that one can act upon all day and every day? The Master said, Perhaps the saying about consideration: "Never do to others what you would not like them to do to you."

15.29. The Master said, To have faults and to be making no effort to amend them is to have faults indeed!

15.31. The Master said, A gentleman, in his plans, thinks of the Way. He does not think how he is going to make a living. Even farming sometimes entails times of shortage; and even learning may incidentally lead to high pay. But a gentleman's anxieties concern the progress of the Way. He has no anxiety concerning poverty.

15.35. The Master said, When it comes to being humane, one need not avoid competing with one's teacher.

Book 17

17.2. The Master said, By nature men are pretty much alike; it is learning and practice that set them apart.

LAO TZU AND TAOISM

Little is known of Lao Tzu, the supposed author of the *Tao te ching*, or "Classic of the Way and its Virtue." He was (probably) an older contemporary of Confucius: legend has it he was visited several times by Confucius, to whom he once said: "Abandon your arrogant ways and countless desires, your suave demeanor and unbridled ambition, for they do not promote your welfare. That is all I have to say to you." Parts of the *Tao te ching* certainly seem to respond to Confucian teachings. Legend also has it that he was the Keeper of the Archives in Chou, where the last of the Chou kings still lived, before disappearing forever into the west in his old age, leaving behind only his small, enigmatic book on the Tao.

   Tao (pronounced "dow") means "way." Confucius and Han Fei Tzu both also use this word, but with a very different meaning from Lao Tzu, and it is to

94   CHAPTER 4   ◆   Individual Ethics and Social Responsibility

Lao Tzu's version of the Way that Chinese history has attached the term *Taoism*. Even more than *The Analects*, the *Tao te ching* is cryptic, poetically mysterious, and open to multiple interpretations (and indeed multiple translations, some of which don't even look like the same work!). In other words, don't look for a logical, linear argument here, but for images, suggestions, and definition by negation. The last may be taken as a metaphor for the Taoist concept of "action through inaction": by doing nothing (or saying what something is not), something (an idea of what something is) is accomplished.

The Tao is, like *The Analects*, partly a handbook for rulers, but it has been taken even more often as a guide to individual life and behavior, and indeed the individualism and emphasis on individual freedom and choice of the *Tao*'s teachings is one of the things that distinguishes it from Confucian thought. This emphasis leads to a clear opposition to ritual in the *Tao*. Read it both as a response and as a potential complement to Confucianism, for the two teachings are not mutually exclusive: One could in certain ways be both a Confucian and a Taoist.

QUESTIONS TO CONSIDER

1. What is the *Tao*? What qualities does Lao Tzu ascribe to it? What metaphors does he use to describe it?

2. A key term in the *Tao* is *wu-wei*, variously translated (loosely) as "inaction" or, more evocatively, "going with the flow." How is *wu-wei* a means to the managing of affairs?

3. What are the principles of social order for Lao Tzu? How do they emerge from the meaning of the *Tao*? What is the role of the individual in fostering social order?

4. Do you think Lao Tzu's Taoism would work as a form of government? As a basis for social order? As an individual lifestyle? Why or why not?

5. What would Lao Tzu think of whistleblowers?

TAO TE CHING

Lao Tzu

Book I: The Book of the Way

1. The Tao that can be told of is not the eternal Tao.
The name that can be named is not the eternal name.
The Nameless is the origin of Heaven and Earth.
The Named is the mother of all things.

Volume 1: –1500

Lao Tzu ◆ *Tao te ching*   95

Therefore let there always be non-being so we may see their subtlety,
And let there always be being so we may see their outcome.
The two are the same.
But after they are produced, they have different names.
They both may be called deep and profound.
Deeper and more profound,
The door of all subtleties!

2. When the people of the world all know beauty as beauty,
There arises the recognition of ugliness.
When they all know the good as good,
There arises the recognition of evil.
Therefore:
Being and non-being produce each other.
Difficult and easy complete each other.
Long and short contrast each other.
High and low distinguish each other.
Sound and voice harmonize with each other.
Front and back follow each other.
Therefore the sage manages affairs without action [*wu-wei*],
And spreads doctrines without words.
All things arise, and he does not turn away from them.
He produces them, but does not take possession of them.
He acts, but does not rely on his own ability.
He accomplishes his task, but does not claim credit for it.
It is precisely because he does not claim credit that his accomplishment remains
    with him.

3. Do not exalt the worthy, so that the people shall not compete.
Do not value goods that are hard to get, so that the people shall not steal.
Do not display objects of desire, so that the people's hearts shall not be disturbed.
Therefore in the government of the sage,
He keeps their hearts vacuous,
Fills their bellies,
Weakens their ambitions,
And strengthens their bones.
He always causes his people to be without knowledge or desire,
And the crafty to be afraid to act.
By acting without action, all things will be in order.

5. Heaven and Earth are not humane [*ren*].
They regard all things as straw dogs.*
The sage is not humane.
He regards all people as straw dogs.

_____

*Dogs made of straw were used for sacrifices in ancient China and then thrown away.

96   CHAPTER 4 ◆ Individual Ethics and Social Responsibility

How Heaven and Earth are like a bellows!
While vacuous, it is never exhausted.
When active, it produces even more.
Much talk will of course come to a dead end.
It is better to keep to the center.

8. The best man is like water.
Water is good; it benefits all things and does not compete with them.
It dwells in lowly places that all disdain.
This is why it is so near to the Tao.
The best man in his dwelling loves the earth.
In his heart, he loves what is profound.
In his associations, he loves humanity.
In his words, he loves faithfulness.
In government, he loves order.
In handling affairs, he loves competence.
In his activities, he loves timeliness.

11. Thirty spokes are united around the hub to make a wheel,
But it is on its non-being that the utility of the carriage depends.
Clay is molded to form a utensil,
But it is on its non-being that the utility of the utensil depends.
Doors and windows are cut out to make a room,
But it is on its non-being that the utility of the room depends.
Therefore turn being into advantage, and turn non-being into utility.

17. The best rulers are those whose existence is merely known by the people.
The next best are those who are loved and praised.
The next are those who are feared.
And the next are those who are despised.
It is only when one does not have enough faith in others that others will have
   no faith in him.

18. When the great Tao declined,
The doctrines of humanity and righteousness arose.
When knowledge and wisdom appeared,
There emerged great hypocrisy.
When the six family relationships* are not in harmony,
There will be the advocacy of filial piety and deep love to children.
When a country is in disorder,
There will be praise of loyal ministers.

---

*Father–son, elder brother–younger brother, husband–wife; these family relationships were important
to Confucian thought.

Book II: The Book of Virtue

48. The pursuit of learning is to increase day after day.
The pursuit of the Tao is to decrease day after day.
It is to decrease and further decrease until one reaches the point of taking no action.
No action is undertaken, and yet nothing is left undone.
An empire is often brought to order by having no activity.
If one likes to undertake activity, he is not qualified to govern the empire.

80. Let there be a small country with few people.
Let there be ten times and a hundred times as many utensils,
But let them not be used.
Let the people value their lives highly and not migrate far.
Even if there are ships and carriages, none will ride in them.
Even if there are armor and weapons, none will display them.
Let the people again knot cords and use them [in place of writing].
Let them relish their food, beautify their clothing, be content with their homes, and
     delight in their customs.
Though neighboring communities overlook one another, and the crowing of cocks
     and barking of dogs can be heard,
Yet the people there may grow old and die without ever visiting one another.

HAN FEI TZU AND LEGALISM

The third writer here differs from the first two in a number of ways. Han Fei Tzu (Master Han Fei) was born a prince of the northern state of Han, one of the successor states of the old state of Chou, and was thus of noble lineage. He lived later—he was born around 280 BCE, near the end of the Warring States era. And therefore the urgency of reform showed itself differently to Han Fei Tzu than it had to Confucius or Lao Tzu: The state of Han's very existence was threatened during Han Fei Tzu's lifetime by the growing power of the state of Qin to its west.

Han Fei had been educated in Confucianism as a young man, but the condition of his own state led him to doubt and eventually reject these teachings as impractical and to focus instead on what could be done to strengthen the state. The result of his concern was a long book, known now as the *Han Fei Tzu,* after its author, that is the clearest statement of the school of thought known as Legalism, or the Way of Law. Han Fei advocated strengthening agriculture and the army, reducing the influence of "enemies of the state" through the impartial application of law, and ruling through an efficient administration. In terms of individual behavior and social order, Han Fei obviously gives primacy to social order and, indeed, subordinates even that to the needs of the state, which are the primary concern in his writing. This formula arrives at very different answers to the problems posed in this chapter from those of Confucius and Lao Tzu.

98   CHAPTER 4 ◆ Individual Ethics and Social Responsibility

Unfortunately, Han Fei's book, aimed at his own king, found no response there and came instead to the attention of the king of Qin. Han Fei met the Qin monarch on a diplomatic mission in 233 BCE and was at first kindly received. But he got caught up in court intrigues and was imprisoned and forced to drink poison. Shortly afterward the ruler of Qin, following some of Han Fei Tzu's advice, conquered Han, then went on to conquer and unite the rest of China by 221 BCE, becoming the First Emperor of China. Han Fei Tzu thus won an ironic victory in the battle of armies and philosophies that characterized the Warring States era. The victory proved short-lived in one way, as the harshness of Qin rule brought the new imperial dynasty down within twenty years. Legalism was discredited in the eyes of later Chinese scholars, mostly Confucian. But the structures of Chinese rule, laid down in the Warring States period by Legalist rulers, persisted beneath the cover of Confucian (and Taoist) philosophy.

QUESTIONS TO CONSIDER

1. Who are the "Five Vermin"? Why are these types of people enemies of a strong state, according to Han Fei Tzu? What are the "Two Handles" and how do they lead to an orderly society?

2. How does Han Fei Tzu propose to measure individual action? Is this a system of ethical decision making for individuals?

3. How does strict adherence to Law (including the use of strict punishments) lead to social order, according to Han Fei Tzu?

4. Does Legalism strike you as a workable system of government? Is it a useful guide to individual action and the creation of social order? What might the advantages and dangers of a strictly Legalist state be?

5. What would Han Fei Tzu think of whistleblowers?

THE FIVE VERMIN

Han Fei Tzu

An enlightened ruler will administer his state in such a way as to decrease the number of merchants, artisans, and other men who make their living by wandering from place to place, and will see to it that such men are looked down upon. In this way he lessens the number of people who abandon primary pursuits [i.e., agriculture] to take up secondary occupations. Nowadays, however, if a man can enlist the private pleading of someone at court, he can buy offices and titles. When offices and titles can be bought, you may be sure that merchants and artisans will not remain despised for long. And when wealth and money, no matter how dishonestly gotten, can buy what is in the market, you may be sure that the number of merchants will not remain small for long. When a man who sits back and collects taxes makes twice as much as the farmer, and enjoys greater honor than the plowman or the soldier, then public-spirited men will grow few, and merchants and tradesmen will increase in number.

These are the customs of a disordered state. Its scholars praise the ways of the former kings and imitate their humanity and righteousness. They put on a fair appearance and speak in elegant phrases, thus casting doubt upon the laws of the time and causing the ruler to be of two minds. Its speechmakers propound false schemes and borrow influence from abroad, furthering their private interests and forgetting the welfare of the state's altars of the soil and grain. Its swordsmen gather bands of followers about them and perform deeds of honor, making a fine name for themselves and violating the prohibitions of the five government bureaus. Those of its people who are worried about military service flock to the gates of private individuals and pour out their wealth in bribes to influential men who will plead for them. In this way they escape the hardship of battle. Its merchants and artisans spend their time making luxury goods, accumulating riches, waiting for the best time to sell, and exploiting the farmers.

These five groups are the vermin of the state. If the rulers do not wipe out such vermin, and in their place encourage men of integrity and public spirit, then they should not be surprised when they look about the area within the four seas, and see states perish and ruling houses wane and die.

On Having Standards

In our present age he who can put an end to private scheming and make men uphold the public law will see his people secure and his state well-ordered. He who can block selfish pursuits and enforce the public law will see his armies growing stronger and his enemies weakening. . . .

Now if able men are selected for promotion on the basis of reputation alone, then the officials will disregard the ruler and seek only the good will of their associates and subordinates. If appointments to office are controlled by cliques, then men will work only to establish profitable connections and will not try to achieve office by regular routes. In such cases, official posts will never be filled by able men, and the state will fall into disorder.

If rewards are handed out on the basis of good report alone, and punishments on the basis of slander, then men who covet rewards and fear punishment will abandon the public interest and pursue only private schemes, banding together to further each other's interests.

A truly enlightened ruler uses the law to select men for him; he does not choose them himself. He uses the law to weigh their merits; he does not attempt to judge them for himself. Hence men of true worth will not be able to hide their talents, nor spoilers to gloss over their faults. Men cannot advance on the basis of praise alone, nor be driven from court by slander. Then there will be a clear understanding of values between the ruler and his ministers, and the state can be easily governed. But only if the ruler makes use of law can he hope to achieve this.

100   CHAPTER 4 ◆ Individual Ethics and Social Responsibility

The Two Handles

The enlightened ruler controls his ministers by means of two handles alone. The two handles are punishment and favor. What do I mean by punishment and favor? To inflict mutilation and death on men is called punishment; to bestow honor and reward is called favor. Those who act as ministers fear the penalties and hope to profit by the rewards. Hence, if the ruler wields his punishments and favors, the ministers will fear his sternness and flock to receive his benefits.

If the ruler of men wishes to put an end to evil-doing, then he must be careful to match up names and results, that is to say, words and deeds. The ministers come forward to present their proposals. The ruler assigns them tasks on the basis of their words, and then concentrates on demanding the accomplishment of the task. If the accomplishment fits the task, and the task fits the words, then he bestows reward. But if they do not match, he doles out punishment.

Hence, if one of the ministers comes forward with big words but produces only small accomplishments, the ruler punishes him—not because the accomplishments are small, but because they do not match the name that was given to the undertaking. Likewise, if one of the ministers comes forward with small words but produces great accomplishments, he too is punished—not because the ruler is displeased at great accomplishments, but because he considers the discrepancy in the name given to the undertaking to be a fault too serious to be outweighed by great accomplishments.

Hence an enlightened ruler, in handling his ministers, does not permit them to gain merit by overstepping their offices, or to speak words that do not tally with their actions. Those who overstep their offices are condemned to die. Those whose words and actions do not tally are punished. If the ministers are made to stick to their proper duties and speak only what is just, then they will be unable to band together in cliques to work for each other's benefit.

THE GREEK TRADITION

The Persian invasions of Greece in 490 and 480 BCE stimulated significant changes in the world of Classical Greece (c. 650–350 BCE). Athens, already one of the largest and most democratic of the many city-states into which Greece was divided, was the main beneficiary of these changes. Athens had gained glory and its citizens pride and confidence by defeating the first Persian invasion at Marathon in 490, and the Athenian navy proved decisive in repelling the second invasion at the Battle of Salamis in 480. Though the Spartan army contributed to the final defeat of the second Persian invasion the following year, Athens took the lead in constructing a coalition of states that carried a naval counteroffensive across the Aegean Sea. Using the revenues generated by the coalition and from a new silver mine, Athens built up its navy and turned the alliance into an empire.

Athenian naval power rested on the participation of the poorer classes of Athenian citizens as rowers in the oar-driven ships of the navy, and this military role was linked to the large role the mass of Athenian citizenry had in running the state. To us, Athenian democracy is an inspiring early example of a form of government common today, an example whose limitations on citizenship and voting rights seem less prominent than its inclusivity. But even in Classical Greece, never mind by the standards of the rest of the world in that age and in all times until at least the nineteenth century, Athens's experiment in mass participatory government was radical. Unlike the firm and centralized control exercised by monarchy, democracy raised serious questions about social order and cohesion and about the freedoms and duties of individual citizens.

It was in this heady atmosphere, combining self-confidence and prosperity with serious philosophical questions open to debate by large numbers of citizens, that Athens created a golden age of cultural output that encompassed virtually every arena of intellectual inquiry and that built on intellectual changes initiated earlier in other parts of the Greek world. We will look at two examples of this output, the historical writing of Thucydides and the drama of the playwright Sophocles. They give us two different perspectives on and ways of talking about the issues of individual ethical action and social order that were so central to this city's culture in the fifth century BCE.

Thucydides, *History of the Peloponnesian War*

The rise of Athenian power raised serious concerns in the other leading Greek city-state, Sparta, and by the 430s most of Greece had divided into two hostile coalitions led by these two cities. War broke out in 431. The Peloponnesian War (named for the Spartan-led Peloponnesian League that fought the Athenian alliance and empire) against monarchical, conservative Sparta challenged not just Athens's political power and leadership but its cultural self-identity.

We know the story of the war from the history written by Thucydides, an Athenian born around 460 to an upper-class family. A relative had served as a general in the Persian wars, and Thucydides was elected general in 424. But an unsuccessful campaign led to his being exiled for the duration of the war. Basing himself on family estates in Thrace, he traveled through Greece and devoted himself to writing a history of the great war. He died sometime after the end of the war (which Athens ultimately lost) in 404, his history unfinished.

We present here a speech Thucydides puts in the mouth of Pericles, the Athenian politician who set Athenian strategy for the early stages of the war and a man admired by Thucydides. Thucydides reports many speeches in the course of his history; in his own words, they are not transcriptions of the actual orations but reconstructions shaped by Thucydides according to what was "fitting" for the occasion. This does not mean that they are inaccurate, just that their truth is at a more general level than verbatim reporting. Pericles was speaking at the state funeral of some of the first Athenian casualties of the war; he took the occasion to defend the Athenian constitution and way of life, including its balance of personal freedom and social order. This is, in other words, an ideal statement of Athenian virtues.

242   CHAPTER 4 ✦ Individual Ethics and Social Responsibility

QUESTIONS TO CONSIDER

1. What are the specific strengths of Athenian democracy, according to Pericles? How do they compare with the characteristics of Sparta—the "enemy" Pericles refers to a number of times in the oration and whose society and government he describes by implication and by contrast with the Athenian system?

2. How does Pericles reconcile the individual freedoms enjoyed by Athenian citizens with the need for social order and cohesion? What costs is he willing to concede as part of the Athenian system?

3. What limits on freedom are visible here? What, in particular, is the place of women in Athens according to the (meager) evidence in this speech?

4. How does the Athenian balance of freedom and order compare with those described by the Chinese authors? What basic assumptions about society and the state are different here from the ones in the Chinese texts?

5. What lessons for individual freedom and social order does Pericles' speech hold for modern democracies such as the United States? What would Pericles and the Athenians think of whistleblowers?

PERICLES' FUNERAL ORATION

Many of those who have spoken here in the past, have praised the institution of this speech at the close of our ceremony. It seemed to them a mark of honour to our soldiers who have fallen in war that a speech should be made over them. I do not agree. These men have shown themselves valiant in action, and it would be enough, I think, for their glories to be proclaimed in action, as you have just seen it done at this funeral organized by the state. . . . However, the fact is that this institution was set up and approved by our forefathers, and it is my duty to follow the tradition and do my best to meet the wishes and the expectations of every one of you. . . .

I have no wish to make a long speech on subjects familiar to you all: so I shall say nothing about the warlike deeds by which we acquired our power or the battles in which we or our fathers gallantly resisted our enemies, Greek or foreign. What I want to do is, in the first place, to discuss the spirit in which we faced our trials and also our constitution and the way of life which has made us great. After that I shall speak in praise of the dead, believing that this kind of speech is not inappropriate to the present occasion, and that this whole assembly, of citizens and foreigners, may listen to it with advantage.

Let me say that our system of government does not copy the institutions of our neighbours. It is more the case of our being a model to others, than of our imitating

Source: From Thucydides in *History of the Peloponnesian War,* trans. Rex Warner, 144–48, 151. Copyright © 1986 Penguin Books. Used by permission of Penguin Putnam Group (USA) Inc.

anyone else. Our constitution is called a democracy because power is in the hands not of a minority but of the whole people. When it is a question of settling private disputes, everyone is equal before the law; when it is a question of putting one person before another in positions of public responsibility, what counts is not membership of a particular class, but the actual ability which the man possesses. No one, so long as he has it in him to be of service to the state, is kept in political obscurity because of poverty. And, just as our political life is free and open, so is our day-to-day life in our relations with each other. We do not get into a state with our next-door neighbour if he enjoys himself in his own way, nor do we give him the kind of black looks which, though they do no real harm, still do hurt people's feelings. We are free and tolerant in our private lives; but in public affairs we keep to the law. This is because it commands our deep respect.

We give our obedience to those whom we put in positions of authority, and we obey the laws themselves, especially those which are for the protection of the oppressed, and those unwritten laws which it is an acknowledged shame to break.

And here is another point. When our work is over, we are in a position to enjoy all kinds of recreation for our spirits. There are various kinds of contests and sacrifices regularly throughout the year; in our own homes we find a beauty and a good taste which delight us every day and which drive away our cares. Then the greatness of our city brings it about that all the good things from all over the world flow in to us, so that to us it seems just as natural to enjoy foreign goods as our own local products.

Then there is a great difference between us and our opponents, in our attitude towards military security. Here are some examples: Our city is open to the world, and we have no periodical deportations in order to prevent people observing or finding out secrets which might be of military advantage to the enemy. This is because we rely, not on secret weapons, but on our own real courage and loyalty. There is a difference, too, in our educational systems. The Spartans, from their earliest boyhood, are submitted to the most laborious training in courage; we pass our lives without all those restrictions, and yet are just as ready to face the same danger, as they are. Here is a proof of this: When the Spartans invade our land, they do not come by themselves, but bring all their allies with them; whereas we, when we launch an attack abroad, do the job by ourselves, and, though fighting on foreign soil, do not often fail to defeat opponents who are fighting for their own hearths and homes. As a matter of fact none of our enemies has ever yet been confronted with our total strength, because we have to divide our attention between our navy and the many missions on which our troops are sent on land. Yet, if our enemies engage a detachment of our forces and defeat it, they give themselves credit for having thrown back our entire army; or, if they lose, they claim that they were beaten by us in full strength. There are certain advantages, I think, in our way of meeting danger voluntarily, with an easy mind, instead of with a laborious training, with natural rather than with state-induced courage. We do not have to spend our time practising to meet sufferings which are still in the future; and when they are actually upon us we show ourselves just as brave as these others who are always in strict training. This is one point in which, I think, our city deserves to be admired. There are also others:

Our love of what is beautiful does not lead to extravagance; our love of the things of the mind does not make us soft. We regard wealth as something to be properly

104   CHAPTER 4   ✦   Individual Ethics and Social Responsibility

used, rather than as something to boast about. As for poverty, no one need be ashamed to admit it: the real shame is in not taking practical measures to escape from it. Here each individual is interested not *only in* his own affairs but in the affairs of the state as well: even those who are mostly occupied with their own business are extremely well informed on general politics—this is a peculiarity of ours: we do not say that a man who takes no interest in politics is a man who minds his own business; we say that he has no business here at all. We Athenians, in our own persons, take our decisions on policy or submit them to proper discussions: for we do not think that there is an incompatibility between words and deeds; the worst thing is to rush into action before the consequences have been properly debated. . . .

Taking everything together then, I declare that our city is an education to Greece, and I declare that in my opinion each single one of our citizens, in all the manifold aspects of life, is able to show himself the rightful lord and owner of his own person, and do this, moreover, with exceptional grace and exceptional versatility. And to show that this is no empty boasting for the present occasion, but real tangible fact, you have only to consider the power which our city possesses and which has been won by those very qualities which I have mentioned. Athens, alone of the states we know, comes to her testing time in a greatness that surpasses what was imagined of her. In her case, and in her case alone, no invading enemy is ashamed at being defeated and no subject can complain of being governed by people unfit for their responsibilities. . . .

Perhaps I should say a word or two on the duties of women to those among you who are now widowed. I can say all I have to say in a short word of advice. Your great glory is not to be inferior to what God has made you, and the greatest glory of a woman is to be least talked about by men, whether they are praising you or criticizing you.

SOPHOCLES, *ANTIGONE*

Sophocles was born in 495 BCE, just outside of Athens, and died in 404 after a long and distinguished career as perhaps the greatest of the Athenian writers of tragedy. He wrote *Antigone* in 442, making it the earliest of his seven surviving plays (out of 120 that he wrote). Sophocles was interested above all in questions of individual psychology, and *Antigone* explores the conflict between the demands of the state and social order against the dictates of individual conscience and ethical choice through the tragedy of the lead character, Antigone.

It is interesting, however, that Sophocles pursues this theme through a female character—one of a number of strong female portrayals in his body of work—adding gender to an already complicated encounter of ideals. Questions of gender roles had, perhaps, special meaning in Athens, where increasing freedom and social responsibility for its male citizens was matched by a far more restricted and subordinate life for its women than was common in other Greek city-states. His work allows us a rare glimpse at the influence of conceptions of gender on questions of social order and individual ethics.

The play is set in the city of Thebes and involves the ill-fated family of Oedipus, the Theban ruler who killed his father and married his mother, producing four children by her: the twin sons Eteocles and Polynices and the sisters Ismene and Antigone. After discovering his horrible fate, Oedipus blinds himself and goes into exile. Eteocles takes the Theban throne, but Polynices contests his rule with an invading army. The two brothers kill each other, and rule of Thebes passes to their uncle Creon, who accords the loyal Theban Eteocles a state burial but decrees that the traitor Polynices's corpse should rot, unburied. Antigone sees this order not through the eyes of the state but as a violation of family relationships and the dictates of religion with regard to proper burial. She defies the order, and eventually dies as a result of her uncle's decision; this proves to have tragic consequences for Creon.

Sophocles therefore presents a conflict of principles with no winners (thus, a tragedy) and no easy answers to the clash between individual conscience and collective responsibility. The key statements of principle by the two central characters are contained in the excerpts that follow.

QUESTIONS TO CONSIDER

1. What principles does Creon appeal to in support of his position? What principles does Antigone appeal to? Are the two positions necessarily incompatible?
2. What are the implications of each position for individual ethical choice and social order?
3. How do you think Antigone's gender influences her position and Creon's reaction to it? What would Pericles say about this dispute?
4. What lessons would an Athenian audience of the sort implied in Pericles' speech have drawn from this tragedy? What comment does it offer on Athenian state and society?
5. What would Creon and Antigone think of whistleblowers? Would they agree?

ANTIGONE

Sophocles

Creon:

My countrymen, the ship of state is safe. The gods who rocked her, after a long, merciless pounding in the storm, have righted her once more. Out of the whole city I have called you here alone. Well I know, first, your undeviating respect for the throne and royal power of King Laius. Next, while Oedipus steered the land of Thebes, and even after he died, your loyalty was unshakable, you still stood by their children. Now

106   CHAPTER 4   ◆   Individual Ethics and Social Responsibility

then, since the two sons are dead—two blows of fate in the same day, cut down by each other's hands, both killers, both brothers stained with blood—as I am next in kin to the dead, I now possess the throne and all its powers.

Of course you cannot know a man completely, his character, his principles, sense of judgment, not till he's shown his colors, ruling the people, making laws. Experience, there's the test. As I see it, whoever assumes the task, the awesome task of setting the city's course, and refuses to adopt the soundest policies but fearing someone, keeps his lips locked tight, he's utterly worthless. So I rate him now, I always have. And whoever places a friend above the good of his own country, he is nothing: I have no use for him. Zeus is my witness, Zeus who sees all things, always—I could never stand by silent, watching destruction march against our city, putting safety to rout, nor could I ever make that man a friend of mine who menaces our country. Remember this: our country is our safety. Only while she voyages true on course can we establish friendships, truer than blood itself.

Such are my standards. They make our city great. Closely akin to them I have proclaimed, just now, the following decree to our people concerning the two sons of Oedipus. Eteocles, who died fighting for Thebes, excelling all in arms: he shall be buried, crowned with a hero's honors, the cups we pour to soak the earth and reach the famous dead. But as for his blood brother, Polynices, who returned from exile, home to his father-city and the gods of his race, consumed with one desire—to burn them roof to roots—who thirsted to drink his kinsmen's blood and sell the rest to slavery: that man—a proclamation has forbidden the city to dignify him with burial, mourn him at all. No, he must be left unburied, his corpse carrion for the birds and dogs to tear, an obscenity for the citizens to behold!

These are my principles. Never at my hands will the traitor be honored above the patriot. But whoever proves his loyalty to the state—I'll prize that man in death as well as life.

Leader of the Chorus:

If this is your pleasure, Creon, treating our city's enemies and our friend this way. . . . The power is yours, I suppose, to enforce it with the laws, both for the dead and all of us, the living.

[The burial of Polynices in contradiction of this order is revealed by a Guard to Creon, who at first suspects the Guard or someone else did this for money.]

Leader of the Chorus:

My king, ever since he began I've been debating in my mind, could this possibly be the work of the gods?

Creon:

Stop before you make me choke with anger—the gods! You, you're senile, must you be insane? You say—why it's intolerable—say the gods could have the slightest concern for that corpse? Tell me, was it for meritorious service they proceeded to bury him, prized him so? The hero who came to burn their temples ringed with pillars, their golden treasures—scorch their hallowed earth and fling their laws to the winds. Exactly when did you last see the gods celebrating traitors? Inconceivable!

No, from the first there were certain citizens who could hardly stand the spirit of my regime, grumbling against me in the dark, heads together, tossing wildly, never keeping their necks beneath the yoke, loyally submitting to their king. These are the instigators, I'm convinced—they've perverted my own guard, bribed them to do their work.

Money! Nothing worse in our lives, so current, rampant, so corrupting. Money—you demolish cities, root men from their homes, you train and twist good minds and set them on to the most atrocious schemes. No limit, you make them adept at every kind of outrage, every godless crime—money!

Everyone—the whole crew bribed to commit this crime, they've made one thing sure at least: sooner or later they will pay the price.

Wheeling on the sentry.

You—I swear to Zeus as I still believe in Zeus, if you don't find the man who buried that corpse, the very man, and produce him before my eyes, simple death won't be enough for you, not till we string you up alive and wring the immorality out of you. Then you can steal the rest of your days better informed about where to make a killing. You'll be learned, at last, it doesn't pay to itch for rewards from every hand that beckons. Filthy profits wreck most men, you'll see—they'll never save your life.

[Antigone is brought before Creon, having been caught in the act of reburying her brother, whose body had been exposed once again.]

Creon:
You, tell me briefly, no long speeches—were you aware a decree had forbidden this?

Antigone:
Well aware. How could I avoid it? It was public.

Creon:
And still you had the gall to break this law?

Antigone:
Of course I did. It wasn't Zeus, not in the least, who made this proclamation—not to me. Nor did that Justice, dwelling with the gods beneath the earth, ordain such laws for men. Nor did I think your edict had such force that you, a mere mortal, could override the gods, the great unwritten, unshakable traditions. They are alive, not just today or yesterday: they live forever, from the first of time, and no one knows when they first saw the light.

These laws—I was not about to break them, not out of fear of some man's wounded pride, and face the retribution of the gods. Die I must, I've known it all my life—how could I keep from knowing?—even without your death-sentence ringing in my ears. And if I am to die before my time I consider that a gain. Who on earth, alive

108   CHAPTER 4   ◆   Individual Ethics and Social Responsibility

in the midst of so much grief as I, could fail to find his death a rich reward? So for me, at least, to meet this doom of yours is precious little pain. But if I had allowed my own mother's son to rot, an unburied corpse—that would have been an agony! This is nothing. And if my present actions strike you as foolish, let's just say I've been accused of folly by a fool.

Leader:

Like father like daughter, passionate, wild . . . she hasn't learned to bend before adversity.

THE INDIAN TRADITION

The Indian religious tradition arose during the long period between the Aryan invasions of India around perhaps 1500 BCE and the emergence of the tradition from oral into written form beginning as early as 400 BCE, though some parts were recorded as late as 600 CE. The development of the ethical and philosophical thought that came to undergird both Hinduism and Buddhism in different forms responded in part to state disorder and warfare, as the Chinese and Greek thinkers did, but the greater challenge met by the development of this tradition seems to have been internally generated: the problem of elaborating and making workable the increasingly rigid and detailed caste system that defined Indian society. Caste, or class divisions defined by birth and admitting of no social mobility, may have developed from the invading Aryans' attempts to maintain an identity separate from their conquered subjects—*varna,* the Sanskrit word for class or caste, means "color," and it may reflect the difference between the lighter-skinned Aryans and the darker pre-Aryan populations. The four major classes were priests, warriors and kings, commoners (farmers and merchants), and servants or slaves; over many centuries following this age numerous subcastes, or *jati,* based on occupation and ranked within the four major classes, evolved. Each caste had its *dharma,* meaning caste-law or sacred duty, to perform.

In one sense it is incorrect to say that there was no social mobility in the caste system, however. For the other crucial part of the context for the emergence of the Hindu and Buddhist religious traditions was the universal Indian belief in *samsara,* or the cycle of reincarnation that all souls were trapped in ("trapped" because rebirth into the world of cares and illusions was a bad thing). What drove *samsara* was *karma,* or the theory of consequences of action (what is translated in the *Bhagavad-Gita* as "fruits of action"). Proper performance of one's *dharma* was reflected in one's *karma,* which in turn determined into what level of the caste system one was reborn (or if one was reborn as a human at all). Finally, only those at the very top of the system, priests and a few great warriors, had a chance for *moksha,* or release from the cycle, meaning that one's undying soul rejoined the universal soul, never to be reborn.

The philosophical and ethical thought of Hinduism and of the Buddha turned to the problems of existence implicit in this view of the cosmos and human life, giving the Indian consideration of individual ethical action and its implications for social order its particular form.

Indian Terms

varna   caste or class

jati   subcastes

dharma   caste-law, sacred duty, duties and responsibilities of each caste

samsara   cycle of reincarnation

karma   consequences or "fruits of action"

moksha   release from *samsara* or the cycle of reincarnation

yoga   discipline

The *Bhagavad-Gita*

The first source we read is probably the most famous and fundamental of all Hindu religious texts, the epic poem known as the *Bhagavad-Gita*.[3] The *Bhagavad-Gita* tells the story of Arjuna, one of the great warrior-kings fighting for the kingdom. The poem opens just as Arjuna is about to go into battle against his cousins and kinsmen from the opposing family line, which sets up the central moral problem of the story. For Arjuna's *dharma* (duty) as a warrior is to fight, but his *dharma* as a family member (and his emotions) tells him not to kill relatives. How to solve a conflict of *dharmas* is the point of the poem, and as such has application to any moral conflict of principles, not just Arjuna's particular dilemma. It is the fundamental Hindu text on the encounter of individual ethical decision making and social order.

Faced with this dilemma, Arjuna freezes in indecision before the battle. Fortunately for Arjuna, he has a charioteer named Krishna who is, in fact, the god Vishnu in disguise. Time stops, in effect, and Krishna holds a dialogue with Arjuna in which he explains why and how he must do his duty as a warrior. This involves his explaining first the fundamental nature of birth, death, and rebirth. Arjuna understands this but remains emotionally unconvinced. Krishna therefore explains the three *yogas,* or disciplines, by which one may attain the proper mental and emotional attitude toward one's *dharma.* The first is the yoga of action, or more accurately the yoga of proper attitude toward action. Achieving this attitude requires that one master the second yoga, the yoga of knowledge, by which one gains control over the illusions that beset the human mind. Achieving this sort of mind control in turn requires that one commit to the yoga of devotion, or complete faith in Vishnu. In the course of explaining the third yoga of devotion, Krishna reveals himself to Arjuna in all his universal, infinite, all-encompassing and awe-inspiring form as Vishnu; Arjuna is the only mortal ever accorded this honor aside from (indirectly) the visionary poet Sanjaya who hears the dialogue and tells us the story. It is this revelation that puts the emotional seal for Arjuna on the philosophical arguments Krishna makes.

110   CHAPTER 4   ◆   Individual Ethics and Social Responsibility

QUESTIONS TO CONSIDER

1. What is it about the nature of death and rebirth that makes it acceptable for Arjuna to kill his relatives?

2. How do the three yogas explain how he is supposed to perform this action? In particular, what does "acting without desiring the fruits of action" mean here?

3. How are these yogas applicable to any individual's ethical decision-making process? What would "acting without desiring the fruits of action" mean in other situations? How is this related to release from the cycle of rebirth?

4. What is the relationship of individual ethical choice to social order presented in the *Gita?* Which side of the equation seems more important to you? What sort of society would result if everyone followed the advice of the *Gita?*

5. What would Krishna think of whistleblowers?

THE *BHAGAVAD-GITA*

The Dilemma

Arjuna
I see omens of chaos,
Krishna; I see no good
in killing my kinsmen
in battle.

Evil will haunt us if we kill them,
even though their bows are drawn to kill.

Honor forbids us to kill
our cousins. . . .

When the family is ruined,
the timeless laws of family duty
perish; and when duty is lost,
chaos overwhelms the family.

In overwhelming chaos, Krishna,
women of the family are corrupted;
and when women are corrupted,
disorder is born in society.

The sins of men who violate
the family create disorder in society
that undermines the constant laws
of caste and family duty.

Death and Rebirth

Lord Krishna
Why this cowardice
in time of crisis, Arjuna?
the cowardice is ignoble, shameful,
foreign to the ways of heaven.

You grieve for those beyond grief,
and you speak words of insight,
but learned men do not grieve
for the dead or the living.

Never have I not existed,
nor you, nor these kings;
and never in the future
shall we cease to exist.

Source: Selections from *The Bhagavad-Gita*, trans. Barbara Stoler Miller. Copyright © 1986. Used by permission of Bantam Books, a division of Random House, Inc.

Just as the embodied self
enters childhood, youth, and old age,
so does it enter another body. . . .

Arjuna, when a man knows the self
to be indestructible, enduring, unborn,
Unchanging, how does he kill
or cause anyone to kill?

Death is certain for anyone born,
and birth is certain for the dead;
since the cycle is inevitable,
you have no cause to grieve!

Look to your own duty;
do not tremble before it;
nothing is better for a warrior
than a battle of sacred duty.

The Yoga of Action

Lord Krishna
Understanding is defined in terms of
    philosophy;
now hear it in spiritual discipline.
Armed with this understanding,
    Arjuna,
you will escape the bondage of
    action.

Be intent on action,
not on the fruits of action;
avoid attraction to the fruits
and attachment to inaction!

Wise men disciplined by understanding
relinquish the fruit born of action;
freed from those bonds of rebirth,
they reach a place beyond decay.

A man cannot escape the force
of action by abstaining from actions;
he does not attain success
just by renunciation.

No one exists for even an instant
without performing an action. . . .

Always perform with detachment
any action you must do;
performing action with detachment,
one achieves supreme good.

These worlds would collapse
if I did not perform action;
I would create disorder in society,
living beings would be destroyed.

The Yoga of Knowledge

Lord Krishna
Without doubt, the mind
is unsteady and hard to hold,
but practice and dispassion
can restrain it, Arjuna.

The Yoga of Devotion

Lord Krishna
Without faith in sacred duty,
men fail to reach me, Arjuna;
they return to the cycle
of death and rebirth.

If he is devoted solely to me,
even a violent criminal
must be deemed a man of virtue,
for his resolve is right.

I am time grown old,
creating world destruction,
set in motion
to annihilate the worlds;
even without you,
all these warriors
arrayed in hostile ranks
will cease to exist.

Therefore, arise
and win glory!
Conquer your foes
and fulfill your kingship!
They are already
killed by me.
Be just my instrument,
the archer at my side!

112   CHAPTER 4 ◆ Individual Ethics and Social Responsibility

Acting only for me, intent on me,
free from attachment,
hostile to no creature, Arjuna,
a man of devotion comes to me.

Action in sacrifice, charity,
and penance is to be performed,
not relinquished—for wise men,
they are acts of sanctity.

But even these actions
should be done by relinquishing to me
attachment and the fruit of action—
this is my decisive idea.

Conclusion

Lord Krishna
The actions of priests, warriors,
commoners, and servants
are apportioned by qualities
born of their intrinsic being.

Tranquility, control, penance,
purity, patience and honesty,
knowledge, judgment, and piety
are intrinsic to the action of a priest.

Heroism, fiery energy, resolve,
skill, refusal to retreat in battle,

charity, and majesty in conduct
are intrinsic to the action of a warrior.

Farming, herding cattle, and commerce
are intrinsic to the action of a
        commoner,
action that is essentially service
is intrinsic to the servant.

Each one achieves success
by focusing on his own action. . . .

Better to do one's own duty imperfectly
than to do another man's well;
doing action intrinsic to his being
a man avoids guilt.

Arjuna
Krishna, my delusion is destroyed,
and by your grace I have regained
        memory;
I stand here, my doubt dispelled,
ready to act on your words.

Sanjaya
Where Krishna is lord of discipline
and Arjuna is the archer,
there do fortune, victory, abundance,
and morality exist, so I think.

BUDDHISM

The Buddha was born Gautama Siddhartha, prince and heir to a small kingdom at the foot of the Himalayas in modern Nepal. But we know little else for certain about his life, for the sources all were written long after his death and reflect conflicting oral traditions. Though they agree that he lived to the age of eighty, different traditions place his birth as early as 624 BCE or as late as 448 BCE. The sources also agree on the outlines of his career: an early life of sheltered luxury, followed by a deeply disturbing encounter with the universal suffering caused by sickness, old age, and death and a quest to find the cause (and so alleviate) this suffering. Finding the answer neither in the teachings of Hindu priests nor in the practice for several years of extreme asceticism,[4] he finally sat under a bo tree and meditated until he achieved enlightenment and became the Buddha, or Enlightened One.

His answer to the problem of suffering is presented here, in a version of his first sermon, along with a lesson about what his teachings do not address and why such things are unimportant. Like the emerging Hindu tradition, Buddhism accepted the reality of *samsara* (cycle of reincarnation) as the central problem of human existence. But the Buddha rejected all divine beings—the universe is instead an uncreated infinity—as well as the restrictions of the caste system: the practice of Buddhism was open to anyone. Properly followed, they led to *nirvana*, which literally means "extinguishment," or the release of the soul from the cycle of rebirth and suffering.

The key concept in Buddhism is variously translated as "desire," "craving," or perhaps most appropriately simply "attachment." It is attachment—to health, loved ones or things, life itself—that causes suffering (a psychological state, not the same as pain, which is physical); attachment is a result of the illusion of the self. Because the universe is for Buddhism in constant flux, attachment to any impermanent constellation of causes and effects, such as a body or a self, constitutes attachment to an illusion. For the Buddha, nonattachment was therefore the key to understanding individual action and its relation to social order.

QUESTIONS TO CONSIDER

1. What is the cause of all suffering for the Buddha? How is suffering then eliminated? Do you agree with the Buddha's diagnosis? Do you agree with his prescription for dealing with the problem?
2. What are the components of the Eightfold Path? How do they reflect the Buddha's emphasis on a Middle Way, neither excessively ascetic nor overly indulgent, as the path to individual moral virtue?
3. What things are unimportant to the Buddha? Why are they unimportant to him? What implications for the relationship of right individual conduct to social order are contained in these views?
4. How does the path to Enlightenment presented here relate to the paths to right conduct and release from *samsara* in the *Bhagavad-Gita*? Is it an easier or a harder path? Who would Buddhism have appealed to in a caste-bound Hindu society?
5. What would the Buddha think of whistleblowers?

THE TEACHINGS OF THE BUDDHA

The Four Noble Truths

The world is full of suffering. Birth is suffering, old age is suffering, sickness and death are sufferings. To meet a man whom one hates is suffering. To be separated from a beloved one is suffering. To be vainly struggling to satisfy one's needs is suffering. In

Source: From *The Teachings of the Buddha,* 1980. Reprinted by permission of Numata Center for Buddhist Translation and Research.

114   CHAPTER 4 ◆ Individual Ethics and Social Responsibility

fact, life that is not free from desire and passion is always involved with distress. This is called the Truth of Suffering.

The cause of human suffering is undoubtedly found in the thirsts of the physical body and in the illusions of worldly passion. If these thirsts and illusions are traced to their source, they are found to be rooted in the intense desires of physical instincts. Thus, desire, having a strong will-to-live as its basis, seeks that which it feels desirable, even if it is sometimes death. This is called the Truth of the Cause of Suffering.

If desire, which lies at the root of all human passion, can be removed, then passion will die out and all human suffering will be ended. This is called the Truth of the Cessation of Suffering.

In order to enter into a state where there is no desire and no suffering, one must follow a certain Path. The stages of this Noble Eightfold Path are: Right Understanding, Right Purpose, Right Speech, Right Behavior, Right Livelihood, Right Effort, Right Mindfulness, and Right Concentration. This is called the Truth of the Noble Path to the Cessation of the Cause of Suffering.

People should keep these Truths clearly in mind, for the world is filled with suffering, and if anyone wishes to escape from suffering, he must sever the ties of worldly passion, which is the sole cause of suffering. The way of life which is free from all worldly passion and suffering can only be known through Enlightenment, and Enlightenment can only be attained through the discipline of the Noble Eightfold Path.

The Search for Enlightenment

In the search for truth there are certain questions that are unimportant. Of what material is the universe constructed? Is the universe eternal? Are there limits or not to the universe? In what way is this human society put together? What is the ideal form of organization for human society? If a man were to postpone his searching and practicing for Enlightenment until such questions were solved, he would die before he found the path.

Suppose a man were pierced by a poisoned arrow, and his relatives and friends got together to call a surgeon to have the arrow pulled out and the wound treated.

If the wounded man objects, saying, "Wait a little. Before you pull it out, I want to know who shot this arrow. Was it a man or a woman? Was it someone of noble birth, or was it a peasant? What was the bow made of? Was it a big bow or a small bow that shot the arrow? Was it made of wood or bamboo? What was the bowstring made of? Was it made of fiber or of gut? Was the arrow made of rattan or of reed? What feathers were used? Before you extract the arrow, I want to know all about these things." Then what will happen?

Before all this information can be secured, no doubt the poison will have time to circulate all through the system and the man may die. The first duty is to remove the arrow, and its poison prevented from spreading.

When a fire of passion is endangering the world, the composition of the universe matters little. What is the ideal form for the human community is not so important to deal with.

The question of whether the universe has limits or is eternal can wait until some way is found to extinguish the fires of birth, old age, sickness, and death. In the presence of lamentation, sorrow, suffering, and pain, one should first search for a way to solve these problems and devote oneself to the practice of that way.

The Buddha's teaching teaches what is important to know and not what is unimportant. That is, it teaches people that they must learn what they should learn, remove what they should remove, train for what they should become enlightened about.

Therefore, people should first discern what is of the first importance, what problem should first be solved, what is the most pressing issue for them. To do all this, they must first undertake to train their minds; that is, they must first seek mind-control.

Those who seek the true path to Enlightenment must not expect an easy task or one made pleasant by offers of respect and honor and devotion. And further, they must not aim with a slight effort, at a trifling advance in calmness or knowledge or insight.

First of all, one should get clearly in mind the basic and essential nature of this world of life and death.

Human Life

There is an allegory that depicts human life. Once there was a man rowing a boat down a river. Someone on the shore warned him, "Stop rowing so gaily down the swift current. There are rapids ahead and a dangerous whirlpool, and there are crocodiles and demons lying in wait in rocky caverns. You will perish if you continue."

In this allegory, "the swift current" is a life of lust. "Rowing gaily" is giving rein to one's passion. "Rapids ahead" means the ensuing suffering and pain. "Whirlpool" means pleasure. "Crocodiles and demons" refers to the decay and death that follow a life of lust and indulgence. "Someone on the shore" who calls out is Buddha.

Everything is changeable, everything appears and disappears. There is no blissful peace until one passes beyond the agony of life and death.

SOUTHWEST ASIAN TRADITIONS

The Indian religious tradition, encompassing both early Hinduism and early Buddhism, infused the entire cosmos with spirituality, seeing gods, nature, and man as all part of the same web of being—indeed, the Buddhists did not even conceive of the universe as created but saw it as infinite in past and future. The two related religious traditions of southwest Asia that we examine next, by contrast, saw a fundamental separation in kind between a Creator and his Creation, the physical universe. But they connected the Creator to Creation through moral laws played out in a human history with a purpose and direction, whereas the very continuity of existence in the Indian tradition seems to have deemphasized the importance of mere human action (and thus history) in favor of metaphysical speculation or attention to the universal problem of suffering. The Persians and Hebrews, therefore, give us another religious take on the problem of individual ethics and social order, but one quite different from the Indian tradition.

Persia: Zarathustra, Sayings of the Prophet

Early Persian religion sprang from the same Indo-European roots as early Aryan-Indian religion. And despite the existence of a single prophet, or carrier of the

116   CHAPTER 4 ◆ Individual Ethics and Social Responsibility

word of god, in the history of the Persian religion, its development is just as difficult to trace in the historical sources as that of Hinduism is. The traditions of the religion that became known as Zoroastrianism[5] put the prophet's life in the half century just after 600 BCE, but the internal linguistic evidence of the earliest sayings of the prophet point to a much earlier date. Complicating the picture is the fact that most of the *Avesta,* the holy written text of Zoroastrianism, dates from after 224 CE. Thus the true role of Zarathustra in the creation of this religion is largely unknowable.

The religion's rise to prominence does fit squarely into the era of world history covered by this chapter, however, as it became the official religion of the Persian royalty under Darius the Great (r. 522–486 BCE). Much of the philosophical development of Zoroastrianism probably dates to the century before Darius, when the Persians began creating their empire. Following Zarathustra's lead, the multiplicity of gods in early Persian religion was pared down to one uncreated creator of the universe, *Ahura* (Lord) *Mazda.* His foe was another uncreated being, *Angra Mainyu* (Hostile Spirit, also known as The Liar), as ageless as Ahura Mazda but lesser in ultimate power, whose evil creations and machinations caused the pain and spiritual pollution in the universe. The story of the cosmos for Zoroastrians, therefore, came down to a struggle between good and evil that good was eventually destined to win but that demanded choice by individuals as to which side they would support. Individual ethical decision making was therefore tied to cosmic standards of right and wrong, as well as to proper social order, and individuals received appropriate eternal rewards and punishments according to the choices made. The ethical philosophy built into this religion may have encouraged good government; it also, however, created a special place for the Persians, the bearers of Zarathustra's Truth, in history, a special place that may well have helped the Persians maintain their separate cultural identity in the vast mix of peoples and cultures—some much older than the Persians—that made up the empire they ruled.

The uncreated nature of Angra Mainyu marks Zoroastrianism as a dualistic religion, and its dualistic view of the universe would later influence Christianity, as well as Islam and some strains of Judaism. But the dualism is also a bit misleading (as calling Christianity dualistic because of the existence of Satan would be), because the emphasis and the ultimate meaning of Zoroastrianism are focused on Ahura Mazda, the principle of good.[6] These views distinguish the Southwest Asian religious and ethical systems from those of China and India and provide a distinctive understanding of the relationship between individual ethical action and social responsibility.

QUESTIONS TO CONSIDER

1. What sorts of beliefs and behaviors does Ahura Mazda demand of his followers? What are the consequences of obedience or disobedience to Mazda's wishes?

2. How do the injunctions about individual choice and behavior connect to social order? What is the role of Mazda's act of creation in structuring the cosmos and society?

3. Ahura Mazda is presented as the single, universal creator. Yet there is no injunction to spread the faith (and in fact Persians were happy to let their subject peoples retain their native religious traditions). Why do you think this was the case? What is the role of the Persian people in the history of Mazda's universe?

4. Persians had a reputation for good government. What do you think the role of Zoroastrianism might have been in promoting good government over conquered peoples? What would be the advantages and disadvantages of a fully Zoroastrian society?

5. What would Zarathustra think of whistleblowers?

YASNAS

Zarathustra

Yasna 19

15. The evil one at once arose (to oppose Him), but He (Ahura) repelled that wicked one with His interdict, and with this repelling renunciation: Neither our minds are in harmony, nor our precepts, nor our comprehensions, nor our beliefs, nor our words, nor our actions, nor our consciences, nor our souls!

16. And this saying, uttered by Mazda, has three stages, or measures, and belongs to four classes (of men as its supporters), and to five chiefs (in the political world, without whom its efficiency is marred), and it has a conclusion ending with a gift. *(Question.)* How are its measures (constituted)? *(Answer.)* The good thought, the good word, and the good deed.

17. *(Question.)* With what classes of men? *(Answer.)* The priest, the charioteer (as the chief of warriors), the systematic tiller of the ground, and the artisan. These classes therefore accompany the religious man throughout his entire duty with the correct thought, the truthful word, and the righteous action. These are the classes and states in life which give attention to the rulers, and fulfill the (laws) of religion; (yea, they are the guides and companions of that religious man) through whose actions the settlements are furthered in righteousness.

18. *(Question.)* How are the chiefs (constituted)? *(Answer.)* They are the house-chief, the village-chief, and the tribe-chief, the chief of the province, and the Zarathushtra* as the fifth. That is, so far as those provinces are concerned which are different from, and outside of the Zarathushtrian regency, or domain. . . . *(Question.)* How are the chiefs of this one constituted? *(Answer.)* They (are) the house-chief, the village-chief, the tribe-chief, and the Zarathushtra as the fourth.

19. *(Question.)* What is the thought well thought? *(Answer.)* (It is that which the holy man thinks), the one who holds the holy thought to be before all other things. *(Question.)* What is the word well spoken? *(Answer.)* It is the Mathra Spenta, the bounteous

---

Source: Translated by L. H. Mills (From *Sacred Books of the East*, American Edition, 1898.)

*The priests of Zoroastrianism and the royal family that ruled in the name of Zoroastrianism.

118   CHAPTER 4 ◆ Individual Ethics and Social Responsibility

word of reason. *(Question.)* What is the deed well done? *(Answer.)* It is that done with praises, and by the creatures who regard Righteousness as before all other things.

20. *(Question.)* Mazda made a proclamation, whom did He announce? *(Answer.)* Some one who was holy, and yet both heavenly and mundane. *(Question.)* What was His character, He who made this sacred enunciation? *(Answer.)* He who is the best (of all), the ruling one. *(Question.)* Of what character (did He proclaim him the coming one)? *(Answer.)* As holy and the best, a ruler who exercises no wanton or despotic power.

Yasna 30

1. Now I will proclaim to those who are willing to hear the things that the understanding man should remember, for hymns unto Ahura and prayers to Good Thought; also the felicity that is with the heavenly lights, which those who think wisely shall behold through Right.

2. Hear with your ears the best things; look upon them with clear-seeing thought, for decision between the two Beliefs, each man for himself before the Great consummation, bethinking you that it be accomplished to our pleasure.

3. Now the two primal Spirits, who reveal themselves in vision as Twins, are the Better and the Bad, in thought and word and action. And between these two the wise ones chose rightly, the foolish not so.

4. And when these two Spirits came together in the beginning, they created Life and Not-Life, and [decided] that at the end the Worst Existence shall be [allotted] to the followers of the Lie, but the Best Existence to him that follows Right.

5. Of these two Spirits he that followed the Lie chose doing the worst things; the holiest Spirit chose Right, he that clothes himself with the massy heavens as a garment. So likewise they that are eager to please Ahura Mazda by dutiful actions.

6. Between these two the Daevas* also chose not rightly, for infatuation came upon them as they took counsel together, so that they chose the Worst Thought. Then they rushed together to Violence, that they might enfeeble the world of men.

7. And to him (i.e. mankind) came Dominion, and Good Mind, and Right and Piety gave continued life to their bodies and indestructibility, so that by Your retributions through (molten) metal he may gain the prize over the others.

8. So when there comes their punishment for their sins, then, O Mazda, at Your command shall Good Thought establish the Dominion in the Consummation, for those who deliver the Lie, O Ahura, into the hands of Right.

9. So may we be those that make this world advance, O Mazda and you other Ahuras, come hither, bestowing (on us) admission into your company . . . , in order that (our) thought may gather together while reason is still shaky.

10. Then truly on the (world of) Lie shall come the destruction of delight; but they who get themselves good name shall be partakers in the promised reward in the fair abode of Good Thought, of Mazda, and of Right.

Source: Translation by C. Bartholomae, from I. J. S. Taraporewala, *The Divine Songs of Zarathushtra.*

*Spirits, originally lesser gods, who were reinterpreted by Zarathustra as demonic creations of Angra Mainyu.

11. If, O you mortals, you mark those commandments which Mazda has ordained—of happiness and pain, the long punishment for the follower of the [Wrong], and blessings for the followers of the Right—then hereafter shall it be well.

Yasna 31

11. When You, O Mazda, in the beginning created the Individual and the Individuality, through Your Spirit, and powers of understanding—when You made life clothed with the body, when (You made) actions and teachings, whereby one may exercise one's convictions at one's free-will;

12. Then lifts up his voice the false speaker or the true speaker, he that knows or he that knows not, (each) according to his own heart and mind. . . .

13. Whatever open or whatever secret (acts) may be visited with punishment, or whether a person for a little sin demands the highest punishment,—of all this . . . You are aware, observing it with Your flashing eye.

THE HEBREWS: SECOND ISAIAH

One of the peoples the Persians conquered were the Chaldeans, who in 586 BCE had themselves conquered the kingdom of Judah and its capital of Jerusalem. Judah was the remaining southern kingdom of the Hebrews, the larger kingdom of Israel to its north having fallen to the Assyrians a century and a half earlier. The Chaldeans destroyed Jerusalem and sent many of the Hebrew elites into exile in their capital at Babylon. But after Cyrus the Great, king of the Persians, destroyed the Chaldean Empire, he freed the Hebrews from what became known as the Babylonian Captivity in 538 BCE.

An otherwise unknown prophet of the time, named Isaiah, took the lead in interpreting these events from the perspective of earlier Hebrew history and faith. His reinterpretation (and the impression the Babylonian Captivity made on the Hebrew elite) proved central to the transformation of early Hebrew religion into the faith now called Judaism. The key shift seems to have been Isaiah's claiming for Yahweh, the exclusive god of the Hebrews, a much larger role as sole God in and creator of the universe, to whom the Hebrews stood in a special relationship. By incorporating Cyrus into the story of the Lord (as Yahweh was increasingly referred to) and his People, Isaiah made all of history part of his God's plan for the universe, with the Chosen People playing a special role in history. Such a conception not only explained the Babylonian Captivity but also contributed to helping the Hebrews (or Jews) maintain their separate cultural identity in the great mix of cultures and peoples that made up the empire of which they were only a small part. At the same time, Isaiah's interpretation put morality, or "righteousness," at the center of his story's (and history's) meaning.

Maintaining their group identity had been a common problem in Hebrew history, especially after this originally pastoral group had settled in Palestine and adopted the settled farming and monarchical ways of their neighbors. The tendency

120   CHAPTER 4   ◆   Individual Ethics and Social Responsibility

for the Hebrew population to drift away from the exclusive worship of Yahweh had given rise to a long string of prophets, or people bearing the word of God, whose role had been to call back the errant Hebrews to Yahweh. The prophets lay outside the power structure of the Hebrew kingdoms but had been essential to the cohesion of the Hebrews before they had kings and to their culture even after the kings arose, and they had already moved the faith, in the process of defending it, toward more universal and moral bases. An earlier great prophet of the eighth century BCE had also been named Isaiah, and the teachings of the Isaiah of the sixth century were appended to those of the first Isaiah in the Bible's book of Isaiah. We are therefore reading the words of the prophet known as Second Isaiah, who synthesized and advanced the development of Judaism so effectively that he was one of the last of the great prophetic line.

QUESTIONS TO CONSIDER

1. What beliefs and actions constitute "righteousness" for Isaiah? What are the consequences for those who do or do not follow the path of righteousness?

2. What is the relationship of individual righteousness to social order in Isaiah? How is this relationship complicated by the Jews' subject status in the Persian Empire? How does Isaiah explain the role of the Persians?

3. Like Ahura Mazda, Yahweh is presented here not as the particular god of the tribes of Hebrews but as the universal and only God, creator of the universe. What is the role of the Hebrews in the history of Yahweh's universe?

4. Given the similarities between Zoroastrianism and Judaism, what do you think the influences of Zoroastrianism were on Isaiah (or vice versa, in fact)? Can we know for sure? What aspects of southwest Asian historical context might account for the similarities?

5. How specific and practical are Isaiah's calls for reform? What would a fully Isaiahan society look like? What would its advantages and disadvantages be? What would Isaiah think of whistleblowers? Was he one himself?

THE BOOK OF ISAIAH

Isaiah 44

24: Thus says the LORD, your Redeemer, who formed you from the womb: "I am the LORD, who made all things, who stretched out the heavens alone, who spread out the earth—Who was with me?—

25: who frustrates the omens of liars, and makes fools of diviners; who turns wise men back, and makes their knowledge foolish;

Source: The Holy Bible, Revised Standard Edition (New York, 1952), 756–58, 769, 770–71.

The Book of Isaiah **121**

26: who confirms the word of his servant, and performs the counsel of his messengers; who says of Jerusalem, 'She shall be inhabited,' and of the cities of Judah, 'They shall be built, and I will raise up their ruins';

27: who says to the deep, 'Be dry, I will dry up your rivers';

28: who says of Cyrus,* 'He is my shepherd, and he shall fulfil all my purpose'; saying of Jerusalem, 'She shall be built,' and of the temple, 'Your foundation shall be laid.'"

Isaiah 45

1: Thus says the LORD to his anointed, to Cyrus, whose right hand I have grasped, to subdue nations before him and ungird the loins of kings, to open doors before him that gates may not be closed:

2: "I will go before you and level the mountains, I will break in pieces the doors of bronze and cut asunder the bars of iron,

3: I will give you the treasures of darkness and the hoards in secret places, that you may know that it is I, the LORD, the God of Israel, who call you by your name.

4: For the sake of my servant Jacob, and Israel my chosen, I call you by your name, I surname you,† though you do not know me.

5: I am the LORD, and there is no other, besides me there is no God; I gird you, though you do not know me,

6: that men may know, from the rising of the sun and from the west, that there is none besides me; I am the LORD, and there is no other.

7: I form light and create darkness, I make weal and create woe, I am the LORD, who do all these things.

8: Shower, O heavens, from above, and let the skies rain down righteousness; let the earth open, that salvation may sprout forth, and let it cause righteousness to spring up also; I the LORD have created it.

9: Woe to him who strives with his Maker, an earthen vessel with the potter! Does the clay say to him who fashions it, 'What are you making?' or 'Your work has no handles'?

10: Woe to him who says to a father, 'What are you begetting?' or to a woman, 'With what are you in travail?'"

11: Thus says the LORD, the Holy One of Israel, and his Maker: "Will you question me about my children, or command me concerning the work of my hands?

12: I made the earth, and created man upon it; it was my hands that stretched out the heavens, and I commanded all their host.

13: I have aroused him in righteousness, and I will make straight all his ways; he shall build my city‡ and set my exiles free, not for price or reward," says the LORD of hosts.

14: Thus says the LORD: "The wealth of Egypt and the merchandise of Ethiopia, and the Sabe'ans, men of stature, shall come over to you and be yours, they shall follow

---

*The Persian king who liberated the Hebrews from Babylon.

†Cyrus the Great; the surname "the Great" is claimed here as a gift from Yahweh.

‡Jerusalem.

122   CHAPTER 4 ◆ Individual Ethics and Social Responsibility

you; they shall come over in chains and bow down to you. They will make supplication to you, saying: 'God is with you only, and there is no other, no god besides him.'"

15: Truly, thou art a God who hidest thyself, O God of Israel, the Savior.*

16: All of them are put to shame and confounded, the makers of idols go in confusion together.

17: But Israel is saved by the LORD with everlasting salvation; you shall not be put to shame or confounded to all eternity.

18: For thus says the LORD, who created the heavens (he is God!), who formed the earth and made it (he established it; he did not create it a chaos, he formed it to be inhabited!): "I am the LORD, and there is no other.

19: I did not speak in secret, in a land of darkness; I did not say to the offspring of Jacob, 'Seek me in chaos.' I the LORD speak the truth, I declare what is right.

20: Assemble yourselves and come, draw near together, you survivors of the nations! They have no knowledge who carry about their wooden idols, and keep on praying to a god that cannot save."

Isaiah 56

1: Thus says the LORD: "Keep justice, and do righteousness, for soon my salvation will come, and my deliverance be revealed.

2: Blessed is the man who does this, and the son of man who holds it fast, who keeps the sabbath, not profaning it, and keeps his hand from doing any evil."

Isaiah 57, 1–2, 15–21

1: The righteous man perishes, and no one lays it to heart; devout men are taken away, while no one understands. For the righteous man is taken away from calamity,

2: he enters into peace; they rest in their beds who walk in their uprightness.

15: For thus says the high and lofty One who inhabits eternity, whose name is Holy: "I dwell in the high and holy place, and also with him who is of a contrite and humble spirit, to revive the spirit of the humble, and to revive the heart of the contrite.

16: For I will not contend for ever, nor will I always be angry; for from me proceeds the spirit, and I have made the breath of life.

17: Because of the iniquity of his covetousness I was angry, I smote him, I hid my face and was angry; but he went on backsliding in the way of his own heart.

18: I have seen his ways, but I will heal him; I will lead him and requite him with comfort, creating for his mourners the fruit of the lips.

19: Peace, peace, to the far and to the near, says the LORD; and I will heal him.

20: But the wicked are like the tossing sea; for it cannot rest, and its waters toss up mire and dirt.

21: There is no peace, says my God, for the wicked."

---

*Scholarly consensus is that Isaiah's use of "Savior" and references to "salvation" and "being saved" refer to earthly peace and prosperity, rather than any sort of eternal reward or punishment.

NOTES

1. Press release at http://www.whistleblowers.org.

2. The understanding of the nature of the universe and humans' place in it.

3. It occurs as a long interlude in an even longer epic poem called the *Mahabharata,* or story of the Great Bharata, legendary king of the state of Dhritarashtra, and of the family feuds of his descendants for control of the kingdom.

4. Self-denial, avoidance of worldly pleasures.

5. From Zoroaster, the Greek version of the name of the prophet Zarathustra, who first preached its basic tenets.

6. The following selections come from the *Yasnas,* or liturgical texts, of the *Avesta,* which contain some of the *Gathas,* or sayings of the Prophet.

CHAPTER 5

Empires, War, and Order

INTRODUCTION

"If you wanna end war 'n stuff you gotta sing loud."

So said Arlo Guthrie in his anti–Vietnam War song "Alice's Restaurant." Because of television coverage and the nature of U.S. war aims—ambiguous and lacking broad public support—Vietnam brought much of the U.S. population into an encounter both with a people, the Vietnamese, whose aspirations and style of warfare seemed foreign to American traditions, and with modern warfare itself. The resulting protests and civic unrest came as a shock to many, whose image of warfare and the U.S. role in the world had been formed thirty or so years earlier in World War II. That had been a "good war," fought against a set of foes universally agreed to be evil and fought for the preservation of freedom and democracy. The encounters of World War II, with enemies who could be beaten and then remade in our own image and with warfare that, however terrible in cost, had a moral purpose, went much better for the United States than the encounters in Vietnam, which left deep scars on an America seen by many as an oppressive imperialist power and on a Vietnam that lost over a million people. This chapter explores encounters of ancient societies with each other in warfare, encounters that raised issues sometimes very similar to those the United States faced in its twentieth-century wars.

The range of questions raised by encounters with others through warfare and with warfare itself can be divided into questions about individuals and questions about states. Why do individuals go to war? In some cases, because they are compelled, either by mechanisms of state control (conscription) or by the demands of their social position. We saw an example of the latter in the previous chapter: Arjuna, the hero of the *Bhagavad-Gita,* has a moral duty to fight arising from his social role as a warrior, a role he was born into. As his dilemma demonstrates, or as the antiwar, draft-protesting sentiments of "Alice's Restaurant" show in a different context, such compulsion need not be accepted unhesitatingly: *Should* individuals go to war is a different question from the question of *why* they do. An individual's moral stance toward war can differ from his state or society's dominant view. But in some cases, individuals go to war willingly. It may be that they do so simply to make a living as a mercenary or out of sheer bloodthirstiness. But it may be that they have personal reasons—defending their homes and families, fighting for a religious or political cause, winning glory—that may also coincide with or support their state's reasons for going to war and that may or may not count as moral, depending on their culture.

Why do states go to war? Like individuals, they may be compelled, either by alliance commitments or by the threat of force. Or they may go to war in defense of their freedom and state interests. But states in the traditional world often went to war for honor, glory, or on the whim of a despotic ruler. As with individuals, the question of whether states *should* go to war is different from the question of *why* they do. And once at war, both individuals and states face the problem of what sorts of behaviors are allowable in war. Almost all warfare has been constrained in some way by cultural conventions and moral rules, putting some wartime behavior off limits to the participants. Some forms of warfare, as between certain Polynesian tribes, were highly ritualized and involved very little killing. In the absence of such rituals and rules, any possible benefits of warfare tend to be exceeded by the costs, right up to and including total mutual destruction by both sides in a conflict. One need not even imagine the global devastation of a full-scale nuclear exchange between the United States and the old Soviet Union to see this. The people of Easter Island, Polynesians and builders of impressive monumental stone heads, virtually wiped each other out hundreds of years ago in a fit of unrestrained warfare. But rules are often broken, and cultures tend not to agree on what the rules are, which is the reason warfare across cultures often seems so much more brutal and unconstrained than intracultural warfare.

And even in intracultural warfare, the realities of war on the ground are mostly brutal. War brings injury, death, destruction, and dislocation directly to portions of the populations involved. In fragile, agriculturally based societies, the indirect effects of war could be even worse. Destruction of crops brought famine and often drove independent farmers into dependence on rich landlords or off the land completely. Armies also acted as carriers of disease by bringing epidemics in their wake or by confining large numbers of people with inadequate food and water in a besieged city, thus fostering the outbreak of diseases. Such indirect consequences were likely to strike women and children especially hard, and women in all ages have been victims of rapes perpetrated by invading armies (and even by the armies supposedly defending them). It is these realities, of course, that make for the deep moral dilemmas created by war, for if warfare involved nothing but glory for winners and shame for losers, it would have no more moral resonance than a big football game.

In the period of world history starting around 200 BCE, following the age of the rise of the great traditions discussed in chapter 4, a number of great empires arose in the areas of the great traditions, drawing on and sometimes synthesizing those emerging traditions to help govern the lands they ruled. The creation of

126   CHAPTER 5   ◆   Empires, War, and Order

these empires inevitably involved the use of military force. Force could unite a set of states that shared a common set of cultural traditions, as in the creation of the Chinese Empire. It could bring foreign peoples under the rule of a conquering society and defend the resulting empire against rebellions by the conquered, as with the creation and defense of the Roman Empire. The creation of the Mauryan Empire in India shared features of both of these models: There were common cultural (especially religious) elements uniting much of the Indian subcontinent, but differences in language, geography, and climate tended to make different areas of India fairly foreign to each other in other ways. Greek warfare produced only the short-lived Athenian Empire within the Greek world, but Greek attitudes toward war informed the approaches to war of both of the imperial powers who subsequently came to control Greece: the Macedon of Alexander the Great and then Rome. Alexander's warfare also brought down the empire of the Persians, earning him a lasting reputation for evil in the Zoroastrian tradition. In all these cases, imperial civilizations faced the same encounters the United States later did in World War II and Vietnam: encounters with other peoples through warfare, and encounters with warfare itself—its purpose, meaning, and moral justification. The preceding questions exercised thinkers in different civilizations, who came to sometimes very different conclusions.

We examine first the classic writing on warfare from the Chinese tradition, Sun Tzu's *The Art of Warfare,* as well as accounts of warfare by the father of Chinese history writing, Sima Qian. As we saw in the last chapter, during the last centuries of the Chou dynasty (771 to 464 BCE) and the period known as the Warring States (464 to 221 BCE), the political unity of China broke down, and China became a land of many small states that tended to engage in constant warfare with each other. Warfare before 464 BCE was mostly an aristocratic affair, fought between chariot armies for honor and symbolic precedence, not conquest. But in the Warring States period, some rulers raised the stakes of warfare, aiming at the conquest of their enemies and the incorporation of enemy territory into their own. The number of states steadily declined, and the survivors grew in size and military power. Eventually, the ruler of the western state of Qin defeated his five remaining rivals and unified China under his autocratic rule. The warfare of the Warring States period called into being increasingly larger armies of disciplined infantry who drove aristocratic forces from the field and engaged in sieges of the walled cities, whence control of states emanated. Such armies in turn required the creation of complex bureaucratic administrations that could raise and support large forces and the formulation of policies and procedures to make effective use of such forces. Whereas philosophers such as Confucius and Han Fei Tzu debated broader questions of governance in this world, Sun Tzu became the most successful and widely read of the writers who focused on the use of military force in this context. Sima Qian describes this new style of warfare and its consequences.

The Greek tradition gives us a set of poems about civic militarism and its alternatives, the first by the Spartan Tyrtaeus, the second by Archilochus of Paros. Warfare was endemic among the Greek *poleis* (city-states, singular *polis*) of the Classical period (650 to 350 BCE). Such wars were at first small, brief affairs between neighboring city-states and involved conflict over disputed agricultural territory separating the combatants. But more than simple economic motivation was at stake. Communal pride became tied to defense of the *polis'* territory, and communal effort by the city's land-owning farmers, serving as citizen soldiers, went into defending the city's land and honor. Tyrtaeus's poem reflects this sort of warfare. The Persian Wars, starting in 490 BCE, however, stimulated alliance systems and larger, more prolonged warfare that resulted in the creation by Athens of a naval-based empire that collapsed in the Peloponnesian Wars against a Spartan coalition. In these longer, more drawn-out wars, mercenaries came to play a larger role in the fighting; Archilochus's poem gives us a glimpse of the way a mercenary's values differed from those of citizen soldiers.

We will see Roman warfare both from the point of view of its grand imperial results, in the *Res Gestae* of Augustus Caesar, and in terms of how it dealt with rebellion in a section from Josephus's *Jewish Wars*. Between 300 BCE and the early years of the first century CE, the Roman Republic built an empire out of a long series of wars against foreign enemies. Its army was at first composed, like those of Greek *poleis*, of citizen soldiers serving in infantry units called legions. It underwent a transformation as wars took longer and the theaters of conflict moved farther from the heartland of the Italian peninsula. Long-serving professionals, often poor and landless when they joined, replaced the land-owning militia. Their loyalty came to focus, therefore, less on the Roman state, to which their ties were more tenuous than those of the farmer-soldiers had been, and more on the generals whose success earned them plunder and land as pensions. Those generals then fought a series of civil wars that brought the republic to an end. Though he never used the title, Augustus was the first emperor of Rome, and his successors maintained the empire against foreign threats and against revolts such as that of the Jews in 70 CE, about which Josephus writes, and attempted with varying success to keep the loyalty of the army focused on the person of the emperor.

Finally, the Indian tradition gives us a very different take on the results of war from the Rock and Pillar Edicts of Emperor Asoka. Indian warfare before 330 BCE or so resembled Chinese warfare under the early Chou: aristocratic, somewhat ritualized, and based on tribute rather than on conquest of territory. But the incursion of Alexander the Great into northwest India in 324 BCE stimulated at least some Indian rulers to think along more Alexandrian lines. One of these princes, Chandragupta Maurya, initiated the conquests that would form the Mauryan Empire, India's largest pre-Muslim polity. His grandson Asoka continued the expansion of the empire, using the large professional army backed by a complex bureaucracy that his grandfather and father had built. But bloodiness and misery caused by the conquest of the south Indian state of Kalinga caused Asoka to reevaluate his view of warfare. He forswore offensive operations, converted to Buddhism, and turned away from military conquest to "spiritual conquest": the spreading of the principles of Buddhism and a practical focus on good government.

Between them, this set of readings provides a wide range of reactions, moral and practical, to the encounter of imperial peoples with others through war and with warfare itself. Look for how different peoples answered the questions posed by warfare: Why do individuals and states go to war? Are they justified in doing so? What restrictions do societies place on the waging of warfare? What was the effect of warfare when it was waged? These issues are as relevant today as they were in 300 BCE.

128   CHAPTER 5 ◆ Empires, War, and Order

CHAPTER QUESTIONS

1. As a group, do these sources take an approach to analyzing warfare that tends more to the moral or to the practical?

2. What are the major motivations for warfare in these sources, and how do they differ from tradition to tradition? Do some seem more motivated by reasons of state and some more motivated by personal reasons?

3. What is the balance between state and individual in these writings on war? How do these two levels of analysis intersect?

4. What conventions do you see with regard to proper behavior in waging war in these sources? In particular, what are the roles of rational calculation versus emotion in conducting war "correctly"?

5. Which source seems most applicable to your own view of warfare? Which offers the best advice to a United States facing conflict in the twenty-first century?

THE CHINESE TRADITION
Conducting Warfare

The Warring States era (464 to 221 BCE) was a crucial turning point in Chinese history. During this time, the many effectively independent states into which China had become divided were at war with each other constantly. But unlike the constant warfare of the period 770 to 453 BCE, which had been aristocratic, based on extracting tribute and admissions of suzerainty, and which had involved small armies of charioteers, Warring States warfare evolved rapidly into a deadly contest of political survival. Some rulers began raising larger, infantry-based armies with which they conducted campaigns of conquest against their neighbors. To raise and support such armies, they refashioned their administrative systems and enhanced the power of kingship against their aristocracies. The fundamental outlines of the later Chinese imperial state were created during this age of military competition.

As rulers looked for every military advantage they could get, there arose a class of military experts who wrote advice on how best to use the new, larger armies in this life-or-death environment. The most famous of these many writers, Sun Tzu, is a shadowy figure about whom we know very little. He lived during the latter half of the Warring States period. Sun Tzu was a scholar of war, and he takes his place with Confucius, Lao Tzu (founder of Taoism), and Han Fei Tzu (founder of Legalism) as one of the Chinese masters. Indeed, the influence of Confucian, Taoist, and Legalist ideas can be seen in Sun Tzu's principles of war. The scholarly nature of Sun Tzu's work and the other Warring States military manuals is important in two ways. First, it shows that the study of warfare and its place in statecraft was taken seriously by Chinese intellectuals. But, second, the intellectualization of war fit into the antiaristocratic, centralizing trends of Chinese states in this age. Sun Tzu and others constructed leadership—and indeed soldierly qualities—in warfare as a matter not of heroism and practical knowledge (as it had been for aristocratic-led armies earlier) but as the implementation of rational principles by a single trained expert; they saw good soldiers as obedient followers of this enlightened leadership. The implications of this model of military leadership for the structure of the state are clear.

The unification of China by the Ch'in in 221 BCE resulted from the successful application of Sun Tzu's principles. It thus proved itself to be a very practical set of principles, so practical that Mao Zedong in the twentieth century read and followed Sun Tzu's advice in his campaigns, and Sun Tzu is still required reading in United States military academies today. But also note that the edition we read includes commentaries by later Chinese scholars on the basic text. These commentaries illustrate the living, expanding nature of the Chinese philosophical tradition and point to the even wider metaphorical use of Sun Tzu's work beyond the military sphere—it has been used as a manual for business executives, for example. It is, in short, a rich text that will repay close study.

QUESTIONS TO CONSIDER

1. What basic principles of warfare does Sun Tzu advocate? How does economics (or logistics—the art of feeding and supplying armies) shape these principles? What role does psychology play in them?

2. What seems to be the ultimate goal of warfare in the Chinese tradition? How does this relate to the downplaying of glory and bravery in the text?

3. What appear to be the influences of Confucian thought on Sun Tzu? Of Taoist thought? Of Legalist thought? Do these schools of thought show up in the commentaries as well?

4. What are the qualities of good military leadership for Sun Tzu? How do these qualities relate to the philosophical influences on the text? Would you have wanted to serve as a spy under a Sun Tzu–trained general?

5. Why has Sun Tzu remained so popular into modern times? How is his advice applicable beyond the problems of warfare?

THE ART OF WARFARE

Sun Tzu

Chapter 1. Estimates

Sun Tzu said:

1. War is a matter of vital importance to the state; the province of life or death; the road to survival or ruin. It is mandatory that it be thoroughly studied.

   Li Ch'üan*: "Weapons are tools of ill omen." War is a grave matter; one is apprehensive lest men embark upon it without due reflection.

Source: From Sun Tzu, *The Art of War*, trans. Samuel B. Griffith. Copyright © 1963 by Oxford University Press, Inc. Used by permission of Oxford University Press, Inc.

*This and the other names before indented paragraphs are the names of later Chinese commentators on the text, followed by their commentary.

130   CHAPTER 5 ◆ Empires, War, and Order

2. Therefore, appraise it in terms of the five fundamental factors and make comparisons of the seven elements later named. So you may assess its essentials.

3. The first of these factors is the Tao; the second, weather; the third, terrain; the fourth, command; and the fifth, law.

4. By the Tao I mean that which causes the people to be in harmony with their leaders, so that they will accompany them in life and unto death without fear of mortal peril.

> *Chang Yü:* When one treats people with humanity, justice, and righteousness, and reposes confidence in them, the army will be united in mind and all will be happy to serve their leaders.

5. By weather I mean the interaction of *yin* and *yang;* the effects of winter's cold and summer's heat and the conduct of military operations in accordance with the seasons.

6. By terrain I mean distances, whether the ground is traversed with ease or difficulty, whether it is open or constricted, and the chances of life or death.

7. By command I mean the general's qualities of wisdom, sincerity, humanity, courage, and strictness.

8. By law I mean organization, control, assignment of appropriate ranks to officers, regulation of supply routes, and the provision of principal items used by the army.

9. There is no general who has not heard of these five matters. Those who master them win; those who do not are defeated.

. . .

15. If a general who heeds my strategy is employed, he is certain to win. Retain him! When one who refuses to listen to my strategy is employed, he is certain to be defeated. Dismiss him!

. . .

17. All warfare is based on deception.

18. Therefore, when capable, feign incapacity; when active, inactivity.

19. When near, make it appear that you are far away; when far away, that you are near.

20. Offer the enemy a bait to lure him; feign disorder and strike him.

> *Tu Mu:* The Chao general Li Mu released herds of cattle with their shepherds; when the Hsiung Nu [Huns] had advanced a short distance he feigned a retirement, leaving behind several thousand men as if abandoning them. When the Khan heard this news, he was delighted, and at the head of a strong force marched to the place. Li Mu put most of his troops into formations on the right and left wings, made a horning attack, crushed the Huns and slaughtered over one hundred thousand of their horsemen.*

21. When he concentrates, prepare against him; where he is strong, avoid him.

22. Anger his general and confuse him.

---

*The Hsiung Nu [Huns] were nomads who caused the Chinese trouble for centuries. The Great Wall was constructed to protect China from their incursions.

23. Pretend inferiority and encourage his arrogance.

24. Keep him under a strain and wear him down.

25. When he is united, divide him.

> *Chang Yü:* Sometimes drive a wedge between a sovereign and his ministers; on other occasions separate his allies from him. Make them mutually suspicious so that they drift apart. Then you can plot against them.

26. Attack where he is unprepared; sally out when he does not expect you.

> *Ho Yen-hsi:* Li Ching of the T'ang* proposed ten plans to be used against Hsiao Hsieh, and the entire responsibility of commanding the armies was entrusted to him. In the eighth month he collected his forces at K'uei Chou.
>
> As it was the season of the autumn floods the waters of the Yangtze were overflowing and the roads by the three gorges were perilous, Hsiao Hsieh thought it certain that Li Ching would not advance against him. Consequently he made no preparations.
>
> In the ninth month Li Ching took command of the troops and addressed them as follows: "What is of the greatest importance in war is extraordinary speed; one cannot afford to neglect opportunity. Now we are concentrated and Hsiao Hsieh does not yet know of it. Taking advantage of the fact that the river is in flood, we will appear unexpectedly under the walls of his capital. As is said: "When the thunder-clap comes, there is no time to cover the ears.' Even if he should discover us, he cannot on the spur of the moment devise a plan to counter us, and surely we can capture him."
>
> He advanced to I Ling and Hsiao Hsieh began to be afraid and summoned reinforcements from south of the river, but these were unable to arrive in time. Li Ching laid siege to the city and Hsieh surrendered.

27. These are the strategist's keys to victory. It is not possible to discuss them beforehand.

> *Mei Yao-ch'en:* When confronted by the enemy respond to changing circumstances and devise expedients. How can these be discussed beforehand?

28. Now if the estimates made in the temple before hostilities indicate victory, it is because calculations show one's strength to be superior to that of his enemy; if they indicate defeat, it is because calculations show that one is inferior. With many calculations, one can win; with few one cannot. How much less chance of victory has one who makes none at all! By this means I examine the situation and the outcome will be clearly apparent.

Chapter 2. Waging War

Sun Tzu said:

1. Generally, operations of war require one thousand fast four-horse chariots, one thousand four-horse wagons covered in leather, and one hundred thousand mailed troops.

---

*Li Ching was a general for the T'ang Dynasty (618–907). The names of people and places in this and other accounts in the commentaries are less important than the general principles the episode illustrates.

132 CHAPTER 5 ◆ Empires, War, and Order

> *Tu Mu:* . . . In ancient chariot fighting, "leather-covered chariots" were both light and heavy. The latter were used for carrying halberds, weapons, military equipment, valuables, and uniforms. The Ssu-ma Fa said: "One chariot carries three mailed officers; seventy-two foot troops accompany it. Additionally, there are ten cooks and servants, five men to take care of uniforms, five grooms in charge of fodder, and five men to collect firewood and draw water. Seventy-five men to one light chariot, twenty-five to one baggage wagon, so that taking the two together one hundred men compose a company."

2. When provisions are transported for a thousand *li*,* expenditures at home and in the field, stipends for the entertainment of advisers and visitors, the cost of materials such as glue and lacquer, and of chariots and armor, will amount to one thousand pieces of gold a day. After this money is in hand, one hundred thousand troops may be raised.

   > *Li Ch'uan:* Now when the army marches abroad, the treasury will be emptied at home.

3. Victory is the main object in war. If this is long delayed, weapons are blunted and morale depressed. When troops attack cities, their strength will be exhausted.

4. When the army engages in protracted campaigns, the resources of the state will not suffice.

5. When your weapons are dulled and ardor damped, your strength exhausted and treasure spent, neighboring rulers will take advantage of your distress to act. And even though you have wise counselors, none will be able to lay good plans for the future.

6. Thus, while we have heard of blundering swiftness in war, we have not yet seen a clever operation that was prolonged.

   > *Tu Yu:* An attack may lack ingenuity, but it must be delivered with supernatural speed.

7. For there has never been a protracted war from which a country has benefited.

8. Thus those unable to understand the dangers inherent in employing troops are equally unable to understand the advantageous ways of doing so.

9. Those adept in waging war do not require a second levy of conscripts nor more than one provisioning.

10. They carry equipment from the homeland; they rely for provisions on the enemy. Thus the army is plentifully provided with food.

11. When a country is impoverished by military operations it is due to distant transportation; carriage of supplies for great distances renders the people destitute.

12. Where the army is, prices are high; when prices rise the wealth of the people is exhausted. When wealth is exhausted, the peasantry will be afflicted with urgent exactions.

---

*Unit of distance; Chinese equivalent of a mile.

13. With strength thus depleted and wealth consumed, the households in the central plains will be utterly impoverished and seven-tenths of their wealth dissipated.

> *Li Ch'üan:* If war drags on without cessation, men and women will resent not being able to marry, and will be distressed by the burdens of transportation.

14. As to government expenditures, those due to broken-down chariots, worn-out horses, armor and helmets, arrows and crossbows, lances, hand and body shields, draft animals and supply wagons will amount to sixty per cent of the total.

15. Hence the wise general sees to it that his troops feed on the enemy, for one bushel of the enemy's provisions is equivalent to twenty of his; one hundredweight of enemy fodder to twenty hundredweight of his.

16. The reason troops slay the enemy is because they are enraged.

17. They take booty from the enemy because they desire wealth.

. . .

19. Treat the captives well, and care for them.

> *Chang Yü:* All the soldiers taken must be cared for with magnanimity and sincerity so that they may be used by us.

20. This is called "winning a battle and becoming stronger."

21. Hence what is essential in war is victory, not prolonged operations. And therefore the general who understands war is the Minister of the people's fate and arbiter of the nation's destiny.

> *Ho Yen-hsi:* The difficulties in the appointment of a commander are the same today as they were in ancient times.

Chapter 13. *Employment of Secret Agents*

5. Now there are five sorts of secret agents to be employed. These are native, inside, double, expendable, and living.

. . .

7. Native agents are those of the enemy's country people whom we employ.

8. Inside agents are enemy officials whom we employ.

9. Double agents are enemy spies whom we employ.

10. Expendable agents are those of our own spies who are deliberately given fabricated information.

11. Living agents are those who return with information.

12. Of all those in the army close to the commander none is more intimate than the secret agent; of all rewards none more liberal than those given to secret agents; of all matters none is more confidential than those relating to secret operations.

> *Mei Yao-ch'en:* Secret agents receive their instructions within the tent of the general, and are intimate and close to him.

13. He who is not sage and wise, humane and just, cannot use secret agents. And he who is not delicate and subtle cannot get the truth out of them.

. . .

134   CHAPTER 5 ◆ Empires, War, and Order

23. And therefore only the enlightened sovereign and the worthy general who are able to use the most intelligent people as agents are certain to achieve great things. Secret operations are essential in war; upon them the army relies to make its every move.

> *Chia Lin:* An army without secret agents is exactly like a man without eyes or ears.

Interpreting Warfare

Sima Qian (c. 145 to after 91 BCE) is to Chinese history writing what Herodotus and Thucydides combined are to Western historical writing. A scholar and official under the Han, he began collecting historical records and sources early in his career. He was eventually appointed Grand Historian of the Han Court in 107 BCE, in which office he composed the *Records of the Grand Historian*. Based on extensive research in the Imperial Library and on the sources he collected, this monumental work traces Chinese history from the legendary Five Sage Emperors down to Sima Qian's own times.

A central section of the work deals with the rise and fall of the Qin (pronounced "chin") dynasty (221 to 206 BCE) and its founder, the fearsome First Emperor, Qin Shi Huangdi (256 to 210 BCE). Military conquest played a central role in the Qin rise and the unification of China, but the Chinese attitude toward war, especially on the part of scholars such as Sima Qian, remained ambivalent. The reputation of the First Emperor is therefore not as favorable as it might have been in other cultures. Compare, for example, the Roman sources later in this chapter for Augustus. It is interesting to note that, to outsiders, the name of China refers to the Qin dynasty, but that the Chinese refer to themselves as "the people of Han."

The Han dynasty under which Sima Qian wrote replaced the Qin after widespread revolts under the second Qin emperor. Although the Han abolished many of the Qin's harshest Legalist measures, especially those aimed against Confucian scholars such as Sima Qian, in many ways it retained the structure of government set in place by the Qin, including uniform government districts, standardized weights and measures, strict law codes, and antiaristocratic measures. But it cloaked the iron hand of the Chinese state in a Confucian velvet glove, founding a Confucian Academy and promoting scholars such as Sima Qian to positions in the bureaucracy. (It also implemented, for a time, a rather Taoist—what we might call laissez-faire—economic policy that worked for a time to promote prosperity.) It was this synthesis, rather than the naked Legalism of the Qin, that would survive into subsequent dynasties, in part because of the view of history promoted by Sima Qian and his successors as official court historians.

QUESTIONS TO CONSIDER

1. In what ways did the First Emperor follow Sun Tzu's advice on conducting warfare, according to this account? How does that advice fit with the Legalist philosophy that guided the First Emperor?

2. The First Emperor was a great conqueror and unifier. In other civilizations he might have been regarded as a martial hero (perhaps, for instance, medieval Western Europe, whose Charlemagne bears some resemblance to the First Emperor). Why is he not seen this way in the Chinese tradition?

3. Sima Qian writes that "the power to attack, and the power to retain what one has thereby won, are not the same." What are the implications of such a view for the role of the military in Chinese government?

4. Given that Sima Qian is writing from the perspective of the dynasty that succeeded the Qin (and that favored scholars such as himself), how reliable and fair does his account seem to you?

5. What can a civilian-run government such as the modern United States learn from Sima Qian's account about the role of the military and the conduct of warfare?

RECORDS OF THE GRAND HISTORIAN

Sima Qian

The First Emperor

. . . [W]hen the power of the Zhou dynasty waned,* the Qin rose to prominence, building its capital in the western borderland. From the time of Duke Mu on,† it gradually ate away at the domains of the other feudal rulers until the process was finally completed by the First Emperor. . . . In the case of Qin, however, while it was in a flourishing state, its manifold laws and stern punishments caused the empire to tremble. But when its power declined, then the people eyed it with hatred and the whole area within the seas rose up in revolt.

Duke Xiao of Qin,‡ relying upon the strength of Mt. Yao and the Hangu Pass and basing himself in the area of Yongzhou,§ with his ministers held fast to his land and eyed the house of Zhou, for he cherished a desire to roll up the empire like a mat, to bind into one the whole world, to bag all the land within the four seas; he had it in his heart to swallow up everything in the eight directions. At this time he was aided by Lord Shang,** who at home set up laws for him, encouraged agriculture and weaving, and built up the instruments of war, and abroad contracted military alliances and

---

Source: Sima Qian, *Records of the Grand Historian,* trans. Burton Watson, 74–83. Copyright © 1993. Reprinted by permission of Columbia University Press.

*The Eastern Zhou (770–256 BCE) lost even nominal control of China during the Warring States era; the last Zhou king was deposed in 256 BCE.

†Mid-seventh century BCE.

‡381–338 BCE.

§The state of Qin was in the west of China and was protected from its enemies by mountain ranges.

**The chief minister of the Qin ruler.

136 CHAPTER 5 ◆ Empires, War, and Order

attacked the other feudal lords.* Thus the men of Qin were able with ease to acquire territory east of the upper reaches of the Yellow River.

After the death of Duke Xiao, kings Huiwen and Wu carried on the undertakings of their predecessor and, following the plans he had laid, seized [a state] in the south and [states] in the west, and acquired rich land in the east and provinces of strategic value. The other feudal lords in alarm came together in council to devise some plan to weaken Qin, sparing nothing in gifts of precious objects and rich lands to induce men from all over the empire to come and join with them in a "vertical alliance," and pool their strength. . . . [The leading] four lords were all men of intelligence and loyalty, generous and kind to others, who honored worthy men and took good care of their followers. They rejected the Horizontal Alliance and instead formed the Vertical Alliance, which united all the forces of [nine] states. . . . With a force of 1,000,000 soldiers drawn from an area ten times that of Qin, they beat upon the Pass and pressed forward toward Qin. But the men of Qin opened the Pass to entice the enemy in, and the armies of the Nine States fled and did not dare advance. Qin, without expending a single arrow or losing a single arrowhead, threatened the feudal rulers of the entire empire.

With this the Vertical Alliance collapsed, its treaties came to naught, and the various states hastened to present Qin with parts of their territory as bribes for peace. With its superior strength Qin pressed the crumbling forces of its rivals, pursued those who had fled in defeat, and overwhelmed and slaughtered the army of 1,000,000 until their shields floated upon a river of blood. Following up the advantages of its victory, Qin gained mastery over the empire and divided up its mountains and rivers. The powerful states begged to submit to its sovereignty and the weaker ones paid homage at its court.

Then followed kings Xiaowen and Zhuangxiang, whose reigns were short and uneventful. After this came the First Emperor who, carrying on the glorious spirit of his six predecessors, cracked his long whip and drove the universe before him, swallowed up the eastern and western Zhou, and overthrew the feudal lords. He ascended the throne of honor and ruled the six directions, scourging the world with his lash, and his might shook the four seas. In the south he seized the land of the hundred tribes . . . and made of it [two] provinces, and the lords of the hundred [tribes] bowed their heads, hung halters from their necks, and pleaded for their lives with the lowest officials of Qin. Then he sent [a general] north to build the Great Wall and defend the borders, driving back the Xiongnu over 700 *li*, so that the barbarians no longer ventured to come south to pasture their horses and their men dared not take up their bows to vent their hatred.

Thereupon he discarded the ways of the former kings and burned the books of the hundred schools of philosophy in order to make the black-headed people† ignorant. He destroyed the walls of the great cities, put to death the powerful leaders, and collected all the arms of the empire, which he had brought to his capital at Xianyang, where the spears and arrowheads were melted down and cast to make twelve human

---

*"Feudal lords" refers to the rulers of the various states of Warring States China, nominally under the rule of the Zhou king.

†That is, the Chinese.

statues. All this he did in order to weaken the black-headed people. After this he ascended and fortified Mt. Hua, set up fords along the Yellow River, and strengthened the heights and precipices overlooking the fathomless valleys, in order to secure his position. He garrisoned the strategic points with skilled generals and strong crossbowmen and stationed trusted ministers and well-trained soldiers to guard the land with arms and question all who passed back and forth. When he had thus pacified the empire, the First Emperor believed in his heart that, with the strength of his capital within the passes and his walls of metal extending 1,000 miles, he had established a rule that would be enjoyed by his sons and grandsons for 10,000 generations.

For a while after the death of the First Emperor the memory of his might continued to awe the common people. Yet Chen She, born in a humble hut with tiny windows and a wattle door, a day laborer in the fields and a garrison conscript, whose abilities could not match even the average, who had neither the worth of Confucius . . . nor wealth . . . , stepped from the ranks of the common soldiers, rose up from the paths of the fields, and led a band of some hundred poor, weary soldiers in revolt against Qin. They cut down trees to make their weapons and raised their flags on garden poles, and the whole world gathered like a cloud, answered like an echo to a sound, brought them provisions, and followed after them as shadows follow a form. In the end the leaders east of the mountains rose up together and destroyed the house of Qin.

. . . Qin, beginning with an insignificant amount of territory, reached the power of a great kingdom and for 100 years made the ancient eight provinces pay homage at its court. Yet, after it had become master of the six directions and established its palaces within the passes, a single commoner opposed it and its seven ancestral temples toppled, its ruler died by the hands of men, and it became the laughing stock of the world. Why? Because it failed to rule with humanity and righteousness, and did not realize that the power to attack, and the power to retain what one has thereby won, are not the same.

. . . [T]he First Emperor was greedy and short-sighted, confident in his own wisdom, never trusting his meritorious officials, never getting to know his people. He cast aside the kingly Way and relied on private procedures, outlawing books and writings, making the laws and penalties much harsher, putting deceit and force foremost and humanity and righteousness last, leading the whole world in violence and cruelty. In annexing the lands of others, one may place priority on deceit and force, but insuring peace and stability in the lands one has annexed calls for a respect for authority. Hence I say that seizing, and guarding what you have seized, do not depend upon the same techniques.

. . . So it is said, a people who feel secure may be led into righteous ways, but a people who feel threatened easily turn to evil. . . .

THE GREEK TRADITION

Greek warfare in the Archaic and Classical, or Hellenic, periods (600 to 323 BCE) was not connected with large empires as Chinese, Roman, and Indian warfare came to be after 200 BCE. But Greek attitudes toward war influenced much of

138   CHAPTER 5 ◆ Empires, War, and Order

southwest Asia after the conquests of Alexander the Great and also influenced the Romans. Greek warfare occurred between small city-states and was conducted by *hoplite phalanxes.* Hoplites were infantrymen armed with bronze body armor, large shields, and spears. They were also the well-off members of the city-state, arming themselves and serving mostly out of civic duty as a militia force. They stood shoulder to shoulder with their friends and neighbors in dense blocks called phalanxes. Two phalanxes would meet on a level piece of ground, charge each other, and push until one side gave way. Such battles were brief but bloody, especially among the front ranks and during the short pursuit after one side broke and ran, and they tested the community solidarity of a city's citizens. Hoplite warfare and its communal virtues were closely connected to the varyingly collective forms of government, from dual monarchies and limited aristocracies to broader oligarchies and even to the democracy of Athens, practiced by Greek city-states. However, the fairly elite character in the small Greek world of those who could afford the hoplite panoply, even if they were only independent farmers, should not be forgotten.

Here we present two poetic visions of hoplite warfare. The first is by Tyrtaeus, a Spartan from c. 650 BCE. Sparta had the most professional and effective of all the phalanx armies, mostly because Sparta based its economy on a large population of rural slaves, called *helots,* who both made possible (through their agricultural production) and necessitated (by their numbers and thus the possibility of a massive revolt) Sparta's maintenance of a full-time, professional force of soldiers. Tyrtaeus praises the virtues that made the trained Spartan phalanx such a formidable force in the Greek world. The second poem is by Archilochus, a contemporary of Tyrtaeus' from the Aegean island of Paros. He served as a mercenary rather than in a regular civic phalanx; mercenary service, or service for pay by members of one *polis* for another, would become increasingly important after 400 BCE in the wake of the Peloponnesian War.

QUESTIONS TO CONSIDER

1. What is the key military virtue for Tyrtaeus? What does this imply about styles of warfare? How does it compare with military virtues in Sun Tzu?

2. What does this style of warfare imply about Greek attitudes toward political participation more broadly? Was participation in warfare an "ennobling" act for Greeks?

3. What does Tyrtaeus' poem tell us about the social setting of warfare—the impact warfare had on the families, friends, and community of the soldiers?

4. What does Archilochus' poem tell us about the potential difference between the ideals and the realities of Greek warfare? How much is his view influenced by his mercenary status?

5. How would these accounts of participation in warfare fit into Chinese warfare as described by Sun Tzu and Sima Qian? How would a Warring States general view a body of Greek hoplites?

PRAISE OF THE VIRTUOSITY
OF THE CITIZEN SOLDIER

Tyrtaeus

I would not say anything for a man nor take account of him
for any speed of his feet or wrestling skill he might have.
Not if he had the size of a Cyclops and strength to go with it,
not if he could outrun Boreas, the North Wind of Thrace.
Not if he were more handsome and gracefully formed than Tithonos,
or had more riches than Midas had, or Kinyras too,
nor if he were more of a king than Tantalid Pelops,
or had the power of speech and persuasion Adrastos had,
not if he had all the splendors except for a fighting spirit.
For no man ever proves himself a good man in war
unless he can endure to face the blood and the slaughter,
go close against the enemy and fight with his hands.
Here is courage, mankind's finest possession,
here is the finest prize that a young man can endeavor to win.

And it is a good thing his city and all the people share with him
when a man plants his feet and stands in the foremost spears relentlessly, all thought
    of foul flight completely forgotten,
and has well trained his heart to be steadfast and to endure,
and with words encourages the man who is stationed beside him.
Here is a man who proves himself to be valiant in war.
With a sudden rush he turns to flight the rugged battalions
of the enemy and sustains the beating waves of the assault.

And he who so falls among the champions and loses his sweet life,
so blessing with honor his city, his father, and all his people,
with wounds in his chest, where the spear that he was facing has transfixed that
    massive guard of his shield,
and gone through his breastplate as well.
Why, such a man is lamented alike by the young and the elders,
and all his city goes into mourning and grieves for his loss.
His tomb is pointed out with pride and so are his children,
and his children's children,
and afterward all the race that is his.
His shining glory is never forgotten, his name is remembered,
and he becomes an immortal, though he lies under the ground,
a brave man who has been killed by the furious War God
standing his ground and fighting hard for his children and land.

Source: Richmond Lattimore, *Greek Lyrics,* 2nd ed., 1960, pp. 14–15. Reprinted by permission of The University of Chicago Press.

140   CHAPTER 5 ✦ Empires, War, and Order

But if he escapes the doom of death, the destroyer of bodies,
and wins his battle and bright renown for the work of his spear,
all men give place to him alike, the youth and the elders,
and much joy comes his way before he goes down to the dead.
Aging he has reputation among his citizens.
No one tries to interfere with his honors or all he deserves.
All men withdraw before his presence and yield their seats to him:
Youth and the men of his age and even those older than he.
Thus a man should endeavor to reach this high place of courage
with all his heart and so trying never be backward in war.

ELEGY

Archilochus

Some barbarian is waving my shield, since I was obliged to
    Leave that perfectly good piece of equipment behind
under a bush. But I got away, so what does it matter?
    Let the shield go; I can buy another one equally good.

THE ROMAN TRADITION
The Benefits of Warfare

After nearly a century of civil war and a series of dictatorships that shook the Roman Republic between about 100 and 27 BCE, Octavian, great-nephew and adopted son of Julius Caesar, last of the dictators, defeated his rivals for power and initiated the era of the *Pax Romana* (Roman Peace). Accorded the title *Augustus* (Revered One, implying divine authority), he is known to us as Augustus Caesar, First Citizen and effectively first emperor of Rome, though he never took that title himself and maintained the outward forms of Republican rule while concentrating all real power in his own hands.

Augustus was a successful military leader, both in civil wars against foes such as Marc Antony (of Cleopatra fame) and against foreign foes (though a general named Varus did lose three of Augustus's legions to Germanic tribes in an ambush in southern Germany in 9 CE), and equally on land and at sea (his final battle against Marc Antony was a naval battle at Actium, off the coast of Greece). The military establishment that Augustus led consisted of a large army of several hundred thousand men organized in legions posted to strategically located bases in

Source: Richmond Lattimore, *Greek Lyrics*, 2nd ed., 1960, p. 2. Reprinted by permission of The University of Chicago Press.

the empire. Movement of the legions was facilitated by the fine Roman road system. (Walls for border defense, such as Hadrian's Wall in Britain, mostly postdate Augustus' time.) The soldiers were full-time professionals who enrolled as young men and served until age sixty, at which point they received their own land, often in a new colony settled by retired soldiers and their families; soldiers also received periodic bonuses from generous emperors, following an example set by Augustus.

Near the end of his reign (27 BCE to 14 CE), Augustus had the following account of his accomplishments engraved on two bronze pillars and set in front of his mausoleum in Rome. The original of "The achievements of the Divine Augustus, by which he brought the world under the empire of the Roman people, and of the expenses which he bore for the state and people of Rome" are lost but are known from copies in Asia Minor. After his death Augustus was worshipped as a diety.

QUESTIONS TO CONSIDER

1. What is Augustus's view of warfare? Is there more to it than a utilitarian tool for establishing peace? How does it compare with Sun Tzu's view? With the Greek view?

2. What is Augustus's relationship to the Roman army? What sorts of measures does Augustus take to ensure the loyalty of the army? What does this tell you about Roman political structures?

3. How does Augustus, as a "first emperor," compare with Qin Shi Huangdi, the Chinese First Emperor? Why are their reputations so different in their own cultures?

4. What does this source tell us about the place of warfare and the Roman army in the Roman world? Were the Romans "militaristic"?

5. What lessons does this source hold for a civilian government such as the United States for civil–military relations? For the exercise of power as an imperial nation?

RES GESTAE DIVI AUGUSTI (THE ACHIEVEMENTS OF THE DIVINE AUGUSTUS)

1) At the age of nineteen [44 BC] on my own responsibility and at my own expense I raised an army, with which I successfully championed the liberty of the republic when it was oppressed by the tyranny of a faction. . . .

Source: Res Gestae Divi Augusti (The Achievements of the Divine Augustus). Edited with an introduction and commentary by P. A. Brunt and J. M. Moore (Oxford, UK: Oxford University Press, 1967).

142   CHAPTER 5 ◆ Empires, War, and Order

2) I drove into exile the murderers of my father,* avenging their crime through tribunals established by law [43 BC]; and afterwards, when they made war on the republic, I twice defeated them in battle [42 BC].

3) I undertook many civil and foreign wars by land and sea throughout the world, and as victor I spared the lives of all citizens who asked for mercy. When foreign peoples could safely be pardoned I preferred to preserve rather than to exterminate them. The Roman citizens who took the soldier's oath of obedience to me numbered about 500,000. I settled rather more than 300,000 of these in colonies or sent them back to their home towns after their period of service; to all these I assigned lands or gave money as rewards for their military service. I captured six hundred ships, not counting ships smaller than triremes.

4) . . . On fifty-five occasions the senate decreed that thanksgivings should be offered to the immortal gods on account of the successes on land and sea gained by me or by my legates acting under my auspices. . . . In my triumphs nine kings or children of kings were led before my chariot. . . .

. . .

13) It was the will of our ancestors that the gateway of Janus Quirinus should be shut when victories had secured peace by land and sea throughout the whole empire of the Roman people; from the foundation of the city down to my birth, tradition records that it was shut only twice, but while I was the leading citizen the senate resolved that it should be shut on three occasions.

. . .

15) To each member of the Roman plebs I paid under my father's will 300 sesterces† [44 BC], and in my own name I gave them 400 each from the booty of war in my fifth consulship [29 BC], and once again in my tenth consulship [24 BC]. . . . In my fifth consulship [29 BC] I gave 1,000 sesterces out of booty to every one of the colonists drawn from my soldiers; about 120,000 men in the colonies received this largesse at the time of my triumph. . . .

16) I paid cash to the towns for the lands that I assigned to soldiers in my fourth consulship. . . . The sum amounted to about 600,000,000 sesterces paid for lands in Italy, and about 260,000,000 disbursed for provincial lands. Of all those who founded military colonies in Italy or the provinces I was the first and only one to have done this in the recollection of my contemporaries. Later, . . . I paid monetary rewards to soldiers whom I settled in their home towns after completion of their service, and on this account I expended about 400,000,000 sesterces.

17) . . . when the military treasury was founded by my advice for the purpose of paying rewards to soldiers who had served for twenty years or more, I transferred to it from my own patrimony 170,000,000 sesterces.

. . .

21) I built the temple of Mars the Avenger and the Forum Augustum on private ground from the proceeds of booty. . . . From the proceeds of booty I dedicated gifts in the

---

*Julius Caesar, his adoptive father.

†A small bronze or silver coin.

Capitol and in the temples of the divine Julius, of Apollo, of Vesta and of Mars the Avenger; this cost me about 100,000,000 sesterces. . . .

22) I gave three gladiatorial games in my own name and five in that of my sons or grandsons; at these games some 10,000 men took part in combat. . . .

23) I produced a naval battle as a show for the people at the place across the Tiber now occupied by the grove of the Caesars, where a site 1,800 feet long and 1,200 broad was excavated. There thirty beaked triremes or biremes and still more smaller vessels were joined in battle. About 3,000 men, besides the rowers, fought in these fleets.

. . .

25) I made the sea peaceful and freed it of pirates. In that war I captured about 30,000 slaves who had escaped from their masters and taken up arms against the republic, and I handed them over to their masters for punishment. The whole of Italy of its own free will swore allegiance to me and demanded me as the leader in the war in which I was victorious at Actium. The Gallic and Spanish provinces, Africa, Sicily and Sardinia swore the same oath of allegiance. More than seven hundred senators served under my standards at that time, including eighty-three who previously or subsequently (down to the time of writing) were appointed consuls, and about one hundred and seventy who were appointed priests.

26) I extended the territory of all those provinces of the Roman people on whose borders lay peoples not subject to our government . . . without waging an unjust war on any people. . . . At my command and under my auspices two armies were led almost at the same time into Ethiopia and Arabia Felix; vast enemy forces of both peoples were cut down in battle and many towns captured. . . .

. . .

29) By victories over enemies I recovered in Spain and in Gaul, and from the Dalmatians several standards lost by other commanders. I compelled the Parthians* to restore to me the spoils and standards of three Roman armies and to ask as suppliants for the friendship of the Roman people. Those standards I deposited in the innermost shrine of the temple of Mars the Avenger.

Maintaining Imperial Rule

Not all the subjects of the Roman Empire were happy with its rule, despite the peace and prosperity of the *Pax Romana*. The Jews, whose exclusive monotheism prevented them from participating in the cult of Augustus, were uncomfortable subjects of the Roman Empire, though the Romans were in fact fairly tolerant of the Jewish population, recognizing their separate religious tradition and allowing them to practice it. Nonetheless, religious and ethnic tensions fanned the flames of Jewish discontent, and the population broke into open revolt in 70 CE.

---

*Originally nomadic horsemen who ruled an empire based in Persia that was Rome's major opponent in the east.

144   CHAPTER 5 ✦ Empires, War, and Order

The war that followed was chronicled by a remarkable historian, Flavius Josephus (c. 37–100 CE). Born in Jerusalem as Joseph ben Matthias, Josephus was developing a career as a scholar and rabbi when he went to Rome on a diplomatic
mission to the Emperor Nero. On his return he was drafted into a command position of the emerging revolt. Captured by the Roman general Vespasian, he earned
the trust of the soon-to-be emperor by prophesying Vespasian's rise to rule. The
emperor adopted Josephus into his family, the Flavians, and Josephus became an
advisor to the Roman war effort, now led by Vespasian's son Titus. Unable to persuade his coreligionists to surrender, he witnessed the sack and destruction of
Jerusalem and its temple. His account of the war is factual but also flattered his
patron the emperor and served as a warning to other peoples who might consider
revolt against the might of the Roman imperium.

Josephus seems from the beginning to have considered the Jewish revolt
doomed, and it is not hard to see why in objective, material terms. Rome was,
along with the Han Empire and the Parthians, one of the world's great powers;
Parthia was contained at this time, and China was so far away as to be nearly legendary (save for the flow of Chinese silk to the Roman elites); thus Rome ruled
nearly the whole world known to Josephus and had proved its military prowess
repeatedly against many foes. The Jews were outnumbered and outorganized—
Josephus had spent much of his time as a commander settling factional disputes
within the Jewish camp, whereas the Romans obeyed a divine emperor. But the
Jews, too, had their notions of divine assistance, and thus this revolt saw a clash of
cultures as much as a clash of politics.

In this selection, Titus, son of Emperor Vespasian and commander of the
Roman forces, exhorts his men before a battle with the Jewish rebels. Note in particular the motivations for fighting Titus ascribes to each side and which he thinks
is more powerful.

QUESTIONS TO CONSIDER

1. What does Titus present as the key motivation for Roman soldiers in battle?
   How does this compare with the Jewish motives for going to war, and how
   does he rank them?

2. What is the balance between passion and rational calculation in what Titus
   says to inspire his troops? Which ultimately seems more important?

3. What does Titus's speech say about the role of warfare in the maintenance
   of order in the empire? How does this compare with Augustus's vision half
   a century earlier?

4. How would Sun Tzu evaluate the Roman conduct of this campaign?
   What advice might he have given the Jewish forces, faced with a vastly
   superior foe?

5. Does the cultural clash visible in this war hold any lessons for current-day
   conflicts? Are Roman attitudes about war useful for a modern superpower?

THE JEWISH WARS

Josephus

Book III
Chapter 10

2. But when Titus perceived that the enemy was very numerous, he sent to his father, and informed him that he should want more forces. But as he saw a great many of the horsemen eager to fight, and that before any succor could come to them, and that yet some of them were privately under a sort of consternation at the multitude of the Jews, he stood in a place whence he might be heard, and said to them,

"My brave Romans! for it is right for me to put you in mind of what nation you are, in the beginning of my speech, that so you may not be ignorant who you are, and who they are against whom we are going to fight. For as to us, Romans, no part of the habitable earth hath been able to escape our hands hitherto; but as for the Jews, that I may speak of them too, though they have been already beaten, yet do they not give up the cause; and a sad thing it would be for us to grow wealthy under good success, when they bear up under their misfortunes. As to the alacrity which you show publicly, I see it, and rejoice at it; yet am I afraid lest the multitude of the enemy should bring a concealed fright upon some of you: let such a one consider again, who we are that are to fight, and who those are against whom we are to fight. Now these Jews, though they be very bold and great despisers of death, are but a disorderly body, and unskillful in war, and may rather be called a rout than an army; while I need say nothing of our skill and our good order; for this is the reason why we Romans alone are exercised for war in time of peace, that we may not think of number for number when we come to fight with our enemies: for what advantage should we reap by our continual sort of warfare, if we must still be equal in number to such as have not been used to war. Consider further, that you are to have a conflict with men in effect unarmed, while you are well armed; with footmen, while you are horsemen; with those that have no good general, while you have one; and as these advantages make you in effect manifold more than you are, so do their disadvantages mightily diminish their number. Now it is not the multitude of men, though they be soldiers, that manages wars with success, but it is their bravery that does it, though they be but a few; for a few are easily set in battle-array, and can easily assist one another, while over-numerous armies are more hurt by themselves than by their enemies. It is boldness and rashness, the effects of madness, that conduct the Jews. Those passions indeed make a great figure when they succeed, but are quite extinguished upon the least ill success; but we are led on by courage, and obedience, and fortitude, which shows itself indeed in our good fortune, but still does not for ever desert us in our ill fortune. Nay, indeed, your fighting is to be on greater motives than those of the Jews; for although they run the hazard of war for liberty, and for their country, yet what can be a greater motive to us than glory? and that it may never be said, that after we have got dominion

Source: Flavius Josephus, *The Works of Flavius Josephus,* trans. William Whiston (Auburn and Buffalo: John E. Beardsley, 1895).

146   CHAPTER 5   ◆   Empires, War, and Order

of the habitable earth, the Jews are able to confront us. We must also reflect upon this, that there is no fear of our suffering any incurable disaster in the present case; for those that are ready to assist us are many, and at hand also; yet it is in our power to seize upon this victory ourselves; and I think we ought to prevent the coming of those my father is sending to us for our assistance, that our success may be peculiar to ourselves, and of greater reputation to us. And I cannot but think this an opportunity wherein my father, and I, and you shall be all put to the trial, whether he be worthy of his former glorious performances, whether I be his son in reality, and whether you be really my soldiers; for it is usual for my father to conquer; and for myself, I should not bear the thoughts of returning to him if I were once taken by the enemy. And how will you be able to avoid being ashamed, if you do not show equal courage with your commander, when he goes before you into danger? For you know very well that I shall go into the danger first, and make the first attack upon the enemy. Do not you therefore desert me, but persuade yourselves that God will be assisting to my onset. Know this also before we begin, that we shall now have better success than we should have, if we were to fight at a distance."

3. As Titus was saying this, an extraordinary fury fell upon the men; and as Trajan was already come before the fight began, with four hundred horsemen, they were uneasy at it, because the reputation of the victory would be diminished by being common to so many. Vespasian had also sent both Antonius and Silo, with two thousand archers, and had given it them in charge to seize upon the mountain that was over against the city, and repel those that were upon the wall; which archers did as they were commanded, and prevented those that attempted to assist them that way; And now Titus made his own horse march first against the enemy, as did the others with a great noise after him, and extended themselves upon the plain as wide as the enemy which confronted them; by which means they appeared much more numerous than they really were. Now the Jews, although they were surprised at their onset, and at their good order, made resistance against their attacks for a little while; but when they were pricked with their long poles, and overborne by the violent noise of the horsemen, they came to be trampled under their feet; many also of them were slain on every side, which made them disperse themselves, and run to the city, as fast as every one of them were able. So Titus pressed upon the hindmost, and slew them; and of the rest, some he fell upon as they stood on heaps, and some he prevented, and met them in the mouth, and ran them through; many also he leaped upon as they fell one upon another, and trod them down, and cut off all the retreat they had to the wall, and turned them back into the plain, till at last they forced a passage by their multitude, and got away, and ran into the city.

THE INDIAN TRADITION
Questioning Warfare

Asoka (304–232 BCE) was third king of the Mauryan dynasty. After taking the throne, he initially pursued the expansionist policies of his father Bindusara and his grandfather Chandragupta Maurya. The Mauryan Empire maintained a large, professional army, complete with an impressive (though militarily unreliable) corps of trained war elephants, supported by a large bureaucratic machine, much like the Han and Roman empires, and indeed the range of terrains and climates in which Mauryan armies campaigned probably exceeded those in either China or the Roman Empire. It is probably this geographic diversity, including the presence within agricultural districts of large tracts of semidesert and scrub land good at best for pastoralism but incapable of supporting agriculture, that accounts for political division, rather than imperial unity, being the rule in India before and even after the Mauryas, by contrast certainly with China and even with Rome (especially the eastern half of the Empire) in later centuries.

It is thus especially noteworthy that, with the conquest of the kingdom of Kalinga on India's southeastern coast, Asoka brought almost the whole of the subcontinent under Mauryan rule. But the cost of that campaign in human lives and misery led Asoka to a spiritual crisis and conversion to Buddhism. He forswore offensive warfare (but did retain his large army and the will to use it defensively when necessary) and instead committed himself and his government to spiritual conquest, the welfare of his subjects, and the promotion of *dharma* (sacred duty, though the term has a number of meanings in Hindu and Buddhist tradition and Asoka construed it broadly and with toleration for religious variety). Adopting the reign name *Priyadarsi* ("One who looks after the welfare of others"), he had stone pillars erected throughout his realms inscribed with his precepts on *dharma*. This selection comes from those Rock and Pillar Edicts and is more about the impact of and reaction to war than about war itself.

QUESTIONS TO CONSIDER

1. What aspects of warfare on the ground most bother Asoka? What are the implications of this list for his view of the world?

2. What view of human nature seems to lie behind Asoka's reaction to warfare and his subsequent policies? Is it one that could be applied elsewhere?

3. A cynic might say that encouraging Buddhism (a pacifist religion) among his subjects would benefit Asoka by reducing resistance to government edicts. How might Asoka answer this charge?

4. What would Sun Tzu say about Asoka's policy of nonaggression? What about Augustus? How would Asoka answer them?

5. Is the moral alternative to warfare expressed here applicable to today's world? How? Is nonaggression a desirable stance for a great power? Is it a possible one?

148   CHAPTER 5   ◆   Empires, War, and Order

ROCK AND PILLAR EDICTS

Asoka

Rock Edict XIII

Beloved-of-the-Gods, King Priyadarsi, conquered the Kalingas eight years after his coronation. One hundred and fifty thousand were deported, one hundred thousand were killed and many more died (from other causes). After the Kalingas had been conquered, Beloved-of-the-Gods came to feel a strong inclination towards the Dharma, a love for the Dharma and for instruction in Dharma. Now Beloved-of-the-Gods feels deep remorse for having conquered the Kalingas.

Indeed, Beloved-of-the-Gods is deeply pained by the killing, dying and deportation that take place when an unconquered country is conquered. But Beloved-of-the-Gods is pained even more by this—that Brahmans, ascetics, and householders of different religions who live in those countries, and who are respectful to superiors, to mother and father, to elders, and who behave properly and have strong loyalty towards friends, acquaintances, companions, relatives, servants and employees—that they are injured, killed or separated from their loved ones. Even those who are not affected (by all this) suffer when they see friends, acquaintances, companions and relatives affected. These misfortunes befall all (as a result of war), and this pains Beloved-of-the-Gods.

There is no country, except among the Greeks, where these two groups, Brahmans* and ascetics, are not found, and there is no country where people are not devoted to one or another religion. Therefore the killing, death or deportation of a hundredth, or even a thousandth part of those who died during the conquest of Kalinga now pains Beloved-of-the-Gods. Now Beloved-of-the-Gods thinks that even those who do wrong should be forgiven where forgiveness is possible.

Even the forest people, who live in Beloved-of-the-Gods' domain, are entreated and reasoned with to act properly. They are told that despite his remorse Beloved-of-the-Gods has the power to punish them if necessary, so that they should be ashamed of their wrong and not be killed. Truly, Beloved-of-the-Gods desires non-injury, restraint and impartiality to all beings, even where wrong has been done.

Now it is conquest by Dharma that Beloved-of-the-Gods considers to be the best conquest. And it (conquest by Dharma) has been won here, on the borders, even six hundred yojanas away, where the Greek king Antiochos rules, beyond there where the four kings named Ptolemy, Antigonos, Magas and Alexander rule,† likewise in the south among the Cholas, the Pandyas, and as far as Tamraparni.‡ Here in the king's domain among the Greeks, the Kambojas, the Nabhakas, the Nabhapamkits, the Bho-

---

Source: The Edicts of King Ashoka, trans. Ven. S. Dhammika. Copyright © 1993 Buddhist Publication Society, Kandy, Sri Lanka. Reprinted by permission of Dhamma Books.

*The priestly class of Hindu society.

†Antiochus, Ptolemy, and the others were Alexander's generals (and their successors) who had divided Alexander's empire into four Successor kingdoms after Alexander's death.

‡Kingdoms in the far south of India, the one area of the subcontinent not under direct Mauryan rule.

jas, the Pitinikas, the Andhras and the Palidas,* everywhere people are following Beloved-of-the-Gods' instructions in Dharma. Even where Beloved-of-the-Gods' envoys have not been, these people too, having heard of the practice of Dharma and the ordinances and instructions in Dharma given by Beloved-of-the-Gods, are following it and will continue to do so. This conquest has been won everywhere, and it gives great joy—the joy which only conquest by Dharma can give. But even this joy is of little consequence. Beloved-of-the-Gods considers the great fruit to be experienced in the next world to be more important.

I have had this Dharma edict written so that my sons and great-grandsons may not consider making new conquests, or that if military conquests are made, that they be done with forbearance and light punishment, or better still, that they consider making conquest by Dharma only, for that bears fruit in this world and the next. May all their intense devotion be given to this which has a result in this world and the next.

---

*The various ethnic and linguistic groups encompassed by the empire.

CHAPTER 6

Women in the Ancient World

INTRODUCTION

In his comedy *Lysistrata* (411 BCE), the Athenian playwright Aristophanes depicted the women of Athens bringing the Peloponnesian War to an end by means of a sex strike. They organized to abstain from sex until the men became so desperate that they made peace. His play is considered a comic masterpiece, but implicit in its plotline is a darker side of Greek society—the systematic disempowerment of women. Because they were denied active involvement in the participatory democracy of the Greek *polis,* the only means they had at their disposal to influence the councils of men was the sex act. The Greek world of the *polis* era is rightly presented as one of the wellsprings of a wide variety of significant aspects of human culture—for example, logic, philosophy, political science, democratic governance, drama, and historical writing. Yet this dynamic, creative society, to an even greater extent than did most ancient societies, relegated women to a position of extreme subordination. The contrast between the accomplishments of the Hellenic Greeks and the treatment of women in that culture throws into stark relief the experiences and roles of women in the ancient world. In the readings that follow, the reader will be asked to assess the nature of women's roles in five different cultures—those of (1) ancient Greece, (2) Rome of the pagan era (ca. 200 BCE), (3) China of the first century CE, (4) the Christian Roman subculture around 200 CE (before Christianity became the established religion of the Roman Empire), and (5) early Hindu India. Of course, questions about the proper relationship between men and women and about the correct role of women in society are still burning issues. Yet, in addition to the contemporary relevance of the exploration of gender issues, the particular subject of gender roles and gender relations allows us to examine the complex social issue of the relatively unempowered and the underclass.

Humans are social animals, and even in situations of extreme disparity in power between social groups—in circumstances such as slavery, prisons, and concentration camps, for example—there is an interaction between those who exercise power and those on whom power is exercised. All the more so, then, in less extreme cases do those lower in the hierarchy of power and status react to, shape, and contest the dominant social values and social systems. Hence, even when excluded from the formal exercise of power by being deprived of the right to participate in government, military affairs, property ownership and management, and higher culture, humans devise ways to exert influence, even if that influence is passive or reactive.

The women represented and presented here were neither completely devoid of influence nor absolutely unable to give voice to their thoughts and feelings. Nonetheless, they were also affected and influenced by the dominant male power structures (known as patriarchies). So an additional subject to examine is the extent to which those lower on the scale of social and political power are molded by and assimilate the reigning social values. Again, an issue of human social life—the complex process by which social norms are created, transmitted, internalized, and transformed—can be addressed by looking at the way women in ancient societies were neither wholly dependent on, nor completely independent of, the male-dominated system of social values.

Two other elements to pay attention to in reading these materials are (1) the common gender split between the public (male) and private or domestic (female) spheres and (2) the different interests of elite and common women. It was not uncommon for women to be accorded some privileges and power inside the walls of the family home or in matters connected with the domestic sphere, even if those matters extended beyond the home. Although it must be recognized that this is a not insignificant realm of responsibility, it still represents less than full empowerment, if the public sphere remained an exclusively or preeminently male domain. An important question to bear in mind is to what extent, if any, women were allowed to extend their influence into the public sphere and how men reacted when they did. Connected with this consideration is the differential power of elite and common women. The sources presented here are "privileged" in the direction of elite women. Penelope, the Roman women, Ban Zhao, and Perpetua all came from the upper class, and none of the authors of these sources can be said to have presented a commoner's point of view. So, again, it is essential to be aware that the situations and values presented here would apply in the first instance to elite women, while also asking ourselves which of these texts might have also affected women who were not from the upper classes.

The first selection comes from the famous epic of ancient Greece, *The Odyssey*. One of the core texts of Classical Greece, the *Odyssey* was probably produced in the 700s BCE. Its story centers on the difficult journey homeward of one of the great heroes of *The Iliad*, Odysseus. Another focus of the work is the home and family, which he struggles to return to. His kingdom and his household were managed in his absence by his faithful wife, Penelope, who has faced her own trials and troubles. Penelope's character and cleverness are displayed in the selection included here, which involves the climactic scene of Odysseus's return and the final test Penelope sets for him to prove his identity.

The second piece excerpted here revolves around a political dispute of ancient Rome. The specific point of contention was the proposal to repeal a law (the

152   CHAPTER 6 ✦ Women in the Ancient World

Oppian Law) that limited the luxury items Roman women could wear in public. Although the law had been passed at a time of great crisis for Rome and that time was long past, the effort to repeal the law became a heated dispute, because women had taken to the streets to protest the law. Thus the law became a symbol of male control over women, and the debate over its repeal reflects different views of the role of women in Roman society. All of the voices in this selection are male, even that of the historian Livy from whose work the selection is taken. Hence this passage provides the dominant masculine perspective and reveals the limits imposed on women's roles in Rome, even by those who supported the women's position on this issue.

The third selection in this chapter comes from a handbook written explicitly to serve as a guide to proper behavior for women in Han China (206 BCE–220 CE) in the second century of our era. The *Nujie*, or *Lessons for Women* (ca. 110 CE), provides us with a comprehensive understanding of the proper role and behavior of women in elite Chinese society. The author, Ban Zhao (ca. 45–ca. 110 CE), was herself an exceptional individual who was chosen to serve the empress directly and whose writing places her among the ranks of the first women scholars in the history of humanity. Although written by a woman of remarkable accomplishments, *Lessons for Women* depicts as the ideal a thoroughly subordinate role for women within the Confucian value system.

The next source in this chapter comes from the prison diary of a woman, Vibia Perpetua, who was executed for her Christian beliefs around 200 CE in the Roman city of Carthage in North Africa. This is a most unusual and distinctive source. Here we have an otherwise unknown woman, speaking to us in her own voice across the centuries. Her decision not to recant her faith when faced with execution and her defiance of her father in the process presents to us a circumstance in which a woman asserted the ultimate power. In a sense, her story demonstrates that, although women in the ancient world were not free to choose the way they lived, they still retained the power to choose the way they died. In addition, her story allows us to examine the role of women in the early Christian world.

The final source in this chapter reflects Hindu religious and social values. It comprises entries in the *Code of Manu* relating to the special responsibilities of women. The *Code of Manu* has been interpreted as an attempt to restore order after a period of turmoil. Although Hindus do not view it as a divinely revealed text, they do believe that the *Code of Manu* is consistent with the proper order of the universe and with the values revealed by the gods in other sources. In that regard, the restrictions and limitations it imposes on women and wives are thought to be divinely sanctioned and to rest on the ultimate authority of the gods.

In different voices and from different cultures and different time periods, the sources excerpted here reveal the social roles of women in the ancient world and the social value systems that defined those roles. Although none of these women were "liberated" in anything like the modern sense, they were not completely disempowered, either. Moreover, even from their inferior position in the power pyramid of the ancient world, they asserted themselves and shaped in significant, though still subordinate, ways the contours of their lives. Their experiences allow us to examine the specific issue of women's role in society and the broader theme of the encounter between the relatively unempowered in society and the dominant social and political systems that constrain them.

CHAPTER QUESTIONS

1. Identify and compare the position of elite women in the different cultures presented here. In what ways do the women presented here exercise power? Are there any differences in the power women exercise in the public sphere versus the private sphere?

2. How do the selections composed by women (Perpetua and Ban Zhao) differ from those written by men? How might the voices of nonelite women differ from the voices of these women?

3. How do the men presented here react to the women? How do the behaviors and opinions of the men differ and what, if anything, do they have in common?

4. In which culture does the elite woman have the most power and privileges? In which the least? Can the difference be explained?

5. What general conclusions can you draw about power relations, based on these readings? What limits are there on the power exercised by the dominant parties, and in what ways is power exercised by those in subordinate social positions?

WOMEN IN THE HOMERIC WORLD: *THE ODYSSEY*

The Odyssey as a literary work is a mixture of fact and fiction. It was probably composed late in the eighth century BCE (i.e., the 700s BCE), but it may have originated even later. Authorship, composition date, and historical accuracy of this text are all highly controversial subjects among classicists. Our concern here is not with these issues, but with the view *The Odyssey* provides of gender relations in an aristocratic society. As far as the story itself goes, *The Odyssey* tells the tale of Odysseus's long and troubled return from the Trojan War, which was the subject of *The Iliad*. Because he has angered Poseidon, the god of the sea, he suffers a series of unfortunate events, such as shipwreck, capture, and escape from the Cyclops, Polyphemus, avoiding the irresistible allure of the Sirens' song, and so on. Odysseus was famous for his judgment and his cleverness—it was he who devised the tactic of the Trojan Horse that led to the conquest of Troy and ultimately ended the Trojan War. His cleverness and perseverance allow him to endure despite his troubles and eventually to succeed in returning home.

The position of noblewomen in the world of *The Odyssey* was mixed. The world of *The Odyssey* was not unlike that of the western Middle Ages without the castles. Noble lords, who were great warriors, lived on self-sufficient manorial estates, worked by peasants. In that world, as in most aristocratic societies, women were valued because of their bloodlines. Aristocracies traditionally assert their

154   CHAPTER 6 ◆ Women in the Ancient World

right to rule on the basis of superior ancestry, so it was important to have noble ancestors on both the father's and the mother's sides. The noblewomen in this society also had important duties, managing the estates and their household economy, especially during the prolonged absences of the noblemen. In Penelope's case, for example, she has successfully run the estate for years in Odysseus's absence. At the same time, noblewomen could not hold property and power on their own. In *The Odyssey*, when Odysseus did not return from the Trojan War along with the other warriors, evil suitors established themselves in his household and were consuming much of what the estate produced. Although Penelope waited faithfully, in the end they would have forced her to choose one of them as her new husband. Until she remarried, she would enjoy a certain degree of autonomy. Here we can detect the ambiguous status of noblewomen: They are valued for their "pedigree," and as members of the upper class they are trained in certain managerial skills, yet ultimately they must accept a subordinate status in a marriage to a nobleman.

The passage presented here represents the culmination of both *The Iliad* and *The Odyssey*, because it returns Odysseus to the embrace of his wife and household, ending his long absence both at Troy and on the journey back. When he finally reaches home, he does not know what to expect, and he is characteristically cautious, concealing his identity until he has appraised the situation. Despite Odysseus's long absence, Penelope continues to wait for him. Hers is an unenviable task. Not only does she bear the burden of worry for her absent husband, but she also has to deal with the insistent pressure from the boorish noble suitors. She reveals an enormous strength of character throughout this ordeal.

Penelope is a worthy match for Odysseus. She demonstrates her own shrewdness in a variety of ways. For example, she devises stratagems to delay the day of decision about a new husband. One way she puts off the suitors is to unravel every night the cloth that she is weaving for her wedding. Her faithfulness and steadfastness has made her name a synonym for fidelity. Another test she uses to hold off the suitors is to require them to string an enormous and extremely powerful bow. In the following scene, she reveals similar cleverness and sagacity in posing one final test for Odysseus to prove his identity.

The suitors are dealt with in the following fashion. Odysseus, still disguised as a homeless wanderer, is allowed by the mocking suitors to have a go at stringing the bow. Of course, he alone is powerful enough to string it, and, after he does so, he uses it to slay all the suitors. At this point, he reveals his true identity to Penelope. Penelope has had her suspicions that this man might actually be her long-lost husband, but she has not endured the long years on her own without developing her own internal resources and caution. She who has held out so long refuses to accept his declaration without first setting him a test. Central to that test is knowledge of the fact that the house was built by Odysseus himself around an olive tree that was topped off and used as a supporting pillar in the middle of the bedroom.

She is fearful, after all her years of faithful waiting, of some trick that would lead her to yield to a clever stranger posing as Odysseus. There are numerous mistaken-identity scenes in both *The Iliad* and *The Odyssey*, often involving deception by the gods. To be sure of his identity, she sets a test for him, ordering her servants to move Odysseus's bed out of the main bedroom. She knows, as the real Odysseus will also know, that the bed is connected to the olive-tree pillar and cannot be moved.

QUESTIONS TO CONSIDER

1. List the elements of Penelope's character that are revealed in this scene. Compare them with the character traits of Odysseus that emerge in this passage.
2. Who holds the power? How is that power utilized? Does this scene involve power in the public or in the private sphere?
3. Odysseus was characterized as "the best of the Achaeans [i.e., Greeks]" because of his wisdom, courage, caution, and cleverness. Assess whether Odysseus demonstrates those attributes in this scene. Analyze Penelope's behavior using those four attributes. Who is "the best of the Achaeans" in this scene?
4. What description does *The Odyssey* provide of Penelope's emotions once she is convinced of Odysseus's identity? How does this description equate her experiences during her husband's long absence with Odysseus's own experiences?
5. Having read the whole passage, how would you describe the relations between Odysseus and Penelope? Is one in a dominant position, or is the relationship on more of an equal footing?

THE ODYSSEY

Homer

The upper servant Eurynome washed and anointed Odysseus in his own house and gave him a shirt and cloak, while Athene* made him look taller and stronger than before; she also made the hair grow thick on the top of his head, and flow down in curls like hyacinth blossoms; she glorified him about the head and shoulders just as a skillful workman who has studied art of all kinds under Hephaestus[†] or Athene—and his work is full of beauty—enriches a piece of silver plate by gilding it. He came from the bath looking like one of the immortals, and sat down opposite his wife on the seat he had left. "My dear," said he, "heaven has endowed you with a heart more unyielding than woman ever yet had. No other woman could bear to keep away from her husband when he had come back to her after twenty years of absence, and after having

---

Source: The Odyssey of Homer, trans. Samuel Butler, 287–90. Copyright © 1944 Walter J. Black, New York.

*Goddess of Wisdom. Odysseus is one of her favorites.

[†]God of fire and volcanoes, and also of metalworking and smiths.

gone through so much. But come, nurse, get a bed ready for me; I will sleep alone, for this woman has a heart as hard as iron."

"My dear," answered Penelope, "I have no wish to set myself up, nor to depreciate you; but I am not struck by your appearance, for I very well remember what kind of a man you were when you set sail from Ithaca. Nevertheless, Euryclea,* take his bed outside the bed chamber that he himself built. Bring the bed outside this room, and put bedding upon it with fleeces, good coverlets, and blankets."

She said this to try him, but Odysseus was very angry and said, "Wife, I am much displeased at what you have just been saying. Who has been taking my bed from the place in which I left it? He must have found it a hard task, no matter how skilled a workman he was, unless some god came and helped him to shift it. There is no man living, however strong and in his prime, who could move it from its place, for it is a marvelous curiosity which I made with my very own hands. There was a young olive growing within the precincts of the house, in full vigor, and about as thick as a bearing-post. I built my room round this with strong walls of stone and a roof to cover them, and I made the doors strong and well-fitting. Then I cut off the top boughs of the olive tree and left the stump standing. This I dressed roughly from the root upwards and then worked with carpenter's tools well and skillfully, straightening my work by drawing a line on the wood, and making it into a bed-prop. I then bored a hole down the middle, and made it the center-post of my bed, at which I worked till I had finished it, inlaying it with gold and silver; after this I stretched a hide of crimson leather from one side of it to the other. So you see I know all about it, and I desire to learn whether it is still there, or whether any one has been removing it by cutting down the olive tree at its roots."

When she heard the sure proofs Odysseus now gave her, she fairly broke down. She flew weeping to his side, flung her arms about his neck, and kissed him. "Do not be angry with me Odysseus," she cried, "you, who are the wisest of mankind. We have suffered, both of us. Heaven has denied us the happiness of spending our youth, and of growing old, together; do not then be aggrieved or take it amiss that I did not embrace you thus as soon as I saw you. I have been shuddering all the time through fear that someone might come here and deceive me with a lying story; for there are many very wicked people going about. Zeus's[†] daughter Helen[‡] would never have yielded herself to a man from a foreign country, if she had known that the sons of Achaeans[§] would come after her and bring her back. Heaven put it in her heart to do wrong, and she gave no thought to that sin, which has been the source of all our sorrows. Now, however, that you have convinced me by showing that you know all about our bed (which no human being has ever seen but you and I and a single maid servant, . . . who was given me by my father on my marriage, and who keeps the doors of our room) hard of belief though I have been I can mistrust no longer."

---

*A domestic slave of Odysseus's father and the woman who wet-nursed Odysseus as a baby.

[†]God of the sky and lightning, king of the gods.

[‡]Helen of Troy ran away from her husband with Paris, son of the king of Troy, which caused the Trojan War.

[§]The Greeks from mainland Greece. They are the ones who attacked Troy.

Then Odysseus in his turn melted, and wept as he clasped his dear and faithful wife to his bosom. As the sight of land is welcome to men who are swimming towards the shore, when Poseidon* has wrecked their ship with the fury of his winds and waves—a few alone reach the land, and these, covered with brine, are thankful when they find themselves on firm ground and out of danger—even so was her husband welcome to her as she looked upon him, and she could not tear her two fair arms from about his neck. Indeed they would have gone on indulging their sorrow till rosy-fingered morn appeared, had not Athene determined otherwise, and held night back in the far west, while she would not suffer Dawn[†] to leave Oceanus, nor to yoke the two steeds Lampus and Phaethon that bear her onward to break the day upon mankind. . . .

Thus did they converse. Meanwhile Eurynome and the nurse took torches and made the bed ready with soft coverlets; as soon as they had laid them, the nurse went back into the house to go to her rest, leaving the bed chamber woman Eurynome to show Odysseus and Penelope to bed by torch light. When she had conducted them to their room she went back, and they then came joyfully to the rites of their own old bed. Telemachus,[‡] Philoetius,[§] and the swineherd now left off dancing, and made the women leave off also. They then laid themselves down to sleep in the cloisters.

When Odysseus and Penelope had had their fill of love they fell talking with one another. She told him how much she had had to bear in seeing the house filled with a crowd of wicked suitors who had killed so many sheep and oxen on her account, and had drunk so many casks of wine. Odysseus in his turn told her what he had suffered, and how much trouble he had himself given to other people. He told her everything, and she was so delighted to listen that she never went to sleep till he had ended his whole story.

A PUBLIC PROTEST DEMONSTRATION BY ELITE ROMAN WOMEN

The second piece excerpted here comes from Titus Livy's *History of Rome*. Livy was born in the last century BCE (either 59 or 64 BCE) in northern Italy. Livy was a Roman patriot, and his history reflected his pride in Rome's accomplishments. Unfortunately, only about a quarter of his original *History* survives. Nonetheless, it is still the best single source for Roman history, and for the parts of his *History* that survive, Livy is an irreplaceable primary source.

---

*God of the Sea.

[†]To the Greeks, Dawn was a goddess who lived in the east by the waters of Oceanus, the body of water that surrounded the land mass in Greek understanding of geography. Every morning, two steeds, Lampus and Phaethon, draw her chariot across the sky.

[‡]The son of Odysseus and Penelope. He was only a baby when Odysseus left for the Trojan War and is still a young man at the time of his father's return. He and Philoetius help Odysseus fight the evil suitors.

[§]An old and loyal servant of Odysseus.

158   CHAPTER 6 ◆ Women in the Ancient World

The incident related in the passage presented here involves an extremely rare instance of public political protest on the part of the women of Rome. The issue was the proposed repeal of the *Lex Oppia*, or Oppian Law. In 215 BCE during the Second Punic Wars, one of Rome's three great conflicts with Carthage over dominance in the western Mediterranean, the famous Carthaginian general Hannibal inflicted a devastating defeat on the Romans at the battle of Cannae. In the wake of that defeat, the Oppian Law was passed, prohibiting women from having more than half an ounce of gold, wearing clothes in public adorned with expensive purple dye, or riding in a carriage except on religious holidays. These restrictions were implemented to suppress public displays of wealth at a time when Romans were forced by Hannibal's successes to undergo enormous sacrifices in order to raise and equip new armies. In 195 BCE a movement arose, supported by public demonstrations by women, to repeal the restrictions. The women appealed to the consuls.[1] One of them, Marcus Porcius Cato, adamantly opposed repeal, and the other consul, Lucius Valerius, supported repeal.

Women were denied political rights in Rome. In fact, Roman law invested the father of the family with extraordinarily broad powers (*patria potestas*), including even the right to kill unwanted children at birth. During the Republic, women were ordinarily under the control (*manus*) of their husbands, and other women had guardians who made all major decisions. The protest was a real-life effort by women to make themselves heard.

For various reasons, the repeal seemed threatening to some Roman leaders. The long Roman wars had left Roman women relatively independent because of their husbands' absences or deaths. In addition, Roman conquests brought a flood of new wealth into the city. Rome was a victim of its own success, and widespread change might transform Roman society beyond recognition. This new wealth, combined with the repeal of Oppian Law restrictions on women's luxury items, called into question the traditional control men wielded over women in Rome.

The most vehement opponent of the repeal of the restrictive law was Marcus Porcius Cato (234–149 BCE), commonly referred to as Cato the Elder. In his remarkable career, Cato had led Roman armies to victory over Carthaginian forces in Spain and had risen to the position of consul. He was known as Cato the Censor for his hard-bitten opposition to what he perceived to be moral decline. Cato opposed displays of wealth and luxury, rigorously enforced laws, and resisted anything he connected with a decline in public morals, including elements of Greek culture, which he deemed to be inferior and effeminate. His objections and arguments were responded to by Lucius Valerius, also consul in 195 but a figure of much less prominence in Roman history and about whom much less is known.

It is also worth mentioning that the Romans carefully studied histories such as Livy's, considering history to be "philosophy teaching by examples." Thus works such as Livy's did not just gather dust on a shelf but were part of the education of the ruling classes in Rome, so the values represented in this selection helped shape Roman attitudes toward women. The circumstances surrounding this public protest by women in Rome constitute an ideal opportunity for us to assess Roman ideas about women and their proper place in the social and political life of humanity.[2]

Livy ◆ *History of Rome*, Book XXXIV I-H   **159**

QUESTIONS TO CONSIDER

1. Considering the restrictions that were being protested, what class of Roman women was probably involved? How might the social class of these women affect the way the male leadership of Rome responded to the protests?

2. What are Cato's arguments for maintaining the ban on gold, purple cloth, and carriages? Is he more concerned with the law itself or with the public protest by the women against it?

3. What distinctions are raised in these passages between the public and the private spheres? Did women have more power in the private sphere in Roman society or were they equally disempowered in both areas?

4. If men are superior to women, as Cato argues, why is it necessary to have a law to enforce rules? Can you identify any ways in which Cato ironically argues that women are actually superior to men? Conversely, although Valerius supports the repeal of the Oppian Law, does he paint a flattering picture of women?

5. The Oppian Law was repealed. In your opinion, does this show that women actually had power in Roman society? How does their power compare with that of Penelope?

HISTORY OF ROME, BOOK XXXIV I-H

Livy

Cato . . . spoke as follows in defense of the law: "If we had, each one of us, made it a rule to uphold the rights and authority of the husband in our own households we should not now have this trouble with the whole body of our women. As things are now our liberty of action, which has been checked and rendered powerless by female despotism at home, is actually crushed and trampled on here in the Forum, and because we were unable to withstand them individually we have now to dread their united strength. . . . [T]here is no class of women from whom the gravest dangers may not arise, if once you allow intrigues, plots, secret cabals to go on. . . .

"It was not without a feeling of shame that I made my way into the Forum through a regular army of women. Our ancestors would have no woman transact even private business except through her guardian, they placed them under the tutelage of parents or brothers or husbands. We suffer them now to dabble in politics and mix themselves up with the business of the Forum and public debates and election contests. . . . Give the reins to a headstrong nature, to a creature that has not been tamed, and then hope that they will themselves set bounds to their license if you do not do it

Source: From Livy in *History of Rome*, Book XXXIV 1-H, Roland Mellor, ed., *The Historians of Ancient Rome*, 1998, 332–33, 335–36, 338. Reprinted with permission of Routledge, a division of Taylor & Francis Books, LTD.

160   CHAPTER 6   ◆   Women in the Ancient World

yourselves. . . . What they really want is . . . license, and if they win on this occasion what is there that they will not attempt? . . .

"If you allow them to . . . finally put themselves on an equality with their husbands, do you imagine that you will be able to tolerate them? From the moment that they become your fellows they will become your masters. . . ."

After this . . . Valerius made the following speech in defense of his proposal: "M. Porcius [Cato] . . . spent . . . more time in castigating the matrons than in arguing against the bill. . . . I shall defend the measure. . . . Because we are now enjoying the blessings of peace and the commonwealth is flourishing and happy, the matrons are making a public request to you that you will repeal a law which was passed against them under the pressure of a time of war. He denounces this action of theirs as a plot, a seditious movement, and he sometimes calls it a female secession. I know how these and other strong expressions are selected to bolster up a case, and . . . Cato is a powerful speaker and sometimes almost menacing. What innovation have the matrons been guilty of by publicly assembling in such numbers for a cause which touches them so closely? Have they never appeared in public before? I will quote your own *Origines** against you. [H]ow often they have done this and always to the benefit of the State."

[Valerius cites several instances from Roman history in which the women of Rome came to its defense.]

"You say that they were actuated by different motives then. It is not my purpose to establish the identity of motives, it is sufficient to clear them from the charge of strange unheard-of conduct. And yet, in matters which concern men and women alike, their action occasioned surprise to no one; why then should we be surprised at their taking the same action in a cause which especially interests them? But what have they done? We must, believe me, have the ears of tyrants if, whilst masters condescend to listen to the prayers of their slaves we deem it an indignity to be asked a favor by honorable women. . . .

"You husbands are at liberty to wear a purple wrap over your dress, will you refuse to allow your wives to wear a purple mantle? Are the trappings of your horses to be more gorgeous than the dress of your wives? . . . No, but most certainly there is general grief and indignation felt among them when they see the wives of our Latin allies† permitted to wear ornaments which they have been deprived of, when they see them resplendent in gold and purple and driving through the City while they have to follow on foot, just as though the seat of empire was in the Latin cities and not in their own. This would be enough to hurt the feelings of men, what then think you must be the feelings of poor little women who are affected by small things? Magistracies, priestly functions, triumphs, military decorations and rewards, spoils of war— none of these fall to their lot. Neatness, elegance, personal adornment, attractive

---

*A seven-volume encyclopedic history of Rome by Cato.

†Non-Roman Latin-speaking peoples of central Italy.

appearance and looks—these are the distinctions they covet, in these they delight and pride themselves; these things our ancestors called the ornament of women. . . . I suppose you think that if you repeal the Oppian Law, and should wish to forbid anything which the law forbids now, it will not be in your power to do so, and that some will lose all legal rights over their daughters and wives and sisters. No; women are never freed from subjection as long as their husbands and fathers are alive; they deprecate the freedom which orphanhood and widowhood bring. They would rather leave their personal adornment to your decision than to that of the law. It is your duty to act as their guardians and protectors and not treat them as slaves; you ought to wish to be called fathers and husbands, instead of lords and masters. . . . Whatever decision you come to, they in their weakness will have to submit to it. The greater your power, so much the more moderate ought you to be in exercising it."

WOMEN AND CONFUCIAN VALUES IN CHINA

The remarkable woman whose work is presented here, Ban Zhao, was born somewhere between 45 and 48 CE and died some time before 120 CE. Later in Chinese history, Ban Zhao was respected for both her scholarship and her ability.[3] Her father, who died when she was a young girl, had begun work on an important imperial history, known as the *Han Shu.* His work was left incomplete at his death, and one of his sons took up the task of completing the father's work, at which he was assisted for a while by his brother. When he also died, Ban Zhao was entrusted with the completion of the work. Although the exact nature of what she added to the final product is a matter of dispute, her contributions were significant, and she ranks as China's earliest woman historian and one of the first woman scholars in world history. She must have had a character as impressive as her scholarly abilities, because she was honored with selection as the governess of the empress and her ladies-in-waiting. The work from which the following extract was taken is the *Nujie,* or *Lessons for Women,* which she wrote somewhere around 110 CE.

As she indicates in the work, it was written as a guide for her own daughters, so that they would have a pattern for their behavior. As such, it is written very much in the Confucian tradition, emphasizing respect for ancestors, elders, and other superiors and the importance of proper behavior to the smooth and correct functioning of society. Although Ban Zhao reached positions of great influence, she highlights the necessity for women to respect and be submissive to other family members, in addition to her husband. These included not only her father- and mother-in-law, but also her brothers- and sisters-in-law. The Confucian system insisted on the recognition of sharply distinguished social hierarchies, and, although a woman might have standing as a member of a high-born family, within the family web itself, she could easily find herself at the base of the pyramid.

By the time of Ban Zhao, Confucianism was firmly rooted in Chinese culture and thought. To review, Confucius, the Western variant of the title Kung Fu Tzu, or "Master Kung," lived from 551 to 479 BCE. His teachings emphasized *li*

162   CHAPTER 6   ◆   Women in the Ancient World

(proper behavior) and *jen* (true manliness) as the foundation of harmony in society and life. Confucianism is a sophisticated extension of the ideas behind the Mandate of Heaven to all aspects of human life, essentially arguing that a harmonious and balanced existence is based on proper personal and ritual behavior. Five key relationships have to be conducted correctly. They are ruler–subject, parents–children, husband–wife, brother–brother, and friend–friend. In virtually every one of these relationships (except for parents/parents-in-law and children) women occupy an inferior position. That *jen* means "true manliness" is equivalent to the linguistic connection between virility and virtue (both with the common Latin root of *vir*, or "man"), and this serves to underline the subordinate position of women in the Confucian value system. At the same time, however, Confucianism emphasizes proper and respectful behavior and criticizes abusive behavior. Moreover, for the system to function properly, women must fulfill their roles and relationships in the correct fashion. Once again, although women occupy secondary and passive roles, Confucianism accords a respectful place to women and attaches significant consequences, both positive and negative, to women's behavior.

QUESTIONS TO CONSIDER

1. According to Ban Zhao, what should be the foremost concerns of a woman? In general terms, how ought she strive to relate to others?

2. What are the two Chinese concepts of *Yin* and *Yang*, and how are they connected to the issue of the proper behavior of women? In your opinion, did the concepts of *Yin* and *Yang* accord women more power in the private sphere as compared with the public sphere, or was the amount of power consistent in both the public and private arenas?

3. Although this work focuses on the obligations of women, judging by it, how ought men to behave in their role as husbands? Does the subordinate role allocated to women in this system have any compensating benefits in the way that men are supposed to behave?

4. Ban Zhao argues that women ought to receive some education and training, just as men do. How can the insistence in the Confucian system that women serve men be used to justify better education and training for women? What class of women do you think would have benefited most if restrictions on education of women had been lifted?

5. How does the position of women in ancient Chinese society compare with that of women in the other societies and cultures presented in this chapter? Would the behavior of Penelope, the Roman women, or Perpetua have been possible in Chinese society? Would she have agreed with the *Code of Manu*?

LESSONS FOR WOMEN

Ban Zhao

Introduction

I, the unworthy writer, am unsophisticated, unenlightened, and by nature unintelligent, but I am fortunate both to have received not a little favor from my scholarly father, and to have had a (cultured) mother and instructresses upon whom to rely for a literary education as well as for training in good manners. More than forty years have passed since at the age of fourteen I took up the dustpan and the broom in the Cao family.* During this time with trembling heart I feared constantly that I might disgrace my parents, and that I might multiply difficulties for both the women and the men (of my husband's family). Day and night I was distressed in heart, (but) I labored without confessing weariness. Now and hereafter, however, I know how to escape (from such fears).

Being careless, and by nature stupid, I taught and trained (my children) without system. Consequently I fear that my son Gu may bring disgrace upon the Imperial Dynasty by whose Holy Grace he has unprecedentedly received the extraordinary privilege of wearing the Gold and the Purple,† a privilege for the attainment of which (by my son, I) a humble subject never even hoped. Nevertheless, now that he is a man and able to plan his own life, I need not again have concern for him. But I do grieve that you, my daughters, just now at the age for marriage, have not at this time had gradual training and advice; that you still have not learned the proper customs for married women. I fear that by failure in good manners in other families you will humiliate both your ancestors and your clan. I am now seriously ill, life is uncertain. As I have thought of you all in so untrained a state, I have been uneasy many a time for you. At hours of leisure I have composed in seven chapters these instructions under the title, "Lessons for Women." . . .

From this time on everyone of you strive to practice these (lessons).

Chapter I Humility

On the third day after the birth of a girl the ancients observed three customs: (first) to place the baby below the bed; (second) to give her a potsherd with which to play; and (third) to announce her birth to her ancestors by an offering. Now to lay the baby below the bed plainly indicated that she is lowly and weak, and should regard it as her primary duty to humble herself before others. To give her potsherds with which to play indubitably signified that she should practice labor and consider it her primary duty to be industrious.

Source: Lessons for Women (Nujie) in Nancy Lee Swann, Pan Chao: Foremost Woman Scholar of China (New York: The Century Co., 1932), 82–90.

*Her husband's family.

†Colors of imperial service.

164 CHAPTER 6 ◆ Women in the Ancient World

To announce her birth before her ancestors clearly meant that she ought to esteem as her primary duty the continuation of the observance of worship in the home.

These three ancient customs epitomize a woman's ordinary way of life and the teachings of the traditional ceremonial rites and regulations. Let a woman modestly yield to others; let her respect others; let her put others first, herself last. Should she do something good, let her not mention it; should she do something bad, let her not deny it.

Let her bear disgrace; let her even endure when others speak or do evil to her. Always let her seem to tremble and to fear. [T]hen she may be said to humble herself before others.

Let a woman retire late to bed, but rise early to duties; let her not dread tasks by day or by night. Let her not refuse to perform domestic duties whether easy or difficult. That which must be done, let her finish completely, tidily, and systematically. Then she may be said to be industrious.

Let a woman be correct in manner and upright in character in order to serve her husband. Let her live in purity and quietness (of spirit), and attend to her own affairs. Let her love not gossip and silly laughter. Let her cleanse and purify and arrange in order the wine and the food for the offerings to the ancestors. Then she may be said to continue ancestral worship.

No woman who observes these three (practices) has ever had a bad reputation or has fallen into disgrace. If a woman fail to observe them, how can her name be honored; how can she but bring disgrace upon herself?

Chapter II Husband and Wife

The Way of husband and wife is intimately connected with *Yin* and *Yang*, and relates the individual to gods and ancestors.* Truly it is the great principle of Heaven and Earth, and the great basis of human relationships. . . . For these reasons the relationship cannot but be an important one.

If a husband be unworthy then he possesses nothing by which to control his wife. If a wife be unworthy, then she possesses nothing with which to serve her husband. If a husband does not control his wife, then the rules of conduct manifesting his authority are abandoned and broken. If a wife does not serve her husband, then the proper relationship (between men and women) and the natural order of things are neglected and destroyed. As a matter of fact the purpose of these two (the controlling of women by men, and the serving of men by women) is the same.

Now examine the gentlemen of the present age. They only know that wives must be controlled, and that the husband's rules of conduct manifesting his authority must be established. They therefore teach their boys to read books and (study) histories. But they do not in the least understand that husbands and masters must (also) be served, and that the proper relationship and the rites should be maintained.

---

*Yin and yang were two cardinal principles in Chinese philosophy of the Han period. Yin and yang were opposing, but mutually necessary and complementary, principles. Yang is the male principle; it is dominant and is also associated with the sun, heat, light, and Heaven. Yin, the female principle, is characterized by yielding and submission. It is connected with the moon, cold, and darkness (winter and fall, for example). Each of them helps create and complement the other, and excess of one principle actually leads into the other. Acting together, they provide harmony and completeness.

Yet only to teach men and not to teach women,—is that not ignoring the essential relation between them? According to the "Rites,"* it is the rule to begin to teach
children to read at the age of eight years, and by the age of fifteen years they ought
then to be ready for cultural training. Only why should it not be (that girls' education
as well as boys' be) according to this principle?

Chapter III Respect and Caution

As *Yin* and *Yang* are not of the same nature, so man and woman have different characteristics. The distinctive quality of the *Yang* is rigidity; the function of the *Yin* is
yielding. Man is honored for strength; a woman is beautiful on account of her gentleness. Hence there arose the common saying: "A man though born like a wolf may, it
is feared, become a weak monstrosity; a woman though born like a mouse may, it is
feared, become a tiger."

Now for self-culture nothing equals respect for others. To counteract firmness
nothing equals compliance. Consequently it can be said that the Way of respect and
acquiescence is woman's most important principle of conduct. . . . Those who are
steadfast in devotion know that they should stay in their proper places; those who are
liberal and generous esteem others, and honor and serve (them). . . .

The correct relationship between husband and wife is based upon harmony and
intimacy, and (conjugal) love is grounded in proper union. Should actual blows be
dealt, how could matrimonial relationship be preserved? Should sharp words be spoken, how could (conjugal) love exist? If love and proper relationship both be destroyed, then husband and wife are divided.

Chapter IV Womanly Qualifications

A woman (ought to) have four qualifications: (1) womanly virtue; (2) womanly words;
(3) womanly bearing; and (4) womanly work. Now what is called womanly virtue
need not be brilliant ability, exceptionally different from others. Womanly words need
be neither clever in debate nor keen in conversation. Womanly appearance requires
neither a pretty nor a perfect face and form. Womanly work need not be work done
more skillfully than that of others. . . .

These four qualifications characterize the greatest virtue of a woman. No woman
can afford to be without them. In fact they are very easy to possess if a woman only
treasure them in her heart. The ancients had a saying: "Is Love afar off? If I desire love,
then love is at hand!" So can it be said of these qualifications.

Chapter V Whole-hearted Devotion

Now in the "Rites" is written the principle that a husband may marry again, but there
is no Canon that authorizes a woman to be married the second time. Therefore it is
said of husbands as of Heaven, that as certainly as people cannot run away from
Heaven, so surely a wife cannot leave (a husband's home).

If people in action or character disobey the spirits of Heaven and of Earth, then
Heaven punishes them. Likewise if a woman errs in the rites and in the proper mode

---

*There were a number of classical texts that all scholar-officials knew intimately. One of the so-called
"Five Classics" was the *Classic of Rites* that discussed court ceremonies and social norms.

166   CHAPTER 6 ❖ Women in the Ancient World

of conduct, then her husband esteems her lightly. The ancient book, "A Pattern for Women," says: "To obtain the love of one man is the crown of a woman's life; to lose the love of one man is to miss the aim in woman's life." For these reasons a woman cannot but seek to win her husband's heart. Nevertheless, the beseeching wife need not use flattery, coaxing words, and cheap methods to gain intimacy. . . .

Chapter VI Implicit Obedience

Now "to win the love of one man is the crown of a woman's life; to lose the love of one man is her eternal disgrace." This saying advises a fixed will and a whole-hearted devotion for a woman. Ought she then to lose the hearts of her father- and mother-in-law?

There are times when love may lead to differences of opinion (between individuals); there are times when duty may lead to disagreement. . . . Nothing is better than an obedience which sacrifices personal opinion. Whenever the mother-in-law says, "Do not do that," and if what she says is right, unquestionably the daughter-in-law obeys. Whenever the mother-in-law says, "Do that," even if what she says is wrong, still the daughter-in-law submits unfailingly to the command.

Let a woman not act contrary to the wishes and the opinions of parents-in-law about right and wrong; let her not dispute with them what is straight and what is crooked. Such (docility) may be called obedience which sacrifices personal opinion. Therefore the ancient book, "A Pattern for Women," says: "If a daughter-in-law (who follows the wishes of her parents-in-law) is like an echo and a shadow, how could she not be praised?"

Chapter VII Harmony with Younger Brothers- and Sisters-in-law

In order for a wife to gain the love of her husband, she must win for herself the love of her parents-in-law. To win for herself the love of her parents-in-law, she must secure for herself the good will of younger brothers- and sisters-in-law. . . . The "Book of Changes"* says:

> "Should two hearts harmonize,
> The united strength can cut gold.
> Words from hearts which agree,
> Give forth fragrance like the orchid."

This saying may be applied to (harmony in the home). . . .

Modesty is virtue's handle; acquiescence is the wife's (most refined) characteristic. All who possess these two have sufficient for harmony with others. In the "Book of Poetry"† it is written that "here is no evil; there is no dart." So it may be said of (these two, modesty and acquiescence).

---

* *Yi jing* (*I Ching*). One of the "Five Classics."
† *Shi jing*, another of the "Five Classics."

A MARTYRED CHRISTIAN WOMAN IN ROMAN NORTH AFRICA

A most fascinating instance of a woman's empowerment is that of Vibia Perpetua, who was executed for her beliefs in 202 or 203 CE in Carthage in Roman North Africa. Very little is known about Perpetua, except that she was still a catechumen—that is, she had not yet been baptized—at the time of her arrest. Her father, who figures prominently in her diary, was a pagan, but her mother and two brothers were Christians. She was executed along with five others who publicly asserted their Christian faith, despite, or perhaps because of, the assurance of execution. As the diary and accompanying materials make clear, Perpetua was a leader and was looked up to as having special spiritual gifts. The supposed day of her death, March 7, is still celebrated as her feast day in the Roman Catholic Church.

The complexity of the issue of women's role in society is very vividly represented in Christianity. On the one hand, Eve is blamed for the fall from grace and the expulsion from the Garden into the troubles of this world. On the other hand, Mary was honored by her selection as the woman who would bear the god-child, Jesus, and the sorrows she endured watching her son be tortured and crucified have earned her unique respect and affection among Christians. Given the subordinate role that women have experienced in almost all cultures, Jesus' special recognition and blessing of the meek in the Sermon on the Mount gave Christianity an additional appeal among women. Yet despite the fact that Christian congregations have often numbered more women than men, most Christian religions have not accorded women equal status. This can be seen very clearly in religion's policies concerning women clergy. Christianity has historically been dominated by men, who are still the only ones deemed worthy of being priests or preachers in the majority of Christian denominations.

This separate and inferior status for women began as early as the Apostle Paul. Paul was arguably the most important founder of the Christian church. He was a converted Jew. Indeed, he was one of the main opponents of the new Christian offshoot of Judaism before his conversion on the Damascus road. He was also a Roman citizen and a man well educated in both rabbinical Judaism and classical Greek learning. As a result, he was exceptionally well placed for and, after his conversion, extraordinarily energetic in organizing and directing the new Christian communities that sprang up across the Mediterranean region and the Middle East. It was primarily Paul who ensured that the new belief would not remain a Jewish sect but would be accessible to non-Jews who did not follow traditional Jewish practices, such as eating kosher foods and practicing circumcision (as even adult male converts to Judaism had to do). As regards women, he established their secondary status in his First Letter to the Corinthians, in which he wrote:

> Be imitators of me, as I am of Christ. . . . But I want you to understand that the head of every man is Christ, the head of a woman is her husband, and the head of Christ is God. . . . For a man . . . is the image and glory of God; but woman is the glory of man. (For man was not made from woman, but woman from man.

168   CHAPTER 6 ◆ Women in the Ancient World

Neither was man created for woman, but woman for man.) . . . Nevertheless, in the Lord woman is not independent of man nor man of woman; for as woman was made from man, so man is now born of woman. And all things are from God.[4]

Although it is simplistic to cite one source as the complete depiction of something as complex as women's proper role in human secular and religious affairs, Paul's characterization of male–female relations in 1 Corinthians is a fair representation of Christian beliefs about gender roles throughout much of the history of that religious system.

Despite the common beliefs to the contrary, there were only two great persecutions of Christians in the Roman Empire, the first of which came in 250 CE. In fact, it was nearly a century after Jesus' death before the Christians reached numbers great enough to get sufficient attention from the Roman authorities as being distinguished from Jews, who had a special religious status under the Romans. It is important to remember that the Romans were religiously, as in most other ways, an extraordinarily pragmatic people, who worshiped an incredible number and variety of gods and spirits. They assumed that their success was due to the patronage of these gods and spirits, who had been properly placated by the Romans in the punctilious public ceremonies honoring the gods. After some time, the Romans had permitted the Jews not to attend these ceremonies, accepting in their stead Jewish prayers to their god on behalf of the emperor. They accepted this in part because Judaism was a small, ancestral religion.

Even though the Roman authorities were opposed to extending these privileges to the Christians, any persecutions of Christians were largely local affairs, erupting under a specific governor in a particular region and then running its course with relatively few victims. In 111 CE Pliny the Younger, who was governor of Bithynia at the time, wrote to the Emperor Trajan for advice on how to handle this new sect. Trajan's response is a model of pragmatism and moderation:

Do not go looking for Christians. If they are brought before you and the charge is proven, they must be punished; with the proviso that if someone denies they are Christian and gives proof of it, by offering reverence to our gods, they shall be acquitted on the grounds of repentance. . . . Anonymous written accusations shall be disregarded as evidence.[5]

Many Christians avoided conflict by bribing an official for a document that indicated the bearer had performed prayers for the Roman gods (which Christians could not do and be true to their belief in one God), by getting servants to perform the rituals, or merely by doing it and keeping their reservations to themselves. In the case that we have this extraordinary record of—Perpetua's prison diary—she refused to recant or to compromise in any way. As a result, she finally got the martyrdom that, as her diary reveals, she so avidly embraced. This record is remarkable for both its rarity and its intimacy. In the rare prison diaries of a female martyr, Perpetua, of early Christianity, we can examine the contradictory empowerment and independence that someone possesses who is willing to give up her life for her beliefs. Her trial, imprisonment, and death throw into stark relief the normal power relations of the late Roman world.

QUESTIONS TO CONSIDER

1. What evidence can you find that indicates that a general persecution of Christians was not underway? What other Christians besides Perpetua and her fellow prisoners do we encounter and what are they doing?

2. How do Perpetua's family members react to her imprisonment, and how can you explain any differences in their behaviors? How would you feel if a member of your family gave herself over to a religion in the way that Perpetua does?

3. How does Perpetua's decision to maintain her faith publicly give her power? How does it change the normal power relations in Roman society? Does it also affect her power in the private sphere?

4. How does Perpetua's power differ from that of Penelope and of the women who protested the Oppian Law in Rome roughly four hundred years earlier? Who had more power, Perpetua, Penelope, or the Roman women?

5. How do you read the scene in Perpetua's vision in which she fights a gladiatorial contest with an Egyptian fighter? Can it be seen as a metaphor for the transformation in power relationships that occurred when Perpetua decided her own fate as a Christian martyr?

THE MARTYRDOM OF PERPETUA, A CHRISTIAN WOMAN IN ROMAN NORTH AFRICA (circa 200 CE)

A number of young catechumens were arrested . . . and with them Vibia Perpetua, a newly married woman of good family and upbringing. Her mother and father were still alive and one of her two brothers was a catechumen like herself. She was about twenty-two years old and had an infant son at the breast. (Now from this point on the entire account of her ordeal is her own, according to her own ideas and in the way that she herself wrote it down.)

While we were still under arrest (she said) my father out of love for me was trying to persuade me and shake my resolution. "Father," said I, "do you see this vase here, for example, or waterpot or whatever?"

"Yes, I do," said he.

And I told him: "Could it be called by any other name than what it is?"

And he said: "No."

"Well, so too I cannot be called anything other than what I am, a Christian."

Source: The Acts of the Christian Martyrs, trans. Herbert Musurillo, 109, 111, 113, 115, 117, 119. Copyright © 1972 by Oxford University Press, Inc. Used by permission of Oxford University Press, Inc.

170   CHAPTER 6   ◆   Women in the Ancient World

At this my father was so angered by the word "Christian" that he moved towards me as though he would pluck my eyes out. But he left it at that and departed, vanquished along with his diabolical arguments.

For a few days afterwards I gave thanks to the Lord that I was separated from my father, and I was comforted by his absence. During these few days I was baptized, and I was inspired by the Spirit not to ask for any other favor after the water but simply the perseverance of the flesh. A few days later we were lodged in the prison; and I was terrified, as I had never before been in such a dark hole. What a difficult time it was! With the crowd the heat was stifling; then there was the extortion of the soldiers; and to crown all, I was tortured with worry for my baby there.

Then Tertius and Pomponius, those blessed deacons who tried to take care of us, bribed the soldiers to allow us to go to a better part of the prison to refresh ourselves for a few hours. Everyone then left that dungeon and shifted for himself. I nursed my baby, who was faint from hunger. In my anxiety I spoke to my mother about the child, I tried to comfort my brother, and I gave the child in their charge. I was in pain because I saw them suffering out of pity for me. These were the trials I had to endure for many days. Then I got permission for my baby to stay with me in prison. At once I recovered my health, relieved as I was of my worry and anxiety over the child. My prison had suddenly become a palace, so that I wanted to be there rather than anywhere else.

Then my brother said to me: "Dear sister, you are greatly privileged; surely you might ask for a vision to discover whether you are to be condemned or freed."

Faithfully I promised that I would, for I knew that I could speak with the Lord, whose great blessings I had come to experience. And so I said: "I shall tell you tomorrow." Then I made my request and this was the vision I had:

I saw a ladder of tremendous height made of bronze, reaching all the way to the heavens, but it was so narrow that only one person could climb up at a time. To the sides of the ladder were attached all sorts of metal weapons: there were swords, spears, hooks, daggers, and spikes; so that if anyone tried to climb up carelessly or without paying attention, he would be mangled and his flesh would adhere to the weapons.

At the foot of the ladder lay a dragon of enormous size, and it would attack those who tried to climb up and try to terrify them from doing so. And Saturus* was the first to go up, he who was later to give himself up of his own accord. He had been the builder of our strength, although he was not present when we were arrested. And he arrived at the top of the staircase and he looked back and said to me: "Perpetua, I am waiting for you. But take care; do not let the dragon bite you."

"He will not harm me," I said, "in the name of Christ Jesus."

Slowly, as though he were afraid of me, the dragon stuck his head out from underneath the ladder. Then, using it as my first step, I trod on his head and went up.

Then I saw an immense garden, and in it a gray-haired man sat in shepherd's garb; tall he was, and milking sheep. And standing around him were many thousands

---

*Another Christian.

of people clad in white garments. He raised his head, looked at me, and said: "I am glad you have come, my child."

He called me over to him and gave me, as it were, a mouthful of the milk he was drawing; and I took it into my cupped hands and consumed it. And all those who stood around said: "Amen!" At the sound of this word I came to, with the taste of something sweet still in my mouth. I at once told this to my brother, and we realized that we would have to suffer, and that from now on we would no longer have any hope in this life.

A few days later there was a rumor that we were going to be given a hearing. My father also arrived from the city, worn with worry, and he came to see me with the idea of persuading me.

"Daughter," he said, "have pity on my grey head—have pity on me your father, if I deserve to be called your father, if I have favored you above all your brothers, if I have raised you to reach this prime of your life. Do not abandon me to be the reproach of men. Think of your brothers, think of your mother and your aunt, think of your child, who will not be able to live once you are gone. Give up your pride! You will destroy all of us! None of us will ever be able to speak freely again if anything happens to you."

This was the way my father spoke out of love for me, kissing my hands and throwing himself down before me. With tears in his eyes he no longer addressed me as his daughter but as a woman. I was sorry for my father's sake, because he alone of all my kin would be unhappy to see me suffer.

I tried to comfort him saying: "It will all happen in the prisoner's dock as God wills; for you may be sure that we are not left to ourselves but are all in his power."

And he left me in great sorrow.

One day while we were eating breakfast we were suddenly hurried off for a hearing. We arrived at the forum, and straight away the story went about the neighborhood near the forum and a huge crowd gathered. We walked up to the prisoner's dock. All the others when questioned admitted their guilt. Then, when it came my turn, my father appeared with my son, dragged me from the step, and said: "Perform the sacrifice—have pity on your baby!"

Hilarianus the governor . . . said to me: "Have pity on your father's grey head; have pity on your infant son. Offer the sacrifice for the welfare of the emperors."

"I will not," I retorted.

"Are you a Christian?" said Hilarianus.

And I said: "Yes, I am."

When my father persisted in trying to dissuade me, Hilarianus ordered him to be thrown to the ground and beaten with a rod. I felt sorry for father, just as if I myself had been beaten. I felt sorry for his pathetic old age.

Then Hilarianus passed sentence on all of us: we were condemned to the beasts, and we returned to prison in high spirits. . . .

The day before we were to fight with the beasts I saw the following vision. Pomponius the deacon came to the prison gates and began to knock violently. I went out and opened the gate for him. He was dressed in an unbelted white tunic, wearing elaborate sandals. And he said to me: "Perpetua, come; we are waiting for you."

172   CHAPTER 6   ◆   Women in the Ancient World

Then he took my hand and we began to walk through rough and broken country. At last we came to the amphitheatre out of breath, and he led me into the centre of the arena.

Then he told me: "Do not be afraid. I am here, struggling with you." Then he left.

I looked at the enormous crowd who watched in astonishment. I was surprised that no beasts were let loose on me; for I knew that I was condemned to die by the beasts. Then out came an Egyptian against me, of vicious appearance, together with his seconds, to fight with me. There also came up to me some handsome young men to be my seconds and assistants.

My clothes were stripped off, and suddenly I was a man. My seconds began to rub me down with oil (as they are wont to do before a contest). Then I saw the Egyptian on the other side rolling in the dust. Next there came forth a man of marvelous stature, such that he rose above the top of the amphitheater. He was clad in a beltless purple tunic with two stripes (one on either side) running down the middle of his chest. He wore sandals that were wondrously made of gold and silver, and he carried a wand like an athletic trainer and a green branch on which there were golden apples.

And he asked for silence and said: "If this Egyptian defeats her he will slay her with the sword. But if she defeats him, she will receive this branch." Then he withdrew.

We drew close to one another and began to let our fists fly. My opponent tried to get hold of my feet, but I kept striking him in the face with the heels of my feet. Then I was raised up into the air and I began to pummel him without as it were touching the ground. Then when I noticed there was a lull, I put my two hands together linking the fingers of one hand with those of the other and thus I got hold of his head. He fell flat on his face and I stepped on his head.

The crowd began to shout and my assistants started to sing psalms. Then I walked up to the trainer and took the branch. He kissed me and said to me: "Peace be with you, my daughter!" I began to walk in triumph towards the Gate of Life. Then I awoke. I realized that it was not with wild animals that I would fight but with the Devil, but I knew that I would win the victory. So much for what I did up until the eve of the contest. About what happened at the contest itself, let him write of it who will.

WOMEN IN CLASSICAL HINDU CULTURE

The last source details the obligations and status of women in the Hindu culture that developed in the Indus Valley. The material included here comes from the *Code of Manu*, which dates from the second to third century CE. The *Code of Manu* deals with many different features of Hindu life, such as the proper behavior of different castes and methods for ritual purification. The "Manu" referred to in the title is the legendary "first man" of Hindu culture (*Manu* and the English word *man* are related linguistically) and also as the first lawgiver. Thus, the *Code of Manu* is thought of within Hinduism as a text based on human traditions (*Smriti*), but it is also believed to be consistent with the values included in texts that are divinely revealed (*Shruti*), such as the "Purusha Hymn." As a result, it restates and reaffirms traditional values and structures, but it does so on the basis of religious authority.

The responsibilities described for women in the *Code of Manu* need to be understood within the context of Hinduism. As was discussed in chapter 2, a central component of Hinduism is the concept of *dharma*. The root meaning of the word *dharma* is "to sustain." Hindus believe that by living up to the religious and social responsibilities attached to one's social position (caste and gender), one sustains the proper order of the universe, gains good karma, and moves up the scale of reincarnation toward unity with the Brahman, or World Soul. Composed following a period of unrest, the *Code of Manu* represents a rigorous attempt to reestablish order within the Hindu world.

QUESTIONS TO CONSIDER

1. What are the duties of a good woman/wife, according to the *Code of Manu*? In general, how would a good woman behave, according to these codes? How would proper behavior differ for an elite woman as opposed to a woman who was not from the upper class?

2. How should men relate to women, according to the *Code*? It has been said that the *Code* was intended to restore order. In what ways are men asked, in their relationships with women, to keep order? Is there any distinction here between the public and private spheres?

3. How would women, by following the codes presented here, adhere to the Hindu concept of *dharma* and help to "sustain" the world?

4. How are women rewarded for behaving the way the *Code* instructs them to? How are the rewards connected with the Hindu belief in reincarnation and *karma*?

5. How does the ideal behavior of a woman and a wife, according to the *Code of Manu,* compare with the standards established for women in the other texts in this chapter? Would it be more desirable to be a woman in Hindu society or in one of the other social systems presented in this chapter?

CODE OF MANU

Hear now the duties of women.

By a girl, by a young woman, or even by an aged one, nothing must be done independently, even in her own house.

Source: The Law of Manu, in *The Sacred Books of the East,* vol. XXV, trans. G. Bühler (Oxford, UK: Clarendon Press, 1886), 194–97, 328–30, 332, 335, 344–45.

174   CHAPTER 6 ❖ Women in the Ancient World

In childhood a female must be subject to her father, in youth to her husband, when her lord is dead to her sons; a woman must never be independent.

She must not seek to separate herself from her father, husband, or sons; by leaving them she would make both (her own and her husband's) families contemptible.

She must always be cheerful, clever in (the management of her) household affairs, careful in cleaning her utensils, and economical in expenditure.

Him to whom her father may give her, or her brother with the father's permission, she shall obey as long as he lives, and when he is dead, she must not insult (his memory). . . .

[B]etrothal (by the father or guardian) is the cause of (the husband's) dominion (over his wife).

The husband who wedded her with sacred texts, always gives happiness to his wife, both in season and out of season, in this world and in the next.

Though destitute of virtue, or seeking pleasure (elsewhere), or devoid of good qualities, (yet) a husband must be constantly worshipped as a god by a faithful wife.

No sacrifice, no vow, no fast must be performed by women apart (from their husbands); if a wife obeys her husband, she will for that (reason alone) be exalted in heaven.

A faithful wife, who desires to dwell (after death) with her husband, must never do anything that might displease him who took her hand, whether he be alive or dead. . . .

[L]et her emaciate her body by (living on) pure flowers, roots, and fruit; but she must never even mention the name of another man after her husband has died.

Until death let her be patient (of hardships), self-controlled, and chaste, and strive (to fulfill) that most excellent duty which (is prescribed) for wives who have one husband only.

A virtuous wife who after the death of her husband constantly remains chaste, reaches heaven, though she have no son, just like those chaste men.

But a woman who from a desire to have offspring violates her duty towards her (deceased) husband, brings on herself disgrace in this world, and loses her place with her husband (in heaven). . . .

By violating her duty towards her husband, a wife is disgraced in this world, (after death) she enters the womb of a jackal, and is tormented by diseases (the punishment of) her sin. . . .

[A] female who controls her thoughts, speech, and actions, gains in this (life) highest renown, and in the next (world) a place near her husband.

Women must particularly be guarded against evil inclinations, however trifling (they may appear); for, if they are not guarded, they will bring sorrow on two families. . . .

No man can completely guard women by force; but they can be guarded by the . . . (following) expedients: Let the (husband) employ his (wife) in the collection and expenditure of his wealth, in keeping (everything) clean, in (the fulfilment of) religious duties, in the preparation of his food, and in looking after the household utensils.

Women, confined in the house under trustworthy and obedient servants, are not (well) guarded; but those who of their own accord keep guard over themselves, are well guarded. . . .

Through their passion for men, through their mutable temper, through their natural heartlessness, they become disloyal towards their husbands, however carefully they may be guarded in this (world).

(When creating them) Manu allotted to women (a love of their) bed, (of their) seat and (of) ornament, impure desires, wrath, dishonesty, malice, and bad conduct. . . .

The production of children, the nurture of those born, and the daily life of men, (of these matters) woman is visibly the cause.

Offspring, (the due performance of) religious rites, faithful service, highest conjugal happiness and heavenly bliss for the ancestors and oneself, depend on one's wife alone.

He only is a perfect man who consists (of three persons united), his wife, himself, and his offspring; thus (says the Veda), and (learned) Brahmanas propound this (maxim) likewise, "The husband is declared to be one with the wife." . . .

The husband receives his wife from the gods, (he does not wed her) according to his own will; doing what is agreeable to the gods, he must always support her (while she is) faithful.

"Let mutual fidelity continue until death," this may be considered as the summary of the highest law for husband and wife.

Let man and woman, united in marriage, constantly exert themselves, that (they may not be) disunited (and) may not violate their mutual fidelity.

NOTES

1. When Rome changed from a monarchy to a republic, the main responsibilities of the king, including military command, were divided between two consuls who shared those powers and duties and who were elected to one-year terms.

2. It was not uncommon for historians in that era to put words into the mouths of historical figures. That is the case in this excerpt, because no record of this speech was available at the time Livy wrote his *History*. Nonetheless, the opinions expressed in this passage still represent Roman views regarding the status and behavior of women.

3. See Arthur Cotterell, *China: A Cultural History* (New York: New American Library, 1988), 117–18.

4. *The Bible*, Revised Standard Version, Paul, 1 Corinthians 11.

5. Cited in Anthony Kamm, *The Romans: An Introduction* (London, UK: Routledge, 1995).

CHAPTER 8

Encountering Transcendent Reality

The Rise of the Salvation Religions

INTRODUCTION

In the 2003 baseball playoffs, both the Boston Red Sox and the Chicago Cubs found themselves up by three runs and only five outs from the promised land of the World Series. Boston had not won a world championship since 1918, Chicago since 1908. Throughout those long wanderings in the wilderness, during which each team was supposedly marked by a "curse," their devoted fans had kept the faith, religiously wearing the regalia—caps, jerseys, t-shirts—of their favorites. They made daily pilgrimages to their Meccas—Fenway Park and Wrigley Field—for every home game. There they worshipped their heroes, sang hymns to them ("Take me out to the ballgame . . ."), and chanted incantations against evil ("Yankees s—". . . well, you get the idea). Surely this year one of the "curses" had to be lifted, and at least one set of baseball faithful would reach nirvana and be rewarded for their suffering.

Alas, it was not to be. Both lost. Lamentations were raised to the sky in the Hub and the Windy City. Boston sacrificed a manager. And yet, in some important way it didn't matter. Their faithful still worship, and they cite the scripture of eternal hope known to baseball fans everywhere: Wait till next year.

This is a chapter about eternal hope. That the story of the 2003 baseball playoffs can be plausibly (if a bit obviously) written in the language of religious devotion shows us the importance of organized sports in the modern world. But it also tells us about the impact that the world's great salvation religions have had on cultural imagination and imagery everywhere. What are the "salvation religions"? They are that set of the world's many religions that promise salvation—eternal life, heavenly rewards, hope for a better existence than this mortal earth offers—to their followers. The four major ones are Mahayana Buddhism, Christianity, Islam, and Devotional Hinduism. All arose sometime in the period 100 BCE to 630 CE, with the major period of development coming after 200 CE. Each offered a version of eternal hope to its followers, a message that proved to have wide resonance in the troubled period of world history between 200 and 700 CE when the age of great empires came to an end, at least partly under pressures from nomadic invaders (see chapters 5 and 7). But invasions and political troubles simply aggravated the uncertainties and problems that have always beset common people in traditional societies, living from harvest to harvest and subject to varying degrees of taxation or rent from those holding power over them. Life for women, too, not just among peasants but at every social level, was full of restrictions (see chapter 6). The major philosophies and religions we examined in chapter 4 addressed some of these problems, but in ways that were not always intellectually accessible to the illiterate masses—they were the philosophies and religions of elites, and in many ways they continued to be so. Creeds that offered hope to the common people, therefore, found a ready audience in this world, though they also found ready converts among the ruling class.

That these faiths found a wide audience was intentional, for a central characteristic of the salvation religions is that their message was meant to be universal and available to all. This was partly a matter of their breaking a "tribal" or inherited notion of membership in a religious community that defined the southwest Asian religions of Persian Zoroastrianism and Hebrew Judaism (see chapter 4).[1] Both Zoroastrianism and Judaism stand as ancestors of or influences on the salvation religions, but each remained the exclusive religion of its people. The salvation religions reached out to different peoples and cultures. Another reason they found a large audience was that they made their message intentionally accessible and their practice "user friendly," to use the computer term. Each of the salvation religions offered a simple message of hope and a straightforward path to salvation. The message was presented not just textually in religious literature but also artistically, through art and architecture, and socially, through community practice and preaching. As a result, they spread widely in the troubled world following the age of empires, and they remain to this day, in one form or another, the most widely practiced religions in the world. In this chapter we present materials related to the spread of these faiths, and, in the next chapter, to the conversion encounters they provoked. In this chapter we look at their doctrines and messages themselves, in terms of both substance and method of presentation.

We include for each of the four religions presented here both a fundamental text and a small selection of visual sources. Neither Buddhism nor Hinduism has a single canonical scripture in the way that Christianity and Islam do, but each had popular texts that shaped the most widely followed Salvationist sects of each faith. For Buddhism, we have excerpted part of *The Lotus Sutra*. *The Lotus Sutra* expounded the fundamental beliefs that came to characterize Mahayana Buddhism, especially the way that Buddhist saints, called *bodhisattvas,* aided humans in the transition up the ten levels of existence to nirvana. The text we use comes from a fifth-century Chinese translation of the work. *The Lotus Sutra* is accompanied by pictures of statues of the sort used in popular Buddhist worship. They show *bodhisattvas,* whose role is explained in *The Lotus Sutra.*

208   CHAPTER 8 ◆ Encountering Transcendent Reality

For Hinduism, we present a section of the *Vishnu Purana*, which is the oldest and most important of the holy texts of Devotional Hinduism. The *Vishnu Purana* guides the reader into the way of devotion to Vishnu, the most popular of the Hindu gods in this form of worship. *Puranas* are collections of myth, folk tales, and teachings, transmitting the belief of Devotional Hinduism that salvation could be achieved through worship of a god. The selection we include is the concluding dialogue of the *Vishnu Purana*. It is not only one of the oldest of the *Puranas*, dating from the 100s CE, but it is also one of the most important. It too is accompanied by pictures of two statues, one of Vishnu and one of Ganesh, another popular Hindu god.

The New Testament of the Bible is the canonical text of Christianity. From it, we present selections from two of its most significant sections: the Book of Romans and the Gospel of Matthew. The passages presented contain the core beliefs of Christianity as laid out in the Sermon on the Mount. In addition, the understanding that Paul had of Christianity and its meaning was crucial to the development of the religion and to Christian beliefs about the nature of and path toward salvation. Both of the selections date from after the death of Jesus. Paul's epistles (letters) to the Romans date from the mid-50s CE, and the date for Matthew's Gospel is usually given as around the 70s CE. In addition, images of early Christian art are included: a mosaic of Christ healing the blind and an icon of Jesus' mother, enthroned and holding the infant Jesus.

Finally, we present passages from the Qur'an, the sacred text of Islam. Muslims believe the Qur'an to be the will and words of God as revealed to Muhammad, the last of his prophets. Scholars think, however, that the Qur'an is the product of the teachings of Muhammad, as shaped by early followers. As was true of the Gospels, a significant passage of time intervened between the death of the religion's founder and the emergence of a canonical text. However that may be, the Qur'an lays out the fundamental beliefs and duties of followers of Islam, and we have excerpted passages central to the salvation message of the faith. These passages are followed by an example of Arab calligraphy, an art form that did not violate Islam's prohibition against representational art.

Hope in the salvation religions was presented as an encounter with a transcendent reality, a higher realm of existence. Suffering in this world would be rewarded in another, better life, a life not bounded by the harsh realities of this material world. Because of the centrality of belief in humans' ability to transcend the physical world, the religions differed among and within themselves on the actual importance of this world and action in this life. They all accommodated some range of both practical, community-based spiritual expression (charity, kindness, and so forth) and more mystical expressions of connection to the divine and even withdrawal from this world. As you read these selections and look at the art associated with them, think about the different ways this encounter with transcendence was conceived of in each tradition, as well as the similarities across all the salvation religions. Above all look for the form in which hope was presented. For all of them offered hope, something to look forward to when the forces of evil and despair seemed triumphant. Wait till next year.

CHAPTER QUESTIONS

1. What elements of belief are common to all these faiths? That is, what do they agree on about life, the universe, and the divine? What elements differ?

2. What elements of practice, of the paths to salvation people could take, are common to all these faiths? That is, what do they agree on about what people should do to achieve a lasting encounter with transcendence? What elements differ? How are the religious practices connected with the belief system?

3. How do the images associated with these texts reinforce or represent the doctrines presented in the written texts? Are there common elements to "salvationist" art?

4. What sort of hope does each salvation religion offer? That is, can you characterize in a word or two the central message of each religion, through which hope appears?

5. Do the similarities or the differences between these faiths seem more important to you? Why have the differences seemed to matter more to the practitioners of these faiths historically?

MAHAYANA BUDDHISM

Buddhism had begun to spread widely within India after the conversion of Asoka (see chapter 5) and his promotion of the religion as part of a syncretic (a combination of elements from different beliefs) emphasis on *dharma* (sacred duty) as the bond between his government and his subjects. It may have been these efforts at popularizing the religion that gave impetus to tendencies within the religion that eventually carried it in a new direction. By the first century CE, these tendencies had begun to come together into a self-conscious new school of Buddhism, described by its practitioners as *Mahayana*, or the Greater Vehicle—meaning that this sect promised to carry far more people to salvation than the older version could. Followers of Mahayana Buddhism referred to the older version as *Hinayana*, or Lesser Vehicle. The followers of the older version, though, preferred to refer to their religion as *Theravada*, or the Teaching of the Elders. This religion continued to exist and itself spread to parts of southeast Asia. It was the Mahayana version of Buddhism that first became widely popular in India and then, during the early centuries CE, spread all over central and East Asia.

In its early form, and largely in the Theravada school, Buddhism was non-theistic—the Buddha was simply a mortal, though a special one—and the search for Enlightenment was a matter of individual practice and achievement, as laid out in the Four Noble Truths and the Noble Eightfold Path (see chapter 4). The tendency to revere the Buddha as a god probably arose even during his own life. The large number of gods and the way that divinity was woven into everyday existence in the Hindu tradition (unlike the separation of divinity and creation in

210   CHAPTER 8 • Encountering Transcendent Reality

the southwest Asian religious traditions) made "godliness" a not uncommon phenomenon. In Mahayana belief, the Buddha has become an all-knowing being, somewhere between a divine person—a mortal man who achieves immortality—and a god, to whom even Hindu gods offer respect. His wisdom surpasses that of the other gods, because he recognizes the uncreated and infinite nature of the universe, whereas some of them imagine themselves as creators.

Accompanying the rise of belief in the Buddha's divinity was a belief in a class of beings known as *bodhisattvas,* or Wise Beings. Essentially these are people who had reached the edge of nirvana, release from the cycle of death and rebirth, only to compassionately turn back to help others cross over into bliss. Nirvana itself evolved from the somewhat abstract notion of "extinguishment"—of the soul becoming one with the cosmos and escaping the illusion of individuality—to a notion of a heavenly paradise.[2] The image often used to explain the role of the bodhisattva is of a ferryman who repeatedly carries masses of devout worshippers over to salvation on his giant barge, while Theravada Buddhists cross the river one at a time and each one only once.

One of the most popular of the bodhisattvas was *Avalokitesvara,* or "Perceiver of the World's Sounds," who first shows up in a book called *The Lotus Sutra,* one of the earliest and most influential of the sacred texts of Mahayana Buddhism. *The Lotus Sutra* describes the ten cosmic levels of existence, from hell up to nirvana, with bodhisattvas on the ninth level working to remove the suffering of the world and to carry people to the highest level. Avalokitesvara is prominent among the bodhisattvas of *The Lotus Sutra,* and his cult spread with the dissemination of the text. The work was first translated into Chinese in 255 CE, and a Chinese translation made in 406 is the basis for this English translation. One interesting note about the transmission of Buddhism to China is that in later centuries Avalokitesvara, called *Guanyin* in China, was transformed into a female. In either form, Perceiver of the World's Sounds illustrates the central characteristics of Mahayana Buddhism's encounter with the transcendent.

QUESTIONS TO CONSIDER

1. What does someone who needs the help of Perceiver of the World's Sounds have to do to get it? How difficult is it to get this help? Are the things a worshipper must do personal or communal?

2. Generate a list of the sorts of help Perceiver of the World's Sounds can offer. What does this list tell you about the concerns and activities of people at the time?

3. How is this Buddhism different from the Buddhism presented in chapter 4? Is its philosophy and practice easier or harder to grasp or perform? What is the significance of the difference?

4. What characteristics of the statues of Amita Buddha and of Avalokitesvara stand out to you? What message do they convey, and how does this message reflect or complement the message of the text?

5. Taking the text and the art together, what strikes you as the central message of Mahayana Buddhism? That is, what is the main avenue to hope in Mahayana Buddhism? What is the appeal of that message?

THE LOTUS SUTRA

At that time the Bodhisattva Inexhaustible Intent immediately rose from his seat, bared his right shoulder, pressed his palms together and, facing the Buddha, spoke these words: "World Honored One, this Bodhisattva Perceiver of the World's Sounds—why is he called Perceiver of the World's Sounds?"

The Buddha said to Bodhisattva Inexhaustible Intent: "Good man, suppose there are immeasurable hundreds, thousands, ten thousands, millions of living beings who are undergoing various trials and suffering. If they hear of this Bodhisattva Perceiver of the World's Sounds and single-mindedly call his name, then at once he will perceive the sound of their voices and they will all gain deliverance from their trials.

"If someone, holding fast to the name of Bodhisattva Perceiver of the World's Sounds, should enter a great fire, the fire could not burn him. This would come about because of this bodhisattva's authority and supernatural power. If one were washed away by a great flood and call upon his name, one would immediately find himself in a shallow place.

"Suppose there were a hundred, a thousand, ten thousand, a million living beings who, seeking for gold, silver, lapis lazuli, seashell, agate, coral, amber, pearls, and other treasures, set out on the great sea, and suppose a fierce wind should blow their ship off course and it drifted to the land of rakshasas* demons. If among those people there is even just one who calls the name of Bodhisattva Perceiver of the World's Sounds, then all those people will be delivered from their troubles with the rakshasas. This is why he is called Perceiver of the World's Sounds.

"If a person who faces imminent threat of attack should call the name of Bodhisattva Perceiver of the World's Sounds, then the swords and staves wielded by his attackers would instantly shatter into so many pieces and he would be delivered.

"Though enough . . . rakshasas to fill all the thousand-million-fold world should try to come and torment a person, if they hear him calling the name of Bodhisattva Perceiver of the World's Sounds, then these evil demons will not even be able to look at him with their evil eyes, much less do him harm.

"Suppose, in a place filled with all the evil-hearted bandits of the thousand-million-fold world, there is a merchant leader who is guiding a band of merchants carrying valuable treasures over a steep and dangerous road, and that one man shouts out

---

Source: The Lotus Sutra, trans. Burton Watson, 298–303. Copyright © 1993 Columbia University Press. Reprinted with permission.

*Divine beings. In the cosmic scheme of things, they are evil, but they also use their powers to protect Buddhism.

212   CHAPTER 8   ◆   Encountering Transcendent Reality

these words: 'Good men, do not be afraid! You must single-mindedly call on the name of Bodhisattva Perceiver of the World's Sounds. This bodhisattva can grant fearlessness to living beings. If you call his name, you will be delivered from these evil-hearted bandits!' When the band of merchants hear this, they all together raise their voices, saying, 'Hail to the Bodhisattva Perceiver of the World's Sounds!' And because they call his name, they are at once able to gain deliverance. Inexhaustible Intent, the authority and supernatural power of the Bodhisattva and Mahasattva* Perceiver of the World's Sounds are as mighty as this!

"If there should be living beings beset by numerous lusts and cravings, let them think with constant reverence of Bodhisattva Perceiver of the World's Sounds and then they can shed their desires. If they have great wrath and ire, let them think with constant reverence of Bodhisattva Perceiver of the World's Sounds and then they can shed their ire. If they have great ignorance and stupidity, let them think with constant reverence of Bodhisattva Perceiver of the World's Sounds and they can rid themselves of stupidity.

"Inexhaustible Intent, the Bodhisattva Perceiver of the World's Sounds possesses great authority and supernatural powers, as I have described, and can confer many benefits. For this reason, living beings should constantly keep the thought of him in mind.

"If a woman wishes to give birth to a male child, she should offer obeisance† and alms to Bodhisattva Perceiver of the World's Sounds and then she will bear a son blessed with merit, virtue, and wisdom. And if she wishes to bear a daughter, she will bear one with all the marks of comeliness,‡ one who in the past planted the roots of virtue and is loved and respected by many persons.

"Inexhaustible Intent, suppose there is a person who accepts and upholds the names of as many bodhisattvas as there are sands in sixty-two million Ganges, and for as long as his present body lasts, he offers them alms in the form of food and drink, clothing, bedding and medicines. What is your opinion? Would this good man or good woman gain many benefits or would he not?"

Inexhaustible Intent replied, "They would be very many, World-Honored One."

The Buddha said: "Suppose also that there is a person who accepts and upholds the name of Bodhisattva Perceiver of the World's Sounds and even just once offers him obeisance and alms. The good fortune gained by these two persons would be exactly equal and without difference. . . . Inexhaustible Intent, if one accepts and upholds the name of Bodhisattva Perceiver of the World's Sounds, he will gain the benefit of merit and virtue that is as immeasurable and boundless as this!"

Bodhisattva Inexhaustible Intent said to the Buddha, "World-Honored One, Bodhisattva Perceiver of the World's Sounds—how does he come and go in this saha§ world? How does he preach the Law for the sake of living beings? How does the power of expedient means apply in this case?"

---

*"Great being."

†Respect.

‡Beauty.

§The saha world is this world, which one must endure in suffering.

The Buddha said to Bodhisattva Inexhaustible Intent: "Good man, if there are living beings in the land who need someone in the body of a Buddha in order to be saved, Bodhisattva Perceiver of the World's Sounds immediately manifests himself in a Buddha body and preaches the Law for them. If they need someone in a pratyekabuddha's* body in order to be saved, immediately he manifests a pratyekabuddha's body and preaches the Law to them. If they need a voice-hearer to be saved, immediately he becomes a voice-hearer and preaches the Law for them. If they need King Brahma† to be saved, immediately he becomes King Brahma and preaches the Law for them. If they need the lord Shakra‡ to be saved, immediately he becomes the lord Shakra and preaches the Law for them. If they need the heavenly being Freedom to be saved, immediately he becomes the heavenly being Freedom and preaches the Law for them. If they need a great general of heaven to be saved, immediately he becomes a great general of heaven and preaches the Law for them. . . . If they need a petty king to be saved, immediately he becomes a petty king and preaches the law for them.

If they need a rich man to be saved, immediately he becomes a rich man and preaches the Law for them. If they need a householder to be saved, immediately he becomes a householder and preaches the Law for them. If they need a chief minister to be saved, immediately he becomes a chief minister and preaches the Law for them. If they need a Brahman to be saved, immediately he becomes a Brahman and preaches the Law for them. If they need a monk, a nun, a layman believer, or a laywoman believer he becomes these and preaches the Law for them. If they need the wife of a rich man, of a householder, a chief minister, or a Brahman to be saved, immediately he becomes those wives and preaches the Law for them. If they need a young boy or a young girl he becomes these and preaches the Law for them. If they need a heavenly being, a dragon, . . . he becomes all of these and preaches the Law for them. . . .

"Inexhaustible Intent, this Bodhisattva Perceiver of the World's Sounds has succeeded in acquiring benefits such as these and, taking on a variety of different forms, goes about among the lands saving living beings. For this reason you and the others should single-mindedly offer alms to Bodhisattva Perceiver of the World's Sounds who can bestow fearlessness on those who are in fearful, pressing or difficult circumstances. That is why in this saha world everyone calls him Bestower of Fearlessness."

Bodhisattva Inexhaustible Intent said to the Buddha, "World-Honored One, now I must offer alms to Bodhisattva Perceiver of the World's Sounds."

Then he took from his neck a necklace adorned with numerous precious gems, worth a hundred or a thousand taels§ of gold, and presented it to [the bodhisattva], saying, "Sir, please accept this necklace of precious gems as a gift in the Dharma."

At that time Bodhisattva Perceiver of the World's Sounds was unwilling to accept the gift.

Inexhaustible Intent spoke once more to Bodhisattva Perceiver of the World's Sounds, saying, "Sir, out of compassion for us, please accept this necklace."

---

*A Buddhist sage who reaches Enlightenment and achieves nirvana without stopping to help others as a bodhisattva does.

†The Hindu god of creation, a protective deity for Mahayana Buddhists.

‡Indra, Hindu god of thunder; another protector deity of Mahayana Buddhists.

§A tael is about one and a half ounces.

214   CHAPTER 8   ◆   Encountering Transcendent Reality

Then the Buddha said to Bodhisattva Perceiver of the World's Sounds, "Out of compassion for this Bodhisattva Inexhaustible Intent and for the four kinds of believers, the heavenly kings, . . . human and nonhuman beings, you should accept this necklace."

Thereupon Bodhisattva Perceiver of the World's Sounds, having compassion for the four kinds of believers and the heavenly beings, dragons, human and nonhuman beings and the others, accepted the necklace and, dividing it into two parts, presented one part to Shakyamuni Buddha* and presented the other to the tower† of the Buddha Many Treasures.

At that time Bodhisattva Inexhaustible Intent posed this question in verse form:

World-Honored One replete with wonderful features,
I now ask you once again
for what reason that Buddha's son
is named Bodhisattva Perceiver of the World's Sounds?
The honored One endowed with wonderful features
replied to Inexhaustible Intent in verse:
Listen to the actions of the Perceiver of Sounds,
how aptly he responds in various quarters.
He has attended many thousands and millions of Buddhas,
setting forth his great pure vow.
I will describe him in outline for you—
listen to his name, observe his body,
bear him in mind, not passing the time vainly,
for he can wipe out the pains of existence.
Suppose you are surrounded by evil-hearted bandits,
each brandishing a knife to wound you.
Think on the power of that Perceiver of Sounds
and at once all will be swayed by compassion!
If living beings encounter weariness or peril,
immeasurable suffering pressing them down,
the power of the Perceiver of Sounds' wonderful wisdom
can save them from the sufferings of the world.
He sends down the sweet dew, the Dharma rain,
to quench the flames of earthly desires.
Endowed with all benefits,
he views living beings with compassionate eyes.

At that time the Bodhisattva Earth Holder immediately rose from his seat, advanced, and said to the Buddha, "World-Honored One, if there are living beings who hear this chapter on Bodhisattva Perceiver of the World's Sounds, on the freedom of his actions, his manifestation of a universal gateway, and his transcendental powers, it should be known that the benefits these persons gain are not few!"

---

*A title for the Buddha, founder of Buddhism.
†A temple.

Figure 8.1 Amita Buddha at Kamakura.

Figure 8.2 Bronze Statue of Avalokitesvara.

Amita Buddha, or Buddha of profound enlightenment (Figure 8.1), is portrayed sitting in the classic meditation position in this 42-foot-tall bronze statue in Kamakura, Japan, cast beginning in 1252. Amita was the bodhisattva Dharmakara, who attained Buddhahood partly by promising to assist others to achieve enlightenment. Amita Buddha is the Buddha of the Pure Land.

Avalokitesvara, Bodhisattva Perceiver of the World's Sounds (Figure 8.2), is shown in this fifteenth-century bronze from Nepal. Done in a style dating back to the sixth century, it shows the bodhisattva with his emblem, a lotus blossom, growing up on either side of him. The lotus was a favorite symbol of enlightenment because its flower rose from muddy waters, as enlightenment rises from the suffering of existence; the wavy form of the stems represents the winding path to enlightenment. Avalokitesvara himself supports a Buddha on his head, making him the literal intermediary between lower and higher planes of existence and the path along which aspirants to enlightenment may rise. His jewelry and other trappings show his ties to this world, meaning that he will not rise to the Pure Land without his followers.

216   CHAPTER 8 ◆ Encountering Transcendent Reality

DEVOTIONAL HINDUISM

The development of Mahayana Buddhism represented a serious challenge to Hinduism's position as the predominant form of religion in India. Hinduism met that challenge with the development of a form of worship called *bhakti,* or devotion, meaning unconditional devotion to a god. Devotional Hinduism built on the *yoga,* or discipline, of devotion that was already one of its central practices. For example, the discipline of devotion was revealed to the warrior Arjuna by his charioteer Krishna in the *Bhagavad-Gita.* Krishna was in reality an *avatar,* or incarnation, of the god Vishnu (see chapter 4). Unlike the Yoga of Action, which required strict and selfless attention to duty at all times, and the Yoga of Knowledge, which required the leisure and temperament for extended study and meditation, the Yoga of Devotion offered salvation to anyone who would worship a god unconditionally. In Devotional Hinduism, the form of that salvation was *moksha,* or release from the cycle of death and rebirth and reunion with Brahman, the universal soul. Because of the salvation that it promised and because it was accessible to everyone, it appealed to many of the same groups who found Mahayana Buddhism attractive, including members of lower castes, women, and others to whom the more traditional, priestly paths toward salvation were largely closed. Bhakti spread rapidly in the period after 300, and in fact by 1500 the combination of resurgent Hinduism and the inroads made by Islam had reduced Buddhism in India to a few scattered outposts.

Sometimes the three main gods of Hinduism are called the Hindu Trinity: namely, Brahma, the Creator; Vishnu, the Preserver; and Shiva, the Destroyer. They are thought to embody the three main aspects of Brahman, the Universal Soul or One. Vishnu and Shiva emerged during this period as the dominant, though not exclusive, subjects of devotional worship throughout India and tended to absorb many of the lesser gods of the Hindu pantheon over time. Though Brahma was thought to be somewhat distant and aloof, having completed his job of creation, Vishnu took an active interest in the world, appearing in different incarnations when he was needed, and Shiva was seen as a loving and interventionist god whose powers of destruction were seen as creative, purifying, and regenerative.

Accompanying the development of the new practice of devotionalism was the rise, between 300 and 100 BCE, of a new body of sacred literature that explained and promoted that practice. These works, known as *puranas,* are compilations of myth, folklore, simplified teachings, and other stories aimed at popular audiences. They were probably meant to be read or recited aloud. Their central message was that unconditional devotion to the worship of a single god would bring salvation. They are long, sometimes disjointed, but full of colorful images and easy-to-grasp ideas. There are eighteen major puranas; the *Vishnu Purana,* which recounts the ten incarnations of the great Vishnu, is one of the oldest and most important of the set. It probably dates to as early as the second century CE. This selection comes from the last chapter of the *Purana* and is in the form of a dialogue between a teacher, Parasara, and his disciple Maitreya. Because of its ideas and its antiquity, it is one of the most important texts for understanding the specific ways that Devotional Hinduism addressed the encounter with transcendence.

QUESTIONS TO CONSIDER

1. What must a worshipper do to receive the blessings of Vishnu? How difficult is it to get these blessings? Are the things a worshipper must do personal or communal?

2. What are the blessings bestowed by devotion to Vishnu? How do they compare with the list of concerns shown in *The Lotus Sutra*?

3. How are the practices required of a good follower of Devotional Hinduism related to its belief system? How did the beliefs and practices combine to offer a more accessible path to salvation than the Hinduism of the *Bhagavad-Gita*? How do the beliefs and practices presented in the *Vishnu Purana* compare with those embodied in Mahayana Buddhism and *The Lotus Sutra*?

4. What characteristics of the statues of Vishnu and the god Ganesh stand out to you? What message do they convey and how does this message reflect or complement the message of the text? How are they similar to or different from the Buddhist statues?

5. Taking the text and art together, what strikes you as the central message of Devotional Hinduism? That is, what is the main avenue to hope in Devotional Hinduism? What is the appeal of that message?

THE *VISHNU PURANA*

Parasara. I have now explained to you, Maitreya, the third kind of worldly dissolution, or that which is absolute and final, which is liberation and resolution into eternal spirit. . . . I have repeated to you, in short, who were desirous of hearing it, the imperishable Vaishnava Purana,* which is destructive of all sins, the most excellent of all holy writings, and the means of attaining the great end of man.

If there is anything else you wish to hear, propose your question, and I will answer it.

Maitreya. Holy teacher, you have, indeed, related to me all that I wished to know; and I have listened to it with pious attention. I have nothing further to inquire. The doubts inseparable from the mind of man have all been resolved by you; and, through your instructions, I am acquainted with the origin, duration, and end of all things. . . . Of all this have I acquired a knowledge, through your favor; and nothing else is worthy to be known, when it is once understood that Vishnu and this world are not (mutually) distinct. Great Muni,† I have obtained, through your kindness, all I desired—the dissipation of my doubts. . . . There is nothing else, venerable Brahman, that I have to inquire of you. And forgive me, if your answers to my questions have

---

Source: The *Vishnu Purana*, trans. H. H. Wilson, vol. 5 (New York and London: Garland Publishing, 1981), 244–55 [facsimile reprint of 1870 ed., London, Trübner & Co.].

*The Purana of Vishnu.

†Teacher, holy man.

218   CHAPTER 8 ◆ Encountering Transcendent Reality

imposed upon you any fatigue. Pardon me the trouble that I have given you, through that amiable quality of the virtuous which makes no distinction between a disciple and a child.

Parasara.   I have related to you this Purana, which is equal to the Vedas* (in sanctity), and by hearing which, all faults and sins whatever are expiated.† In this have been described to you the primary and secondary creation, [the hierarchy of heavenly beings and earthly kings]; the (distinctions of the) four castes, and the actions of the most eminent amongst men; holy places on the earth, holy rivers and oceans, sacred mountains, and legends of the (truly) wise; the duties of the different tribes, and the observances enjoined by the Vedas. By hearing this, all sins are at once obliterated. In this, also, the glorious Hari‡ has been revealed—the cause of the creation, preservation, and destruction of the world; the soul of all things, and himself all things; by the repetition of whose name man is, undoubtedly, liberated from all sins, which fly like wolves that are frightened by a lion. The repetition of his name with devout faith is the best remover of all sins; destroying them, as fire purifies the metal from the dross. The stain of the Kali age,§ which ensures to men sharp punishments in hell, is, at once, effaced by a single invocation of Hari. He who is all that is—the whole egg of Brahma,** with [all the divine beings], the stars, asteroids, planets, . . . men, Brahmans, and the rest, animals tame and wild, insects, birds, ghosts and goblins, trees, woods, mountains, rivers, oceans, the subterranean regions, the divisions of the earth, and all perceptible objects, he who is all things, who knows all things, who is the form of all things, being without form himself, and of whom whatever is, from Mount Meru†† to an atom, all consists—he, the glorious Vishnu, the destroyer of all sin—is described in this Purana. By hearing this Purana an equal recompense is obtained to that which is derived from the performance of an Aswamedha sacrifice,‡‡ or from fasting at the holy places. . . . Hearing this Purana but once is as efficacious as the offering of oblations in a perpetual fire for a year. The man who, with well-governed passions, bathes at [a holy place and time], and beholds the image of Hari, obtains a great recompense; so does he who, with mind fixed upon [Vishnu], attentively recites this Purana. . . . The same degree of merit that a man reaps from [a series of traditional devotions] and effecting the liberation of his progenitors by offering to them on such an occasion obsequial cakes,§§ he derives, also, from hearing, with equal devotion, a section of this Purana. This Purana is the best of all preservatives for those who

---

*The Vedas, or "Wisdoms," are the earliest religious texts of Hinduism, dating from somewhere around 1000 BCE (see chapter 2).

†Atoned for.

‡Vishnu.

§The last of four repeating ages of the universe, a period of 360,000 years of corruption and decline named for Kali, the goddess consort of Shiva. Shiva's destruction ends the Kali Age, and the universe is then reborn to an age of virtue. The Puranas all assert that we are living in the Kali Age.

**The universe.

††Home of the Gods.

‡‡An ancient Aryan horse sacrifice.

§§Offerings at funeral rites for ancestors.

are afraid of worldly existence, a certain alleviation of the sufferings of men and remover of all imperfections.

This Purana . . . was communicated by Brahma to [a series of gods, monarchs and holy men, through whom] it came to my knowledge; and I have, now, Maitreya, faithfully imparted it to you. . . . Whoever hears this great mystery, which removes the contamination of the Kali, shall be freed from all his sins. He who hears this every day, acquits himself of his daily obligations to ancestors, gods, and men. The great and rarely attainable merit that a man acquires by the gift of a brown cow he derives from hearing ten chapters of this Purana. He who hears the entire Purana, contemplating in his mind Achyuta*—who is all things, and of whom all things are made; who is the stay of the whole world, the receptacle of spirit; who is knowledge, and that which is to be known; who is without beginning or end, and the benefactor of the gods—obtains, assuredly, the reward that attends the uninterrupted celebration of the Aswamedha rite. He who reads and retains with faith this Purana, in the beginning, middle, and end of which is described the glorious Achyuta, the lord of the universe in every stage, the master of all that is stationary or moveable, composed of spiritual knowledge, acquires such purity as exists not in any world—the eternal state of perfection which is Hari. The man who fixes his mind on Vishnu goes not to hell. He who meditates upon him regards heavenly enjoyment only as an impediment; and he whose mind and soul are penetrated by him thinks little of the world of Brahma;† for, when present in the minds of those whose intellects are free from soil, he confers upon them eternal freedom. What marvel it is, therefore, that the sins of one who repeats the name of Achyuta should be wiped away? Should not that Hari be heard of whom those devoted to acts‡ worship with sacrifices continually as the god of sacrifice; whom those devoted to meditation§ contemplate as primary and secondary, composed of spirit; by obtaining whom, man is not born, nor nourished, nor subjected to death; who is all that is, and that is not, who is both cause and effect; who, as the progenitors, receives the libations made to them; who, as the gods, accepts the offerings addressed to them; the glorious being who is without beginning or end; . . . who is the abode of all spiritual power; in whom the limits of finite things cannot be measured; and who, when he enters the ear, destroys all sin?

[Closing prayer to Vishnu:]

I adore him, that first of gods, Purushottama,** who is without end and without beginning, without growth, without decay, without death; who is substance that knows not change. I adore that ever inexhaustible spirit who assumed sensible qualities;††

---

*Another name for Vishnu, meaning "The Unfallen One."

†In other words, the material world created by Brahma.

‡Those who follow the Discipline (*yoga*) of Action (see *Bhagavad-Gita*, chapter 4) to obtain *moksha*, or release from the cycle of death and rebirth.

§Those who follow the Discipline of Knowledge.

**"The Substance of Purusha" (see "Purusha Hymn," chapter 2); that is, the original material from which the universe was created; another name for Vishnu.

††Who appears as various avatars such as Krishna, the charioteer of the *Bhagavad-Gita*.

220   CHAPTER 8   ✦   Encountering Transcendent Reality

who, though one, became many; who, though pure, became as if impure, by appearing in many and various shapes; who is endowed with divine wisdom and is the author of the preservation of all creatures. I adore him, who is the one conjoined essence and object of both meditative wisdom and active virtue; who is watchful in providing for human enjoyments; who is one with the three qualities;* who, without undergoing change, is the cause of the evolution of the world; who exists of his own essence, ever exempt from decay. I constantly adore him, who is entitled heaven, air, fire, water, earth, and ether; who is the bestower of all the objects which give gratification to the senses; who benefits mankind with the instruments of fruition; who is perceptible, who is subtle, who is imperceptible. May that unborn, eternal Hari, whose form is manifold, and whose essence is composed of both nature and spirit, bestow upon all mankind that blessed state which knows neither birth nor decay!

Figure 8.3 Vishnu   **Figure 8.4** Ganesh

*Creation, preservation, destruction, the qualities of Brahma, Vishnu, and Shiva, the Hindu "trinity."

The Vishnu statue in Figure 8.3 is from the early Chola period, around 850; it is a bronze figure just over 14 inches tall. It shows the god standing in repose and reaching out one of his four arms in blessing and assistance. The Chola kingdom was in the southeast part of India and thrived between about 850 and 1100. Vishnu, Shiva, and Ganesh were all popular figures in Chola art.

The Ganesh in Figure 8.4 is high Chola, from around 1071, and stands almost 20 inches tall. Ganesh is one of the most popular of the non-Trinity gods. According to the legend in the *Shiva Purana,* one version of many, he was the son of Shiva and his consort Parvati, who created him to guard her rooms after Shiva had interrupted her bath. Shiva beheaded the boy when he blocked his way the next time, but when Parvati proved inconsolable, he replaced the missing boy's head with that of an elephant and brought him back to life. He is revered as a protector of families and as the Remover of Obstacles; he is thus worshipped at the commencement of important activities (including the worship of other gods) and projects (such as term papers). He holds an axe from Shiva in his upper right arm, his own tusk in the lower right arm, a noose that snares delusion in the upper left arm, and a sweet that he tastes with his trunk (thus the large belly) in the lower right arm.

CHRISTIANITY

The eastern Mediterranean around the beginning of the first century CE was a world of religious ferment. In addition to the civic and emerging imperial cults of the ruling Roman Empire, mystery religions—often secret groups who looked to some particular god for eternal life, Truth, and so forth, usually by means of sacrificial ceremonies and other rituals—were gaining popularity. Prominent also were many of the ideas associated with Persian Zoroastrianism (see chapter 4) and a variety of dualistic, proto-salvationist faiths influenced by it. Finally, a number of Jewish sects took varying approaches to the problem posed by Roman control of Palestine, the land they believed had been promised to them by their god. A militant strain in Judaism would rise in revolt against Rome in 69 CE, leading to the war chronicled by Josephus (see chapter 5). But before then, a different sort of Jewish rabbi, or teacher, and his followers had already made their mark on the religious world.

Joshua, or Jesus in Greek, of Nazareth (c. 4 BCE–c. 30 CE) was a prophet in the tradition of Second Isaiah (chapter 4), who preached the coming, not of a military Messiah (Anointed One, a sacred leader) who would lead the Jews to repossession of the promised land, but of the coming of a spiritual Messiah who would lead not just Jews but all of mankind to the promised land of salvation and heavenly reward. At some point, his followers became convinced that he was that Messiah. Despite his emphasis on a heavenly Kingdom, his popularity among the Jewish population made both the Romans and the leaders of the Jewish community (who had no desire to irritate the Romans) nervous, and they had him executed by crucifixion. His followers, however, believed that he rose from the dead and ascended to his Father in heaven, promising to return to sit in judgment on mankind.

222 CHAPTER 8 ◆ Encountering Transcendent Reality

The teachings of Jesus himself clearly formed the basis of what became a new religion, Christianity, so called because Jesus' title of Messiah in Greek is *Christos,* and his followers were therefore Christians. But because Jesus left no writings of his own, the working out and refining of Jesus' message in theological terms, as well as defining who the message was aimed at and what constituted the community of believers, was largely the work of a Jew named Saul (3 BCE–64 or 67 CE) from Tarsus in Asia Minor. Trained as a rabbi and scholarly religious leader in the Jewish tradition, he underwent a sudden conversion experience, changed his name to Paul, and became early Christianity's most influential missionary and teacher. He wrote many epistles, or letters, to different communities of converts, explaining and developing the new faith and, most crucially, opening it up decisively to Gentiles, or non-Jews. His letter to a group of Christians in Rome is his fullest, most complete statement of the tenets of the new religion, and it came to be part of the authoritative texts of the faith. These texts, including Paul's Epistle to the Romans, came to be known collectively as the New Testament of the Bible, to distinguish it from the Old Testament, the Jewish portion of the Bible. A section of this epistle is the first reading here.

Also included as the foundation of the New Testament were accounts of Jesus' life and teachings, known as *Gospels,* or Good News. Four came to be considered canonical, with pride of place taken by that of Matthew. Early Christians attributed this book to the Matthew who was one of Jesus' original twelve Apostles, but modern scholarship places the author as a second-generation Christian, probably from Antioch, and writing around 80 CE. Included here is the section of the Gospel of Matthew known as the Sermon on the Mount, which almost certainly represents not a verbatim transcription of a single speech but Matthew's summary of Jesus' key teachings set in an appropriate setting, similar to Thucydides' account of Pericles' funeral oration (see chapter 4). Together, the writings of Paul and Matthew give a good sense of the foundations of this new salvation religion.

QUESTIONS TO CONSIDER

1. What must a worshipper do to receive the blessings of Christ? How difficult is it to receive these blessings? Are the things a worshipper must do personal or communal? What classes of people would find the message of the Sermon on the Mount attractive? Why?

2. What are the blessings bestowed by adherence to the teachings of Jesus? How do they compare with those bestowed in *The Lotus Sutra* and the *Vishnu Purana*—what are the similarities and differences?

3. What are the differences between Christianity and the Judaism of Second Isaiah? What are the differences and similarities between the doctrine developed by Paul and the doctrine presented as Jesus' by Matthew?

4. What characteristics of the mosaics of Jesus and Mary stand out to you? What message do they convey, and how does this message reflect or complement the

message of the text? How are they similar to or different from the Buddhist and Hindu statues?

5. Taking the text and art together, what strikes you as the central message of Christianity? That is, what is the main avenue to hope in Christianity? What is the appeal of that message?

THE NEW TESTAMENT

Romans 1

[1]Paul, a servant of Christ Jesus, called to be an apostle and set apart for the gospel of God. . . .
[7]To all in Rome who are loved by God and called to be saints:
Grace and peace to you from God our Father and from the Lord Jesus Christ.
[11]I long to see you so that I may impart to you some spiritual gift to make you strong—
[12]that is, that you and I may be mutually encouraged by each other's faith. . . .
[14]I am obligated both to Greeks and non-Greeks, both to the wise and the foolish.
[15]That is why I am so eager to preach the gospel also to you who are at Rome.
[16]I am not ashamed of the gospel, because it is the power of God for the salvation of everyone who believes: first for the Jew, then for the Gentile. [17]For in the gospel a righteousness from God is revealed, a righteousness that is by faith from first to last, just as it is written: "The righteous will live by faith."

Romans 5

[1]Therefore, since we have been justified through faith, we have peace with God through our Lord Jesus Christ, [2]through whom we have gained access by faith into this grace in which we now stand. And we rejoice in the hope of the glory of God. [3]Not only so, but we also rejoice in our sufferings, because we know that suffering produces perseverance; [4]perseverance, character; and character, hope. [5]And hope does not disappoint us, because God has poured out his love into our hearts by the Holy Spirit, whom he has given us.
[6]You see, at just the right time, when we were still powerless, Christ died for the ungodly. [7]Very rarely will anyone die for a righteous man, though for a good man someone might possibly dare to die. [8]But God demonstrates his own love for us in this: While we were still sinners, Christ died for us.
[9]Since we have now been justified by his blood, how much more shall we be saved from God's wrath through him! [10]For if, when we were God's enemies, we were reconciled to him through the death of his Son, how much more, having been reconciled, shall we be saved through his life! [11]Not only is this so, but we also rejoice in God through our Lord Jesus Christ, through whom we have now received reconciliation.

Source: The Holy Bible, Revised Standard Edition (New York: American Bible Society, 1952), Romans 1, 5, 10; Matthew 5, 6.

224   CHAPTER 8 ◆ Encountering Transcendent Reality

Romans 10

"The word is near you; it is in your mouth and in your heart," that is, the word of faith we are proclaiming: [9]That if you confess with your mouth, "Jesus is Lord," and believe in your heart that God raised him from the dead, you will be saved. [10]For it is with your heart that you believe and are justified, and it is with your mouth that you confess and are saved. [11]As the Scripture says, "Anyone who trusts in him will never be put to shame."
[12]For there is no difference between Jew and Gentile—the same Lord is Lord of all and richly blesses all who call on him, [13]for, "Everyone who calls on the name of the Lord will be saved."
[14]How, then, can they call on the one they have not believed in? And how can they believe in the one of whom they have not heard? And how can they hear without someone preaching to them? [15]And how can they preach unless they are sent? As it is written, "How beautiful are the feet of those who bring good news!"

Matthew 5

[1]Now when he saw the crowds, he went up on a mountainside and sat down. His disciples came to him, [2]and he began to teach them saying:

[3]"Blessed are the poor in spirit,
for theirs is the kingdom of heaven.
[4]Blessed are those who mourn,
for they will be comforted.
[5]Blessed are the meek,
for they will inherit the earth.
[6]Blessed are those who hunger and thirst for righteousness,
for they will be filled.
[7]Blessed are the merciful,
for they will be shown mercy.
[8]Blessed are the pure in heart,
for they will see God.
[9]Blessed are the peacemakers,
for they will be called sons of God.
[10]Blessed are those who are persecuted because of righteousness,
for theirs is the kingdom of heaven.

[11]"Blessed are you when people insult you, persecute you and falsely say all kinds of evil against you because of me. [12]Rejoice and be glad, because great is your reward in heaven, for in the same way they persecuted the prophets who were before you.
[13]"You are the salt of the earth. But if the salt loses its saltiness, how can it be made salty again? It is no longer good for anything, except to be thrown out and trampled by men.
[14]"You are the light of the world. A city on a hill cannot be hidden. [15]Neither do people light a lamp and put it under a bowl. Instead they put it on its stand, and it gives light to everyone in the house. [16]In the same way, let your light shine before men, that they may see your good deeds and praise your Father in heaven.
[17]"Do not think that I have come to abolish the Law or the Prophets; I have not come to abolish them but to fulfill them. [18]I tell you the truth, until heaven and earth disap-

pear, not the smallest letter, not the least stroke of a pen, will by any means disappear from the Law until everything is accomplished. ¹⁹Anyone who breaks one of the least of these commandments and teaches others to do the same will be called least in the kingdom of heaven, but whoever practices and teaches these commands will be called great in the kingdom of heaven. ²⁰For I tell you that unless your righteousness surpasses that of the Pharisees and the teachers of the law, you will certainly not enter the kingdom of heaven.

²¹"You have heard that it was said to the people long ago, 'Do not murder, and anyone who murders will be subject to judgment.' ²²But I tell you that anyone who is angry with his brother will be subject to judgment. . . . .

³³"Again, you have heard that it was said to the people long ago, 'Do not break your oath, but keep the oaths you have made to the Lord.' ³⁴But I tell you, Do not swear at all: either by heaven, for it is God's throne; ³⁵or by the earth, for it is his footstool; or by Jerusalem, for it is the city of the Great King. ³⁶And do not swear by your head, for you cannot make even one hair white or black. ³⁷Simply let your 'Yes' be 'Yes,' and your 'No,' 'No'; anything beyond this comes from the evil one.

³⁸"You have heard that it was said, 'Eye for eye, and tooth for tooth.' ³⁹But I tell you, Do not resist an evil person. If someone strikes you on the right cheek, turn to him the other also. ⁴⁰And if someone wants to sue you and take your tunic, let him have your cloak as well. ⁴¹If someone forces you to go one mile, go with him two miles. ⁴²Give to the one who asks you, and do not turn away from the one who wants to borrow from you.

⁴³"You have heard that it was said, 'Love your neighbor and hate your enemy.' ⁴⁴But I tell you: Love your enemies and pray for those who persecute you, ⁴⁵that you may be sons of your Father in heaven. He causes his sun to rise on the evil and the good, and sends rain on the righteous and the unrighteous. ⁴⁶If you love those who love you, what reward will you get? Are not even the tax collectors doing that? ⁴⁷And if you greet only your brothers, what are you doing more than others? Do not even pagans do that? ⁴⁸Be perfect, therefore, as your heavenly Father is perfect.

Matthew 6

¹"Be careful not to do your 'acts of righteousness' before men, to be seen by them. If you do, you will have no reward from your Father in heaven.

²"So when you give to the needy, do not announce it with trumpets, as the hypocrites do in the synagogues and on the streets, to be honored by men. I tell you the truth, they have received their reward in full. ³But when you give to the needy, do not let your left hand know what your right hand is doing, ⁴so that your giving may be in secret. Then your Father, who sees what is done in secret, will reward you.

⁵"And when you pray, do not be like the hypocrites, for they love to pray standing in the synagogues and on the street corners to be seen by men. I tell you the truth, they have received their reward in full. ⁶But when you pray, go into your room, close the door and pray to your Father, who is unseen. Then your Father, who sees what is done in secret, will reward you. ⁷And when you pray, do not keep on babbling like pagans, for they think they will be heard because of their many words. ⁸Do not be like them, for your Father knows what you need before you ask him.

⁹"This, then, is how you should pray:

"'Our Father in heaven,

226 CHAPTER 8 ◆ Encountering Transcendent Reality

hallowed be your name,
[10]your kingdom come,
your will be done
on earth as it is in heaven.
[11]Give us today our daily bread.
[12]Forgive us our debts,
as we also have forgiven our debtors.
[13]And lead us not into temptation,
but deliver us from the evil one.'

[14]For if you forgive men when they sin against you, your heavenly Father will also forgive you. [15]But if you do not forgive men their sins, your Father will not forgive your sins.

[19]"Do not store up for yourselves treasures on earth, where moth and rust destroy, and where thieves break in and steal. [20]But store up for yourselves treasures in heaven, where moth and rust do not destroy, and where thieves do not break in and steal. [21]For where your treasure is, there your heart will be also.

[22]"The eye is the lamp of the body. If your eyes are good, your whole body will be full of light. [23]But if your eyes are bad, your whole body will be full of darkness. If then the light within you is darkness, how great is that darkness!

[24]"No one can serve two masters. Either he will hate the one and love the other, or he will be devoted to the one and despise the other. You cannot serve both God and Money.

[25]"Therefore I tell you, do not worry about your life, what you will eat or drink; or about your body, what you will wear. Is not life more important than food, and the body more important than clothes? [26]Look at the birds of the air; they do not sow or reap or store away in barns, and yet your heavenly Father feeds them. Are you not much more valuable than they? [27]Who of you by worrying can add a single hour to his life? [28]"And why do you worry about clothes? See how the lilies of the field grow. They do not labor or spin. [29]Yet I tell you that not even Solomon in all his splendor was dressed like one of these. [30]If that is how God clothes the grass of the field, which is here today and tomorrow is thrown into the fire, will he not much more clothe you, O you of little faith? [31]So do not worry, saying, 'What shall we eat?' or 'What shall we drink?' or 'What shall we wear?' [32]For the pagans run after all these things, and your heavenly Father knows that you need them. [33]But seek first his kingdom and his righteousness, and all these things will be given to you as well. [34]Therefore do not worry about tomorrow, for tomorrow will worry about itself. Each day has enough trouble of its own."

The picture in Figure 8.5 illustrates an episode from the Gospels in which Jesus cures the blind with his touch. It is a mosaic from a wall of a church in Ravenna, Italy, and dates from around 500 CE. The picture in Figure 8.6 is an *icon*, or a painting of a religious figure intended to be carried around as an object of devotion; its beauty and subject matter were supposed to lift the attention of the

Figure 8.5 Christ Healing the Blind

Figure 8.6 Enthroned Mother of God

viewer to heaven—a sort of artistic intermediary between this world and the spiritual realm. This one comes from Mt. Sinai in Palestine and dates to about 550 CE. In it, Jesus as a baby sits on the lap of his mother Mary, who became a major object of devotion in both the eastern, Greek branch of Christianity and somewhat later in the western, Latin branch. Mary sits enthroned with a Patriarch, or high Church official, on one side of her and the Eastern Roman Emperor on the other, with archangels behind her looking up toward heaven.

ISLAM

Islam was the last of the major salvation religions to arise, and in some ways it is surprising that it did appear. Arabia is basically a vast desert that for most of its history has supported little more than nomadic Arab herders known as bedouins, with a fringe of merchant towns along the coast and some settled farmers on Arabia's northwestern edge where it joins to Palestine. The nomads of Arabia, unlike the nomads of the central Asian steppes, were too poor to generate their own political organization internally and both too poor and too few in numbers to play a major military role in most eras. Some Arab groups occasionally made alliances with the great powers of the area, but Arab leaders were more the clients than the equal allies of sedentary kings and emperors. On the other hand, Arabia lacked the constant political turnover and migration of populations that characterized the steppes and that made any ethnic, linguistic, or cultural grouping there temporary and shallowly rooted. As a result, the Arab tribes by 600 CE had a long,

228   CHAPTER 8 ◆ Encountering Transcendent Reality

stable cultural history and deeply rooted group identities and divisions. Finally, a mix of religious traditions characterized pre-Islamic Arabia. Many Arabs still followed old pagan ways; Jewish communities coexisted with Arab ones; and Christianity by 600 was making major inroads. This is one reason the emergence of a new faith is surprising, for a salvation religion was already established in the area.

But a combination of circumstances derailed expectations and launched a new religion. First, Arabia between 600 and 630 became an arena of competition between the Christian Byzantine Empire and the Zoroastrian Persian Empire of the Sassanid dynasty. Engaged in a protracted struggle for dominance in southwest Asia and Egypt, the two empires both looked for Arab allies, putting new resources into Arab society and raising the political pressure in the area. At the same time, an Arab merchant from Mecca began preaching messages from Allah, *the* god—the same god of the Jews and Christians, but with a new and final message specially for the Arabs. Muhammad became the prophet of a new Arab creed. According to Muslim belief, he was the last of the line of prophets running from Abraham and Moses through Isaiah and Jesus with the final revelation from God. But his success was far from immediate. He preached for twelve years in Mecca, gaining only a small following and much opposition. In 622 he took his followers to an oasis village that became known as Medina, the City of the Prophet, and established the first *umma*, or community of the faithful. (The *hejira*, the break with Mecca and move to Medina, became the act marking the beginning of the Islamic calendar.) Now a political and military leader, as well as a prophet, Muhammad was able to attract new followers to Medina and eight years later to reenter Mecca in triumph. Almost all of Arabia fell under his leadership. Even before Muhammad's death in 632, he had begun leading his Arab coalition against the now exhausted empires on the borders of Arabia. His first two successors in leadership of the *umma*, Abu Bakr and Umar, rapidly created a vast Arab empire, swallowing religiously dissident provinces of Byzantium and the whole of the Persian Empire.

Islam means "submission," and a Muslim is one who submits to the will of Allah. The holy book of the Muslims is the Qur'an. Like Jesus, Muhammad did not write down his own teachings, though Islamic tradition holds that the Qur'an was recited by Muhammad, to whom it was revealed by Allah. But unlike Christianity, which had a single Paul to define much of its doctrine, the developed doctrines of Islam emerged from a much broader, more communal and contested recording, reordering, and refining of the words of the Prophet. What we actually know of very early Islamic doctrine is therefore minimal. But what emerged after eighty years or so has remained ever since the core of Islam, the last of the great encounters with transcendence via a salvation religion.

QUESTIONS TO CONSIDER

1. What are the key duties that a Muslim must perform to receive the blessing of Allah? How difficult are they? Are they communal or personal?

2. What are the blessings of Allah? What do they tell us of the concerns of the Arab world at the time? What punishments are reserved for those who do not seek the blessings of Allah?

Volume 1: –1500

3. What similarities and differences does Islam show as a salvation religion compared with the other three faiths presented in this chapter? What characteristics of Islam seem to reflect its late entry into the field, and what characteristics seem to reflect the particular historical circumstances that surrounded the emergence of Islam?

4. The greatest sin in Islam is worship of idols. How could this have influenced Muslim art in the direction of "nonrepresentational" art, such as that of the Arab calligraphy? What differences in the use of art in religion are implied by a nonrepresentational artistic tradition?

5. Considering both the text and the calligraphy, what strikes you as the central message of Islam? That is, what is the main avenue to hope in Islam? What is the appeal of that message?

THE QUR'AN

*The Cow**

In the name of Allah, the Beneficent, the Merciful.

[2.2] This Book, there is no doubt in it, is a guide to those who guard (against evil).

[2.3] Those who believe in the unseen and keep up prayer and spend out of what We have given them.

[2.4] And who believe in that which has been revealed to you and that which was revealed before you and they are sure of the hereafter.

[2.5] These are on a right course from their Lord and these it is that shall be successful.

[2.6] Surely those who disbelieve, it being alike to them whether you warn them, or do not warn them, will not believe.

. . .

[2.21] O men! serve your Lord Who created you and those before you so that you may guard (against evil).

[2.22] Who made the earth a resting place for you and the heaven a canopy and (Who) sends down rain from the cloud then brings forth with it subsistence for you of the fruits; therefore do not set up rivals to Allah while you know.

[2.23] And if you are in doubt as to that which We have revealed to Our servant, then produce a chapter like it and call on your witnesses besides Allah if you are truthful.

. . .

[2.25] And convey good news to those who believe and do good deeds, that they shall have gardens in which rivers flow; whenever they shall be given a portion of the fruit thereof, they shall say: This is what was given to us before; and they shall

Source: The Holy Qur'an, trans. M. H. Shakir, 1983. Reprinted by permission of Tahrike Tarsile Qur'an, Inc.

*The names of sections in the Qur'an reflect items discussed in those sections. Sometimes, as in this section known as "The Cow," these strike non-Muslims, who do not know the entire text, as odd.

230   CHAPTER 8 ◆ Encountering Transcendent Reality

be given the like of it, and they shall have pure mates in them, and in them, they shall abide.

. . .

[2.28] How do you deny Allah and you were dead and He gave you life? Again He will cause you to die and again bring you to life, then you shall be brought back to Him.

. . .

[2.30] And when your Lord said to the angels, I am going to place in the earth a khalif,* they said: What! wilt Thou place in it such as shall make mischief in it and shed blood, and we celebrate Thy praise and extol Thy holiness? He said: Surely I know what you do not know.

. . .

[2.40] O children of Israel! call to mind My favor which I bestowed on you and be faithful to (your) covenant with Me, I will fulfill (My) covenant with you; and of Me, Me alone, should you be afraid.

. . .

[2.43] And keep up prayer and pay the poor-rate† and bow down with those who bow down.

[2.44] What! do you enjoin men to be good and neglect your own souls while you read the Book; have you then no sense?

[2.45] And seek assistance through patience and prayer, and most surely it is a hard thing except for the humble ones,

[2.46] Who know that they shall meet their Lord and that they shall return to Him.

. . .

[2.62] Surely those who believe, and those who are Jews, and the Christians, and the Sabians,‡ whoever believes in Allah and the Last day and does good, they shall have their reward from their Lord, and there is no fear for them, nor shall they grieve.

. . .

[2.79] Woe, then, to those who write the book with their hands and then say: This is from Allah, so that they may take for it a small price; therefore woe to them for what their hands have written and woe to them for what they earn.

. . .

[2.82] And (as for) those who believe and do good deeds, these are the dwellers of the garden; in it they shall abide.

. . .

---

*Khalif, or Caliph, means "Successor of the Prophet [Muhammad]." The caliphs were the head of the Islamic community as a whole, and they therefore held a position that combined aspects of a Catholic pope and an emperor.

†The tax or tithe that embodied the Islamic duty of being charitable.

‡Gnostic, or rationalist, Christians in Persia; therefore, a "people of the book"—Jews, Christians, and Muslims—and worthy of toleration in Islamic thought, since they were not idol worshippers.

[2.87] And most certainly We gave Musa the Book and We sent apostles after him one after another; and We gave Isa, the son of Marium,* clear arguments and strengthened him with the holy spirit, What! whenever then an apostle came to you with that which your souls did not desire, you were insolent so you called some liars and some you slew.

. . .

[2.105] Those who disbelieve from among the followers of the Book do not like, nor do the polytheists, that the good should be sent down to you from your Lord, and Allah chooses especially whom He pleases for His mercy, and Allah is the Lord of mighty grace.

[2.106] Whatever communications We abrogate or cause to be forgotten, We bring one better than it or like it. Do you not know that Allah has power over all things?

[2.107] Do you not know that Allah's is the kingdom of the heavens and the earth, and that besides Allah you have no guardian or helper?

. . .

[2.110] And keep up prayer and pay the poor-rate and whatever good you send before for yourselves, you shall find it with Allah; surely Allah sees what you do.

. . .

[2.112] Yes! whoever submits himself entirely to Allah and he is the doer of good (to others) he has his reward from his Lord, and there is no fear for him nor shall he grieve.

. . .

[2.115] And Allah's is the East and the West, therefore, whither you turn, thither is Allah's purpose; surely Allah is Amplegiving, Knowing.

. . .

[2.119] Surely We have sent you with the truth as a bearer of good news and as a warner, ...

. . .

[2.125] And when We made the House a pilgrimage for men and a (place of) security, and: Appoint for yourselves a place of prayer on the standing-place of Ibrahim. And We enjoined Ibrahim and Ismail† saying: Purify My House for those who visit (it) and those who abide (in it) for devotion and those who bow down (and) those who prostrate themselves.

. . .

[2.129] Our Lord! and raise up in them an Apostle from among them who shall recite to them Thy communications and teach them the Book and the wisdom, and purify them; surely Thou art the Mighty, the Wise.

---

*Musa is Moses; Isa is Jesus, and Marium is Mary.

†Ibrahim is Abraham, and Ismail is Ishmail. The Arabs considered themselves the descendants of Abraham through his son Ishmail, whom he had with the slave girl Hagar, while the Jews were Abraham's descendants through Isaac, his son by his wife Sarah.

232   CHAPTER 8   ◆   Encountering Transcendent Reality

[2.130] And who forsakes the religion of Ibrahim but he who makes himself a fool, and most certainly We chose him in this world, and in the hereafter he is most surely among the righteous.

[2.131]When his Lord said to him, Be a Muslim, he said: I submit myself to the Lord of the worlds.

. . .

[2.147] The truth is from your Lord, therefore you should not be of the doubters.

[2.148] And every one has a direction to which he should turn, therefore hasten to (do) good works; wherever you are, Allah will bring you all together; surely Allah has power over all things.

[2.149] And from whatsoever place you come forth, turn your face towards the Sacred Mosque; and surely it is the very truth from your Lord, and Allah is not at all heedless of what you do.

[2.150] And from whatsoever place you come forth, turn your face towards the Sacred Mosque; and wherever you are turn your faces towards it, so that people shall have no accusation against you, except such of them as are unjust; so do not fear them, and fear Me, that I may complete My favor on you and that you may walk on the right course.

[2.151] Even as We have sent among you an Apostle* from among you who recites to you Our communications and purifies you and teaches you the Book and the wisdom and teaches you that which you did not know.

[2.152] Therefore remember Me, I will remember you, and be thankful to Me, and do not be ungrateful to Me.

[2.153] O you who believe! seek assistance through patience and prayer; surely Allah is with the patient.

[2.154] And do not speak of those who are slain in Allah's way as dead; nay, (they are) alive, but you do not perceive.

[2.155] And We will most certainly try you with somewhat of fear and hunger and loss of property and lives and fruits; and give good news to the patient,

[2.156] Who, when a misfortune befalls them, say: Surely we are Allah's and to Him we shall surely return.

[2.157] Those are they on whom are blessings and mercy from their Lord, and those are the followers of the right course.

[2.158] Surely the . . . whoever makes a pilgrimage to the House or pays a visit (to it), there is no blame on him if he goes round them both; and whoever does good spontaneously, then surely Allah is Grateful, Knowing.

. . .

[2.190] And fight in the way of Allah with those who fight with you, and do not exceed the limits, surely Allah does not love those who exceed the limits.

[2.191] And kill them wherever you find them, and drive them out from whence they drove you out, and persecution is severer than slaughter, and do not fight with them

---

*Muhammad.

at the Sacred Mosque until they fight with you in it, but if they do fight you, then slay them; such is the recompense of the unbelievers.

[2.192] But if they desist, then surely Allah is Forgiving, Merciful.

[2.193] And fight with them until there is no persecution, and religion should be only for Allah, but if they desist, then there should be no hostility except against the oppressors.

. . .

[2.196] And accomplish the pilgrimage and the visit for Allah, but if, you are prevented, (send) whatever offering is easy to obtain, and do not shave your heads until the offering reaches its destination; but whoever among you is sick or has an ailment of the head, he (should effect) a compensation by fasting or alms or sacrificing, then when you are secure, whoever profits by combining the visit with the pilgrimage (should take) what offering is easy to obtain; but he who cannot find (any offering) should fast for three days during the pilgrimage and for seven days when you return; these (make) ten (days) complete; this is for him whose family is not present in the Sacred Mosque, and be careful (of your duty) to Allah, and know that Allah is severe in requiting (evil).

. . .

[2.263] Kind speech and forgiveness is better than charity followed by injury; and Allah is Self-sufficient, Forbearing.

. . .

[2.270] And whatever alms you give or (whatever) vow you vow, surely Allah knows it; and the unjust shall have no helpers.

[2.271] If you give alms openly, it is well, and if you hide it and give it to the poor, it is better for you; and this will do away with some of your evil deeds; and Allah is aware of what you do.

. . .

[2.277] Surely they who believe and do good deeds and keep up prayer and pay the poor-rate they shall have their reward from their Lord, and they shall have no fear, nor shall they grieve.

. . .

[2.284] Whatever is in the heavens and whatever is in the earth is Allah's; and whether you manifest what is in your minds or hide it, Allah will call you to account according to it; then He will forgive whom He pleases and chastise whom He pleases, and Allah has power over all things.

Alms

In the name of Allah, the Beneficent, the Merciful.

[107.1] Have you considered him who calls the judgment a lie?

[107.2] That is the one who treats the orphan with harshness,

[107.3] And does not urge (others) to feed the poor.

[107.4] So woe to the praying ones,

[107.5] Who are unmindful of their prayers,

[107.6] Who do (good) to be seen,

[107.7] And withhold the necessaries of life.

234   CHAPTER 8 ◆ Encountering Transcendent Reality

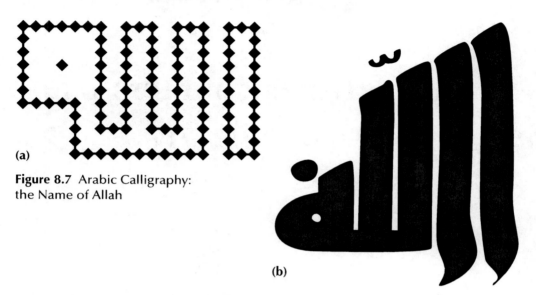

(a)

Figure 8.7 Arabic Calligraphy:
the Name of Allah

(b)

Islam, like Judaism, taught that the making of representational images of Allah, people, or animals was a form of idolatry that was therefore prohibited. But this does not mean that Islamic religion was without artistic expression. In addition to a long tradition of beautiful abstract geometric decorations on buildings and in the margins of manuscripts, calligraphy, or the art of beautiful handwriting, became a means of artistic expression in itself, not just a means of conveying the written word. (A similar calligraphic tradition had already evolved in China, whose ideographic system of writing lent itself to expressive textual production, though in China calligraphy often accompanied and complemented a thriving tradition of representational art.) The two pictures in Figure 8.7 both show the name of Allah written in Kufic script. Figure 8.7a is a detail of a mosaic inscription from a mosque in Samarqand in Central Asia, Figure 8.7b is calligraphy from the Maghrib in North Africa, written on gazelle skin.

NOTES

1. To some extent, Hinduism remained largely a religion one was born into as well, but the size and variety of the population that embraced this manifold tradition distinguished it from these other two faiths, and Hinduism did spread, if only in somewhat limited ways, beyond India into southeast Asia.

2. For example, it is called the "Pure Land" in the Mahayana Buddhist sect of that name.

CHAPTER 10

The Artist Encounters Life

Literature and Social Values

INTRODUCTION

In a famous formulation, Supreme Court Justice Potter Stewart asserted, "I shall not today attempt further to define . . . [pornography] . . . but I know it when I see it." Justice Stewart was trying to distinguish between art and pornography, and his statement echoes the common American assertion that "I don't know art, but I know what I like." In the same way that the Supreme Court found Justice Stewart's formulation inadequate to the task of defining pornography—the issues of free speech proved too thorny—the common attempt to reduce arguments about art to issues of aesthetics (the study of the beautiful) has not really succeeded in defining art. Art and its role in human society is simply too complex an issue to sum up adequately in the saying "Beauty is in the eye of the beholder." One reason for this is that beauty is not the only dimension to art. Another way of looking at art is to consider what function art plays in human societies. The question then becomes, "What is (the role of) art?" An individual work would then be "art" only if it performed whatever role one thinks art should perform.

Many different answers have been given to that problem. One response is captured in the expression *Ars gratia ars*, which appears under the roaring lion at the beginning of movies produced by MGM. It is a Latin expression, meaning "Art for art's sake." According to this understanding, art performs no other function than to embody the human need to express itself in artistic creation. Another consideration concerning the role of art is that art must perform a positive social function. This is both a traditional religious view of art and a contemporary modern understanding. Art, from this perspective, must instill correct values and hold up proper models, whatever those are judged to be. Clearly, this point of view rejects the idea of "art for art's sake," and it maintains that art has a "higher" function. Some anthropologists take an entirely different tack, in assessing the role of art in human life as a form of playful self-expression. In all of these understandings, art is a fundamental part of the human encounter with the world.

268   CHAPTER 10 ◆ The Artist Encounters Life

These three ways of viewing art can be summarized as (1) art as an independent and natural process of human self-expression, (2) art as shaper of social values, and (3) art as a complex form of human play. In this chapter, we address the relationship of art to human life, keeping in mind these three understandings of what constitutes art. We do so by considering selections from four "classics" of world literature: Murasaki Shikibu's *The Tale of Genji,* the famous *Arabian Nights, The Song of Roland,* and Geoffrey Chaucer's *The Canterbury Tales.* The works and the passages from them have been chosen to represent a variety of cultures and of social groups within those cultures. An additional consideration taken into account is the genesis of the works themselves, the way these artistic works were created. These selections allow you to sample eminent elements of the global cultural heritage, as well as to grapple with the relationship between art and human social values. Whether it is true, as it is often said, that "art imitates life," it is undoubtedly true that art encounters life, and this chapter is devoted to that encounter.

Our first text comes from Murasaki Shikibu's *The Tale of Genji.* This text from Heian Japan (794–1185 CE) is very interesting for a number of reasons. First of all, it was written by a lady-in-waiting for the empress. As a result, it provides a unique "interior" perspective of elite Japanese values of that time period from the point of view of a woman. Furthermore, because sexual politics were a prominent part of Heian elite culture, gender issues are even more dramatically highlighted. Because of the absence in that time period of significant military threats, elite Japanese reflected highly sophisticated artistic standards. The selection presented here comes from a chapter titled "The Picture Competition," so considerations of art's role in human life come into play on several levels of this text.

Our second selection comes from the *Arabian Nights,* one of the most famous pieces of world literature. The story we present here is "The Story of Ali Cogia, a Merchant of Bagdad." As the title indicates, this tale involves the ethics and practices of the merchant and trading culture of the Middle East. In addition, it allows us to glimpse the values that structured the behavior of political authorities. Finally, the story incorporates children playing a game as a key part of the resolution of the conflict, so that another aspect of art is foregrounded in the narrative itself. In general, this story incorporates the values of Middle Eastern culture in a rich, vibrant, and sophisticated Islamic era.

Following *Arabian Nights,* we present excerpts from a classic epic of medieval western Europe, *The Song of Roland.* The tale is about an incident that occurred in the late eighth century, but the text we have is an Anglo-Norman version, composed around 1100 CE. The world and the values represented here are those of the armed nobility of the Middle Ages. The tension and narrative in *Roland* revolve around the issue of what constitutes a good vassal. Insofar as it, too, deals with the problem of "true" nobility, *Roland* has similarities with both *Genji* and the selection from *The Canterbury Tales.* In addition, although the warrior spirit of *Roland* gives it a very different feel from *The Tale of Genji,* it also involves a competition—in this case a very deadly game of trial by combat.

The final text is "The Wife of Bath's Tale" from Geoffrey Chaucer's *The Canterbury Tales.* Chaucer composed these tales between 1387 and his death in 1400. The overall work was left incomplete at his death, but the tale we include in this chapter is in finished form. Like two of the other works included here, it involves a nobleman and a discussion—playful, to be sure—of what true nobility entails. In addition, like *Genji,* it raises gender issues. Perhaps more than any of the other texts, Chaucer's piece poses for us the question of whether this work of art embodies the human need to express itself in artistic form (art for art's sake), an enduring human effort to use art to shape social values, or an artistic instance of the recurring human attribute of playfulness. Art encounters life in a variety of forms and expressions, and to that encounter we now turn.

CHAPTER QUESTIONS

1. Which works or which parts of each work seem to you to represent "art for art's sake"? Identify those aspects of the works here that seem to involve art as a form of human self-expression. What benefit or purpose do you think the artist who composed these works might have sought or achieved through the process of creating these works?

2. In what ways do the following works seek to identify and hold up for imitation certain values? Do the works represent different, perhaps conflicting, values? If so, how are they reconciled, or how is the tension between them handled?

3. What role does the seemingly irrepressible human instinct for play occupy in these works of elite literature? How do the authors utilize play to move the action of their narratives? How is play used to represent and promote certain values?

4. What is distinctive about the cultures and societies that produced these works of art? What common elements do they have? How does the culture and society affect the nature of the art that is produced? What is the role of gender in these works and societies, and how does its role differ from contemporary social practices?

5. How does the treatment of human cultures and social values in these works differ from the way those subjects are dealt with in other works (for example, the Bible or the Qur'an)? Can you identify with the subjects and issues dealt with in these works? Do they speak to you across the ages and the cultural divides? In what ways?

ELITE VALUES IN HEIAN JAPAN

Murasaki Shikibu's *The Tale of Genji* is a product of Japan's Heian period (794–1185). In that era, Japan was greatly influenced by Chinese governmental and cultural forms, which were nativized and adapted to fit the Japanese environment. For example, the extreme centralization and imperial power of the Chinese system were never replicated in Japan. Because Japan consists of islands and faced no great foreign threat at that time, the emperor and the central government ruled in concert with a powerful aristocracy organized on clan lines. In fact, over time

270   CHAPTER 10 ◆ The Artist Encounters Life

a branch of one of the leading aristocratic clans, the northern Fujiwara, succeeded in dominating the emperors and effectively ruling Japan in their place (866–1068). Ultimately, the Fujiwara were outmaneuvered and some imperial autonomy was restored, but nothing approaching the Chinese system ever existed. Similarly, Chinese culture in the forms of written language, the Buddhist religion, and art and architecture exercised a powerful attraction for the Japanese. In the seventh century, the Chinese system of writing was adopted as the first written language in Japan, used for government, laws, records, and histories. Around 900 CE a written, phonetic Japanese script (*hiragana*) was devised, and a lively literary culture evolved.

As in most other societies before modern times, Japan was dominated politically and culturally by the aristocratic elite, especially the court notables. One remarkable feature of Japanese elite culture in this era is the prominent position occupied by a couple of extraordinary women. Although knowledge and use of written Chinese had been largely restricted to men and to male-dominated fields, such as government and law, *hiragana* was more accessible to aristocratic women, and it was more suitable to the intimate and personal issues—especially marital politics—that played a central role in their lives. The two literary products of the Heian era that are best known in the West—Sei Shonagon's *Pillow Book* and Murasaki's *The Tale of Genji*—were written by aristocratic women. As was true in the political system, the absence of external military threat allowed the Japanese elite the luxury of concentrating on aristocratic cultural aesthetics and court politics. In this environment, and equipped with the flexible and familiar *hiragana*, women writers could assume a prominence unheard of in other systems.

The Tale of Genji is a remarkable work written by a remarkable woman, Murasaki Shikibu, who is so completely identified with this work that she actually earned the name "Murasaki" as a nickname based on the name of the leading female character in *Genji*. She was born around 973 into a minor branch of the Fujiwara clan, the powerful aristocratic family that dominated politics in Heian Japan from 866 to 1068 CE, and she died sometime after 1031. Her father served in minor posts, such as provincial governor, but, as far back as her great-grandfather, the family had enjoyed a certain literary eminence. After the death of her husband, she became a sort of lady-in-waiting tutor of a young empress, so she was ideally placed to observe the highly stylized but fiercely pursued sexual politics of the Japanese court. The Fujiwara had achieved dominance by succeeding in marrying a succession of daughters to the emperors, who were in turn pressured by the Fujiwara to abdicate early. As a result, there was usually more than one fairly young former emperor in the background of the political picture, and the ruling emperor was often a minor, for whom the senior Fujiwara served as guardian and effective ruler of the country. The combination of this political constellation with the relatively lax sexual mores of the Heian upper class meant that there were at any given moment a number of currents of sexual and marital intrigue swirling about the court. Such are the court politics and aristocratic characters that make up the crux of Murasaki's story.[1]

The Tale of Genji has been called with some justification the world's first novel. It is the story of an especially gifted son of an emperor, Genji. In the course of the story, Genji evolves from a sort of courtly playboy who is most concerned with court conquests and politics to a man who finds his greatest pleasure with his wife and who understands the impermanence of this world. For most of the novel, though, he exists in the rarified atmosphere of the higher realms of Heian aristocratic and court life. It was a world of exquisite cultural nuance and extraordinary sensibility to aesthetic (that is, relating to beauty) distinctions and etiquette, not unlike that of Louis XIV's Versailles. The complex interrelations in the story are worthy of a modern-day soap opera, and they can be somewhat dizzying. Here is the basic outline. Genji's father was an emperor who fell in love with a woman of inappropriate rank, Genji's mother. Ultimately, Genji's father's first wife, Lady Kokiden, a powerful Fujiwara, forces him to declare Genji ineligible to become an emperor (that is what *Genji* means). Lady Kokiden's son becomes emperor Suzaku, though by the time of the passage excerpted here he has already abdicated, and so he is the ex-emperor. Genji's mother is persecuted and dies. Eventually, another woman becomes the emperor's wife and replaces Genji's mother in his affections. She is Fujitsubo, who has her own complex relations with Genji. Genji adopts a young woman, Murasaki, who it turns out is Fujitsubo's niece. In the passage included here, Murasaki's presentation at court has been arranged by Genji, who seeks to promote her interests by introducing her to the underage current emperor. (Ultimately, Genji will decide that he is in love with Murasaki; he will take her as his wife and find sincere happiness with her.) His main rival at the court is To no Chujo, Genji's brother-in-law (Genji is married to his sister, but he neglects her in favor of relationships with other women) and at this time still his close friend. The main point of contention becomes showing the young emperor that his ward, Murasaki, has greater sensitivity and cultural sophistication connected with painting than does To no Chujo's daughter.

The characters in this selection are

Genji

the young emperor

Murasaki[2]—Genji's ward and eventually his main wife

Fujitsubo—Genji's father's wife and surrogate mother to him; also Murasaki's aunt

To no Chujo—Genji's brother-in-law, friend, and rival

Princess Chujo—To no Chujo's young daughter, the young current emperor's favorite court lady

Emperor Suzaku—a young ex-emperor, Genji's stepbrother

QUESTIONS TO CONSIDER

1. Identify all the traits or behaviors in the characters presented in this selection that seem to be represented as desirable or admirable. Define the attributes of an ideal individual in that society based on the traits you have identified.

2. As the chapter title indicates, the action revolves around a "picture competition." Assess the kinds of subjects and treatments that they valued most in paintings.

272   CHAPTER 10   ◆   The Artist Encounters Life

3. In your opinion, what values, if any, was Murasaki Shikibu holding up for imitation? Perhaps she was presenting values and behaviors in order to criticize them. Do you see any of that at work in this selection? How do the values presented here compare with those of modern American society?

4. The anthropological understanding of the role of art in human society also includes "play." In this selection, play is presented as a competition between Genji and To no Chujo. Assess the way each one conducts himself in this competition. How might this depiction have "shaped" or affected the behavior of subsequent generations of Japanese? How does it compare with American competitive behavior?

5. Finally, art has also been understood as "an independent and natural process of human self-expression." Murasaki Shikibu was widowed young and assigned to the service of a limited and prudish imperial wife. What might *The Tale of Genji* have allowed her to express? What kind of outlet might the process of literary creation have provided for her? If you have produced any art, what purposes did the creative process serve for you?

THE TALE OF GENJI, "THE PICTURE COMPETITION"

Murasaki Shikibu

To no Chujo had presented his daughter at Court with the express intention that she should one day share the Throne. The presence of this formidable rival at the Palace could not fail to cause him considerable anxiety. . . .

[The Emperor's] favor seemed to be pretty equally divided between the two existing claimants. He was particularly interested in pictures and had as a result of this taste himself acquired considerable skill. It happened that Murasaki painted very charmingly, and so soon as he discovered this the Emperor began constantly sending for her to paint pictures with him. Among the serving-women in the Palace he had always taken an interest in any who were said to be fond of pictures; and it was natural that when he discovered painting to be the favorite occupation of the pretty princess he should become very much attached to her. Hers were not solemn pictures, but such clever, quick sketches; so that just to watch her do them was an exciting game. And when, sitting so charmingly beside him on the divan, she paused and held her brush in the air for a moment wondering where to put the next stroke, she looked so daring that the little Emperor's heart was completely captivated. Soon he was going to her rooms at all hours, and To no Chujo became seriously alarmed lest his own daugh-

---

Source: Murasaki Shikibu, *The Tale of Genji,* trans. Arthur Waley (New York: The Modern Library, 1960), 331, 332–34, 336–37, 338–39, 341–42.

ter should lose her primacy. But he was determined not to be outdone, and being of an extremely ingenious and resourceful nature he soon had a plan for putting an end to this menacing situation. He sent for all the most skillful painters in the land and under strict bond of secrecy set them to work upon a collection of pictures which was to be like nothing that had ever been seen before. They were to be illustrations to romances, which would be preferable to purely ingenious subjects, the significance being more easily grasped by a young mind and all the most interesting and exciting stories were chosen. In addition to these illustrations there was to be a set of "Months," a very attractive subject, with texts specially written for the occasion. In due time Princess Chujo showed them to the Emperor, who was naturally very much interested and soon afterwards asked for them again, saying that he thought Murasaki would like to see them. At this Princess Chujo began to make difficulties, and though His Majesty promised to show them to no one else and carry them with the greatest care straight to the other princess's apartments, she refused to part with them. Genji heard of this and was amused to see that To no Chujo could still throw himself into these absurd conspiracies with the same childish excitement as in their young days. "I am very sorry," he said to the Emperor, "to hear that Princess Chujo hides her pictures from you and will not let you take them away and study them at your ease. It seems, too, that she was quite cross and quarrelsome about it, which was most reprehensible. But I have some very nice pictures, painted a long while ago. I will send them to you: . . . there were whole cupboards full of pictures both old and new. Taking Murasaki with him he now inspected their contents and together they went through the whole collection, putting on one side those which were most likely to appeal to modern taste. . . . [I]t occurred to Genji that his own sketches made during his sojourn at Suma and Akashi might be of interest, and sending for the box in which they were kept he took advantage of this occasion to go through them with Murasaki. Even someone seeing them without any knowledge of the circumstances under which they were painted would, if possessed of the slightest understanding of such matters, have at once been profoundly moved by these drawings. . . .

On hearing of the preparations that were taking place . . . , To no Chujo went through his pictures again and had them all fitted out with the most elegant ivory-rollers, backings and ribbons. It was about the tenth day of the third month. The weather was delightful, things were looking at their best and everyone was in a good temper; moreover it was a time at which no particular fetes or ceremonies occupied the Court, so that uninterrupted attention could be now given to those lighter pastimes in which the Emperor so much delighted, and whole days were spent unrolling painting after painting. The one ambition of everyone at Court was to rout out and bring to the Palace some picture which should particularly catch the young Emperor's fancy. Both Murasaki's partisans and those of Lady Chujo had brought forward vast numbers of scrolls. On the whole, illustrated romances proved to be the most popular. Murasaki's side was strongest in ancient works of well-established reputation; while Lady Chujo patronized all the cleverest modern painters, so that her collection, representing as it did all that most appealed to the fashionable tastes of the moment, made at first sight a more dazzling impression. . . .

It happened that Fujitsubo was paying one of her periodical visits to the Court, and having given a casual inspection to the exhibits of both parties she decided to

274   CHAPTER 10   ◆   The Artist Encounters Life

suspend her usual religious observances and devote herself to a thorough study of all these works, for painting was a matter in which she had always taken a deep interest. Hearing the animated discussions which were taking place between the supporters of modern and ancient art, she suggested that those present should be formed into two teams [Murasaki's and Lady Chujo's]. . . . These were considered the cleverest women of the day, and Fujitsubo promised herself very good entertainment from such an interchange of wit and knowledge as their rivalry was likely to afford. . . .

Presently Genji arrived at the Palace and was greatly diverted by the spectacle of this disorderly and embittered combat. "If you will get up another competition," he said, "I will arrange for the Emperor to be present and will myself make the awards." In preparation for this event, which he had indeed been contemplating for some time, he made a further selection from the pictures which he had recently put aside, and having done so he could not resist inserting among them the two scrolls of his sketches made at Suma and Akashi. To no Chujo meanwhile, determined not to be outdone, was straining every nerve in preparation for the new contest. It was indeed a moment in the history of our country when the whole energy of the nation seemed to be concentrated upon the search for the prettiest method of mounting paper-scrolls. In arranging the conditions of the contest Genji had said: "My idea is that it should be confined to paintings already in existence; we do not want a lot of new work hurriedly executed for this special purpose. . . ." But To no Chujo could not resist the temptation to set some of his favorite masters to work, and improvising a little studio with a secret door he strove to steal a march on his rivals. The secrecy was not however as well maintained as he could have desired; even Suzaku, in his secluded apartments, heard the story and determined to put his own collection at the service of Murasaki. He had a series of "Festivals All the Year Round," painted by various famous old masters; texts explaining these pictures had been added by no less a hand than that of the [former] Emperor Daigo. . . .

When the great day came, though there had not been much time for preparation everything was arranged in the most striking and effective manner. The ladies-in-waiting belonging to the two sides stood drawn up in line on either side of the Imperial Throne; the courtiers, very much on the alert, were ranged up in the verandah of the small back room. Lady Chujo's party (the left) exhibited their pictures in boxes of purple sandalwood mounted on sapanwood stands, over which was thrown a cover of Chinese brocade worked on a mauve ground. The carpet on which the boxes stood was of Chinese fine-silk, dyed to the color of grape-juice. Six little girls were in attendance to assist in handling the boxes and scrolls; they were dressed in mantles with white scarves lined with pink; their tunics were of scarlet, worn with facings blue outside and light green within.

Murasaki's boxes were of aloeswood arranged on a low table of similar wood, but lighter in color. The carpet was of Korean brocade on a blue-green ground. The festoons hanging round the table and the design of the table-legs were carefully thought out and in the best taste. The little girls in attendance wore blue mantles, with willow-colored scarves; their tunics, brown outside and yellow within. When all the boxes were duly arranged on their stands, the Emperor's own ladies took up their places, some with Lady Chujo's supporters, some with the opposing side. At the sum-

Murasaki Shikibu ◆ *The Tale of Genji,* "The Picture Competition" **275**

mons of the herald Genji and To no Chujo now appeared. . . . An amazing collection of paintings had been assembled and assuredly the task of the judges was no light one. A great impression was made when Murasaki's side produced the famous series of "Four Seasons" by noted masters of antiquity. Both the charming fancy displayed in the choice of episodes for illustration and the easy, flowing character of the brush-strokes rendered these works highly attractive; and the modern paintings on paper, being necessarily limited in size, sometimes, especially in landscape, made a certain impression of incompleteness. Yet the far greater richness both of brushwork and invention gave even to the more trivial of these modern works a liveliness which made them compare not unfavorably with the masterpieces of the past. Thus it was very difficult indeed to reach any decision, save that today, as on the previous occasion, both sides had produced many works of absorbing interest. . . .

At last the moment arrived when there was only one more picture to show on each side. Amid intense excitement Murasaki's side produced the roll containing Genji's sketches at Suma. To no Chujo was aghast. His daughter's side too had reserved for their last stroke one of the most important works at their disposition; but against the prospect of so masterly a hand working at complete leisure and far from the distracting influences which beset an artist in town, Lady Chujo's supporters at once knew that they could not hope to prevail. An additional advantage was given to Genji's paintings by the pathos of the subject. That during those years of exile he had endured a cheerless and monotonous existence those present could well conjecture. But when they saw, so vividly presented, both the stern manner of his life and in some sort even the feelings which this rustic life had aroused in one used to every luxury and indulgence, they could not but be deeply moved, and there were many . . . who could scarcely refrain from tears. Here were presented in the most vivid manner famous bays and shores of the Suma coast, so renowned in story yet to these city folk so utterly unknown and unimagined. The text was written in cursive Chinese characters, helped out here and there with a little native script, and unlike the business day-to-day journals that men generally keep it was varied by the insertion of an occasional poem or song. The spectators now clamored only for more specimens of Genji's handiwork, and it would have been impossible at that moment to interest them in anything else. It seemed to them as though all the interest and beauty of the many pictures which they had been examining had in some strange manner accumulated and attached themselves to this one scroll. By universal and ungrudging consent Murasaki's side was awarded the victory. . . .

Genji gave instructions that the Suma scroll should be left with Fujitsubo. Hearing that it was only one of a series, she begged to be shown the rest. "You shall see them all in good time," Genji said; "there are far too many of them to go through at one sitting." The little Emperor, too, seemed to have thoroughly enjoyed the proceedings, which was a great comfort to those who had engineered them.

When To no Chujo saw with what zest Genji supported his ward Murasaki even in such trifling matters as this contest he again became a little uneasy about Lady Chujo's position. But observing the situation closely, he noted that the young Emperor, who certainly began by being very deeply attached to his little playmate, after his first excitement of recognizing this new companion with her interesting grownup

276 CHAPTER 10 ◆ The Artist Encounters Life

accomplishments had passed away, settled down again quite happily to his old love. For the present at any rate there was no need for anxiety.

THE *ARABIAN NIGHTS* AND ISLAMIC CULTURE

With the possible exception of the Qur'an itself, no other work of Arab–Muslim culture is as widely known in the west as is the *Arabian Nights*. The story that we present here, "The Story of Ali Cogia, a Merchant of Bagdad," is included to represent the culture of the Arab Muslim world before 1000 CE. This era is one of the golden ages of the Arab Islamic zone, a time when a sophisticated, vibrant, and cohesive culture permeated much of the Muslim world, the *dar al-Islam*. Within a hundred years of the death of Muhammad in 632 CE, the region from Persia across North Africa to Spain was under the control of Muslim rulers. Most of the former Persian and Byzantine empires were Islamic in faith and governance, and Islamic thinkers absorbed the Persian and Greek intellectual and cultural legacies. Its dynamic economy included some of the richest and most productive portions of the Persian and Mediterranean worlds, and the Islamic world enjoyed high levels of both urbanization and literacy. The region was far in advance of western Europe. Caliph Harun al-Rashid, who figures prominently in many of the stories in the *Arabian Nights* and who is famous for a magnificent and enlightened reign in the late 700s and early 800s, is emblematic of the brilliant, culturally synthetic intellectual life of medieval Islam.

The history of the text of the *Arabian Nights* is a long, complex story in itself. By 1000 CE a version of the *Arabian Nights* existed, though we do not know what its exact contents were. The current version consists of stories that were versions of older, pre-Islamic tales and some that were added after the year 1000 and even from other collections. As a result, it has been called a "book without authors," and we cannot assert with any certainty either the individual author or in many cases even the origin of many stories in the *Arabian Nights*. Hence, as opposed to *The Tale of Genji*, there is no biography of an author on the basis of which we can conjecture about authorial intent or the process of self-expression. What we can say about the *Arabian Nights* is that a variety of genres is represented, such as heroic epics, fables, and humorous tales. Many of the stories, such as those involving Aladdin, Ali Baba, and Sinbad, are already well known in the west. The pretext for the telling of these diverse tales is the story of the narrator herself, Sheherazade. The story is that a cruel king, Shariyar, had women killed after he had slept with them one time. When it was her turn, Sheherazade told him an unfinished story, and he put off having her killed in order to hear the end of it. This story telling cycle continued for the thousand and one nights, after which Shariyar had decided not to have her beheaded. As regards the overall explanation for a series of unrelated tales and in terms of the use of narratives within narratives, the *Arabian Nights* resembles Chaucer's *The Canterbury Tales*.

The *Nights* is a very useful source for the social history of the Islamic Middle East in that era. Thus we can examine material from the *Nights* as both shaping and reflecting Muslim social values. The story presented here involves a Baghdad merchant and his search for justice from the caliph for a wrong done to him while he is on an extended journey that includes his pilgrimage to Mecca. Learning of other trading opportunities, he travels widely in the Islamic world and is away for several years, during which time his supposed friend steals some gold from him. The story involves the social status and values of the merchantry in Islamic society, an Islamic religious element, and a representation of governmental authority. It is important to note that the merchantry enjoyed a higher status in Islamic society than was true of the Christian West until relatively recent times. Both the Prophet Muhammad himself and many of his leading early followers came from trading families. At the time of this story, 'Abbasid Baghdad was the economic, political, and cultural center of Islam, and the apex of 'Abbasid power and eminence occurred under Caliph Harun al-Rashid (786–809), who is also known as a great patron of the arts. Finally, the practice of taking items to sell in order to finance the pilgrimage, or *hajj*, to Mecca was considered quite acceptable. Ali Cogia was following good Muslim practice.

QUESTIONS TO CONSIDER

1. Because of its moral, we can assume that this story "encodes" certain social messages about proper behaviors and values in Muslim society of that era. By examining the actions of both Ali Cogia and the man with whom he left the jar of "olives," describe how a merchant should behave in Muslim society. How does it compare with contemporary American values concerning merchants?

2. One element that the anthropological interpretation of art insists on is "play." How is play incorporated into this story? How does play in this story compare with that in "The Picture Competition" from *The Tale of Genji*?

3. Consider the way that political authority is represented in this story. How many different instances can you identify in which authority is represented as responsive and legitimate? How do the political concerns presented here compare with the ideal behavior expected of a merchant?

4. How do the caliph and his subordinates compare with the political elite presented in *The Tale of Genji*? Which system and sets of behaviors seems closer to our own? Why? What do Ali Cogia's travels tell us about the nature of Islamic society in that era?

5. How does this story compare with "The Picture Competition" from *The Tale of Genji*? Does it have a different "artistic" feel? How would you describe any difference you detect? What do you think explains any difference?

278   CHAPTER 10 ✦ The Artist Encounters Life

THE STORY OF ALI COGIA,
A MERCHANT OF BAGDAD

In reign of the caliph Haroun Alraschid, there lived at Bagdad a merchant, whose name was Ali Cogia, that was neither one of the richest nor meanest sort. He was a bachelor, and lived master of his own actions, in the house which was his father's, very well content with the profit he made of his trading; but happening to dream for three nights together that a venerable old man came to him, and, with a severe look reprimanded him for not having made a pilgrimage to Mecca, he was very much troubled.

As a good Muslim, he knew he was obliged to undertake a pilgrimage; but as he had a house, shop, and goods, he always believed that they might stand for a sufficient reason to excuse him, endeavoring by his charity, and good deeds, to atone for that neglect. But after this dream, his conscience was so much pricked, that the fear lest any misfortune should befall made him resolve not to defer it any longer; and, to be able to go that year, he sold off his household goods, his shop, and with it the greatest part of his merchandises; reserving only some which he thought might turn to a better account at Mecca; and meeting with a tenant for his house, let* that also.

Things being thus disposed, he was ready to go when the Bagdad caravan set out for Mecca; the only thing he had to do, was to secure a sum of a thousand pieces of gold, which would be troublesome to carry along with him, besides the money he had set apart to defray his expenses. To this end he made choice of a jar, of a proportionable size, put the thousand pieces of gold into it, and covered them over with olives. When he had closed the mouth of the jar, he carried it to a merchant, a particular friend of his, and said to him, You know, brother, that in two or three days time I set out with the caravan on my pilgrimage to Mecca; and I beg the favor of you, that you would take upon you the charge of keeping a jar of olives for me till I return. The merchant promised him he would, and in an obliging manner said, Here, take the key of my warehouse, and set your jar where you please; I promise you shall find it there when you come again.

On the day the caravan was to set out, Ali Cogia added himself to it, with a camel, (loaded with what merchandises he thought fit to carry along with him,) which served him to ride on, and arrived safe at Mecca, where he visited, along with other pilgrims, the temple so much celebrated and frequented by all Muslims every year, who come from all parts of the world and observe religiously the ceremonies prescribed them; and when he had acquitted himself of the duties of his pilgrimage, he exposed the merchandises he had brought with him, to sell or exchange them.

Two merchants passing by, and seeing Ali Cogia's goods, thought them so fine and choice, that they stopped some time to look at them, though they had no occasion for them; and when they had satisfied their curiosity, one of them said to the

Source: Arabian Nights' Entertainment, ed. Robert L. Mack, 787–96. Copyright © 1995 Oxford University Press, Inc. Used by permission of Oxford University Press, Inc. Spelling has been modified to accord with standard American usage, and *mussulman* has been changed to *Muslim* for clarity.

*He rented his house.

other, as they were going away, If this merchant knew to what profit these goods would turn at Cairo, he would carry them thither, and not sell them here, though this is a good market.

Ali Cogia heard these words; and as he had often heard talk of the beauties of Egypt, he was resolved to take the opportunity of seeing them, and take a journey thither; therefore, after having packed up his goods again, instead of returning to Bagdad, he set out for Egypt with a caravan to Cairo; and when he came thither, he found his account in his journey, and in a few days sold all his goods to a greater advantage than he hoped for. . . .

[Using his profits to buy goods for sale back in Baghdad, he journeys homeward, but is lured into visiting other places by curiosity and business opportunity. Hence, he is gone from Baghdad for a long time.]

All this time, his friend, with whom he had left his jar of olives, neither thought of him nor them; but . . . one evening, when this merchant was supping at home with his family, and the discourse happening to fall upon olives, his wife was desirous to eat some, saying, that she had not tasted any for a long while. Now you talk of olives, said the merchant, you put me in mind of a jar which Ali Cogia left with me seven years ago, when he went to Mecca, and put it himself in my warehouse, for me to keep it for him against he returned; and what is become of him I know not; though, when the caravan came back, they told me he was gone for Egypt. Certainly he must be dead, since he has not returned in all this time; and we may eat the olives, if they prove good. Lend me a plate and a candle, and I will go and fetch some of them, and we will see.

For God's sake, good husband, said the wife, do not commit so base an action; you know that nothing is more sacred than what is committed to one's care and trust: you say Ali Cogia has been gone to Mecca, and is not returned; and they say, that he is gone to Egypt; and how do you know but that he may be gone farther? As you have no news of his death, he may return to-morrow, for any thing you can tell; and what a disgrace would it be to you and your family, if he should come, and you not restore him his jar in the same condition he left it? I declare I have no desire for the olives, and will not taste of them; for when I mentioned them, it was only by way of discourse; besides, do you think that they can be good, after they have been kept so long? They must be all moldy, and spoiled; and if Ali Cogia should return, as I have a great fancy he will, and should find they have been opened, what will he think of your honor? I beg of you to let them alone.

The wife had not argued so long with her husband, but that she read his obstinacy in his face. In short, he never regarded what she said, but got up, took a candle and a platter, and went into the warehouse. Well, husband, said the wife again, remember I have no hand in this business, and that you cannot lay any thing to my charge if you should have cause to repent of this action.

The merchant's ears were deaf to these remonstrances of his wife, and he still persisted in his design. When he came into the warehouse, he opened the jar, and found the olives all moldy; but, to see if they were all so at the bottom, he turned the jar topsy-turvy upon the plate; and by shaking the jar, some of the gold tumbled out.

280   CHAPTER 10   ◆   The Artist Encounters Life

At the sight of the gold, the merchant, who was naturally covetous, looked into the jar, and perceived that he had shaken out almost all the olives, and what remained was gold coin fast wedged in: he immediately put the olives into the jar again, and returned to his wife. Indeed, my dear, said he, you was [sic] in the right to say that the olives were all moldy; for I have found it so, and have made up the jar just as Ali Cogia left it; so that he will not perceive that they have been touched, if he should return. You had better have taken my advice, said the wife, and not meddled with them: God grant that no mischief may come of it.

The merchant was not in the least affected with his wife's last words, but spent almost the whole night in thinking how he might appropriate Ali Cogia's gold to his own use, in case Ali Cogia should return, and ask him for the jar. The next morning he went and bought some olives of that year, took out the old, with the gold, and filled the jar with the new, covered it up, and put it in the same place.

About a month after the merchant had committed so base an action, (for which he ought to pay dear,) Ali Cogia arrived at Bagdad. . . .

The next morning, Ali Cogia went to pay a visit to the merchant his friend, who received him in the most obliging manner imaginable, and expressed a great deal of joy at his return, after so many years absence; telling him that he had begun to lose all hopes of ever seeing him again.

After the usual compliments on such a meeting, Ali Cogia desired the merchant to return him the jar of olives which he had left with him, and to excuse the liberty he had taken in giving him so much trouble.

My dear friend, Ali Cogia, replied the merchant, you are to blame to make all these apologies on such an occasion; I should have made as free with you; there, take the key of the warehouse, go and take it; you will find it in the same place where you left it.

Ali Cogia went into the merchant's warehouse, took his jar, and after having returned him the key, and thanks for the favor he had done, returned with it to the inn where he lodged; and opening the jar, and putting his hand down to the bottom, to see for his gold, was very much surprised to find none. At first he thought he might perhaps be mistaken; and, to discover the truth, poured out all the olives, without so much as finding one single piece of money. His astonishment was so great, that he then stood for some time motionless: lifting up his hands and eyes to heaven, he cried out, Is it possible that a man whom I took for my very good friend, should be guilty of so base an action?

Ali Cogia, cruelly frightened at so considerable a loss, returned immediately to the merchant. My good friend, said he, do not be surprised to see me come back so soon: I own the jar of olives to be the same put into your magazine; but with the olives I put a thousand pieces of gold into it, which I do not find: Perhaps you might have had an occasion for them, and used them in your traffic: if so, they are at your service; only put me out of my pain, and give me an acknowledgment, and pay me them again at your own convenience.

The merchant, who expected that Ali Cogia would come with such a complaint, had meditated upon a ready answer. Friend Ali Cogia, said he, when you brought your jar of olives to me, I never touched it, but gave you the key of my warehouse, whither you carried it yourself; and did not you find it in the same place, and covered in the same manner as when you left it? And if you put gold in it, you have found it again: You told me that they were olives, and I believed so. This is all I know of the matter; and you may believe me, if you please, for I never touched them.

Ali Cogia made use of all the mild ways he could think of, to oblige the merchant to do him right. I love peace and quietness, said he to him, and shall be very sorry to come to those extremities which will bring the greatest disgrace upon you: Consider, that merchants, as we are, ought to forsake all interest to preserve a good reputation. Once again, I tell you, I should be very much concerned, if your obstinacy should oblige me to force you to do me justice; for I would rather, almost, lose what is my right, than have recourse to law.

Ali Cogia, replied the merchant, you agree that you left the jar of olives with me; and now you have taken it away, you come and ask me for a thousand pieces of gold. Did you ever tell me that such a sum was in the jar? I knew nothing but that they were olives. I wonder you do not as well ask me for diamonds and pearls: Be gone about your business, and do not raise a mob about my shop.

These last words were pronounced in so great an heat and passion, as not only made those who stood about the shop already, stay longer, and created a great mob, but made the neighboring merchants come out of their shops to see what was the difference between Ali Cogia and the merchant, and endeavor to reconcile them; and when Ali Cogia had informed them of his grievance, they asked the merchant what he had to say.

The merchant owned that he had kept the jar for Ali Cogia in his warehouse, but denied that ever he meddled with it, and swore, that he knew nothing but that it was full of olives, as Ali Cogia told him, and bid them all bear witness of the insult and affront offered him. You bring it upon yourself, said Ali Cogia, taking him by the arm; but since you use me so basely, I cite you according to the law of God: Let us see whether you will have the assurance to say the same thing before the cady.*

The merchant could not refuse this summons, which every good Muslim is bound to observe, or be declared a rebel against his religion; but said, With all my heart, we shall soon see who is in the wrong.

Ali Cogia carried the merchant before the cady, before whom he accused him of cheating him of a thousand pieces of gold, which he had left with him. The cady asked him if he had any witnesses; to which he replied that he had not taken that necessary precaution, because he believed the person he trusted his money with, to be his friend, and always took him for an honest man.

The merchant made the same defense he had done before the merchants his neighbors, offering to make oath that he never had the money he was accused of, and that he did not so much as know there was such a sum; upon which the cady took his oath, and afterwards dismissed him.

Ali Cogia, extremely mortified to find that he must sit down with so considerable a loss, protested against the sentence the cady gave, declaring that he would appeal to the caliph Haroun Alraschid, who would do him justice; which protestation the

---

*An Islamic judge.

282   CHAPTER 10 ✶ The Artist Encounters Life

cady only looked upon as the effect of the common resentment of all those who lose their cause; and thought he had done his duty, in acquitting a person accused without witnesses.

While the merchant returned home, triumphing over Ali Cogia, and overjoyed at his good fortune, Ali Cogia went to get a petition drawn up; and the next day, observing the time when the caliph came from prayers in the afternoon, he placed himself in the street he was to pass through; and holding out his hand with the petition, an officer appointed for that purpose, who always goes before the caliph, came and took it from him.

As Ali Cogia knew that it was the caliph's custom to read the petitions as he went into the palace, he went into the court, and waited till the officer came out of the caliph's apartment, who told him the hour the caliph had appointed to hear him; and then asking him where the merchant lived, he sent to him to signify the caliph's pleasure.

The same evening, the caliph, the grand visier Giafar, and Mesrour, the chief of the eunuchs,* went all disguised through the town, as . . . it was usual so to do; and passing through a street, the caliph heard a noise, and mending his pace, he came to a gate which led into a little court, where, through a hole, he perceived ten or twelve children playing by moon-light.

The caliph, who was curious to know at what play these children played, sat down upon a bench which he found just by; and still looking through the hole, he heard one of the briskest and liveliest of the children say, Come, let us play at the cady. I will be cady; bring Ali Cogia and the merchant who cheated him of the thousand pieces of gold before me.

These words of the child put the caliph in mind of the petition Ali Cogia had given him that day, and made him redouble his attention. As Ali Cogia's affairs and the merchant's made a great noise, and were in every body's mouth in Bagdad, it had not escaped the children, who all accepted the proposition with joy, and agreed on the parts each was to act; not one of them refused him that made the proposal to be cady; and when he had taken his seat, which he did with all the seeming gravity of a cady, another, as an officer of the court, presented two before him; one as Ali Cogia, and the other as the merchant against whom he complained.

Then the pretended cady, directing his discourse to the feigned Ali Cogia, asked him what he had to lay to that merchant's charge?

Ali Cogia, after a low bow, informed the young cady of the fact, and related every particular, and afterwards begged that he would use his authority, that he might not lose so considerable a sum of money.

Then the cady, turning about to the merchant, asked him why he did not return the money which Ali Cogia demanded of him.

The young merchant alleged the same reasons as the real merchant had done before the cady himself, and proffered to confirm it by an oath, that what he had said was truth.

---

*The grand vizier was a sort of prime minister. Eunuchs were frequently used in palaces, because they had no family interests to promote.

Not so fast, replied the pretended cady; before you come to your oath, I should be glad to see the jar of olives. Ali Cogia, said he, addressing himself to the lad who acted that part, have you brought the jar? No, replied he: Then go and fetch it immediately.

The pretended Ali Cogia went immediately, and returning as soon, feigned to bring a jar before the cady, telling him, that it was the same he left with the accused person, and took away again. But to omit no part of the formality, the supposed cady asked the merchant if it was the same; and as, by his silence, he seemed not to deny it, he ordered it to be opened. He that represented Ali Cogia, seemed to take off the cover, and the pretended cady made as if he looked into it. They are fine olives, said he; let me taste them; and then pretending to eat of them, added, they are excellent: But, continued he, I cannot think that olives will keep seven years, and be so good: Send for two olive merchants, and let me hear what is their opinion. Then the two boys, as olive merchants, presented themselves. Are you olive merchants, said the sham cady? Tell me how long olives will keep to be fit to eat.

Sir, replied the two merchants, let us take what care we can, they will hardly be worth any thing at the third year; for they have neither taste nor colour. If it be so, answered the cady, look into that jar, and tell me how old those olives are.

The two merchants pretended to examine and to taste the olives, and told the cady they were new and good. You are deceived, said the young cady; there is Ali Cogia, who says they were put into the jar seven years ago.

Sir, replied the merchants, we can assure you they are of this year's growth; and we will maintain, there is not a merchant in Bagdad but will say the same.

The sham merchant that was accused would fain have objected against the evidence of the olive merchants; but the cady would not suffer him. Hold your tongue, said he; you are a rogue, and ought to be hanged. Then the children put an end to their play, by clapping their hands with a great deal of joy, and seizing the criminal, to carry him to execution.

I cannot express how much the caliph Haroun Alraschid admired the wisdom and sense of the boy who had passed so just a sentence, in an affair which was to be pleaded before him the next day; and rising up off the bench he sat on, he asked the grand visier, who heard all that passed, what he thought of it. Indeed, Commander of the True Believers, answered the grand visier Giafar, I am surprised to find so much sense in one so young.

But, answered the caliph, dost thou know one thing? I am to pronounce sentence in this very cause tomorrow, and that the true Ali Cogia presented his petition to me today: And do you think, continued he, that I can judge better? I think not, answered the visier, if the case is as the children represented it. Take notice then of this house, said the caliph, and bring the boy to me tomorrow, that he may judge of this affair in my presence; and also order the cady who acquitted the roguish merchant to attend, to take example by a child: Besides, take care to bid Ali Cogia bring his jar of olives with him, and let two olive merchants be present. After this charge, he pursued his rounds, without meeting with any thing worth his attention.

The next day, the visier went to the house where the caliph had been a witness of the children's play, and asked for the master of it; but he being abroad, his wife came

284   CHAPTER 10 ◆ The Artist Encounters Life

to him. He asked her if she had any children. To which she answered, she had three; and called them. My brave boys, said the visier, which of you was the cady, when you played together last night? The eldest made answer, he was: But not knowing why he asked the question, colored.* Come along with me, child, said the grand visier, the Commander of the Faithful wants to see you.

The mother was in a great fright when she saw the grand visier would take her son with him, and asked him upon what account the caliph wanted him. The grand visier promised her that he should return again in an hour's time, when he would tell her; assuring her he should come to no harm. But pray, sir, said the mother, give me leave to dress him first, that he may be fit to appear before the Commander of the Faithful; which the visier readily complied with.

As soon as the child was dressed, the visier carried him, and presented him to the caliph, at the time he had appointed Ali Cogia and the merchant. The caliph, who saw that the boy was dashed,† to encourage him, said, Come to me, child, and tell me if it was you that determined the affair between Ali Cogia and the merchant that cheated him of his money. I saw and heard you, and am very well pleased with you. The boy answered modestly, that it was he. Well, my dear, replied the caliph, come and sit down by me, and you shall see the true Ali Cogia and the true merchant.

Then the caliph set him on the throne by him, and asked for the two parties. When they were called, they came and prostrated themselves before the throne, bowing their heads quite down to the tapestry. Afterwards, the caliph said to them, Plead both of you your causes before this child, who shall do you both justice; and if he be at any loss, I will rectify it.

Ali Cogia and the merchant pleaded one after the other, as before; but when the merchant proposed his oath, the child said, It is too soon; it is proper that we should see the jar of olives.

At these words, Ali Cogia presented the jar, placed it at the caliph's feet, and opened it. The caliph looked upon the olives, and took one, and tasted of it. Afterwards the merchants were called, who examined the olives, and reported that they were good, and of that year. The boy told them, that Ali Cogia assured him that it was seven years since he put them up; and they returned the same answer as the children who represented them the night before.

Though the merchant who was accused saw plainly that these merchants' opinion would condemn him, yet he would say something in his own justification: When the child, instead of ordering him to be hanged, looked upon the caliph, and said, Commander of the Faithful, this is no jesting matter; it is your majesty that must condemn him to death, and not me, though I did it yesterday in my play.

The caliph, fully satisfied of the merchant's villany,‡ gave him into the hands of the ministers of justice, to be hanged; which sentence was executed upon him, after he had confessed where he had hid the thousand pieces of gold, which were re-

---

*Blushed.

†Awed by being in the presence of the caliph and the court.

‡Crime.

stored to Ali Cogia. Then the monarch, who was all just and equitable, turning to the cady, bid him learn of the child how to acquit himself of his duty; and embracing the boy, sent him home with a purse of a hundred pieces of gold, as a token of his liberality.*

FEUDAL VALUES IN MEDIEVAL WESTERN EUROPE: *THE SONG OF ROLAND*

The contrast between the two cultures of Heian Japan and medieval Islam and that of the medieval west could hardly be greater. Even under Roman rule, western Europe had never been as urban and developed as the eastern Mediterranean lands. But the period dealt with in *The Song of Roland* is not known as the Dark Ages for no reason. Economic life, public administration and safety, cities, and even the population itself were cratering. The population of England, for example, fell from about 4.5 million in the Roman period to a low of about 1.5 million. Such higher culture as existed was restricted to monasteries, as the collapse of the Roman system, a cycle of bad weather, and devastating invasions reduced life to very basic levels. The great lord of *Roland* is Charlemagne, who was indeed the most powerful and dynamic ruler in the west for hundreds of years. Yet despite the mini-Renaissance that occurred during his reign, Charlemagne himself was illiterate and, at 20,000 inhabitants, his capital of Aachen was a provincial burg compared with the caliph's Baghdad, with nearly half a million residents. By 1100, when *Roland* was composed somewhere in the Anglo-Norman realms of England or northern France, Europe had rebounded a great deal from the worst experiences of the Early Middle Ages. Still, it would be some time yet before western Europe passed the Islamic world of the Middle East in wealth, knowledge, population, and power. Although some aspects of so-called courtly love and medieval romances could be compared with aspects of the *Genji* tale and the romantic intrigues of the Heian court, there is nothing in the west to compare with the aesthetic sophistication and style of the medieval Japanese aristocracy.

As Charlemagne was the greatest ruler of the Early Middle Ages, it is only fitting that the greatest epic of that era should involve an expedition launched by him into northern Spain in 778. One of the Moorish rulers of Iberia had invited Charlemagne into Spain to help him against a rival. The main French action was the siege of the northern Iberian city of Saragossa, which siege Charlemagne was forced to lift prematurely because of a revolt in his northern territories. As his forces were leaving Spain through the Pyrenees pass at Roncesvalles, a Basque force attacked and destroyed the rear guard in retaliation for destruction caused

---

*Generosity.

286   CHAPTER 10   ◆   The Artist Encounters Life

by Charlemagne and his forces. This attack occurred on August 15, 778, and it became the basis for the medieval *chanson de geste*, or epic poem, known as *The Song of Roland*. As indicated, it was probably written down close to 1100 CE, either in Normandy or in Anglo-Norman England.

The events as depicted in *The Song of Roland* diverge from the actual historical record. Essentially, the story of the *chanson* goes as follows: The campaign of Charlemagne in northern Spain has lasted seven years, and only Saragossa, under the Moorish king Marsile, remains to be conquered. To preserve himself and his kingdom, Marsile gives Charlemagne expensive gifts and prominent hostages and promises (falsely) to come north later to be baptized into Christianity and to become Charlemagne's vassal. The great warrior Roland, who is Charlemagne's nephew and his favorite vassal, counsels him to refuse, suspecting treachery, because earlier two negotiators had been killed by Marsile. Roland's stepfather and rival Ganelon urges Charlemagne to accept. Ganelon then becomes very angry when Roland suggests that he be Charlemagne's emissary to Marsile, an indication that he does not truly believe Marsile. Ganelon hatches a plot to ensure that Roland will lead a relatively small rear guard, allowing Marsile's forces to destroy them. The plan works; Roland and his force are destroyed. But Ganelon is arrested by Charlemagne, who knows he is responsible. After Charlemagne has avenged Roland's death by capturing Saragossa, he subjects Ganelon to trial by combat.

Two great clashes occur in *The Song of Roland,* one religious and the other political. The first is the relatively straightforward struggle between Christianity and infidels. Although the attacking force in the real events of 778 were Christian Basques, by the time of the composition of *The Song of Roland* the enemy has become the Muslims of Spain. They are variously referred to as "Saracens" and "pagans," and there are confusing references to "their gods, Tervagant and Muhammad/And Apollo."[3] This aspect of the poem may provide a justification for the recently launched First Crusade to "regain" the Holy Land. Moreover, Charlemagne prays for and receives divine help in making the day last longer, so that he can catch and destroy Marsile's forces. He is also visited and aided by "saint Gabriel." After Saragossa has been taken:

> He has the city searched by a thousand Franks,
> The synagogues and the mosques as well.
> With iron hammers and hatchets which they held
> They shatter the statues and all the idols.
> Neither sorcery nor falseness will be left there.
> The king believes in God; he wants to hold a service
> And his bishops bless the water.
> They take the pagans up to the baptistery;
> If there is anyone who withstands Charles,
> He has him hanged or burned or put to death.
> More than a hundred thousand are baptized
> True Christians, with the exception of the queen.
> She will be taken as a captive to fair France;
> The king wishes her to become a convert through love.[4]

Clearly, *The Song of Roland* is intended in part to show that, as Roland put it, "The pagans are wrong and the Christians are right."[5]

The second and more central contest in *Roland* involves the more complicated issue of what constitutes a true or faithful vassal. Roland's father had already died, and his mother—Charlemagne's sister—married Ganelon. Despite this connection, there is no love lost between Roland and Ganelon. Roland is Ganelon's rival for primacy among Charlemagne's vassals. Moreover, Ganelon has a son by Roland's mother, and it is to this boy, Baldwin, that he bequeaths his lands when he sets out on the mission to Marsile. Ganelon has evil in his heart from the outset. He first recommends that Roland be sent on the mission, but Charlemagne will not hear of it. Then, when Roland suggests Ganelon as the emissary, his stepfather's hatred bursts into the open. He states to Charlemagne:

> . . . "this is all Roland's doing;
> As long as I live, I shall have no love for him,
> Nor Oliver, since he is his companion,
> Nor the twelve peers, because they love him so.
> I challenge them here, lord, in your presence."[6]

To Ganelon, all of Roland's actions are those of a rival feudal lord. When Roland offers to go in his place, he responds, "You will not go in my place; You are not my vassal and I am not your lord."[7] Hence, for Ganelon, his act of vengeance against Roland is a private feud between two independent feudal lords and has no bearing on Ganelon's relationship to Charlemagne as vassal.

The story of *The Song of Roland*, then, is about what constitutes true or faithful behavior and who is a better nobleman—Roland or Ganelon. It is also a story about the contest for power among members of the elite. In that regard it resembles the *Genji* tale, but in a far different culture with vastly different values. As the action begins, Roland, his faithful friend Oliver, and Archbishop Turpin (who is also a warrior knight) realize that they face an enormous army and that they have been set up. Oliver has thrice asked Roland to blow his great horn to summon Charlemagne and the main forces to return and face the Saracens with them, and three times Roland has refused. They will eventually be overwhelmed by the sheer size of the Moorish force, but not before killing incredible numbers of the enemy.

QUESTIONS TO CONSIDER

1. According to the title, Roland is the hero of this piece. Describe his most important attributes and assess what they tell us about ideal behavior of knights and vassals, according to this work.

2. Ganelon is Roland's archenemy. Identify how he is treated by Charlemagne and by others in these passages, and interpret what values the author is trying to impart by having him dealt with in these ways.

3. What do the other knights think of Ganelon's justification of his own actions? What do you make of the fact that only one knight will come forward to serve as Charlemagne's champion in the trial by combat?

288   CHAPTER 10   ◆   The Artist Encounters Life

4. This tale was part of an oral tradition and then was given shape by a single, unknown author around 1100. Hence it has aspects of the long oral tradition behind the *Arabian Nights* and the singular, authorial voice of *The Tale of Genji*. How does it compare artistically with those two works? Does it seem more similar to one than to the other to you? Or is it distinctive, and, if so, what in your opinion distinguishes it?

5. Here again, we have a different sort of elite, representing a different cultural tradition. Compare the warrior values depicted in this tale with the courtly ways of Heian Japan and the Islamic values of medieval Baghdad. Are there any common elements among the different elites? In the ways that authority is represented? How justice is determined?

THE SONG OF ROLAND

Roland is brave and Oliver is wise;
Both are marvelous vassals.
Now that they are armed and mounted
    on their horses,
Neither will avoid the fray for fear of
    death.
The counts are brave and their words
    lofty;
The treacherous pagans ride on in great
    fury.
Oliver said: "Roland, just see all this;
The enemy is near us, Charles is so far
    away.
You did not deign to blow your horn;
If the king were here, we should suffer
    no harm.
Look up towards the Spanish pass;
The rearguard, as you see, is in a sorry
    plight.
Those who are part of this one will never
    form another."
Roland replies: "Do not speak of such
    outrage;
A curse on the heart which cowers in
    the breast!
We shall stand firm and hold our
    ground,

It is we who shall deal the blows and
    hack men down."

88

When Roland sees that battle will begin,
He becomes fiercer than a lion or a
    leopard.
He hails the Franks and calls to Oliver:
"Lord companion, friend, such words
    should not be spoken;
The emperor who left the Franks with us
Allotted us twenty thousand men,
And to his knowledge there was not a
    coward amongst them.
For his lord a vassal must suffer great
    hardship
And endure both great heat and great
    cold;
He must also part with flesh and blood.
Strike with your lance and I with
    Durendal,
My good sword, which was a gift from
    the king.
If I die here, the man who owns it next
    can say
That it belonged to a noble vassal."

Source: The Song of Roland, trans. Glyn Burgess, 64–65, 87, 148–55. Copyright © 1990 Penguin Books. Used by permission of Penguin Putnam Group (USA) Inc.

89

Archbishop Turpin, some way across the
    field,
Spurs on his horse and gallops up a hill.
With these solemn words he calls upon
    the Franks:
"Lord barons, Charles has left us here;
For our king we must be prepared to die.
Help us now to sustain the Christian
    faith:
You will have to engage in battle, as you
    well know;
For you see the Saracens with your own
    eyes.
Confess your sins, pray for the grace
    of God;
To save your souls I shall absolve you all.
If you die, you will be blessed martyrs
And take your place in paradise on
    high."
The Franks dismount and kneel upon
    the ground;
In God's name the archbishop blessed
    them.
As penance he orders them to strike.

90

The Franks rise and get to their feet;
They are fully absolved and freed of
    their sins
And the archbishop in God's name has
    blessed them.
Then they mounted their swift war-
    horses,
Armed in knightly fashion
And all well equipped for battle.
Count Roland summons Oliver:
"Lord companion, you realized full well
That Ganelon has betrayed us all.
He has accepted gold, riches and
    money;
It is the emperor's duty to avenge us.
King Marsile has struck a bargain for
    our lives;

But he will have to pay for it with the
    sword."

*[Finally, when it has become evident
that the Moorish army will defeat them
unless help arrives, Roland blows his
mighty horn. It is too late, but even
then Ganelon counsels Charlemagne
not to turn back, because it is just
Roland calling attention to himself.
Charlemagne realizes what has happened, and, before turning his forces
around to ride to Roland's defense,
he orders Ganelon arrested.]*

137

The evening sky becomes brighter
And their weapons gleam in the sun;
Hauberks and helmets give off dashes
    of light,
And so do their shields, which are richly
    painted with flowers,
And their spears and their gilded
    pennons.
Full of wrath the emperor rides
And the Franks as well, grieving and
    sorrowful.
There is no one who does not weep
    profusely
And they are greatly afraid for Roland.
The king has Count Ganelon seized
And he handed him over to his
    household cooks.
He summons the master cook, Besgun:
"Guard him for me well, as befits a
    criminal;
He has betrayed my household."
The cook takes him and assigns to
    the task
A hundred scullions, both best and
    worst.
They pluck out his beard and his
    moustache
And each gives him four blows with
    his fist.

290   CHAPTER 10 ✦ The Artist Encounters Life

They beat him soundly with sticks and
    staves;
They put an iron collar round his neck
And place him in fetters like a bear.
To his shame they set him upon a pack-
    horse,
Guarding him until they deliver him to
    Charles.

*[Having defeated the Moorish armies,
captured Saragossa and avenged Roland,
Charlemagne returns north, and he turns
to the task of dealing with Ganelon. It
turns out, though, that Charlemagne's
greatest vassals now think that punishment of Ganelon would be pointless. They recommend leniency and
restoration of Ganelon to his noble
position. One of Ganelon's vassals,
Pinabel, has offered to step forward for
Ganelon in a trial by combat that will
determine Ganelon's fate. Only one
knight, Thierry, comes forward to back
Charlemagne, and he offers to represent
the king in the trial by combat. This
action, the combat itself and the judgement that befell Ganelon are presented
in the section that follows.]*

276

The emperor has returned to Aix;
Ganelon the traitor, in iron chains,
Is in the citadel before the palace.
The servants have tied him to a post;
They bind his hands with thongs of
    deer-hide
And beat him thoroughly with sticks and
    staves.
He has not deserved a different fate;
In great anguish he awaits his trial there.

277

It is written in the ancient chronicle
That Charles summons vassals from
    many lands.

They are assembled in the chapel in Aix.
The day is solemn, the festival is great;
Many say it was Saint Sylvester's day.
Then the trial and the case begin
Of Ganelon who committed treason.
The emperor had him dragged before
    him.

278

"Lord barons," said King Charlemagne,
"Give me a true judgement with regard
    to Ganelon.
He came with me in my army as far as
    Spain
And robbed me of twenty thousand of
    my Franks
And my nephew, whom you will never
    see again,
Oliver too, the brave and the courtly.
He betrayed the twelve peers for money."
Ganelon said: "A curse on me, if I
    conceal this!
Roland wronged me in respect of gold
    and wealth;
For which reason I sought his death and
    his woe.
But I admit to no treason in this act."
The Franks reply: "Now we shall hold a
    council."

279

Ganelon stood there before the king;
His body is robust, his face of noble hue;
If he were loyal, he would seem the
    perfect baron.
He sees the men of France and all the
    judges
And thirty of his kinsmen who are with
    him.
Then he shouted out loudly in clear
    tones:
"For the love of God, listen to me,
    barons.
Lords, I was in the army with the
    emperor;

I served him in faith and in love.
Roland his nephew conceived a hatred
   for me
And nominated me for death and woe.
I was a messenger to King Marsile;
Through my wisdom I managed to
   escape.
I challenged Roland the warrior
And Oliver and all his companions;
Charles heard it and his noble barons.
I avenged myself, but there is no treason
   in it."
The Franks reply: "We shall begin our
   council."

280

When Ganelon sees that his great trial
   is under way,
He had thirty of his kinsmen with him;
There is one to whom the others pay
   attention
He is Pinabel from Castel de Sorence.
He is a skilled talker and a good
   spokesman
And also a good vassal for defending
   his arms.

281

Ganelon said: "In you . . . friend . . .
Now save me from death and from this
   accusation."
Pinabel said: "You will soon be free.
There is no Frank who dares sentence
   you to hang,
To whom, if the emperor brings us
   together,
I shall not give the lie with my steel
   sword."
In thanks Count Ganelon kneels at
   his feet.

282

Bavarians and Saxons have gone to
   the council

And Poitevins and Normans and Franks.
There are many Germans and Teutons
   there.
Those from the Auvergne are the most
   skilled in law;
Because of Pinabel they are inclined to
   peace.
They said to each other: "It is best to let
   matters drop.
Let us abandon the trial and beseech the
   king
To absolve Ganelon this time;
Let him then serve him in love and
   faith.
Roland is dead, never will you see him
   again.
He will not be recovered for gold or any
   sum of money;
Anyone who fought over this would be a
   fool."
There is no one who does not grant this
   and agree,
Except for Thierry, the brother of Lord
   Geoffrey.

283

Charlemagne's barons return to him;
They say to the king: "Lord, we beseech
   you
To absolve Count Ganelon,
Then let him serve you in faith and love.
Let him live, for he is a very noble man.
Never, even if he dies, will this baron
   [i.e., Roland] be seen again
And no amount of money will ever get
   him back for us."
The king said: "You are traitors to me."

284

When Charles sees that everyone has
   failed him,
He bows his head and keeps his face
   down low;
The sorrow he feels makes him bewail
   his fate.

292   CHAPTER 10 ◆ The Artist Encounters Life

But see, before him stands a knight, Thierry,
The brother of Geoffrey, a duke of Anjou.
His body was spare and slim and slender,
His hair black and his face somewhat tanned.
He is not big, but nor is he too small.
In courtly fashion he spoke to the emperor:
"Fair lord king, do not distress yourself so.
You know that I have served you very well;
By virtue of my ancestors I must make this case:
Whatever Roland may have done to Ganelon,
The act of serving you should have protected him.
Ganelon is a traitor in that he betrayed him;
He committed perjury against you and wronged you.
For this I judge that he be hanged and put to death
And his body should be placed . . .
As befits a man who has committed treason.
If he now has a kinsman who would give me the lie,
With this sword I have girded on
I am willing to uphold my verdict at once."
The Franks reply: "You have spoken well."

285

Pinabel then came before the king.
He is tall and strong, brave and swift;
The man he strikes has come to the end of his days.
He said to the king: "Lord, this trial is yours;
Order that this confusion should cease.
I see Thierry here who has given judgement;

I declare it false and shall do battle with him."
He places in the king's hand his right deerskin gauntlet;
The emperor said: "I required good surety."
So thirty kinsmen make a pledge of loyalty;
The king said: "And I shall set him at liberty."
He has them guarded until the trial takes place.

286

When Thierry sees that there will now be a battle,
He presented his right gauntlet to Charles.
The emperor secures him with hostages;
Then he has four benches brought on to the spot.
Those who are to fight take their seats there;
They are summoned to battle by the agreement of the rest.
Ogier of Denmark explained the procedures;
And then they ask for their horses and their arms.

287

Now that the battle is arranged,
They make confession and are absolved and blessed.
They hear mass and receive communion
And place generous offerings in the churches.
Then they both came back before Charles.
They have their spurs fitted to their feet
And don shining hauberks, strong and light;
Their bright helmets are fastened upon their heads.

They gird on their swords with pommels
    of pure gold;
Around their necks they hang their
    quartered shields
And in their right hands they carry their
    sharp spears.
Then they mounted their swift war-
    horses,
Whereupon a hundred thousand knights
    began to weep.
Because of Roland they feel pity for
    Thierry.
God well knows how it will all end.

288

Beneath Aix the meadow is very broad;
The combat between the two barons has
    begun.
They are valiant men of great courage
And their horses are swift and lively.
They spur them on well, letting go the
    reins;
With all their might they go to strike
    each other.
Their entire shields are shattered and
    smashed;
They tear their hauberks and burst their
    saddle girths.
Their bows are turned round and their
    saddles fall;
A hundred thousand men weep as they
    watch them.

289

Both the knights are together on the
    ground,
Swiftly they jump back on to their feet.
Pinabel is strong and swift and agile;
They attack each other without their
    horses.
With swords whose pommels are of
    pure gold
They strike repeatedly on their steel
    helmets.

Mighty are the blows which tear apart
    the helmets;
Great is the lament of the Frankish
    knights.
"O God," said Charles, "make justice
    shine forth!"

290

Pinabel said: "Thierry, surrender;
I shall become your vassal in love and
    faith
And shall give you as much as you
    desire of my wealth.
But let Ganelon be reconciled with the
    king."
Thierry replies: "I shall not hear of it.
A curse on me, if I ever agree to this.
Let God show this day which of us is
    right."

291

Thierry said: "Pinabel, you are very
    brave;
You are tall and strong and your body is
    well formed.
Your peers recognize your courage.
Let this combat cease right now;
I shall reconcile you with Charlemagne.
Justice will be done to Ganelon;
No day will dawn without it being
    spoken of."
Pinabel said: "May the Lord God forbid!
I want to support all my kinsmen
And shall not surrender for any man
    alive.
I should sooner die than be reproached
    for this."
With their swords they renew their blows
On their helmets, studded with pure
    gold and gems;
Bright sparks fly up towards heaven.
It is not possible to separate them now;
Only when one of them is dead will the
    battle end.

294   CHAPTER 10 ◆ The Artist Encounters Life

292

Pinabel of Sorence is very brave
And he strikes Thierry on his helmet
  from Provence;
The sparks fly on to the grass, setting
  it alight.
The point of his sword of steel bears
  down
On his forehead . . .
He brings it right down on to his face;
His right cheek is covered in blood.
His hauberk is burst open right down
  to his waist;
God protects him from being cast
  down dead.

293

Thierry sees that he is wounded in the
  face;
The clear blood falls on to the grassy
  meadow.
He strikes Pinabel on his helmet of
  burnished steel;
He broke and split it right down to the
  nasal.
His brains spilled forth from his head;
Thierry raised his sword and flung him
  dead.
With this blow the combat is won.
The Franks shout out: "God has
  performed a miracle.
It is right for Ganelon to be hanged
And his kinsmen who upheld his suit."

294

When Thierry has won his combat,
The Emperor Charles came up to him,
Together with forty of his barons,
Duke Naimes, Ogier of Denmark,
Geoffrey of Anjou and William of Blaye.
The king took Thierry in his arms;
He wipes his face with his great marten
  skins;

He lays these aside, then they put others
  on him.
They disarm the knight very gently
And sit him astride a mule from Arabia.
He returns in joy and jubilation.
They arrive at Aix and dismount in the
  square.
At that time the execution of the others
  commences.

295

Charles addresses his counts and his
  dukes:
"What is your advice concerning those
  whom I detained?
They came to support Ganelon in his
  trial;
For Pinabel they agreed to become
  hostages."
The Franks reply: "Not a single one shall
  live."
The king commands his provost,
  Basbrun:
"Go and hang them all from the gallows-
  tree.
By this beard whose hair is hoary white,
If one escapes, you are dead and ruined."
He replies: "What else could I do?"
With a hundred serving-men he leads
  them away by force;
There are thirty of them who were
  hanged.
A traitor kills himself and his fellows.

296

Then the Bavarians and the Germans
  came back,
Together with the Poitevins, Bretons and
  Normans.
Above all others the Franks agreed
That Ganelon should die in terrible
  agony.
They have four war-horses brought
  forward;

Then they bind him by his hands and feet.	All his ligaments are stretched taut
The horses are mettlesome and swift;	And he is torn limb from limb;
Four servants goad them on	His clear blood spills out on to the green grass.
Towards a stream which flows through a field.	Ganelon died a traitor's death.
Ganelon was given over to total perdition.	A man who betrays another has no right to boast of it.

ELITE VALUES IN GEOFFREY CHAUCER'S *CANTERBURY TALES*

By Chaucer's day (ca. 1340–1400), both England and western Europe had changed a great deal. They were still probably less advanced than the Muslim world, and warfare continued to bedevil the region. Nonetheless, they were wealthier, both more urban and more urbane, and had come a long way from the worst period of the great collapse in the Early Middle Ages. The great events of Chaucer's era were the Hundred Years' War and the onset of the bubonic plague. The former would not end till 1453, its conclusion greatly accelerated, as was the Ottoman conquest of Constantinople, by the impact of gunpowder weapons. It marked an important transition in politics, ending the Anglo-Norman arrangements that had the English king with holdings both in Britain and on the mainland in France. The latter was an unprecedented demographic disaster, cutting the population nearly in half in 1348–1349. The socioeconomic development, geopolitical transformations, and demographic convulsions of this time period sent shock waves through the theoretically static and unchanging social hierarchy of medieval England. Workers immediately benefited from the drastic drop in the labor force, as wages rose precipitously. Peasant life was affected as well, and by 1381 the social unrest contributed to the Peasants' Revolt (see chapter 12) led by Wat Tyler. By the time of Chaucer's death in 1400, the Renaissance would be under way across Europe. The simplistic estate structure of an earlier day that had divided the population into "those who pray, those who fight, and those who work" no longer coincided in even the remotest fashion to the social diversity and dynamism of Western Europe.

This most interesting of times found a fitting chronicler in the author of *The Canterbury Tales*. Geoffrey Chaucer was born in 1340 or later, the first child of John Chaucer, a reasonably successful rising man, who pursued both court and business interests. Chaucer himself served in a variety of court and government posts in his lifetime, even holding briefly a position as a member of Parliament. He knew a variety of languages. His government work involved him in missions to the continent, including to Italy, and he was strongly influenced by Italian writers, especially Boccaccio. From 1387 onward (perhaps up to the very end of his life), Chaucer worked on *The Canterbury Tales*. Although he authored other works, it is for this great collection of stories that he is best known. After his death

296 CHAPTER 10 ◆ The Artist Encounters Life

in 1400, he was buried in Westminster Abbey, the first resident of a section that came to be known as "Poet's Corner."

The Canterbury Tales begins with a prologue that introduces the reader to the twenty-nine pilgrims who are joined together on this common journey, and Chaucer reveals much of the character of each in his brief capsule summaries. The work shares certain features with both the *Arabian Nights* in general and the story of Ali Cogia in particular. It has in common with the *Arabian Nights* the presence of multiple stories within the story. Chaucer's device for introducing the tales is a sort of wager or competition proposed to lighten their journey by having each member of the company tell tales on their journey to Canterbury and on the way back. The traveler whose story is judged the best by the general company will be hosted to a sumptuous dinner on the completion of their journey. And like the tale of Ali Cogia, it involves a pilgrimage, in this case to the sacred shrine of Thomas à Becket at Canterbury Cathedral. Also similar to *Arabian Nights* is the presence of characters from diverse social groups. We provide here his characterization of one of his more memorable personalities, the Wife of Bath, followed by her tale.

QUESTIONS TO CONSIDER

1. List the main character traits and life experiences of the Wife of Bath. How does she compare with the female characters in the other stories? Do you think she represents an "ideal woman" of the time?

2. What is the role of play in Chaucer's work in general and in this story in particular? Do you think that the message of this story is intended to be taken seriously, or does the "playful" element undercut the message?

3. How is the knight depicted in this story? What kind of "quest" is the knight on, and how does it compare with the heroic ideal of knighthood presented in *Roland*? What does the fairy-hag have to say about the nobility and commoners? And how does this compare with the image of the noble elite in the other stories?

4. As has been discussed, Chaucer lived in an era of change in politics to more of a national orientation and also a time of great social stress. In that context, is the Wife of Bath's story subversive of traditional medieval values? Does it "encode" a new set of values in terms of gender and class roles? How do the gender and class roles presented in this story compare with the traditional understanding of those roles?

5. Most commentators agree that the narrator of the story represents Chaucer's point of view. What do you think of the artistic self-expression as relates to the character and story of the Wife of Bath? Is Chaucer merely creating a saucy and vital character who tells a humorous story, or does he take seriously both the woman herself and the messages implicit in her story?

Geoffrey Chaucer ◆ "The Wife of Bath's Tale" from *The Canterbury Tales*   **297**

"THE WIFE OF BATH'S TALE" FROM *THE CANTERBURY TALES*

Geoffrey Chaucer

A worthy woman there was from near
    the city
Of Bath, but somewhat deaf, and more's
    the pity
For weaving she possessed so great a
    bent
She outdid the people of Ypres and of
    Ghent.
No other woman dreamed of such a
    thing
As to precede her at the offering,
Or if any did, she fell in such a wrath
She dried up all the charity in Bath.
She wore fine kerchiefs of old-fashioned
    air,
And on a Sunday morning, I could
    swear,
She had ten pounds of linen on her
    head.
Her stockings were of finest scarlet-red,
Laced tightly, and her shoes were soft
    and new.
Bold was her face, and fair, and red in
    hue.
She had been an excellent woman all
    her life.
Five men in turn had taken her to wife,
Omitting other youthful company—
But let that pass for now! Over the sea
She had traveled freely; many a distant
    stream
She crossed, and visited Jerusalem
Three times. She had been at Rome and
    at Boulogne,
At the shrine of Compostella, and at
    Cologne.

She had wandered by the way through
    many a scene.
Her teeth were set with little gaps
    between.
Easily on her ambling horse she sat.
She was well wimpled, and she wore a
    hat
As wide in circuit as a shield or targe.
A skirt swathed up her hips, and they
    were large.
Upon her feet she wore sharp-roweled
    spurs.
She was a good fellow; a ready tongue
    was hers.
All remedies of love she knew by name,
For she had all the tricks of that old
    game.

The Wife of Bath's Tale

In the old days when King Arthur ruled
    the nation,
Whom Welshmen speak of with such
    veneration,
This realm we live in was a fairy land.
The fairy queen danced with her jolly
    band
On the green meadows where they held
    dominion.
This was, as I have read, the old opinion;
I speak of many hundred years ago.
But no one sees an elf now, as you
    know,
For in our time the charity and prayers
And all the begging of these holy friars
Who swarm through every nook and
    every stream

Source: Geoffrey Chaucer, *The Portable Chaucer,* ed. Theodore Morrison, 73–74, 243–53. Copyright © 1967 Penguin Books. Used by permission of Viking Books, a division of Penguin Putnam Group (USA) Inc.

298   CHAPTER 10 ◆ The Artist Encounters Life

Thicker than motes of dust in a sunbeam,
Blessing our chambers, kitchens, halls,
    and bowers
Our cities, towns, and castles, our high
    towers,
Our villages, our stables, barns, and
    dairies,
They keep us all from seeing any fairies,
For where you might have come upon
    an elf
There now you find the holy friar himself
Working his district on industrious legs
And saying his devotions while he begs.
Women are safe now under every tree.
No incubus is there unless it's he,
And all they have to fear from him is
    shame.
        It chanced that Arthur had a knight
        who came
Lustily riding home one day from
    hawking,
And in his path he saw a maiden
    walking
Before him, stark alone, right in his
    course.
This young knight took her maidenhead
    by force,
A crime at which the outcry was so keen
It would have cost his neck, but that the
    queen,
With other ladies, begged the king so
    long
That Arthur spared his life, for right or
    wrong,
And gave him to the queen, at her own
    will,
According to her choice, to save
    or kill.
        She thanked the king, and later
        told this knight.
Choosing her time, "You are still in such
    a plight
Your very life has no security.
I grant your life, if you can answer me
This question: what is the thing that most
    of all

Women desire? Think, or your neck will
    fall
Under the ax! If you cannot let me know
Immediately, I give you leave to go
A twelvemonth and a day, no more, in
    quest
Of such an answer as will meet the test.
But you must pledge your honor to
    return
And yield your body, whatever you may
    learn."
        The knight sighed; he was rueful
        beyond measure.
But what! He could not follow his own
    pleasure,
He chose at last upon his way to ride
And with such answer as God might
    provide
To come back when the year was at the
    close.
And so he takes his leave, and off he
    goes.
        He seeks out every house and
        every place
Where he has any hope, by luck or
    grace,
Of learning what thing women covet
    most.
But it seemed he could not light on any
    coast
Where on this point two people would
    agree,
For some said wealth and some said
    jollity,
Some said position, some said sport in
    bed
And often to be widowed, often wed.
Some said that to a woman's heart what
    mattered
Above all else was to be pleased and
    flattered.
That shaft, to tell the truth, was a close
    hit.
Men win us best by flattery, I admit,
And by attention. Some say our greatest
    ease

Geoffrey Chaucer ◆ "The Wife of Bath's Tale" from *The Canterbury Tales* **299**

Is to be free and do just as we please,
And not to have our faults thrown in our
    eyes,
But always to be praised for being wise.
And true enough, there's not one of us all
Who will not kick if you rub us on a gall.
Whatever vices we may have within,
We won't be taxed with any fault or sin.
    Some say that women are
    delighted well
If it is thought that they will never tell
A secret they are trusted with, or
    scandal.
But that tale isn't worth an old rake
    handle;
We women, for a fact, can never hold
A secret. Will you hear a story told?
Then witness Midas! For it can be read
In Ovid that he had upon his head
Two ass's ears that he kept out of sight
Beneath his long hair with such skill and
    sleight
That no one else besides his wife could
    guess.
He loved her well, and trusted her no
    less.
He begged her not to make his blemish
    known,
But keep her knowledge to herself alone.
She swore that never, though to save her
    skin,
Would she be guilty of so mean a sin,
And yet it seemed to her she nearly died
Keeping a secret locked so long inside.
It swelled about her heart so hard and
    deep
She was afraid some word was bound to
    leap
Out of her mouth, and since there was
    no man
She dared to tell, down to a swamp she
    ran—
Her heart, until she got there, all agog—
And like a bittern booming in the bog
She put her mouth close to the watery
    ground:

"Water, do not betray me with your
    sound!
I speak to you, and you alone," she said.
"Two ass's ears grow on my husband's
    head!
And now my heart is whole, now it is
    out.
I'd burst if I held it longer, past all
    doubt."
Safely, you see, awhile you may confide
In us, but it will out; we cannot hide
A secret. Look in Ovid if you care
To learn what followed; the whole tale
    is there.
    This knight, when he perceived he
    could not find
What women covet most, was low in
    mind;
But the day had come when homeward
    he must ride,
And as he crossed a wooded countryside
Some four and twenty ladies there by
    chance
He saw, all circling in a woodland
    dance,
And toward this dance he eagerly drew
    near
In hope of any counsel he might hear.
But the truth was, he had not reached
    the place
When dance and all, they vanished into
    space.
No living soul remained there to be seen
Save an old woman sitting on the green,
As ugly a witch as fancy could devise.
As he approached her she began to rise
And said, "Sir knight, here runs no
    thoroughfare.
What are you seeking with such anxious
    air?
Tell me! The better may your fortune be.
We old folk know a lot of things," said
    she.
    "Good mother," said the knight,
    "my life's to pay,
That's all too certain, if I cannot say

300   CHAPTER 10   ◆   The Artist Encounters Life

What women covet most. If you could
     tell
That secret to me, I'd requite you well."
     "Give me your hand," she
          answered. "Swear me true
That whatsoever I next ask of you,
You'll do it if it lies within your might
And I'll enlighten you before the night."
     "Granted, upon my honor," he replied.
"Then I dare boast, and with no empty
     pride,
Your life is safe;" she told him. "Let me
     die
If the queen herself won't say the same
     as I.
Let's learn if the haughtiest of all who
     wear
A net or coverchief upon their hair
Will be so forward as to answer 'no'
To what I'll teach you. No more; let us
     go."
With that she whispered something in
     his ear,
And told him to be glad and have no
     fear.
     When they had reached the court,
          the knight declared
That he had kept his day, and was
     prepared
To give his answer, standing for his life.
Many the wise widow, many the wife,
Many the maid who rallied to the scene,
And at the head as justice sat the queen.
Then silence was enjoined; the knight
     was told
In open court to say what women hold
Precious above all else. He did not stand
Dumb like a beast, but spoke up at
     command
And plainly offered them his answering
     word
In manly voice, so that the whole court
     heard.
     "My liege and lady, most of all,"
          said he,
"Women desire to have the sovereignty

And sit in rule and government above
Their husbands, and to have their way in
     love.
This is what most you want. Spare me or
     kill
As you may like; I stand here by your
     will."
     No widow, wife, or maid gave any
          token
Of contradicting what the knight had
     spoken.
He should not die; he should be spared
     instead;
He was worthy of his life, the whole
     court said.
     The old woman whom the knight
          met on the green
Sprang up at this. "My sovereign lady
     queen,
Before your court has risen, do me right!
It was I who taught this answer to the
     knight,
For which he pledged his honor in my
     hand,
Solemnly, that the first thing I demand,
He would do it, if it lay within his might.
Before the court I ask you, then, sir
     knight,
To take me," said the woman, "as your
     wife,
For well you know that I have saved your
     life.
Deny me, on your honor, if you can."
     "Alas," replied this miserable
          man,
"That was my promise, it must be
     confessed.
For the love of God, though, choose a
     new request!
Take all my wealth, and let my body be."
     "If that's your tune, then curse both
          you and me,"
She said. "Though I am ugly, old, and
     poor,
I'll have, for all the metal and the ore
That under earth is hidden or lies above,

Geoffrey Chaucer   •   "The Wife of Bath's Tale" from *The Canterbury Tales*   **301**

Nothing, except to be your wife and
  love."
    "My love? No, my damnation, if
    you can!
Alas," he said, "that any of my clan
Should be so miserably misallied!"
    All to no good; force overruled his
    pride,
And in the end he is constrained to wed,
And marries his old wife and goes to
  bed.
    Now some will charge me with an
    oversight
In failing to describe the day's delight,
The merriment, the food, the dress at
  least.
But I reply, there was no joy nor feast;
There was only sorrow and sharp misery.
He married her in private, secretly,
And all day after, such was his distress,
Hid like an owl from his wife's ugliness.
    Great was the woe this knight had
    in his head
When in due time they both were
  brought to bed.
He shuddered, tossed, and turned, and
  all the while
His old wife lay and waited with a smile.
"Is every knight so backward with a
  spouse?
Is it," she said, "a law in Arthur's house?
I am your love, your own, your wedded
  wife.
I am the woman who has saved your life.
I have never done you anything but
  right.
Why do you treat me this way the first
  night?
You must be mad, the way that you
  behave!
Tell me my fault, and as God's love can
  save,
I will amend it, truly, if I can."
    "Amend it?" answered this
    unhappy man.
"It can never be amended, truth to tell.

You are so loathsome and so old as well,
And your low birth besides is such a
  cross
It is no wonder that I turn and toss.
God take my woeful spirit from my
  breast!"
    "Is this," she said, "the cause of
    your unrest?"
    "No wonder!" said the knight. "It
    truly is:"
"Now sir," she said, "I could amend all
  this
Within three days, if it should please me
  to,
And if you deal with me as you should
  do.
    "But since you speak of that
    nobility
That comes from ancient wealth and
  pedigree,
As if that constituted gentlemen,
I hold such arrogance not worth a hen!
The man whose virtue is pre-eminent,
In public and alone, always intent
On doing every generous act he can,
Take him—he is the greatest gentleman!
Christ wills that we should claim nobility
From him, not from old wealth or family.
Our elders left us all that they were
  worth
And through their wealth and blood we
  claim high birth,
But never, since it was beyond their
  giving,
Could they bequeath to us their virtuous
  living;
Although it first conferred on them the
  name
Of gentlemen, they could not leave that
  claim!
    "Dante the Florentine on this was
    wise:
'Frail is the branch on which man's
  virtues rise'—
Thus runs his rhyme—"God's goodness
  wills that we

302   CHAPTER 10   ◆   The Artist Encounters Life

Should claim from him alone nobility
Thus from our elders we can only claim
Such temporal things as men may hurt
    and maim.
        "It is clear enough that true
        nobility
Is not bequeathed along with property,
For many a lord's son does a deed of
    shame
And yet, God knows, enjoys his noble
    name.
But though descended from a noble
    house
And elders who were wise and virtuous,
If he will not follow his elders, who are
    dead,
But leads, himself, a shameful life
    instead,
He is not noble, be he duke or earl.
It is the churlish deed that makes the
    churl.
And therefore, my dear husband, I
    conclude
That though my ancestors were rough
    and rude,
Yet may Almighty God confer on me
The grace to live, as I hope, virtuously.
Call me of noble blood when I begin
To live in virtue and to cast out sin.
        "As for my poverty, at which you
        grieve;
Almighty God in whom we all believe
In willful poverty chose to lead his life,
And surely every man and maid and
    wife
Can understand that Jesus, heaven's king,
Would never choose a low or vicious
    thing.
A poor and cheerful life is nobly led;
So Seneca and others have well said,
The man so poor he doesn't have a
    stitch,
If he thinks himself repaid, I count him
    rich.
He that is covetous, he is the poor man,
Pining to have the things he never can.

It is of cheerful mind, true poverty.
Juvenal says about it happily:
'The poor man as he goes along his way
And passes thieves is free to sing and
    play.'
Poverty is a good we loathe, a great
Reliever of our busy worldly state,
A great amender also of our minds
As he that patiently will bear it finds.
And poverty, for all it seems distressed,
Is a possession no one will contest.
Poverty, too, by bringing a man low,
Helps him the better both God and self
    to know,
Poverty is a glass where we can see
Which are our true friends, as it seems to
    me.
So, sir, I do not wrong you on this score;
Reproach me with my poverty no more.
        "Now, sir, you tax me with my age;
        but, sir,
You gentlemen of breeding all aver
That men should not despise old age, but
    rather
Grant an old man respect, and call him
    'father':
        "If I am old and ugly, as you have
        said,
You have less fear of being cuckolded,
For ugliness and age, as all agree,
Are notable guardians of chastity.
But since I know in what you take
    delight,
I'll gratify your worldly appetite.
        "Choose now, which of two
        courses you will try:
To have me old and ugly till I die
But evermore your true and humble
    wife,
Never displeasing you in all my life,
Or will you have me rather young and
    fair
And take your chances on who may
    repair
Either to your house on account of me
Or to some other place, it well may be.

Now make your choice, whichever you
    prefer."
        The knight took thought, and
        sighed, and said to her
At last, "My love and lady, my dear wife,
In your wise government I put my life.
Choose for yourself which course will
    best agree
With pleasure and honor, both for you
    and me.
I do not care, choose either of the two;
I am content, whatever pleases you."
        "Then have I won from you the
        sovereignty,
Since I may choose and rule at will?"
    said she.
        He answered, "That is best, I think,
        dear wife."
        "Kiss me," she said. "Now we are
        done with strife,
For on my word, I will be both to you,
That is to say, fair, yes, and faithful too.
May I die mad unless I am as true
As ever wife was since the world was
    new.
Unless I am as lovely to be seen
By morning as an empress or a queen
Or any lady between east and west,
Do with my life or death as you think best.

Lift up the curtain, see what you may
    see."
        And when the knight saw what
        had come to be
And knew her as she was, so young, so
    fair,
His joy was such that it was past
    compare.
He took her in his arms and gave her
    kisses
A thousand times on end; he bathed in
    blisses.
And she obeyed him also in full measure
In everything that tended to his pleasure.
        And so they lived in full joy to the
        end.
And now to all us women may Christ
    send
Submissive husbands, full of youth in
    bed,
And grace to outlive all the men we
    wed.
And I pray Jesus to cut short the lives
Of those who won't be governed by their
    wives;
And old, ill-tempered niggards who hate
    expense,
God promptly bring them down with
    pestilence!

NOTES

1. Richard Bowring, *Muraski Shikibu: The Tale of Genji* (Cambridge and New York: Cambridge University Press, 1988), 4–5.

2. In the original, she is also referred to as Princess Akikonomu. To make the already complicated story a little less confusing, we refer to her as Murasaki throughout.

3. *The Song of Roland*, trans. Glyn Burgess (London: Penguin Books, 1990), 114.

4. Ibid., 145–46.

5. Ibid., p. 61.

6. Ibid., p. 39.

7. Ibid., p. 38.

CHAPTER 11

The Encounter between War and Religion

INTRODUCTION

In the wake of September 11, 2001, President George W. Bush called for a "crusade" against terrorism. The crusading label was almost instantly withdrawn and repudiated because of the very problematic historical resonances it raised for the Islamic world, whose cooperation would be necessary in any attempt to deal with global terrorism. But in the Bush Administration's "war on terrorism" and in the subsequent real wars in Afghanistan and Iraq, the idea of a "clash of civilizations" (to use Samuel P. Huntington's simplistic phrase), of a set of wars at least partially informed by differences in religion, lurked just below the surface of official rhetoric and received explicit expression by religious extremists on both sides.

Yet talk of "holy war" in the modern world makes many people uncomfortable. The idea of aggressive warfare, in particular, being sanctioned by major religions whose central message focuses on peace, love, and brotherhood in a world whose United Nations Charter calls for religious freedom, tolerance, and respect for human rights strikes many as anachronistic and wrongheaded. In other words, war and religion in our modern world do not mix well. The very history that made President Bush's use of the term *crusade* problematic, however, shows that religion and warfare have long been linked historically—that religion and warfare encountered each other from early on. Why? And what was the nature of this encounter? This chapter explores some of the answers to those questions and examines the ways in which religious precepts, religiously inspired worldviews, and religiously based theories of "Just War" encountered and interacted with the practice of war itself.

Even before the rise of the salvation faiths, religion had been central to the worldview of most traditional civilizations, as we saw in chapter 4. This centrality became even more pronounced after the rise of the salvation religions, which we examined in chapters 8 and 9, as these religions assumed important roles even in areas such as China, where a dominant strand of that civilization's worldview was

308   CHAPTER 11   *   The Encounter between War and Religion

based in a secular philosophy, Confucianism. As a central part of a civilization's worldview, religion not only explained the cosmos and guided ethical thinking but also tended to be a, if not the, pillar of legitimacy for the governments of traditional states. This is where it came into contact with war making, for as we saw in chapter 5, and in a different form in chapter 7, states (and their nomadic neighbors) invariably and consistently conducted warfare for a whole range of reasons. What was a religion, especially one adopted as the official creed of an empire, to say about making war? The rise of the salvation religions, with their universalist claims, had the potential to raise the stakes in terms of government and warfare, for the outcome of wars could be seen from this perspective as signaling God's divine favor for one political faction or faith over another—religion and war could now produce, in short, "holy war." One key, then, to understanding the relationship of war and religion is to understand the relationship of religion to states, or the encounter of faith and power.

Attitudes compatible with holy war have their roots, especially in southwest Asia, in presalvationist religions that were closely tied to a particular people and so to a particular state. The Hebrew Scriptures are full of tales of God smiting the foes of the Israelites or ordering His people to fight for a homeland or their freedom. This sanctioning of warfare worked most easily when a Hebrew kingdom still existed, of course; once it ceased to, prophets such as Isaiah reinterpreted warfare in terms of God's universal plan for history. Yet the Persians, beneficiaries of this reinterpretation, already had their own universal-seeming but essentially exclusive religion in Zoroastrianism that also sanctioned the warfare of the Persian state unproblematically. In a similar but more restricted way in south Asia, Hinduism also sanctioned warfare on the part of the warrior caste, as represented in the *Bhagavad-Gita* and its tale of Arjuna's ethical dilemma. While subordinating warrior authority to priestly authority, at least in theory, Hindu thought still carved out a place for warfare among the tools of statecraft. (See chapter 4 for the *Gita*, Zoroastrianism, and Isaiah.)

The attitudes of Christianity, Islam, and Buddhism toward warfare were more complicated, and they are explored in the sources for this chapter. They stem from the "foundational events" of each religion, discussed in the introduction to chapter 9: the conversion of the Mauryan emperor Asoka in 261 BCE, the conversion of the Roman emperor Constantine in 312, and the career of Muhammad in the 620s. After his conversion, Asoka forswore offensive warfare, and as a rule afterward Buddhism had little to do with direct sanctioning of warfare, though in Japan after c. 1000 Buddhism, especially though not exclusively in its Zen form, came to be associated with the ethos of the *bushi*, the Japanese warrior class. But the tradition of *in hoc signo vinces*—"under this sign you will conquer"—established by Constantine linked Christianity with warfare from its earliest days as a state-favored religion, and Muhammad fought from early in his career to establish his community of believers, again linking warfare to the religion from its inception. It is not accidental that both religions between 300 and 1000 developed conceptions of holy war unknown in Buddhism. Some historians identify the first Christian "crusade" in the campaigns of the East Roman emperor Heraclius in the early 600s against the Persians, who themselves campaigned under the banner of a militant Zoroastrianism. The first wave of Islamic *jihad* then burst on both sides, swallowing the Persians and reducing the Byzantine Empire to a Holy Land under siege.

Still, there is a subtle but important difference in the way each religion was connected to warfare. Christianity always accepted the existence (indeed the necessity) of the state, having grown up under the Roman Empire at its height. Even as a minority and sometimes persecuted religion, the notion of "rendering unto Caesar" recognized the state and its functions, including warfare. (Christian pacifism was always the view only of a small minority.) Once Christianity became the state religion, the efforts of Christian thinkers were directed not toward arguing against war but toward arguing about when it was justified. Christian Just War theory was largely a product of the writings of Augustine of Hippo (354–430) and equated warfare with the other exercise of coercive force on the part of the state, law and justice. In short, Christianity accepted the state and therefore had to accept (and justify) at least some warfare.

Islam, on the other hand, developed from Arab tribal traditions that set themselves against the imperial state structures of Rome and Persia that dominated Southwest Asia in 600. Thus, as the scholars and jurists of the Islamic *ulema* came to define Islam in the two centuries after the initial Islamic conquests, a curious result emerged. Warfare in the form of *jihad* (literally "struggle") against unbelievers was unproblematic as an activity of the Islamic community, having been established by the Prophet himself. But the state, because it usually resembled by necessity the imperial structures of the Romans and Persians against whom the *ulema* defined Islam, came easily to be seen as essentially illegitimate, though not by definition. This left Islamic warfare as being acceptable in itself (though not against other Muslims), while the only structure capable of organizing such warfare was often not acceptable. As a result, there was a significant strain of Muslim thought that defined *jihad* in terms of the internal, individual struggle of individuals against evil, not in terms of a state-organized activity. At the same time, Islamic military systems came to rely on slave soldiers and frontier tribes—groups outside the mainstream of Islamic society—for manpower. In short, by rejecting the state (at least practical states), Islam made problematic the practice of warfare by Islamic communities.

Ironically, it was the Crusades, the culmination of the development of Christian notions of holy war, that by bringing holy war to Islam did much to revive the alternate tradition of *jihad* as real warfare rather than individual struggle. The First Crusade (1097–1101) is thus a crucial episode in the history of holy war for both Christianity and Islam, and it set the tone for relationships between the two civilizations for the next 400 years and beyond.

Despite all these differences, however, Christianity, Islam, and Buddhism all attempted in various ways to place restrictions on warfare—in practice, for example, Muslim Just War theory came to resemble Christian Just War theory fairly closely. On the other hand, religious differences often seemed not to restrict but to inflame the passions of war when peoples of different faiths fought each other. Our exploration of the encounter between religion and warfare in the period from 1100 to 1500 will examine both the similarities and the important divergences in the connection between war and different religions.

CHAPTER QUESTIONS

1. What is the relationship in each religion between cosmic order and earthly order? That is, what role does the religion take in ensuring peace in this life, as well as salvation in the next?

2. What impact does this connection have for individual followers of each religion in terms of waging warfare? Is it a duty? A necessary evil? A desired activity?

3. How did the nature of a belief system affect its interpretation of war? Did the ethical values of each religion require adjustment in the encounter with war? What are the overall similarities and differences in each religion's relationship to warfare compared with the others?

4. What do you think accounts for these similarities and differences?

5. Which view of the connection of religion and warfare seems most applicable to warfare in the twenty-first century? Why?

CHRISTIANITY AND WAR

Thomas Aquinas (1224–1274) was the greatest medieval Christian theologian, a teacher at universities in Paris and Rome and a prolific writer. His masterpiece, the *Summa Theologiae*, or *Summation of Theology*, explored Catholic Christian scholarship in a huge range of fields and represents the highpoint of the medieval synthesis of faith and reason. He wrote during the second century of crusading, when the major Crusades were being led by Louis IX of France. (Louis earned sainthood for his piety, not necessarily for the results of his crusades, which were consistently disasters.) He was therefore very familiar with the theological and ethical questions surrounding the exercise of force by Christian states.

Drawing on a number of sources, but most crucially on various writings of St. Augustine, Aquinas summarized Christian theories of Just War in one small part of the *Summa*. The structure of this section, like all the sections of the *Summa*, presents first the views with which Aquinas disagrees, stated as answers to a specific question (in this case "Is it always a sin to wage war?"). Aquinas then cites, under the heading "On the Other Hand," a quote from Scripture or some earlier theologian that calls the opposing position into question. Finally, under the heading "Reply," he presents his own case, which answers the points presented initially.

QUESTIONS TO CONSIDER

1. What conditions does Aquinas say are necessary for a war to be waged justly? What kinds of Christian behaviors must a warrior practice in order to make war just, according to Aquinas?

2. Do Aquinas's justifications of war answer adequately the arguments for war as a sin presented in the first part of the reading? How does this encounter between Christianity and war result in a "Christianized" ideal of warfare?

3. What sorts of authorities or sources back up his argument? In other words, how does the history of Christianity inform his answers? How important does religion seem to this theory?

4. How easy to fulfill are the conditions Aquinas lays out? Are they sufficient? Too restrictive? Not restrictive enough? In your opinion, is it possible while engaged in actual combat to maintain the Christian principles Aquinas lays out?

5. Are Aquinas's conditions universal? That is, do they work to describe the justness of modern wars, even if they are not waged by Christian states, or is this a culturally restricted view of the justness of war?

SUMMA THEOLOGIAE

Thomas Aquinas

Second Part of the Second Part, Question 40: Concerning War
Article 1. Is it always a sin to wage war?

THE FIRST POINT: 1. It would seem that it is always a sin to wage war. Punishments are meted out only for sin. But our Lord named the punishment for people who wage war when he said, "All who draw the sword will die by the sword" (Matthew 26.52). Every kind of war, then, is unlawful.

2. Moreover, whatever goes against a divine command is a sin. But war does that. Scripture says, "But I say this to you, offer the wicked man no resistance." (Matthew 5.39). Also, "Not revenging yourselves, my dearly beloved, but give place to [the] wrath [of God]" (Romans 12.19). War is always a sin then.

3. Besides, the only thing that stands as a contrary to the act of virtue is a sin. Now war is the contrary of peace. Therefore, it is always a sin.

4. Besides, if an action is lawful, practicing for it would be lawful, as is obvious in the practice involved in the sciences [e.g. medicine]. But warlike exercises which go on in tournaments are forbidden by the church, since those killed in such trials are denied ecclesiastical burial. Consequently, war appears to be plainly wrong.

ON THE OTHER HAND, Augustine says [commenting on John the Baptist's advice to the Roman soldiers in Luke 3.14], "If Christian teaching forbade war altogether, those looking for the salutary advice of the Gospel would have been told to get rid of their arms and give up soldiering. But instead they were told, 'Do violence to no man, be content with your pay.' If this ordered them to be satisfied with their pay, then it did not forbid a military career."

REPLY: Three things are required for any war to be just. The first is the authority of the sovereign on whose command war is waged. Now, a private person has no business

Source: Thomas Aquinas, *Summa Theologiae* in *Latin Text and English Translation, Introductions, Notes, Appendices, and Glossaries* (New York: McGraw-Hill, 1964–), Pt. 2, Qu. 40, Art. 1.

312 CHAPTER 11 ✦ The Encounter between War and Religion

declaring war. He can seek redress by appealing to the judgment of his superiors. Nor can he summon together whole people, which has to be done to fight a war. Since the care of the commonweal is committed to those in authority, they are the ones to watch over the public affairs of the city, kingdom, or province in their jurisdiction. And just as they use the sword in lawful defense against domestic disturbance when they punish criminals, as Paul says—"He does not bear the sword in vain, for he is God's minister, an avenger to execute wrath upon him that does evil" (Romans 13.4)—so they lawfully use the sword of war to protect the commonweal from foreign attacks. Thus it is said to those in authority, "Rescue the weak and the needy, save them from the clutches of the wicked" (Psalms 82.3). Hence Augustine writes, "The natural order conducive to human peace demands that the power to counsel and declare war belongs to those who hold the supreme authority."

Secondly, a just cause is required, namely that those who are attacked are attacked because they deserve it on account of some wrong they have done. So Augustine says, "We usually describe a just war as one that avenges wrongs, that is, when a nation or state has to be punished either for refusing to make amends for outrages done by its subjects, or to restore what it has seized injuriously."

Thirdly, the right intention of those waging war is required, that is, they must intend to promote the good and to avoid evil. Hence Augustine writes, "Among true worshippers of God, those wars are looked on as peace-making which are waged neither from aggrandizement nor cruelty, but with the object of securing peace, of repressing the evil and supporting the good." Now it can happen that, even given a legitimate authority and a just cause for declaring war, it may yet be wrong because of a perverse intention. So again Augustine says, "The craving to hurt people, the cruel thirst for revenge, the unappeased and unrelenting spirit, the savageness of fighting on, the lust to dominate, and suchlike—all these are rightly condemned in wars."

Hence: 1. On the first point, as Augustine says, "'To draw the sword' is to arm oneself and to spill blood without command or permission of superior or lawful authority." But if a private person uses the sword by the authority of the sovereign or judge, or a public person uses it through zeal for justice, and by the authority, so to speak, of God, then he himself does not 'draw the sword,' but is commissioned by another to use it. He thus does not deserve punishment. Still, even those who do use it sinfully are not always slain with the sword. Yet they will always 'die by the sword,' since they will be punished eternally for their sinful use of it unless they repent.

2. On the second point, these words, as Augustine says, must always be borne in readiness of mind, so that a man must always be prepared to refrain from resistance or self-defense if the situation calls for it. Sometimes, however, he must act otherwise for the common good or even for the good of his opponents. Thus Augustine writes, "One must do many things with a kind of benign severity with those who must be punished against their will. Now whoever is stripped of the lawlessness of sin is overcome for his own good, since nothing is unhappier than the happiness of sinners. It encourages guilty impunity, and strengthens bad will, the enemy inside us."

3. On the third point, even those who wage a just war intend peace. They are not then hostile to peace, except that evil peace which our Lord "did not come to send on the earth" (Matthew 10.34). So Augustine again says, "We do not seek peace in order to

wage war, but we go to war to gain peace. Therefore be peaceful even while you are at war, that you may overcome your enemy and bring him to the prosperity of peace."

4. On the fourth point, warlike exercises are not completely forbidden—only those which are excessive and dangerous, and end in killing and looting. In olden time, they presented no such danger. So, as Jerome writes, they were called "practices of arms" or "wars without blood."*

CHRISTIAN ACCOUNTS OF THE FIRST CRUSADE

In response to requests from the Byzantine Empire for mercenaries to help them fight the Sejuk Turks, who had overrun the heart of Asia Minor and taken much of the Holy Land in the decades after defeating the Byzantines at Manzikert in 1071, Pope Urban II (1088–1099) called for an armed pilgrimage to Jerusalem to free the Holy Land from the hands of the Saracens. Preaching first at Claremont, in France, in 1095, his call met an immediate and overwhelmingly enthusiastic response. A crusade (so called from the crosses those who took the pledge sewed onto their surcoats) resulted, the first of many, as it turned out. Our first selection is one version (of five that we have) of the speech Pope Urban II gave at Claremont in 1095 that launched the First Crusade.

It took two years for the expedition to get under way, and it was led not by any of the kings of Europe but by a motley assortment of second-rank rulers, mostly French, including the Count of Aquitaine and the Duke of Normandy. It achieved success beyond any reasonable expectation, defeating several Turkish armies along the way and surviving a ten-month siege at Antioch, the major city of northern Syria, in 1097–1098. After a siege during which the Crusaders nearly starved to death, they captured the city, only to be besieged in turn by a Turkish Muslim army under the Turkish amir of Mosul, Kerbogha. With morale at a critical low, the events described in the third selection took place. In June 1099 they reached Jerusalem, which was captured in a bloody massacre on July 15, 1099. Fulk of Chartres, the author of our fourth selection, participated in the storming of the city. This victory capped the creation of a set of Christian-ruled states along the eastern Mediterranean seaboard.

QUESTIONS TO CONSIDER

1. What are Pope Urban's reasons for urging the Franks (a term for the French and for western Europeans generally in much Crusading literature) to take up arms and go to the Holy Land? Could someone motivated to join the

---

*This is actually from a treatise on Roman military practices called *A Summary of Military Matters*, written around 400 CE by an imperial Roman administrator named Flavius Vegetius Renatus, and widely studied in the Middle Ages.

Crusade by Urban's speech approach the war in the way that Aquinas required for just war?

2. What is the tone of his speech in presenting these reasons? Is this a rational appeal, or an emotional one? Or both? How important is religion in the appeal? What motivations other than religious ones does Urban give? Does his presentation of the reasons for this war conform to the requirements for a Just War laid out by Aquinas?

3. How does the religion of Aquinas and Pope Urban compare with the popular conception of the connection of religion and war seen in the events at Antioch?

4. Does what happened at Jerusalem strike you as a logical outcome of Urban's appeal? Is it in conformity with Aquinas's conditions for a Just War?

5. What is the relationship of Christianity and warfare as it appears in this set of sources?

POPE URBAN PREACHES THE FIRST CRUSADE (1095)

The Version of Robert the Monk

Oh, race of Franks, race from across the mountains, race chosen and beloved by God as shines forth in very many of your works, set apart from all nations by the situation of your country, as well as by your catholic faith and the honor of the holy church! To you our discourse is addressed and for you our exhortation is intended. We wish you to know what a grievous cause has led us to your country, what peril threatening you and all the faithful has brought us.

From the confines of Jerusalem and the city of Constantinople a horrible tale has gone forth and very frequently has been brought to our ears, namely, that a race from the kingdom of the Persians,* an accursed race, a race utterly alienated from God, a generation forsooth which has not directed its heart and has not entrusted its spirit to God, has invaded the lands of those Christians and has depopulated them by the sword, pillage and fire; it has led away a part of the captives into its own country, and a part it has destroyed by cruel tortures; it has either entirely destroyed the churches of God or appropriated them for the rites of its own religion. They destroy the altars, after having defiled them with their uncleanness. They circumcise the Christians, and the blood of the circumcision they either spread upon the altars or pour into the vases of the baptismal font. When they wish to torture people by a base death, they perforate their navels, and dragging forth the extremity of the intestines, bind it to a stake; then with flogging they lead the victim around until the viscera having gushed forth the victim falls prostrate upon the ground. Others they bind to a post and pierce with arrows. Others they compel to extend their necks and then, attacking them with naked swords, at-

Source: Selected from Dana C. Munro, "Urban and the Crusaders," *Translations and Reprints from the Original Sources of European History*, Vol 1:2 (Philadelphia: University of Pennsylvania, 1895), 5–8.
*An archaic way of referring to the Turks.

Pope Urban Preaches the First Crusade (1095)   315

tempt to cut through the neck with a single blow. What shall I say of the abominable rape of the women? To speak of it is worse than to be silent.* The kingdom of the Greeks is now dismembered by them and deprived of territory so vast in extent that it can not be traversed in a march of two months. On whom therefore is the labor of avenging these wrongs and of recovering this territory incumbent, if not upon you? You, upon whom above other nations God has conferred remarkable glory in arms, great courage, bodily activity, and strength to humble the hairy scalp of those who resist you.

Let the deeds of your ancestors move you and incite your minds to manly achievements; the glory and greatness of king Charles the Great,[†] and of his son Louis, and of your other kings, who have destroyed the kingdoms of the pagans, and have extended in these lands the territory of the holy church. Let the holy sepulcher of the Lord our Savior, which is possessed by unclean nations, especially incite you, and the holy places which are now treated with ignominy and irreverently polluted with their filthiness. Oh, most valiant soldiers and descendants of invincible ancestors, be not degenerate, but recall the valor of your progenitors.

But if you are hindered by love of children, parents and wives, remember what the Lord says in the Gospel, "He that loveth father or mother more than me, is not worthy of me." "Every one that hath forsaken houses, or brethren, or sisters, or father, or mother, or wife, or children, or lands for my name's sake shall receive an hundred-fold and shall inherit everlasting life." Let none of your possessions detain you, no solicitude for your family affairs, since this land which you inhabit, shut in on all sides by the seas and surrounded by the mountain peaks, is too narrow for your large population; nor does it abound in wealth; and it furnishes scarcely food enough for its cultivators. Hence it is that you murder one another, that you wage war, and that frequently you perish by mutual wounds. Let therefore hatred depart from among you, let your quarrels end, let wars cease, and let all dissensions and controversies slumber. Enter upon the road to the Holy Sepulcher; wrest that land from the wicked race, and subject it to yourselves. That land which as the Scripture says "floweth with milk and honey," was given by God into the possession of the children of Israel. Jerusalem is the navel of the world; the land is fruitful above others, like another paradise of delights. This the Redeemer of the human race has made illustrious by His advent, has beautified by residence, has consecrated by suffering, has redeemed by death, has glorified by burial. This royal city, therefore, situated at the center of the world, is now held captive by His enemies, and is in subjection to those who do not know God, to the worship of the heathens. She seeks therefore and desires to be liberated, and does not cease to implore you to come to her aid. From you especially she asks succor, because, as we have already said, God has conferred upon you above all nations great glory in arms. Accordingly undertake this journey for the remission of your sins, with the assurance of the imperishable glory of the kingdom of heaven.

When Pope Urban had said these and very many similar things in his urbane discourse, he so influenced to one purpose the desires of all who were present, that they cried out, "It is the will of God! It is the will of God!" When the venerable Roman pontiff heard that, with eyes uplifted to heaven he gave thanks to God and, with his hand commanding silence, said:

---

*This list of charges is vastly exaggerated.

†Charlemagne.

316   CHAPTER 11   ◆   The Encounter between War and Religion

Most beloved brethren, today is manifest in you what the Lord says in the Gospel, "Where two or three are gathered together in my name there am I in the midst of them." Unless the Lord God had been present in your spirits, all of you would not have uttered the same cry. For, although the cry issued from numerous mouths, yet the origin of the cry was one. Therefore I say to you that God, who implanted this in your breasts, has drawn it forth from you. Let this then be your war-cry in combats, because this word is given to you by God. When an armed attack is made upon the enemy, let this one cry be raised by all the soldiers of God: It is the will of God! It is the will of God!

And we do not command or advise that the old or feeble, or those unfit for bearing arms, undertake this journey; nor ought women to set out at all, without their husbands or brothers or legal guardians. For such are more of a hindrance than aid, more of a burden than advantage. Let the rich aid the needy; and according to their wealth, let them take with them experienced soldiers. The priests and clerks of any order are not to go without the consent of their bishop; for this journey would profit them nothing if they went without permission of these. Also, it is not fitting that laymen should enter upon the pilgrimage without the blessing of their priests.

Whoever, therefore, shall determine upon this holy pilgrimage and shall make his vow to God to that effect and shall offer himself to Him as a living sacrifice, holy, acceptable unto God, shall wear the sign of the cross of the Lord on his forehead or on his breast. When, truly, having fulfilled his vow be wishes to return, let him place the cross on his back between his shoulders. Such, indeed, by the twofold action will fulfill the precept of the Lord, as He commands in the Gospel, "He that taketh not his cross and followeth after me, is not worthy of me."

THE FINDING OF THE HOLY LANCE AT ANTIOCH (1098)

The Account of the **Gesta Francorum**

There was a certain pilgrim of our army, whose name was Peter, to whom before we entered the city St. Andrew, the apostle, appeared and said: "What art thou doing, good man?"

Peter answered, "Who art thou?"

The apostle said to him: "I am St. Andrew, the apostle. Know, my son, that when thou shalt enter the town, go to the church of St. Peter. There thou wilt find the Lance of our Saviour, Jesus Christ, with which He was wounded as He hung on the arm of the cross." Having said all this, the apostle straightway withdrew.

But Peter, afraid to reveal the advice of the apostle, was unwilling to make it known to the pilgrims.

Source: August C. Krey, *The First Crusade: The Accounts of Eyewitnesses and Participants* (Princeton, NJ: Princeton University Press, 1921), 174–76.

However, he thought that he had seen a vision, and said: "Lord, who would believe this?" But at that hour St. Andrew took him and carried him to the place where the Lance was hidden in the ground. When we were a second time situated in such (straits) as we have stated above, St. Andrew came again, saying to him: "Wherefore hast thou not yet taken the Lance from the earth as I commanded thee? Know verily, that whoever shall bear this Lance in battle shall never be overcome by an enemy." Peter, indeed, straightway made known to our men the mystery of the apostle.

The people, however, did not believe (it), but refused, saying: "How can we believe this?" For they were utterly terrified and thought that they were to die forthwith. Thereupon, this man came forth and swore that it was all most true, since St. Andrew had twice appeared to him in a vision and had said to him: "Rise, go and tell the people of God not to fear, but to trust firmly with whole heart in the one true God and they will be everywhere victorious. Within five days the Lord will send them such a token that they will remain happy and joyful, and if they wish to fight, let them go out immediately to battle, all together, and all their enemies will be conquered, and no one will stand against them." Thereupon, when they heard that their enemies were to be overcome by them, they began straightway to revive and to encourage one another, saying: "Bestir yourselves, and be everywhere brave and alert, since the Lord will come to our aid in the next battle and will be the greatest refuge to His people whom He beholds lingering in sorrow."

Accordingly, upon hearing the statements of that man who reported to us the revelation of Christ through the words of the apostle, we went in haste immediately to the place in the church of St. Peter which he had pointed out. Thirteen men dug there from morning until vespers. And so that man found the Lance, just as he had indicated. They received it with great gladness and fear, and a joy beyond measure arose in the whole city.

BATTLE WITH KERBOGHA OUTSIDE ANTIOCH (1098)

The Account of the Gesta Francorum

[Inspired by the "discovery" of the Holy Lance, the Crusaders sallied out to do battle with their besiegers.]

At length, when the three days fast had been fulfilled, and a procession had been held from one church to another, they confessed their sins, were absolved, and faithfully took the communion of the body and blood of Christ; and when alms had been given they celebrated mass. Then six battle lines were formed from the forces within the city [taking the Holy Lance with them]. . . . Our bishops, priests, clerics, and monks, dressed in holy vestments, came out with us with crosses, praying and

Source: August C. Krey, *The First Crusade: The Accounts of Eyewitnesses and Participants* (Princeton, NJ: Princeton University Press, 1921), 182–85.

beseeching the Lord to make us safe, guard us, and deliver us from all evil. Some stood on the wall of the gate, holding the sacred crosses in their hands, making the sign (of the cross) and blessing us. Thus were we arrayed, and, protected with the sign of the cross, we went forth through the gate which is before the mosque.

After Kerbogha saw the lines of the Franks, so beautifully formed, coming out one after the other, he said: "Let them come out, that we may the better have them in our power!" But after they were outside the city and Kerbogha saw the huge host of the Franks, he was greatly frightened. He straightway sent word to his Emir, who had everything in charge, that if he saw a light burn at the head of the army he should have the trumpets sounded for it to retreat, knowing that the Turks had lost the battle. . . . Duke Godfrey, the Count of Flanders, and Hugh the Great rode near the water, where the enemy's strength lay. These men, fortified by the sign of the cross, together attacked the enemy first. When the other lines saw this, they likewise attacked. The Turks and the Persians in their turn cried out. Thereupon, we invoked the Living and True God and charged against them, and in the name of Jesus Christ and of the Holy Sepulchre we began the battle, and, God helping, we overcame them. But the terrified Turks took to flight, and our men followed them to the tents. Thereupon, the knights of Christ chose rather to pursue them than to seek any spoils. . . . The enemy, indeed, left their pavilions there, gold, silver, and many ornaments, also sheep, cattle, horses, mules, camels, asses, grain, wine, butter, and many other things which we needed. When the Armenians and Syrians who dwelt in those regions heard that we had overcome the Turks, they ran to the mountain to meet them and killed as many of them as they could catch. We, however, returned to the city with great joy and praised and blessed God, who gave the victory to His people. . . .

This battle was fought on the fourth day before the Kalends of July, on the vigil of the apostles Peter and Paul, in the reign of our Lord Jesus Christ, who has honor and glory forever and ever. Amen. And after our enemies had now been completely conquered, we gave fitting thanks to God, Three and One, and the Highest. Some of the enemy, exhausted, others, wounded in their flight hither and thither, succumbed to death in valley, forest, fields, and roads. But the people of Christ, that is, the victorious pilgrims, returned to the city, rejoicing in the happy triumph over their defeated foes.

THE SIEGE AND CAPTURE OF JERUSALEM (1099)

On the seventh of June the Franks besieged Jerusalem. . . . The Saracens defended themselves vigorously, and, with slings, very skillfully hurled back burning firebrands,

---

Source: Fulk (or Fulcher) of Chartres, *Gesta Francorum Jerusalem Expugnantium [The Deeds of the Franks Who Attacked Jerusalem]*, in Frederick Duncan and August C. Krey, eds., *Parallel Source Problems in Medieval History* (New York: Harper & Brothers, 1912), pp. 109–15.

The Siege and Capture of Jerusalem (1099)   319

which had been dipped in oil and fresh fat. Many on both sides, fighting in this manner, often found themselves in the presence of death.

. . . On the following day the work again began at the sound of the trumpet, and to such purpose that the rams, by continual pounding, made a hole through one part of the wall. The Saracens suspended two beams before the opening, supporting them by ropes, so that by piling stones behind them they would make an obstacle to the rams. However, what they did for their own protection became, through the providence of God, the cause of their own destruction. For, when the tower was moved nearer to the wall, the ropes that supported the beams were cut; from these same beams the Franks constructed a bridge, which they cleverly extended from the tower to the wall. About this time one of the towers in the stonewall began to burn, for the men who worked our machines had been hurling firebrands upon it until the wooden beams within it caught fire. The flames and smoke soon became so bad that none of the defenders of this part of the wall were able to remain near this place. At the noon hour on Friday, with trumpets sounding, amid great commotion and shouting "God help us," the Franks entered the city. When the pagans saw one standard planted on the wall, they were completely demoralized, and all their former boldness vanished, and they turned to flee through the narrow streets of the city. Those who were already in rapid flight began to flee more rapidly.

Count Raymond and his men, who were attacking the wall on the other side, did not yet know of all this, until they saw the Saracens leap from the wall in front of them. Forthwith, they joyfully rushed into the city to pursue and kill the nefarious enemies, as their comrades were already doing. Some Saracens, Arabs, and Ethiopians took refuge in the tower of David, others fled to the temples of the Lord and of Solomon. A great fight took place in the court and porch of the temples, where they were unable to escape from our gladiators. Many fled to the roof of the temple of Solomon, and were shot with arrows, so that they fell to the ground dead. In this temple almost ten thousand were killed. Indeed, if you had been there you would have seen our feet colored to our ankles with the blood of the slain. But what more shall I relate? None of them were left alive; neither women nor children were spared.

This may seem strange to you. Our squires and poorer footmen discovered a trick of the Saracens, for they learned that they could find byzants [note: a gold coin] in the stomachs and intestines of the dead Saracens, who had swallowed them. Thus, after several days they burned a great heap of dead bodies, that they might more easily get the precious metal from the ashes. Moreover, Tancred broke into the temple of the Lord and most wrongfully stole much gold and silver, also precious stones, but later, repenting of his action, after everything had been accounted for, be restored all to its former place of sanctity.

The carnage over, the crusaders entered the houses and took whatever they found in them. However, this was all done in such a sensible manner that whoever entered a house first received no injury from any one else, whether he was rich or poor. Even though the house was a palace, whatever he found there was his property. Thus many poor men became rich.

Afterward, all, clergy and laymen, went to the Sepulcher of the Lord and His glorious temple, singing the ninth chant. With fitting humility, they repeated prayers and made their offering at the holy places that they had long desired to visit.

ISLAM AND WAR

The fountainhead of any Islamic theory is the Qur'an. In the Qur'an, the Prophet Muhammad sanctioned warfare as one form of *jihad*, or the struggle to establish and spread the peace and justice of an Islamic community. By the time of the Crusades, Islamic jurists had developed the tenets of an Islamic theory of Just War. In this view, the world was divided into *Dar al-Islam*, the realm of peace and justice, and *Dar al-Harb*, the realm of chaos and war that brings misery to its inhabitants and whose continued existence poses an ongoing threat to the security of *Dar al-Islam*. It was the duty of true Islamic states to expand the realm of *Dar al-Islam* by preaching, writing, and if necessary conquest, so as to bring Muslim law and its benefits of peace and justice to the whole world. But certain conditions had to be met before a *jihad* was justified. There had to be a just cause for starting the war—note the essentially defensive injunction in Sura 2 in the reading. The targets of the *jihad* had first to be invited to convert or to pay tribute to the Islamic authority. A properly constituted Islamic authority had to declare the *jihad* (though what constituted a "proper Islamic authority" was open to dispute). Finally, the war had to be conducted according to broader Islamic values.

The selections from the Qur'an presented here are the key ones relating directly to warfare. As you read them, bear in mind the passages from the Qur'an presented in chapter 8 that define those broader Islamic values.

QUESTIONS TO CONSIDER

1. What are the key elements of *jihad* as presented in these passages? Is this about warfare alone?

2. Do they seem to support the Islamic theory of Just War outlined in the introduction to the selection? Do alternate interpretations seem possible?

3. How do these passages compare with Aquinas's writings in terms of the place of warfare in a faith-based world? Is religion more or less important than in Aquinas's theory?

4. Are the Qur'anic conditions for Just War universal? That is, do they work to describe the justness of modern wars, even if they are not waged by Muslim states, or is this a culturally restricted view of the justness of war? How do they compare with Aquinas in this sense?

THE QUR'AN

2. The Cow

*In the name of God,
Most Gracious, Most Merciful*

190.   Fight in the cause of God
Those who fight you,
But aggress not.
For God does not love aggressors.

191.   And slay them
Wherever you catch them,
And turn them out
From where they have
Turned you out.
For tumult and oppression
Are worse than slaughter.
But do not fight them
At the Sacred Mosque,
Unless they first
Fight you there.
But if they fight you,
Slay them.
Such is the reward
Of those who suppress
faith.

192.   But if they cease,
God is Oft-forgiving,
Most Merciful.

193.   And fight them on
Until there is no more
Tumult or oppression,
And there prevail
Justice and faith in God.
But if they cease,
Let there be no hostility,
Except to those
Who practice oppression.

9. The Repentance

5.   But when the forbidden months
Are past, then fight and slay
The pagans wherever you find
them,
And seize them, beleaguer
them,
And lie in wait for them
In every stratagem of war.
But if they repent
And establish regular prayers
And practice regular charity,
Then open the way for them.
For God is Oft-Forgiving,
Most Merciful.

6.   If one amongst the pagans
Ask you for asylum,
Grant it to him,
So that he may hear the Word
Of God. And then escort him
To where he can be secure.
That is because they are
Men without knowledge.

22. Pilgrimage

*In the name of God,
Most Gracious, Most Merciful*

78.   And strive [*jihad*] in His cause
As you ought to strive,
With sincerity and under
discipline.
He has chosen you, and has
Imposed no difficulties on you
In religion. It is the cult
Of your father Abraham.
It is He Who has named
You Muslims, both before

Source: The Holy Qur'an, trans. M. H. Shakir, 1983. Reprinted by permission of Tahrike Tarsile Qur'an, Inc.

322 CHAPTER 11 ◆ The Encounter between War and Religion

And in this Revelation,
That the Messenger may be
A witness for you, and you
Be witnesses for mankind!
So establish regular prayer,
Give regular charity,
And hold fast to God.
He is your Protector—
The best to protect
And the best to help.

25. The Criterion

In the name of God,
Most Gracious, Most Merciful

47. And He it is Who makes
The night as a robe
For you, and sleep as repose
And makes the day
As if it were a resurrection.

48. And He it is Who sends
The winds as heralds
Of glad tidings, going before
His Mercy, and We send down
Pure water from the sky—

49. That with it, We may give
Life to a dead land,
And slake the thirst
Of things We have created—
Cattle and men in great numbers.

50. And We have distributed
The water amongst them,
    in order
That they may celebrate
Our praises, but most men
Are averse to anything but
Rank ingratitude

51. Had it been Our Will,
We could have sent
A warner to every center
Of population,

52. Therefore listen not
To the Unbelievers,
But strive [*jihad*]
Against them with the utmost
Strenuousness, with the
    Qur'an.

Muslim Accounts of the First Crusade

Ibn al-Athir, whom we met in chapter 7 describing the Mongol attacks on Islamic lands, was a Muslim scholar whose most important work was *al-Kamil fi at-tarikh* ("The Complete History"), a history of the world. Born in Jazirat in 1160, he lived most of his life in Mosul but traveled widely in the Muslim lands of southwest Asia, including several trips to Baghdad, and later lived in Aleppo and Damascus. As a young man he spent time with Saladin's army in Syria as Saladin fought the Crusader states. He died in 1233 in Mosul. Here he tells the story of the origin of the Crusades as he had it and then describes the Frankish conquest of Jerusalem in 1099.

QUESTIONS TO CONSIDER

1. What were the causes of the Frankish attack on Muslim lands, according to al-Athir? What specific events characterize the events at Antioch and the conquest of Jerusalem for al-Athir?

2. How do his descriptions of these causes and events compare with the Christian accounts of the launching of the First Crusade, the siege of Antioch, and the conquest of Jerusalem? What are the differences and similarities? Al-Athir describes the same incidents as do the Western sources cited previously. What does his account tell us about Muslim attitudes concerning Just War?

3. Are the values and ideas expressed in the poem al-Athir quotes consistent with the Muslim ideal of Just War presented in the passages from the Qur'an? Can the values in this passage be reconciled with al-Athir's condemnation of the Christian Crusaders?

4. Does al-Athir think Muslim actions in these wars accord with Islamic values and the duty to *jihad*? Why or why not? Is this a Just War from the Muslim perspective? How do al-Athir's ideas on war compare with those expressed in the Qur'an? How do they compare with those expressed in Aquinas?

5. What is the relationship of Islam and warfare as it appears in this set of sources?

THE COMPLETE HISTORY

Ibn al-Athir

Origin of the Franks' Attack on Islam

The power of the Franks first became apparent when in the year 478/1085–86* they invaded the territories of Islam and took Toledo and other parts of Andalusia, as was mentioned earlier. Then in 484/1091 they attacked and conquered the island of Sicily[†] and turned their attention to the African coast. Certain of their conquests there were won back again but they had other successes, as you will see.

In 490/1097 the Franks attacked Syria. This is how it all began: Baldwin, their King,[‡] a kinsman of Roger the Frank who had conquered Sicily, assembled a great army and sent word to Roger saying: "I have assembled a great army and now I am on my way to you, to use your bases for my conquest of the African coast. Thus you and I shall become neighbours."

Roger called together his companions and consulted them about these proposals. "This will be a fine thing both for them and for us!" they declared, "for by this means these lands will be converted to the Faith!" At this Roger raised one leg and farted loudly and swore that it was of more use than their advice.[§] "Why?" "Because if

---

Source: From Francesco Gabrieli, *Arab Historians of the Crusades*, 3–4, 7–9, 10–12. Copyright © 1957 The Regents of the University of California. Reprinted with permission.

*Islamic date followed by CE date.

[†]This date clearly refers to the end of the Norman conquest [of Sicily].

[‡]This Baldwin (Bardawīl) is a composite character, compounded of the various Baldwins of Flanders and Jerusalem; or else the first Baldwin is mistakenly thought to have been already a king in the West.

[§]It is disagreeable to find the great count acting like a barbarian on the very first page, but the passage is characteristic of the contemptuous crudity with which the Muslims usually spoke of their enemies, as well as giving a fairly accurate picture of Roger's political acumen.

this army comes here it will need quantities of provisions and fleets of ships to transport it to Africa, as well as reinforcements from my own troops. Then, if the Franks succeed in conquering this territory they will take it over and will need provisioning from Sicily. This will cost me my annual profit from the harvest. If they fail they will return here and be an embarrassment to me here in my own domain. As well as all this Tamīm* will say that I have broken faith with him and violated our treaty, and friendly relations and communications between us will be disrupted. As far as we are concerned, Africa is always there. When we are strong enough we will take it."

He summoned Baldwin's messenger and said to him: "If you have decided to make war on the Muslims your best course will be to free Jerusalem from their rule and thereby win great honour. I am bound by certain promises and treaties of allegiance with the rulers of Africa." So the Franks made ready and set out to attack Syria.

Another story is that the Fatimids of Egypt were afraid when they saw the Seljuqids extending their empire through Syria as far as Gaza, until they reached the Egyptian border and Atsiz† invaded Egypt itself. They therefore sent to invite the Franks to invade Syria and so protect Egypt from the Muslims.‡ But God knows best.

The Finding of the Holy Lance and the Battle at Antioch

When Kerbogha heard that the Franks had taken Antioch he mustered his army and advanced into Syria. . . . All the Turkish and Arab forces in Syria rallied to him except for the army from Aleppo. . . . When the Franks heard of this they were alarmed and afraid, for their troops were weak and short of food. The Muslims advanced and came face to face with the Franks in front of Antioch. Kerbogha, thinking that the present crisis would force the Muslims to remain loyal to him, alienated them by his pride and ill-treatment of them. They plotted in secret anger to betray him and desert him in the heat of battle.

After taking Antioch the Franks camped there for twelve days without food. The wealthy ate their horses and the poor ate carrion and leaves from the trees. Their leaders, faced with this situation, wrote to Kerbogha to ask for safe-conduct through his territory but he refused, saying "You will have to fight your way out." . . . There was also a holy man [among the Franks] who had great influence over them, a man of low cunning, who proclaimed that the Messiah had a lance buried in the Qusyin, a great building in Antioch. "And if you find it you will be victorious and if you fail you will surely die." Before saying this he had buried a lance in a certain spot and concealed all trace of it. He exhorted them to fast and repent for three days, and on the fourth day he led them all to the spot with their soldiers and workmen, who dug everywhere and found the lance as he had told them. Whereupon he cried "Rejoice! For victory is secure." So on the fifth day they left the city in groups of five or six. The Muslims said to Kerbogha: "You should go up to the city and kill them one by one as they come out; it is easy to pick them off now that they have split up." He replied: "No, wait until

---

*The Zirid amir of Tunisia, Tarmīm ibn Mu'izz.

†A general of the Seljuqid [Turkish] Sultan Malikshāh, who in 1076 attacked Egypt from Palestine.

‡Of course the Fatimids [rulers of Egypt] were also Muslims, but they were *shi'a* "heretics" and so opposed to the rest of *sunni* Islam.

they have all come out and then we will kill them." He would not allow them to attack the enemy and when some Muslims killed a group of Franks, he went himself to forbid such behaviour and prevent its recurrence. When all the Franks had come out and not one was left in Antioch, they began to attack strongly, and the Muslims turned and fled. This was Kerbogha's fault, first because he had treated the Muslims with such contempt and scorn, and second because he had prevented their killing the Franks. The Muslims were completely routed without striking a single blow or firing a single arrow. . . . The only Muslims to stand firm were a detachment of warriors from the Holy Land, who fought to acquire merit in God's eyes and to seek martyrdom. The Franks killed them by the thousand and stripped their camp of food and possessions, equipment, horses and arms, with which they re-equipped themselves.

The Franks Conquer Jerusalem

Taj ad-Daula Tutūsh* was the Lord of Jerusalem but had given it as a fief to the amir Suqmān ibn Artūq the Turcoman. When the Franks defeated the Turks at Antioch the massacre demoralized them, and the Egyptians, who saw that the Turkish armies were being weakened by desertion, besieged Jerusalem under the command of al-Afdal ibn Badr al-Jamali.[†] Inside the city were Artūq's sons, Suqmān and Ilghazi, their cousin Sunij and their nephew Yaquti. The Egyptians brought more than forty siege engines to attack Jerusalem and broke down the walls at several points. The inhabitants put up a defense, and the siege and fighting went on for more than six weeks. In the end the Egyptians forced the city to capitulate, in sha'bān 489/August 1096.[‡] Suqmān, Ilghazi and their friends were well treated by al-Afdal, who gave them large gifts of money and let them go free. They made for Damascus and then crossed the Euphrates. Suqmān settled in Edessa and Ilghazi went on into Iraq. The Egyptian governor of Jerusalem was a certain Iftikhār ad-Daula, who was still there at the time of which we are speaking.

After their vain attempt to take Acre by siege, the Franks moved on to Jerusalem and besieged it for more than six weeks. They built two towers, one of which, near Sion, the Muslims burnt down, killing everyone inside it. It had scarcely ceased to burn before a messenger arrived to ask for help and to bring the news that the other side of the city had fallen. In fact Jerusalem was taken from the north on the morning of Friday 22, sha'bān 492/15 July 1099. The population was put to the sword by the Franks, who pillaged the area for a week. A band of Muslims barricaded themselves into the Oratory of David[§] and fought on for several days. They were granted their lives in return for surrendering. The Franks honoured their word, and the group left by night for Ascalon. In the Masjid al-Aqsa the Franks slaughtered more than 70,000

---

*A Syrian Seljuqid, Malikshlāh's brother.

†The Fatimid vizier.

‡If this date were correct, the connection with the fall of Antioch would no longer exist. In fact, the date given here is wrong: the Egyptians took Jerusalem in August 1098.

§The *Mihrāb Dawūd*, called the Tower of David in the European sources, is the citadel at Jerusalem. Not to be confused with a small sanctuary of the same name in the Temple precinct.

people, among them a large number of Imams and Muslim scholars, devout and ascetic men who had left their homelands to live lives of pious seclusion in the Holy Place. The Franks stripped the Dome of the Rock* of more than forty silver candelabra, each of them weighing 3,600 drams, and a great silver lamp weighing forty four Syrian pounds, as well as a hundred and fifty smaller silver candelabra and more than twenty gold ones, and a great deal more booty. Refugees from Syria reached Baghdad in Ramadan, among them the qadi Abu Sa'd al Hārawi. They told the Caliph's ministers a story that wrung their hearts and brought tears to their eyes. On Friday they went to the Cathedral Mosque and begged for help, weeping so that their hearers wept with them as they described the sufferings of the Muslims in that Holy City: the men killed, the women and children taken prisoner, the homes pillaged. Because of the terrible hardships they had suffered, they were allowed to break the fast.

It was the discord between the Muslim princes, as we shall describe, that enabled the Franks to overrun the country. Abu l-Muzaffar al-Abiwardi[†] composed several poems on this subject, in one of which he says:

We have mingled blood with flowing tears, and there is no room left in us
  for pity(?)
To shed tears is a man's worst weapon when the swords stir up the embers of war.
Sons of Islam, behind you are battles in which heads rolled at your feet.
Dare you slumber in the blessed shade of safety, where life is as soft as an orchard
  flower?
How can the eye sleep between the lids at a time of disasters that would waken any
  sleeper?
While your Syrian brothers can only sleep on the backs of their chargers, or in
  vultures' bellies!
Must the foreigners feed on our ignominy, while you trail behind you the train of a
  pleasant life, like men whose world is at peace?
When blood has been spilt, when sweet girls must for shame hide their lovely faces
  in their hands!
When the white swords' points are red with blood, and the iron of the brown lances
  is stained with gore!
At the sound of sword hammering on lance young children's hair turns white.
This is war, and the man who shuns the whirlpool to save his life shall grind his teeth
  in penitence.
This is war, and the infidel's sword is naked in his hand, ready to be sheathed again
  in men's necks and skulls.

---

*The rock from which, the Muslims believe, Muhammad ascended into heaven. Over it was built the so-called Mosque of 'Umar, the chief Islamic monument in Jerusalem. It was from this mosque that the conquerors took their booty. Nearby, but separate from it, is the 'Farthest Mosque' (al-Masjid al-Aqsa), where according to Ibn al-Athir the armies of the Cross showed even greater barbarity. The two sanctuaries are often confused in both Arabic and European sources.

[†]An Iraqi poet of the eleventh and twelfth centuries.

This is war, and he who lies in the tomb at Medina seems to raise his voice and cry: "O sons of Hashim!*

I see my people slow to raise the lance against the enemy: I see the Faith resting on feeble pillars.

For fear of death the Muslims are evading the fire of battle, refusing to believe that death will surely strike them."

Must the Arab champions then suffer with resignation, while the gallant Persians shut their eyes to their dishonour?

BUDDHISM AND WARFARE

The closest association between Buddhism and warfare developed in Japan. Because it was imported as the religion of the ruling courtly class, Buddhism was attractive for political reasons to the rural warrior class, the *bushi*, that began to emerge into prominence as the military arm of the court in the eleventh and twelfth centuries. Mahayana sects such as Pure Land Buddhism also carried the promise of life after death to a class whose profession forced it to face death frequently, though later, in the thirteenth and fourteenth centuries, Zen, which emphasized the ephemeral nature of life and laid stress on personal discipline and living each moment fully, became the most popular form of Buddhism for the *bushi*. Yet the promise of salvation carried a price, for Buddhism, like the other salvation religions, considered killing a sin, and made fewer concessions to the worldly, essentially political necessity that states exercise coercive force to maintain order. The potential conflicts this created for warriors whose role in government involved killing are illustrated in this selection.

The Tale of the Heike is the most famous of a whole set of medieval Japanese war tales. It tells the story of the Gempei War (1180–1185), the culmination of a civil war that split Japan between 1156 and 1185. It takes its name from the Chinese name of the losing side, a coalition of families led by the Heike (or Taira, in Japanese)—the Japanese war tales often focus on heroic losers rather than winners. Though initially successful, the Taira eventually met defeat at the hand of a set of clans led by the Genji (*Minamoto* in Japanese), whose leader, Minamoto Yoritomo, became Japan's first shogun in 1185. Even on the winning side, however, the emphasis is on tragic heroes, for the central figure of the tale is the Genji general Yoshitsune, Yoritomo's cousin, a brilliant general but naïve politician. After leading the Genji forces to victory, he is eliminated by Yoritomo as a potential rival. As you read this selection, think about the image of winners and losers from the perspective of Buddhist religious precepts.

---

*The Prophet, who from the tomb raises his voice to rebuke his descendants (the sons of Hashim), that is, the unworthy Caliphs whose opposition to the Crusades is only halfhearted.

328   CHAPTER 11   ◆   The Encounter between War and Religion

QUESTIONS TO CONSIDER

1. As it is shown here, what is the attitude of Japanese warriors toward killing and death?

2. What are the key precepts of Buddhism as the warriors understood them? How do these relate to their attitudes toward waging warfare?

3. How is the relationship of Japanese warriors to their religion and their duty similar to or different from that of Christian and Muslim warriors? Can you imagine a Christian Crusader anguishing over killing a foe in the way that Naozone does? Why or why not?

4. Given what we see here, do you think there could be a Buddhist theory of Just War?

5. What is the relationship of Buddhism and warfare as it appears in this set of sources?

THE TALE OF THE HEIKE

9.16. The Death of Atsumori

[Naozone, a warrior on the Genji side of the battle, captures Atsumori, a young court aristocrat from the Heike side. The following exchange then takes place.]

"I would like to spare you," he said, restraining his tears, "but there are Genji warriors everywhere. You cannot possibly escape. It will be better if I kill you than if someone else does it, because I will offer prayers on your behalf."

"Just take my head and be quick about it."

Overwhelmed by compassion, Naozone could not find a place to strike. His senses reeled, his wits forsook him, and he was scarcely conscious of his surroundings. But matters could not go on like that forever: in tears, he took his head.

"Alas, no lot is as hard as a warrior's. I would never have suffered such a dreadful experience if I had not been born into a military house. How cruel I was to kill him!"

He pressed his sleeve to his face and shed floods of tears. . . .

After that, Naozone thought increasingly of becoming a monk.

10.5. A Statement of Precepts

[Shigehira, a leader of the defeated Heike side, is captured. When he learns he is to be sent to the Genji headquarters to be executed, he requests of his captors that he be allowed to enter religious life.]

He summoned Toi no Jirō Sanehira. "I would like to become a monk. Do you think it could be arranged?"

Source: From *The Tale of the Heike*, trans. Helen Craig McCullough, 317, 333–35. Copyright © 1988 Stanford University Press. Reprinted with permission.

Sanehira transmitted the request to Yoshitsune, who reported it to Retired Emperor Go-Shirakawa. "We can probably do something about that after Yoritomo interviews him. It cannot be allowed at present," the Retired Emperor said.

"In that case," Shigehira said when he was told, "might I see a holy man who has been my teacher for many years? I would like to talk to him about the next life."

"What is his name?"

"He is the man known as Hōnenbō of Kurodani."

Sanehira assented. "I see no objection."

Overjoyed, the Middle Captain sent for the monk. "I must have been taken prisoner because I was destined to meet you again," he said in tears. "What ought I to do about the life to come? In the days when I was a man of some importance, I let myself be distracted by official duties and fettered by public affairs, too proud and arrogant to worry about my fate in the next world. And it was even worse after our luck ended and the disorders broke out: battling here and contending there, I was hampered by the evil desire to destroy others and save myself, perpetually unable to achieve purity of heart. In particular, there is the matter of the burning of the southern capital. Under orders from the court and the military, and because I could not refuse to serve the Emperor or to comply with the demands of the times, I went to Nara to end the monks' violence. The destruction of the temples was quite unanticipated—quite beyond anyone's power to prevent—but I was Commander-in-Chief at the time; and that, I suppose, is why all the blame fell on me. (I hear there is a saying, 'The man at the top is the man responsible,' or something of the sort.) I have come to realize that these present dreadful humiliations must all be regarded as punishments.

"Now I would like to shave my head, receive the precepts, and devote myself heart and soul to religious pursuits, but a man in my situation is not free to do as he pleases. Alas! Because today or tomorrow may bring my end, I fear I can perform no pious acts that would suffice to erase a single one of my sins. When I review my life, I understand that my evil deeds tower higher than Mount Sumeru, that my good ones amount to less than a speck of dust. Beyond any question, I am doomed to the Three Evil Paths if I die in this state. Please, Your Holiness, be compassionate and merciful. If there is a way to save such a sinner, tell me of it."

The holy man remained silent for a time, choked with tears. By and by, he began to speak. "It is a sorrow beyond sorrow that you should face the prospect of returning to the Three Evil Paths after having enjoyed the rare good fortune of being born a man. But the Buddhas of the Three Worlds must surely feel happiness because you have now abandoned wicked thoughts and embraced good ones, desirous of rejecting the impure world and achieving rebirth in the Pure Land. There are various ways of escaping from the world of illusion, but in these unclean, tumultuous latter days of the Law, the best one is to recite the name of Amida Buddha. The goal, the Pure Land, has been divided into nine grades, and the necessary pious acts have been compressed into six syllables, which even the most slow witted person can chant.* You must not depreciate yourself because you think you have committed grave sins: even those who are guilty of the Ten Evils and the Five Deadly Sins can attain rebirth if they

---

* *Namu amida butsu* ("Hail, Amida Buddha!").

330   CHAPTER 11   ◆   The Encounter between War and Religion

repent. Nor must you lose hope because you think you have performed few meritorious acts: Amida will come to meet anyone who has it in his heart to intone the sacred name one time or ten times. It is explained, 'He who intones the sacred name with all his heart will enter the Western Paradise.' It is taught, 'To intone Amida's name is to repent sins constantly.' Demons cannot approach the person who trusts in the words, 'Amida's name is a sharp sword.' It is written that a man's sins will all vanish if he recites, 'A single Buddha invocation washes away all sins.'

"I have tried to summarize the essential elements of the Pure Land faith: these quotations may be considered its basic teachings. But belief is the key to rebirth. You must believe with all your heart: never, never entertain a doubt. If you believe these teachings without reservation, and if you meditate on Amida Buddha in your heart and keep his name on your lips, always and everywhere, whether you are walking, standing, sitting, or lying down, there can be no doubt that at the hour of death you will leave this cruel world for the Pure Land from which there is no return."

The instructive discourse delighted the Middle Captain. "I would like to receive the commandments now. May I do so without becoming a monk?"

"It is quite common for a layman to receive them." The holy man touched a razor to Shigehira's forehead, made shaving motions, and administered the Ten Commandments. Shigehira received the precepts with tears of joy streaming down his face, and Hōnen also wept as he spoke, moved by deep compassion and sympathy.

Shigehira told Tomotoki to fetch a certain inkstone, one he had deposited with a samurai whose house he had frequented for poetry and music sessions. Then he presented it to the holy man as a pious offering. "Please do not give this away," he said, weeping. "Keep it where you can see it always, and whenever you remember, 'That object belonged to Shigehira once,' think of it as though it were myself and recite the sacred name. I would be truly grateful if you could chant an occasional scroll of holy writ on my behalf when you have the time." Unable to reply, Hōnen put the inkstone in his bosom and went home in tears, wringing the sleeves of his black robe.

CHAPTER 15

Expanding Global Encounters in the Fourteenth through Sixteenth Centuries

INTRODUCTION

Beginning in the mid-fifteenth century, European nations began to send explorers, merchants, missionaries, and colonizers throughout the rest of the world. Historians have often called this the "Age of Discovery," in which enterprising Portuguese and Spanish explorers took the lead in developing new sailing skills to traverse the unknown seas, discovering new lands and peoples, and initiating a new phase of global encounters that was unprecedented and unmatched in human history. In other words, the so-called Age of Discovery has commonly been portrayed as exclusively European and historically unique. But such accounts of world history are misleading and incomplete. It was certainly not a unique event, for exploration and expansion are as old as the history of mankind.[1] It was also not uniquely European. Centuries before Columbus set out from Spain in 1492, Muslim and Chinese explorers and traders had pioneered routes overland and by sea that served to link together the peoples, goods, and ideas of Asia, Arabia, and Africa. Moreover, such historical accounts do not reveal much about the essence of these voyages—the motivations, attitudes, and cross-cultural perceptions that were to have long-term consequences far beyond the initial period of "discovery."

This chapter explores the theme of exploration through the voyage diaries and chronicles of four of the most widely traveled men of the fourteenth through sixteenth centuries: Ibn Battuta, whose journeys in the mid-fourteenth century took him throughout the vast extent of the Islamic world; Zheng He, a Chinese admiral who sailed as far as the coast of east Africa in the mid-fifteenth century; Vasco da Gama, the Portuguese sea captain who was the first European to reach India by sea in 1498; and Christopher Columbus, who inadvertently "discovered" the Americas as he sought a western sea route to the spice markets of Asia. The accounts of these travelers are fascinating and useful for the detailed historical information they convey about different civilizations and cultures in the fourteenth through sixteenth centuries.[2] Moreover, they allow us to examine and assess the personal motives and actions of explorers, the nature of their experiences and contacts, and, most important, the formation of cross-cultural perceptions and attitudes.

The first voyager we shall examine is Ibn Battuta (1304–1369), a Muslim from Morocco, who was so enthralled by the sights he witnessed on his way to complete the *hajj*[3] in Mecca that he afterward devoted his life to traveling throughout most of the Muslim world, covering an estimated 75,000 miles. Such distances should not be too surprising, for the Islamic world had grown to be one of the largest, wealthiest, and most dynamic civilizations in the world by the fourteenth century. In the years following Muhammad's proclamation of the new faith in Arabia during the seventh century, Islam had spread quickly westward across north Africa and into Iberia (Spain and Portugal) and eastward into Syria and Persia (Iran). In subsequent centuries, Islam continued to expand into northern India and Asia, along the coast of east Africa, and even across the Sahara Desert into west Africa.

Although the Islamic world was rarely unified politically, Muslims were partially bound by religion and commerce. Islam offered a set of common laws and values to its adherents that helped to provide a bond of unity and common identity that transcended ethnic and regional differences. Equally important, the establishment of long-distance trading networks linked Muslim producers and consumers from different regions, as well as with peoples of different religions. In their quest for spices, gold, and other luxury commodities, Muslim traders organized camel caravans to the frontiers of India and across the Sahara in Africa, while organizing equally profitable trade routes by sea across the Indian Ocean. By the time of the first European arrivals in the late fifteenth century, most of the lands bordering the Indian Ocean were linked together in a dynamic and prosperous trade that was under the near monopolistic control of Muslim traders and businessmen.

Such extensive trade networks had important consequences for world history. First, it promoted a parallel development in industry and export production throughout the Islamic world. By the fourteenth century, for example, Persia was renowned for its exquisite glassware, jewelry, and pottery; Morocco for its finely-worked leather goods; and Syria for its durable cotton fabrics. Trade and industry also helped to create an urban, cosmopolitan society. The hub of Islamic civilization lay in its great cities, such as Cairo, Damascus, Baghdad, Timbuktu, and Zanzibar, that straddled major trade routes. The commercial opportunities and sophisticated culture found in these cities attracted residents from far-flung regions, resulting in a rich intermingling of different cultures. Finally, the expansion of trade and cultural contacts helped to spread Islam and elements of Islamic culture to more distant regions, such as the Delhi Sultanate (India) and the west African kingdom of Mali. In fact, some scholars suggest that one of Ibn Battuta's primary goals in his travels was to observe and record the successful expansion of Islam in much of the known world.

In terms of wealth, advanced industry, and technology, China was at least the equal of the Islamic world. But whereas Islam was expanding along with its commerce in the mid-fourteenth century, China was just emerging from a period of foreign conquest and occupation by the Mongols.[4] Eager to assert its power and influence, the first emperors of the new Ming dynasty (1368–1644) launched an

424   CHAPTER 15   ◆   Expanding Global Encounters in the Fourteenth through Sixteenth Centuries

ambitious new foreign policy based on sea power. Although China has traditionally been viewed as a land power, it has had a long seafaring tradition, and Chinese vessels had sailed to India as early as the Han dynasty (202 BCE–200 CE). China also possessed important maritime technologies to make long-distance travel possible, including the compass, large multimasted ships, and shipboard rockets. Under the early Ming emperors, China organized seven major expeditions between 1405 and 1422, which were led by the capable and daring Chinese admiral Zheng He.

In sheer scope and scale, Zheng He far surpassed the European maritime voyages that occurred later. His armada was several times the size of the fleets commanded by Columbus, and his ships were more than six times bigger. With approximately 300 vessels and 27,000 sailors, Zheng He visited ports in southeast Asia, India, Persia, Arabia, and east Africa. His primary mission was political: to display Chinese might, to collect tribute from subordinate "barbarians" in other lands, and to ferry foreign diplomats to the Chinese emperor's court. In exchange for tribute, Zheng He delivered gifts of fine porcelain dishes, silks, gold and silver, and manufactured goods. But as his travel record also shows, he was prepared and able to use military force to demand deference and to assert his superiority.

After 1422, the great maritime expeditions of China ended abruptly. Historians have proposed several different theories to explain this sudden halt, suggesting that the voyages were too costly, that funds were needed for the construction of the Great Wall, or that the expeditions were seen as counter to Confucian ideals.[5] Nonetheless, the seven voyages of Zheng He had long-term impact. They extended China's political hegemony overseas, promoted the emigration of Chinese into regions of southeast Asia, and reinforced an international tribute system that continued into the nineteenth century.

In comparison with Chinese and Islamic civilizations, Europe was relatively poor, undeveloped, and isolated during much of the fourteenth and fifteenth centuries. The economy was still small, largely agricultural, and organized to meet local needs. Although the Crusades had created a new demand for spices and luxury items from Asia, Europeans remained mostly dependent on Muslim merchants and middlemen. Europe was also politically fragmented, and scarce resources and manpower were spent in innumerable wars and conflicts. And finally, beginning in the mid-fourteenth century, the Black Death (bubonic plague) struck Europe, killing millions, further weakening economies, and creating a widespread climate of fear and xenophobia.[6] From a global perspective, Europe was insular, backward, and unsophisticated.

The initial European drive to explore and expand began in Iberia, and it was fueled by a mixture of political, religious, and commercial motives. For centuries, Portuguese and Spanish Christians had struggled to expel the Moors (Muslim Arabs) who had ruled their lands ever since the eighth century. The *Reconquista*[7] of Iberia by Christian armies created an intense religious fervor and missionary zeal among the warring Christians, and it also generated a new sense of unity and national identity. With the successful expulsion of Muslims from Iberia in the fourteenth and fifteenth centuries, Spain and Portugal emerged as strong, dynamic, and consolidated monarchies, eager to continue the offensive against the hated Moors.

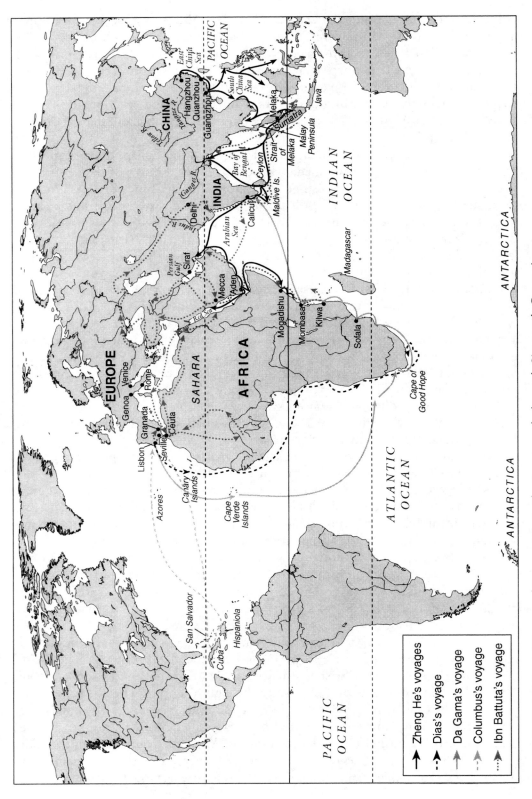

Map 15.1 Global Expeditions and Encounters in the Fourteenth through Sixteenth Centuries

426   CHAPTER 15   ◆   Expanding Global Encounters in the Fourteenth through Sixteenth Centuries

One of the major proponents and patrons of expansion was Prince Henry the Navigator (1394–1460), the third son of King John I of Portugal. Under Henry's auspices, the Portuguese improved ship designs and sailing technologies that allowed voyages to venture farther from their home ports, which culminated in the 1488 voyage of Bartholomeu Dias around Africa's southern Cape of Good Hope (South Africa). Equally important, Henry provided a grand strategy to gain profit and fight the Muslim enemy at the same time by outflanking their trade routes and establishing direct European contact with the rich markets and producers of Africa and Asia. It was also Henry's goal that Europeans discover and make alliances with long-lost Christian monarchs such as Prester John, a wayward Crusader who was believed to have established a large Christian kingdom somewhere in the east. Although Prester John proved to be a myth, such intense religious ideals profoundly shaped European attitudes and actions in their initial encounters with peoples from distant lands.

Less than four decades after Prince Henry's death, Vasco da Gama departed from Portugal in 1497, determined to find a direct sea route to India and Asia. After rounding the Cape of Good Hope in four medium-sized boats with only 168 men, his first stops were at several wealthy city-states situated along the east coast of Africa in what is now Mozambique, Tanzania, and Kenya. Here he found cosmopolitan cities and a thriving trading network controlled by Muslims, but no Christians, and his stay was marked by mutual suspicion and violence. Da Gama then sailed on to India, but here his efforts to conclude commercial treaties with rulers were largely unsuccessful because European trade goods were not highly desired. Still, he returned to Portugal with his ships filled with spices and precious stones, inspiring more commercial ventures and a greater determination than ever to seize control of the Indian Ocean trade from the Muslims.

While the Portuguese were exploring eastern trade routes to India and Asia, Christopher Columbus was determined to find a western route. In 1492, after winning the patronage and financial support of the Spanish monarchy, Columbus set sail from Europe in three small ships with only 120 men. After a voyage of just over thirty days, Columbus sighted the Bahamas and then found and explored Cuba and Haiti, which he initially confused with Japan and China. Although Columbus remained disappointed that he did not find the western route to Asia (and he tried again on three more subsequent voyages), he declared himself "enchanted" with the land and peoples he "discovered," which he described in great detail in a letter to the Spanish monarchs King Fernando and Queen Ysabel.

The early voyages of the Portuguese and Spanish had immediate and long-term consequences for world history. By the sixteenth and seventeenth centuries, these initial European travelers were joined (and eventually overshadowed) by explorers and merchants from the Netherlands, Britain, and France, who joined in the conquest and colonization of the Americas and in the establishment of trading routes and depots elsewhere. With superior military might, as well as the willingness to use it, Europeans were eventually able to extend their commercial and political influence over large parts of the world. This age of expansion also initiated a process of biological exchange, whereby plants, animals, and various diseases were able to migrate beyond their original ecological environments into new areas. Historical research has shown that the so-called Columbian Exchange[8] has had a very uneven historical impact. Although the introduction of crops such as corn and the potato from the Americas to Europe may have initiated a dramatic increase in population by the eighteenth century, the global dispersion of diseases such as smallpox, syphilis, and bubonic plague decimated entire regional populations.

The readings included in this chapter provide the opportunity to explore the process of exploration and expansion in greater depth and to make comparisons between the four case studies. One of the most important themes to keep in mind is the formation and impact of cross-cultural perceptions and attitudes. Are there any commonalities in the ways people first viewed "others"? What are the most important factors that shape opinions, beliefs, and behaviors? How does one's own culture and values shape one's view of the world? What lasting impact might these initial encounters have had on subsequent meetings?

CHAPTER QUESTIONS

1. When the four travel accounts are compared, what were the most important motivations that underlay the age of expansion? How did explorers see themselves and their mission? How did their expressed motives compare with the ones that are revealed in their descriptions of their discoveries and experiences?

2. What kinds of observations and experiences were recorded by the explorers? What do they tell us about different cultures? Existing trade routes? What kind of information seems to be missing from these accounts?

3. What role did religion play in the motives and experiences of the explorers? How were beliefs used to justify actions? What are the implications?

4. How were cross-cultural ideas formed? Were they the result of actual experiences and observations? Or were they the result of preexisting values and cultural biases? What general conclusions can be made?

5. In what ways, if any, were the European voyages of exploration unique? Examine the relationship between motives, experiences, attitudes, and long-term consequences. Do you think world history would have been radically different if China and Zheng He had "discovered" Europe in the early fifteenth century?

IBN BATTUTA'S TRAVELS IN THE ISLAMIC WORLD

Even by our modern measures, the travels of Abu Abdullah Muhammad Ibn Battuta (1304–1369) are extraordinary. Over a period of nearly thirty years, he is estimated to have traveled 75,000 miles and visited regions that now comprise over forty modern nations (see Map 15.2). Born in 1304 at Tangier, Morocco, to a family of legal scholars, Ibn Battuta initially planned to become a judge, and he pursued a legal education. But his journey to Mecca for the *hajj* when he was

428 CHAPTER 15 ◆ Expanding Global Encounters in the Fourteenth through Sixteenth Centuries

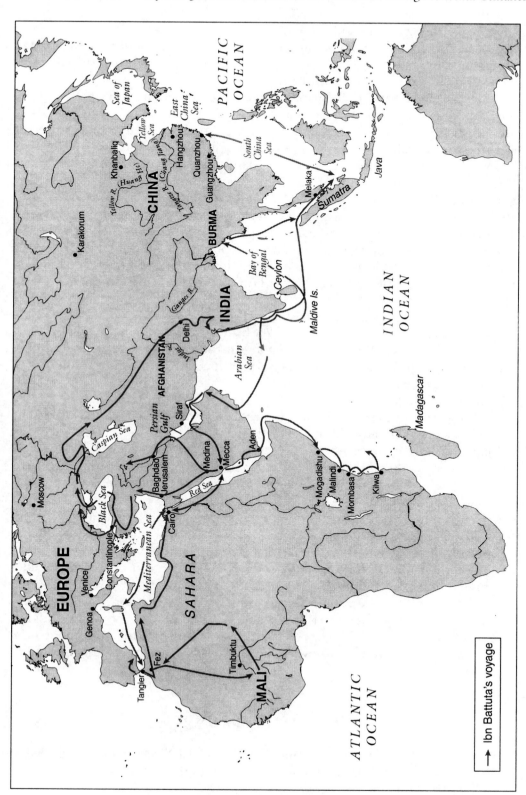

Map 15.2 Ibn Battuta's Travels

→ Ibn Battuta's voyage

twenty-one forever changed his life. Fascinated by his long journey across north Africa, he determined to devote his entire life to traveling in different lands and observing different cultures. He reportedly had only two rules: to visit only Muslim countries, and never to travel the same road twice.

For the most part, Ibn Battuta followed his own rules. He first traveled the lands of the Middle East, crossed the Arabian desert, and visited the cities of present-day Iraq and Iran. In 1330, he changed directions and sailed down the Red Sea to the Indian Ocean, stopping along the way at trading towns situated along the coast of east Africa. Two years later, he journeyed through southern Russia and Afghanistan to India, where he was appointed a regional judge by the Sultan of Delhi. After five years' service, he recommenced his journeys and traveled to China, Burma, and Sumatra (Indonesia). After a short return home to Tangier, he departed on his last major trip in 1349, a trek across the Sahara Desert to visit the kingdom of Mali in west Africa. Upon his return, he finished writing his travel accounts while residing as an honored guest at the court of Sultan Abu Inan of Morocco. Unfortunately, little is known about the final two decades of his life before he died in 1369.

Some historians contend that Ibn Battuta's chronicles are occasionally fictional and sometimes prone to errors. Yet his record of observations and experiences provides a wealth of information about the social structures and cultural values of many different lands in the fourteenth century. In some regions of the world, such as the interior regions of Africa, his account of different African societies is one of the few remaining recorded sources for this time period. Although he focused most of his attention on the ruling classes in the areas he visited, he also recorded a wide range of human activities, from the royal ceremonies of the Malian king to farming techniques in imperial China. Indeed, some biographers of Ibn Battuta contend that it was his deep personal interest in people and their customs that led him to record and assess in such great detail the practices, beliefs, and daily life of different societies.

The reading that follows provides brief excerpts from three of Ibn Battuta's trips. The first excerpt recounts his visit to the holy sites of Medina and Mecca[9] in 1326, early in his career as a world traveler. Here his account is very favorable, focusing on the kindness and cleanliness of residents. The second excerpt includes his observations while visiting China around 1340, one of the few non-Muslim areas that he visited. Although he was impressed with the prosperity found in China, he ultimately judged that the country "did not attract me" because of its "heathendom." The final excerpt focuses on Ibn Battuta's journey to the Kingdom of Mali in west Africa, where he finds cultural attributes to praise and to condemn.

QUESTIONS TO CONSIDER

1. Compare and contrast Ibn Battuta's descriptions of Mecca, China, and Mali. What commonalities are found in each description? What does he find to praise? What does he condemn?

430   CHAPTER 15   ◆   Expanding Global Encounters in the Fourteenth through Sixteenth Centuries

2. Using his descriptions as evidence, what were some of the underlying motives that inspired his travels? In what ways might these motives shape or distort his observations?

3. Identify the most important assumptions, values, or attitudes that helped shape his assessments about other cultures. Is it possible to be an "objective" world traveler?

4. Given his selective observations and value judgments, can Ibn Battuta's travel accounts be used as a reliable source of historical information?

5. Imagine that Ibn Battuta had been able to visit France or England during his travels. What kind of observations do you think he might have made? Would he have had a favorable impression of Europe during this time period? Why?

MY TRAVELS (1355)

Ibn Battuta

I left Tangier, my birthplace, on June 14, 1325, being at that time twenty-one years of age with the intention of making the Pilgrimage to the Holy House [at Mecca] and the Tomb of the Prophet [at Medina].

I set out alone, finding no companion to cheer the way with friendly intercourse, and no party of travelers with whom to associate myself. Swayed by an overmastering impulse within me, and a long-cherished desire to visit those glorious sanctuaries, I resolved to quit all my friends and tear myself away from my home. As my parents were still alive, it weighed grievously upon me to part from them, and both they and I were afflicted with sorrow. . . .

Visiting the Holy Sites of Medina & Mecca

[One] evening . . . we entered the holy sanctuary and reached the illustrious mosque, halting in salutation at the Gate of Peace; then we prayed in the illustrious garden between the tomb of the Prophet and the noble pulpit, and reverently touched the fragment that remains of the palm-trunk against which the Prophet stood when he preached. Having paid our respects to the lord of men from first to last, the intercessor for sinners, the Prophet of Mecca, Muhammad . . . we returned to our camp, rejoicing at this great favor bestowed upon us, praising God for our having reached the former abodes and the magnificent sanctuaries of His Holy Prophet, and praying [to] Him to grant that this visit should not be our last and that we might be of those whose pilgrimage is accepted.

On this journey, our stay at Medina lasted four days. We used to spend every night in the illustrious mosque, where the people, after forming circles in the courtyard and, lighting large numbers of candles, would pass the time either in reciting the Koran from volumes set on rests in front of them, or in intoning litanies, or in visiting

Source: Ibn Battuta, *Travels in Asia and Africa, 1325–1354,* trans. H. A. R. Gibb (London: Routledge, 1929), 43, 74–76, 282–84, 292, 321–25, 329.

the sanctuaries of the holy tomb. . . . We departed at night . . . with hearts full of joy at reaching the goal of our hopes, and in the morning arrived at the City of Surety, Mecca (may God ennoble her!), where we immediately entered the holy sanctuary and began the rites of pilgrimage.

The inhabitants of Mecca are distinguished by many excellent and noble activities and qualities, by their beneficence to the humble and weak, and by their kindness to strangers. When any of them makes a feast, he begins by giving food to the religious devotees who are poor and without resources, inviting them first with kindness and delicacy. The majority of these unfortunates are to be found by the public bakeries, and when anyone has his bread baked and takes it away to his house, they follow him and he gives each one of them some share of it, sending away none disappointed. Even if he has but a single loaf, he gives away a third or a half of it, cheerfully and without any ill-feeling.

Another good habit of theirs is this. The orphan children sit in the bazaar, each with two baskets, one large and one small. When one of the townspeople comes to the bazaar and buys cereals, meat and vegetables, he hands them to one of these boys, who puts the cereals in one basket and the meat and vegetables in the other and takes them to the man's house, so that his meal may be prepared. Meanwhile the man goes about his devotions and his business. There is no instance of any of the boys having ever abused their trust in this matter, and they are given a fixed fee of a few coppers.

The Meccans are very elegant and clean in their dress, and most of them wear white garments, which you always see fresh and snowy. They use a great deal of perfume and kohl and make free use of toothpicks of green arak-wood. The Meccan women are extraordinarily beautiful and very pious and modest. They too make great use of perfumes to such a degree that they will spend the night hungry in order to buy perfumes with the price of their food. They visit the mosque every Thursday night, wearing their finest apparel; and the whole sanctuary is saturated with the smell of their perfume. When one of these women goes away the odor of the perfume clings to the place after she has gone.

Voyage to China

The land of China is of vast extent, and abounding in produce, fruits, gold, and silver. In this respect there is no country in the world that can rival it. It is traversed by the river called the "Water of Life."* It is bordered by villages, fields, fruit gardens, and bazaars, just like the Egyptian Nile, only that [China] is even more richly cultivated and populous. . . . All of the fruits we have in our country are to be found here, either the same or better quality. . . . [As for Chinese pottery], it is exported to India and other countries, even reaching us as far as our own lands in the West, and it is the finest of all makes of pottery.

The Chinese themselves are infidels, who worship idols and burn their dead like the Hindus. The king of China is a Tatar [Mongol], one of the descendants of Genghis Khan. In every Chinese city there is a quarter for Muslims, in which they live by themselves, and in which they have mosques both for Friday services and for other religious

---

*Most scholars believe that Ibn Battuta is referring to China's "Grand Canal," one of the world's oldest (begun in 486 BCE) and largest (over 1,000 miles long) man-made waterways.

432   CHAPTER 15   ◆   Expanding Global Encounters in the Fourteenth through Sixteenth Centuries

purposes. The Muslims are honored and respected. The Chinese infidels eat the flesh of swine and dogs, and sell it in their markets. They are wealthy folk and well-to-do, but they make no display [of wealth] in their food or their clothes. You will see a principal merchant, a man so rich that his wealth cannot be counted, wearing a coarse cotton tunic. But one thing that the Chinese do take a pride in is gold and silver plate. Everyone of them carries a stick, on which they lean in walking, and which they call the third leg. . . .

The land of China, in spite of all that is agreeable in it, did not attract me. On the contrary, I was sorely grieved that heathendom had such a strong hold over it. Whenever I went out of my house I used to see any number of revolting things, and that distressed me so much that I used to keep indoors and go out only in case of necessity. When I met Muslims in China, I always felt just as though I were meeting with my own faith and kin. . . .

Travels to the Kingdom of Mali in West Africa

When I decided to make the journey to Mali, which is reached in twenty-four days from Walata [an oasis in the Sahara] if the traveler pushes on rapidly, I hired a guide . . . for there is no necessity to travel in a company on account of the safety of that road, and set out with three of my companions. . . .

A traveler in this country carries no provisions, whether plain food or seasonings, and neither gold nor silver. He takes nothing but pieces of salt and glass ornaments, which the people call beads, and some aromatic goods. When he comes to a village the womenfolk of the blacks bring out millet, milk, chickens, pulped fruit, rice . . . and pounded beans. The traveler buys whatever of these foods he wants. . . .

Thus I reached the city of Mali, the capital of the king of the blacks. I stopped at the cemetery and went to the quarter occupied by the whites [Arab merchants], where I asked for Muhammad ibn al-Faqih. I found that he had hired a house for me and went there. His son-in-law brought me candles and food, and next day Ibn al-Faqih himself came to visit me, with other prominent residents. I met the judge of Mali, Abd ar-Rahman, who came to see me; he is a Negro, a devout Muslim, and a man of fine character. I met also the interpreter Dugha, who is one of the principal men among the blacks. All these persons sent me hospitality gifts of food and treated me with the utmost generosity. May God reward them for their kindnesses! . . .

The sultan of Mali is Mansa Sulayman, "mansa" meaning [in Mandingo*] sultan, and Sulayman being his proper name. He is a miserly king, not a man from whom one might hope for a rich present. It happened that I spent these two months without seeing him, on account of my illness. Later on he held a banquet . . . to which the commanders, doctors, judges, and preachers were invited, and I went along with them. Reading desks were brought in, and the Koran was read through, then they prayed for . . . Mansa Sulayman.

When the ceremony was over I went forward and saluted Mansa Sulayman. The judge, the preacher, and [my host] Ibn al-Faqih told him who I was, and he answered them in their tongue. They said to me, "The sultan says to you 'Give thanks to God,'"

---

*Mandingo is an African language spoken by the Malinke people who reside in the grasslands south of the Sahara Desert.

so I said, "Praise be to God and thanks under all circumstances." When I withdrew, the [sultan's] welcoming gift was sent to me. . . . Ibn al-Faqih came hurrying out of his house barefooted, and entered my room saying, "Stand up; here comes the sultan's gift to you." So I stood up, thinking that it would consist of robes of honor and money, and behold! It was three cakes of bread, and a piece of beef fried in native oil, and a calabash of sour curds. When I saw this I burst out laughing, and thought it a most amazing thing that they could be so foolish and make so much of such a paltry matter. . . .

The Negroes possess some admirable qualities. They are seldom unjust, and have a greater abhorrence of injustice than any other people. Their sultan shows no mercy to anyone who is guilty of the least act of it. There is complete security in their country. Neither traveler nor inhabitant in it has anything to fear from robbers or men of violence. They do not confiscate the property of any white man who dies in their country, even if it be uncounted wealth. On the contrary, they give it into the charge of some trustworthy person among the whites, until the rightful heir takes possession of it. They are careful to observe the hours of prayer, and assiduous in attending them in congregations, and in bringing up their children to them. On Fridays, if a man does not go early to the mosque, he cannot find a corner to pray in, on account of the crowd. It is a custom of theirs to send each man his boy [to the mosque] with his prayer-mat; the boy spreads it out for his master in a place befitting him [and remains on it] until he comes to the mosque. Their prayer-mats are made of the leaves of a tree resembling a date-palm, but without fruit.

Another of their good qualities is their habit of wearing clean white garments on Fridays. Even if a man has nothing but an old worn shirt, he washes it and cleans it, and wears it to the Friday service. Yet another is their zeal for learning the Koran by heart. They put their children in chains if they show any backwardness in memorizing it, and they are not set free until they have it by heart. I visited the *qadi* [judge] in his house on the day of the festival. His children were chained up, so I said to him, "Will you not let them loose?" He replied, "I shall not do so until they learn the Koran by heart."

Among their bad qualities are the following. The women servants, slave-girls, and young girls go about in front of everyone naked, without a stitch of clothing on them. Women go into the sultan's presence naked and without coverings, and his daughters also go about naked. Then there is their custom of putting dust and ashes on their heads, as a mark of respect, and the grotesque ceremonies we have described when the poets recite their verses. Another reprehensible practice among many of them is the eating of carrion, dogs, and asses.

THE CHINESE NAVAL EXPEDITIONS OF ZHENG HE

In 1935, a Chinese official in Fujian province found a long-forgotten stone tablet that recounted one of the greatest series of naval expeditions in world history. The tablet briefly describes the seven voyages of the Chinese admiral, explorer, and diplomat Zheng He (1371–1435), who traveled as far as Arabia and the east coast

434 CHAPTER 15 ◆ Expanding Global Encounters in the Fourteenth through Sixteenth Centuries

of Africa and visited more than thirty present-day countries. Born in 1371 in Yun-nan (Kunyang) province, he was drafted at age ten to serve as an orderly in the army, which had just succeeded in overthrowing the Mongols and reestablishing Chinese authority under the Ming dynasty. Under the command of the Prince of Yen, Zheng He rose rapidly in rank, proving himself strong, loyal, ambitious, and a skilled junior officer. In 1403, when the Prince of Yen seized the Celestial Throne from a rival, Zheng He fought bravely on his behalf and was rewarded with an administrative position within the royal household. Two years later, he was promoted to commander in chief of one of the largest flotillas in world history.

From 1405 to 1422, Zheng He led six different expeditions that took him as far as Java, Sumatra, Vietnam, India, and Arabia and to trading centers in east Africa (see Map 15.3). For the most part, these were diplomatic missions, centered on the exchange of ambassadors, presents, and tribute. Among the gifts he brought back to China for the Yongle Emperor[10] were giraffes and lions. In exchange for tribute, Zheng He presented gifts from the emperor that included finely made porcelain dishes, rare silks, precious metals, and manufactured goods. But in places where the local "barbarians" did not adequately show deference and respect to representatives of the Celestial Empire, Zheng He and his crew used their power to impose their will on others.

When the Yongle Emperor died in 1424, Zheng He lost his most important ally and benefactor. Although he made one last great voyage in 1431, subsequent Ming emperors turned their primary attention to overland ventures and defense, most notably the construction of the Great Wall. To underscore their change in foreign policy, court officials destroyed the official travel logs of Zheng He, leaving us with only the stone tablet inscriptions and some notes kept by his crew as evidence of his achievements. The last years of his life also remain shrouded in mystery, and it is believed that he died in 1435 at the age of sixty-five.

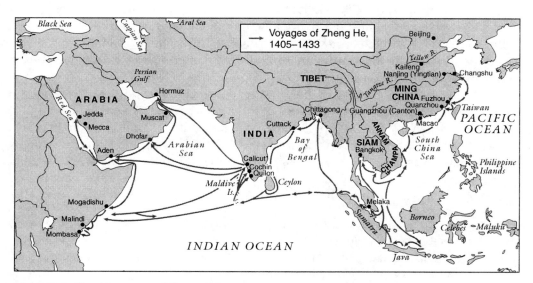

Map 15.3 The Voyages of Zheng He

QUESTIONS TO CONSIDER

1. According to the inscription, what were the goals of the voyages? In what ways might the Ming dynasty have hoped to benefit from these expeditions?

2. What role was played by the Celestial goddess? How did religious beliefs shape Zheng He's perceptions of his mission and his relations with others? How did it motivate him to leave a record of his voyages?

3. What kinds of interactions did Zheng He have with the peoples he encountered? What factors explain his different experiences and reactions?

4. In his voyage to China, Ibn Battuta was impressed with the economy and society but criticized their "heathen" practices. How might Zheng He, himself a Muslim, have responded?

5. After 1431, the Chinese abruptly stopped their overseas voyages. Based on Zheng He's account, what might have happened if they had continued into the next century? Would they have altered world history in a significant manner? What might have been different if China had "discovered" Europe, instead of Europe "discovering" China?

INSCRIPTION OF WORLD VOYAGES

Zheng He

A record of the miraculous answer [to prayer] to the goddess the Celestial Spouse.*

The Imperial Ming Dynasty unifying seas and continents, surpassing the three dynasties even goes beyond the Han and Tang dynasties. The countries beyond the horizon and from the ends of the earth have all become subjects and to the most western of the western or the most northern of the northern countries, however far they may be, the distance and the routes may be calculated. Thus the barbarians from beyond the seas, though their countries are truly distant . . . have come to audience bearing precious objects and presents.

The Emperor, approving of their loyalty and sincerity, has ordered us, Zheng He and others at the head of several tens of thousands of officers and flag-troops to ascend more than one hundred large ships to go and confer presents on them in order to make manifest the transforming power of the (imperial) virtue and to treat distant people with kindness. From the third year of Yongle[†] [1405] till now we have seven times received the commission of ambassadors to countries of the western ocean. The barbarian countries which we have visited are Zhancheng [Vietnam], Zhaowa [Java,

---

Source: Teobaldo Filesi, *China and Africa in the Middle Ages*, trans. David Morison, 1972, 61–65. Reprinted by Frank Cass Publishers.

*The Celestial Spouse was a goddess in Taoism, one of the major religions of China. She was considered to be the protector of travelers on the sea.

[†]In these inscriptions, years are measured by the emperor's reign.

436 CHAPTER 15 ◆ Expanding Global Encounters in the Fourteenth through Sixteenth Centuries

Indonesia], Sanfoqi [Sumatra, Indonesia], and Xianlo [Siam] crossing straight over to Xilanshan [Sri Lanka] in South India, Calicut [India], and Kezhi [India], we have gone to the western regions of Hulumosi [Ormuz], Aden [Yemen], Mogadishu [Somalia], altogether more than thirty countries large and small. We have traversed more than one hundred thousand *li** of immense water spaces and have beheld in the ocean huge waves like mountains rising sky-high, and we have set eyes on barbarian regions far away hidden in a blue transparency of light vapors, while our sails loftily unfurled like clouds day and night continued their course rapidly like that of a star, traversing those savage waves as if we were treading a public thoroughfare. Truly this was due to the majesty and the good fortune of the Imperial Court and moreover we owe it to the protecting virtue of the divine Celestial Spouse.

The power of the goddess having indeed been manifested in previous times has been abundantly revealed in the present generation. In the midst of the rushing waters it happened that, when there was a hurricane, suddenly there was a divine lantern shining in the mast, and as soon as this miraculous light appeared[†] the danger was appeased, so that even in the danger of capsizing one felt reassured that there was no cause for fear. When we arrived in the distant countries we captured alive those of the native kings who were not respectful and exterminated those barbarian robbers who were engaged in piracy, so that consequently the sea route was cleansed and pacified and the natives put their trust in it. All this is due to the favors of the goddess.

It is not easy to enumerate completely all the cases where the goddess has answered [my prayers]. Previously in a memorial to the Court we have requested that her virtue be recognized . . . and a temple be built at Nanking on the bank of the river where regular sacrifices should be made forever. We have respectfully received an Imperial commemoration exalting her miraculous favors, which is the highest recompense and praise indeed. However, the miraculous power of the goddess resides wherever one goes. . . .

We have received the high favor of a gracious commission from our sacred Lord [the Yongle Emperor], we carry to the distant barbarians the benefits of respect and good faith [on their part]. Commanding the multitudes on the fleet and being responsible for a quantity of money and valuables in the face of the violence of the winds and the nights, our one fear is not to be able to succeed. How, then, dare we not to serve our dynasty with . . . all our loyalty and the gods with the utmost sincerity? How would it be possible not to realize what is the source of the tranquillity of the fleet and the troops and the salvation on the voyage both going and returning? Therefore, we have inscribed the virtue of the [Celestial Spouse] on stone and have also recorded the years and months of the voyages to the barbarian countries . . . in order to leave the memory forever.

---

*Scholars estimated that Zheng He traveled over 35,000 miles during his seven voyages.

[†]Scholars believe that this miraculous light may have been St. Elmo's fire, static electricity that is not an uncommon sight to seafarers. Because the sailors had prayed to the Taoist goddess, they believed that the light was a sign of her beneficent protection. This helps explain why Zheng He later placed a pillar of thanksgiving at the Temple of the Celestial Spouse in Fujian province.

I. In the third year of Yongle [1405] commanding the fleet we went to Calicut [India] and other countries. At that time the pirate Chen Zuyi had gathered his followers in the country of Sanfoqi [island of Sumatra], where he plundered the native merchants. When he also advanced to resist our fleet, supernatural soldiers secretly came to the rescue so that after one beating of the drum he was annihilated. In the fifth year [1407] we returned.

II. In the fifth year of Yongle [1407] commanding the fleet we went to Zhaowa [Java], Calicut, Kezhi [India], and Xianle [Siam]. The kings of these countries all sent as tribute precious objects, precious birds and rare animals. In the seventh year [1409] we returned.

III. In the seventh year of Yongle [1409] commanding the fleet we went to the countries (visited) before and took our route by the country of Xilanshan [Sri Lanka]. Its king Alagakkonara was guilty of a gross lack of respect and plotted against the fleet. Owing to the manifest answer to prayer of the goddess, [the plot] was discovered and thereupon that king was captured alive. In the ninth year [1411] on our return the captured king was presented [to the throne as a prisoner]; subsequently he received the Imperial [forgiveness and] favor of returning to his own country.

IV. In the eleventh year of Yongle [1413] commanding the fleet we went to Hulumosi [Ormuz] and other countries. In the country of Samudra [northern tip of Sumatra] there was a false king [named Sekandar] who was marauding and invading his country. The [true] king [Zaynu-'l-Abidin] had sent an envoy to the Palace Gates in order to lodge a complaint. We went there with the official troops under our command and exterminated some and arrested [other rebels], and owing to the silent aid of the goddess, we captured the false king alive. In the thirteenth year [1415] on our return he was presented [to the Emperor as a prisoner]. In that year the king of the country of Manlajia [Malacca, Malaysia] came in person with his wife and son to present tribute.

V. In the fifteenth year of Yongle [1417] commanding the fleet we visited the western regions. The country of Ormuz presented lions, leopards with gold spots and large western horses. The country of Aden [Yemen] presented [giraffes], as well as the long-horned [oryx]. The country of Mogadishu [Somalia] presented [zebras] as well as lions. The country of Brava [Somalia or Kenya] presented camels which run one thousand *li*, as well as camel-birds [ostriches]. The countries of Zhaowa [Java] and Calicut [India] presented animal *miligao* [hides]. They all vied in presenting the marvelous objects preserved in the mountains or hidden in the seas and the beautiful treasures buried in the sand or deposited on the shores. Some sent a maternal uncle of the king, others a paternal uncle or a younger brother of the king in order to present a letter of homage written on gold leaf as well as tribute.

VI. In the nineteenth year of Yongle [1421] commanding the fleet we escorted the ambassadors from Ormuz and the other countries who had been in attendance at the capital for a long time back to their countries. The kings of all these countries prepared even more tribute than previously.

438 CHAPTER 15 ◆ Expanding Global Encounters in the Fourteenth through Sixteenth Centuries

VII. In the sixth year of Exeunt* [1431] once more commanding the fleet we have left for the barbarian countries in order to read to them [an Imperial edict] and to confer presents.

We have anchored in this port awaiting a north wind to take the sea, and recalling how previously we have on several occasions received the benefits of the protection of the divine intelligence we have thus recorded an inscription in stone.

VASCO DA GAMA'S VOYAGE TO AFRICA AND INDIA

Vasco da Gama's (1460–1524) two voyages to India (1497–1498; 1502–1503) are significant because they initiated direct and profitable trading routes between Europe and Asia that marked the beginning of a new phase of global commerce. Equally important, they foreshadow the use of European military power to assert its economic and political interests in new areas of the world. In both regards, Vasco da Gama played a central and pivotal role.

Born into the Portuguese nobility in 1460, da Gama received an education in mathematics and navigation and then followed his father (and most aristocrats) into the military, where he proved himself an effective officer. In the mid-1490s, when King John of Portugal ordered a naval expedition to India to open up trade, outflank the Muslims, and find new Christian allies, Vasco da Gama was placed in command of the fleet. In stark contrast to the large armada led by Zheng He more than a century earlier, da Gama had only four ships and less than two hundred men under his command when he left Lisbon in July 1497 (Map 15.4).

Five months later, as the ships rounded the tip of southern Africa, two of his vessels were leaking and many of the crew were sick with scurvy.[11] He therefore stopped along the coast of east Africa for fresh food and repairs and took the opportunity to visit some of the wealthy Swahili city-states (Mozambique, Mombasa [Kenya], Mylanta [Kenya]) that had been engaged in maritime trade with Arabia, Persia, and India for centuries.[12] But as the journal describes in great detail, the Portuguese visit to these city-states was not entirely successful nor amicable, and da Gama was frustrated in his failure to locate the lost Christian kingdom of Prester John. After a 23-day voyage across the Indian Ocean, da Gama became the first European to reach Calicut, one of the most important commercial ports of India. But his efforts to arrange a business pact with the local Hindu ruler proved unsuccessful because of mutual suspicions, the hostility of local Muslim government advisors and merchants, and, most interestingly, the general lack of interest in European trade goods. Misfortune followed da Gama after his departure from India: bad winds caused a very slow return, and many of his crew died of scurvy. Despite these setbacks, his return to Portugal in 1499 was accompanied

---

*The Emperor Zhu Zhang ordered one final voyage planned for 1431, the sixth year of his reign.

by a hero's welcome, and his prized and profitable cargoes of spices and jewels encouraged additional commercial ventures and investments.

In 1502, Vasco da Gama returned to east Africa and India with a larger, better armed fleet at his disposal. His primary mission was to avenge the murder of several Portuguese seamen who had visited Calicut in the intervening years, but his subsequent actions suggest that he was equally intent upon establishing Portuguese supremacy in the Indian Ocean. Arriving back at the east African city-state of Mombasa, da Gama threatened to burn the town and destroy its Muslim inhabitants if they did not submit to Portuguese authority (which they promptly did). The fleet then sailed to Calicut, where the Portuguese admiral demanded that all Muslims be banished from the port. To demonstrate his determination and strength, he then bombarded the city with cannon fire and routed the Muslim ships that tried to put up a fight. Following his return to Portugal in 1503, he seems to have lived in relative obscurity until called to duty again in 1524 to become a diplomat at one of the permanent outposts that the Portuguese had established in India in the meantime. But shortly after his arrival in India, he died suddenly and unexpectedly.

The original written sea logs of Vasco da Gama disappeared and are lost. Consequently, the only detailed account we possess was written by a crew member of the expedition. Although his exact identity remains somewhat a mystery, his account has been mostly verified by comparison with some of da Gama's letters and Portuguese government documents from that era. The excerpts that follow describe da Gama's experiences in the city-states of east Africa, as well as his misadventures in India. In both instances, it is valuable to examine Portuguese motives and perceptions of others, and how these shaped their particular experiences.

QUESTIONS TO CONSIDER

1. What kinds of observations and impressions are recorded in the journal? Are these shaped more by Vasco da Gama's motives and preexisting cultural values or by actual experiences? How important is physical appearance in making cultural judgments?

2. What role did religion play in shaping Portuguese motives and their views of others? How were religious beliefs used to justify their actions?

3. Why did the Swahili and Indians show such little interest in Portuguese trade goods and gifts? What dilemma did this cause? What might have been a solution to this problem?

4. In Africa and Asia, the Portuguese encountered both hospitality and hostility. What might have explained the varying reaction? To what degree, if any, did the Portuguese bring this hostility upon themselves?

5. How would you describe the cross-cultural attitudes formed during da Gama's first voyage? What kind of future relations did they portend?

440 CHAPTER 15 ◆ Expanding Global Encounters in the Fourteenth through Sixteenth Centuries

Map 15.4 Vasco da Gama's First Voyage to Africa and India

A JOURNAL OF THE FIRST VOYAGE
OF VASCO DA GAMA (1497–1499)

In the name of God. Amen. In the year 1497, King Dom Manuel . . . despatched four vessels to make discoveries and go in search of spices. Vasco da Gama was the captain of these vessels. . . .

1497. Mozambique. The people of this country are of ruddy complexion and well made. They are Muhammadans [Muslims], and their language is the same as

Source: A Journal of the First Voyage of Vasco da Gama, 1497–1499, trans. E. Ravenstein, Hakluyt Society Series 1, vol. 99 (London: The Hakluyt Society, 1898), 22–25, 28–30, 34–36, 37–38, 48–68.

A Journal of the First Voyage of Vasco da Gama (1497–1499)   441

that of the Moors.* Their dresses are of fine linen or cotton stuffs, with variously colored stripes, and of rich and elaborate workmanship. They all wear robes with borders of silk embroidered in gold. They are merchants, and have transactions with white Moors,† four of whose vessels were at the time in port, laden with gold, silver, cloves, pepper, ginger, and silver rings, as also with quantities of pearls, jewels, and rubies, all of which are used by the people of this country. We understood them to say that all these things, with the exception of the gold, were brought thither by these Moors; and that further on to where we were going, they abounded, and that precious stones, pearls and spices were so plentiful that there was no need to purchase them as they could be collected in baskets. All this we learned through a sailor the Captain [Vasco da Gama] had with him, and who, having formerly been a prisoner among the Moors, understood their language.

These Moors, moreover, told us that along the route which we were about to follow we should meet . . . many cities along the coast, and also an island, where one half the population consisted of Moors and the other half of Christians, who were at war with each other. This island was said to be very wealthy. We were told, moreover, that Prester John resided not far from this place; that he held many cities along the coast, and that the inhabitants of those cities were great merchants and owned big ships. The residence of Prester John was said to be far in the interior, and could be reached only on the back of camels. . . . This information, and many other things which we heard, rendered us so happy that we cried with joy, and prayed God to grant us health, so that we might behold what we so much desired.

In this place and island of Mozambique, there resided a chief who had the title of Sultan. He often came aboard our ships attended by some of his people. The Captain gave him many good things to eat, and made him a present of hats, shirts, corals and many other articles. He was, however, so proud that he treated all we gave him with contempt, and asked for scarlet cloth, of which we had none. We gave him, however, of all the things we had. . . . During our stay here the Sultan of Mozambique sent word that he wanted to make peace with us and to be our friend. His ambassador was a white Moor and a nobleman, and at the same time a great drunkard. . . .

One evening, as we left the ship for the mainland to obtain drinking water, we saw about twenty men on the beach. They were armed with spears, and forbade our landing. After the Captain heard this, he ordered three bombards [small cannon] to be fired upon them, so that we might land. Having effected our landing, these men fled into the bush, and we took as much water as we wanted. [The next day], a Moor rowed out to our ships, and told us that if we wanted more drinking water, that we should go for it, suggesting that we would encounter more trouble and be forced to turn back. The Captain no sooner heard this [threat] than he resolved to go, in order to show that we were able to do them harm if we desired it. We then armed our boats, placing bombards in their poops, and started for the shore. The Moors had constructed [a defensive wall] by lashing planks together . . . [but as we approached] they were at the time walking along the beach, armed with spears, knives, bows, and slingshots,

---

*The Portuguese are describing the Swahili people of east Africa.

†"White Moors" was a term used to identify Muslim Arabs.

442   CHAPTER 15   ◆   Expanding Global Encounters in the Fourteenth through Sixteenth Centuries

with which they hurled stones at us. But our bombards soon made it so hot for them that they fled behind their walls, but this turned out to their injury rather than their profit. During the three hours that we were occupied in this manner [bombarding the beach] we saw at least two men killed, one on the beach and the other behind the wall. When we were weary of this work we retired to our ships to dine. . . .

[Vasco da Gama and his fleet left Mozambique shortly thereafter and arrived two weeks later at the Swahili city-state of Mombasa.]

On Saturday, we cast anchor off Mombasa, but did not enter the port. . . . In front of the city there lay numerous vessels, all dressed in flags.* And we, anxious not to be outdone, also dressed our ships, and we actually surpassed their show. . . . We anchored here with much pleasure, for we confidently hoped that on the following day we might go on land and hear [Catholic] mass jointly with the Christians reported to live there in a neighborhood separate from that of the Moors. . . .

But those who had told us [about the Christians] had said it [to trap us], for it was not true. At midnight there approached us a *dhow* with about a hundred men, all armed with cutlasses and shields. When they came to the vessel of the Captain they attempted to board her, armed as they were, but this was not permitted, only four or five of the most distinguished men among them being allowed on board. They remained about a couple of hours, and it seemed to us that they paid us this visit merely to find out whether they might not capture one or the other of our vessels. . . .

[The next day] the King of Mombasa sent the Captain a sheep and large quantities of oranges, lemons and sugar-cane, together with a ring, as a pledge of safety, letting him know that in case of his entering the port he would be supplied with all he stood in need of. . . . The Captain sent the king a string of coral-beads as a return present, and let him know that he planned to enter the port on the following day. . . . Two men were sent by the Captain to the king, still further to confirm these peaceful assurances. . . . The king received them hospitably, and ordered that they should be shown the city. . . . When they had seen all, the king sent them back with samples of cloves, pepper and sorghum, articles he would allow us to purchase and load on our ships. . . .

That evening, the Captain questioned two Moors whom we had captured, by dropping boiling oil upon their skin, so that they might confess to any treachery intended against us. They said that orders had been given to capture us as soon as we entered the port, and thus to avenge what we had done at Mozambique. And when this torture was being applied a second time, one of the Moors, although his hands were tied, threw himself into the sea, whilst the other did so during the morning watch.

About midnight two *dhows*, with many men in them, approached. The *dhows* stood off whilst the men entered the water, swimming in the direction of our ships. . . . Our men on watch thought at first that they were fish, but when they perceived their mistake they shouted to the other vessels. They [Moors] had already boarded one ship and got hold of the rigging of the mizzen-mast, but seeing themselves discovered,

---

*The Swahili traditionally "dress" their vessels with flags and pennants to mark the feast that ends the month-long fast of Ramadan. Ramadan is an important Islamic holiday that commemorates Allah's gift of the Qur'an to mankind, a time when Muslims fast and spend more time concentrating on their faith.

they silently slipped down and fled. These and other wicked tricks were practiced upon us by these dogs, but our Lord did not allow them to succeed, because they were unbelievers.

[After a 23-day voyage across the Indian Ocean, aided by a Muslim navigator lent by the Sultan of Mozambique, the Portuguese arrived at Calicut, one of the most prosperous and important trading centers in southern India. Although the local ruler and much of the population were Hindu, there were also many merchants, traders, and government officials who were Muslims.]

After we were at anchor, four boats approached us from the land, and they asked of what nation we were. We told them, and they then pointed out Calicut to us. . . . The city of Calicut is inhabited by Christians.* They are of tawny complexion. Some of them have big beards and long hair, whilst others clip their hair short or shave the head, merely allowing a tuft to remain on the crown as a sign that they are Christians. They also wear moustaches. They pierce the ears and wear much gold in them. They go naked down to the waist, covering their lower extremities with very fine cotton stuffs. But it is only the most respectable who do this, for the others manage as best they are able.† The women of this country, as a rule, are ugly and of small stature. They wear many jewels of gold round the neck, numerous bracelets on their arms, and rings set with precious stones on their toes. All these people are well-disposed and apparently of mild temper. At first sight they seem covetous and ignorant. . . .

When we arrived at Calicut the king was away. The Captain sent two men to him with a message, informing him that an ambassador had arrived from the King of Portugal with letters. . . . [The king] sent word to the Captain bidding him welcome [and sent] a pilot . . . with orders to take us to [an anchorage] in front of the city of Calicut. We were told that the anchorage at the place to which we were to go was good . . . and that it was customary for the ships which came to this country to anchor there for the sake of safety. We ourselves did not feel comfortable . . . and we did not anchor as near the shore as the king's pilot desired. . . .

On the following morning . . . the Captain set out to speak to the king, and took with him thirteen men. We put on our best attire, put bombards [small cannon] in our boats, and took with us trumpets and many flags. On landing, the Captain was received by government officials, along with a crowd of many men, armed and unarmed. The reception was friendly, as if the people were pleased to see us, though at first appearances looked threatening, for they carried naked swords in their hands. A palanquin‡ was provided for the captain, such as is used by men of distinction in that country. . . . When we arrived [at the king's palace], men of much distinction and great lords came out to meet the Captain, and joined those who were already in attendance upon him. . . .

---

*With no prior knowledge of Indian culture or religion, Vasco da Gama and his crew mistook Hindus for Christians.

†The differences in dress witnessed by the Portuguese were most likely related to the caste system prevalent in Indian society.

‡A palanquin is a mode of transportation consisting of a chair mounted on poles and carried on the shoulders of four to six men.

444 CHAPTER 15 ◆ Expanding Global Encounters in the Fourteenth through Sixteenth Centuries

The king was in a small court, reclining upon a couch covered with a cloth of green velvet, above which was a good mattress, and upon this again a sheet of cotton stuff, very white and fine, more so than any linen. . . . The Captain, on entering, saluted in the manner of the country: by putting the hands together, then raising them towards Heaven, as is done by Christians when addressing God, and immediately afterwards opening them and shutting fists quickly. . . .

And the Captain told him he was the ambassador of the King of Portugal, who was Lord of many countries and the possessor of great wealth of every description, exceeding that of any king of these parts; that for a period of sixty years his people had annually sent out vessels to make discoveries in the direction of India, as they knew that there were Christian kings there like themselves. This, he said, was the reason which induced them to order this country to be discovered, not because they sought for gold or silver, for of this they had such abundance that they needed not what was to be found in this country. . . . There reigned a king now whose name was Dom Manuel, who had ordered [da Gama] to build three vessels, of which he had been appointed Captain, and who had ordered him not to return to Portugal until he should have discovered this King of the Christians, on pain of having his head cut off. That two letters had been intrusted to him to be presented in case he succeeded in discovering him . . . and, finally, he had been instructed to say by word of mouth that he [the King of Portugal] desired to be his friend and brother.

In reply to this the king said that he was welcome; that, on his part, he held him as a friend and brother, and would send ambassadors with him to Portugal. . . . These and many other things passed between the two in this chamber, and as it was already late in the night, the king asked the Captain with whom he desired to lodge, with Christians or with Moors? And the Captain replied, neither with Christians nor with Moors, and begged as a favor that he be given a lodging by himself. The king said he would order it thus, upon which the Captain took leave of the king and came to where his men were. . . .

By that time four hours of the night had already gone . . . and the time occupied in passing through the city was so long that the captain at last grew tired, and complained to the king's advisor, a Moor of distinction, who attended him to the lodgings. The Moor then took him to his own house, and we were admitted to a court within it. . . . Many carpets had been spread, and there were two large candlesticks like those at the Royal palace. . . .

[The next morning], the captain got ready the following gifts to be sent to the king: twelve pieces of *lambel*,* four scarlet hoods, six hats, four strings of coral, a case containing six wash-hand basins, a case of sugar, two casks of oil, and two of honey. And as it is the custom not to send anything to the king without the knowledge of the Moor [his financial advisor], and other officials, the Captain informed them of his intention. They came, and when they saw the present they laughed at it, saying that it was not a thing to offer to a king, that the poorest merchant from Mecca, or any other part of India, gave more, and that if he wanted to make a present it should be in gold, as the king would not accept such things. When the Captain heard this he grew sad, and said that he had brought no gold, that, moreover, he was no merchant, but an ambassador; that he gave of that which he had, which was his own private gift and

---

*Striped cotton cloth.

not the king's; that if the King of Portugal ordered him to return he would intrust him with far richer presents; and that if the king would not accept these things he would send them back to the ships. Upon this they [the government officials] declared that they would not forward his presents, nor consent to his forwarding them himself. When they had gone there came certain Moorish merchants, and they all mocked the presents which the Captain desired to be sent to the king.

When the Captain saw that they were determined not to forward his presents, he [asked] to speak to the king, and would then return to the ships. [The officials] approved of this, and told [the Captain] that if he would wait a short time they would return and accompany him to the palace. And the Captain waited all day, but they never came back. The Captain was very angry at being among so phlegmatic and unreliable a people, and intended, at first, to go to the palace without them. On further consideration, however, he thought it best to wait until the following day. . . .

On Wednesday morning the Moors returned, and took the captain to the palace. The palace was crowded with armed men. Our Captain was kept waiting . . . for fully four long hours, outside a door, which was only opened when the king sent word to admit him. . . . The king said that he [the Captain] had claimed that he came from a very rich kingdom, and yet had brought him nothing; that he had also told him that he was the bearer of a letter, which had not yet been delivered. To this the Captain rejoined that he had brought nothing, because the object of his voyage was merely to make discoveries, but that when other ships came he would then see what they brought him; as to the letter, it was true that he had brought one, and would deliver it immediately.

The king then asked what it was he had come to discover: stones or men? If he came to discover men, as [the Captain] had claimed, why had he brought nothing? Moreover, he had been told that [the ships] carried . . . the golden image of a Santa Maria. The Captain said that the Santa Maria was not of gold, and that even if she were he would not part with her, as she had guided him across the ocean, and would guide him back to his own country. . . .

The king then asked what kind of merchandise was to be found in [Portugal]. The Captain said there was much corn, cloth, iron, bronze, and many other things. The king asked whether he had any merchandise with him. The captain replied that he had a little of each sort, as samples, and that if permitted to return to the ships he would order it to be landed, and that meantime four or five men would remain at the lodgings assigned them. The king refused [and was not interested]. The Captain might take all his people with him, securely moor his ships, land his merchandise, and attempt to sell it himself to the best advantage. Having taken leave of the king, the Captain returned to his lodgings, and we with him. As it was already late no attempt was made to depart that night.

[After two days of waiting], the Captain again asked for boats to take him to his ships. [The king's advisors] began to whisper among themselves, and said that we should have them if we would order our vessels to come nearer the shore. The Captain replied that if he ordered his vessels to approach his brother* would think that he was being held a prisoner, and would hoist the sails and return to Portugal. They said that if we refused to order the ships to come nearer we should not be permitted to

---

*Vasco da Gama's younger brother was second in command of the fleet.

446 CHAPTER 15 ◆ Expanding Global Encounters in the Fourteenth through Sixteenth Centuries

leave . . . [and] they immediately closed all the doors, and many armed men entered to guard us, none of us being allowed to go outside without being accompanied by several of these guards. . . .

The Captain and we others felt very down-hearted, though outwardly we pretended not to notice what they did. . . . The Captain did not wish the ships to come within the port, for it seemed to him—as it did to us—that once inside they could easily be captured, after which they would first kill him, and us others, as we were already in their power. We passed all that day most anxiously. At night more people surrounded us than ever before, and we were no longer allowed to walk in the compound, within which we were, but confined within a small tiled court, with a multitude of people around us. We quite expected that on the following day we should be separated, or that some harm would befall us, for we noticed that our jailers were much annoyed with us. This, however, did not prevent our making a good supper off the things found in the village. Throughout that night we were guarded by over a hundred men, all armed with swords, two-edged battle-axes, shields, and bows and arrows. Whilst some of these slept, others kept guard, each taking his turn of duty throughout the night.

On the following day, these gentlemen [the Moors and government officials] came back, and this time they wore better faces. They told the Captain that . . . as it was the custom of the country that every ship on its arrival should at once land the merchandise it brought, as also the crews, and that the sellers should not return on board until the whole of it had been sold. The Captain consented, and said he would . . . see to its being done. They said this was well, and that immediately after the arrival of the merchandise he would be permitted to return to his ship. . . . At this there was great rejoicing, thanks being rendered to God for having extricated us from the hands of people who had no more sense than beasts. . . .

The merchants whom the king had sent . . . instead of buying our merchandise merely ridiculed it. The Moors no longer visited the house where the merchandise was, but they bore us no good-will, and they spat on the ground, saying "Portugal, Portugal." Indeed, from the very first they had sought to take and kill us. . . .

COLUMBUS'S FIRST VOYAGE TO THE "NEW WORLD"

Christopher Columbus (1451–1506) is probably the most famous—and infamous—explorer in world history. He has long been viewed as a heroic figure, a master navigator whose four voyages (1492–1504) across the Atlantic Ocean paved the way for the triumphant European exploration and colonization of the Americas, and his exploits have been celebrated with a national holiday, monuments and parades, and innumerable place names. But more recently, Columbus has been seen in a different, more critical perspective. He was a man driven by flawed and selfish motives, whose personal actions and ambitions opened the way for the European exploitation of the resources and peoples of the New World.

Unlike his contemporary Vasco da Gama, Columbus began life with humble origins. He was born in Genoa (Italy) in 1451, the eldest son of a Genoese wool-worker and small-time trader. He began his career on the seas in the Portuguese merchant marine, which took him as far as Iceland to the north and the coast of west Africa to the south. These experiences gave him invaluable navigation and sailing experience, and they fueled his curiosity and desire to find a western route to Asia. In 1484, he began seeking financial support for an Atlantic crossing, and he was rebuffed at least three times by the Portuguese and Spanish monarchs before he finally received support from King Fernando and Queen Ysabel in early 1492. In the initial contract, Columbus bargained to win promotion to admiral, admittance to the Spanish nobility, and a 10 percent claim to the riches of new lands discovered upon successful completion of the first voyage.

On August 3, 1492, Columbus set sail in three small ships with 120 crewmen. After a relatively uneventful voyage of thirty-three days, the fleet sighted the Bahama islands and then landed and explored parts of Cuba and Hispaniola (the island currently divided between Haiti and the Dominican Republic). With assistance of a local leader, he established a fort on Hispaniola called *Villa de Navidad* and left about forty crewmen there to guard it until his return. The Spanish monarchs were so impressed with Columbus's gifts of gold, spices, exotic birds, and human captives that he secured the financial backing for a second voyage. In 1493, Columbus left with a much larger flotilla of seventeen ships, filled with colonists, investors, and a small troop of cavalry. But his return to the fort at *Villa de Navidad* was too late, for he discovered the fort ruined and all of the crew gone.

Altogether, Columbus made four voyages across the Atlantic under the sponsorship of Fernando and Ysabel. By the end of the second voyage (1493–1496), he had sighted most of the Caribbean islands, and he rebuilt his base in Hispaniola. During the third and fourth trips (1498–1500; 1502–1504), Columbus explored the coasts of Central and South America, from present-day Honduras to Venezuela. But his last trip was marred by his difficulties with Spanish colonists, increased hostility from indigenous peoples, and his frustrating inability to discover the westward route to Asia. Back in Spain, his attempts to join the nobility and to recover his governorship of the "Indies" from King Fernando were unsuccessful. By many accounts, Columbus died a disappointed man.

The outcome of Columbus's voyages are open to interpretation and debate. His discoveries undoubtedly brought Europe and the Americas into sustained contact with each other and ultimately led to European immigration and the transplantation of their culture and values. But others might add that it also led to the exploitation and genocide of native Americans. On the island of Hispaniola, for example, Spanish actions against the indigenous population dramatically reduced their population from an estimated 250,000 in 1492 to under 500 by 1538. Moreover, the genocide of native Americans throughout the Caribbean, by conquest or disease, was one of the principal factors behind the importation of African slave labor in subsequent centuries.

We possess two accounts of Columbus's first voyage to the Americas, and excerpts from each are included in this chapter. The first source is the logbook kept

448   CHAPTER 15 ◆ Expanding Global Encounters in the Fourteenth through Sixteenth Centuries

by Columbus during the trip and presented in 1493 to the Spanish monarchs. The prologue to the log highlights his stated motives and objectives prior to his departure. The second source is a letter written by Columbus prior to his return, in which he summarized his discoveries and assessments, with the goal of securing additional financial support for a second voyage. The letter describes his enchantment with the natural beauty of the islands and his impressions of the "innocent" inhabitants. But it is also evident that Columbus was somewhat disappointed and remained uncertain whether he had discovered anything of great importance. He found neither great cities nor civilized peoples, and although the islands might hold potential wealth, they were not his intended object of discovery.

QUESTIONS TO CONSIDER

1. What were Columbus's primary motives, as declared in the prologue to his logbook? How do these compare with the ones revealed in his descriptions of Hispaniola and Cuba? How might one account for the differences?

2. Columbus portrays most of the island inhabitants as "innocent" and "timid." What led him to these conclusions? What impact did this perception have on his behavior? In your estimation, did Columbus take advantage of the innocence and generosity of the inhabitants?

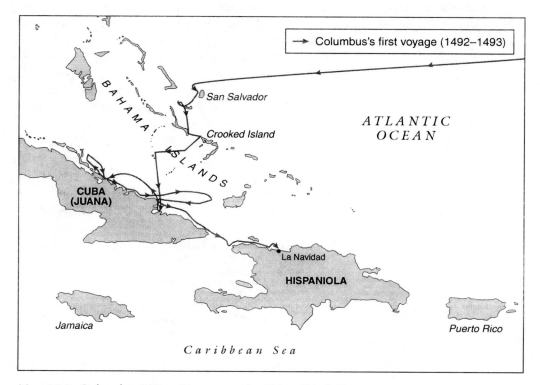

Map 15.5 Columbus's First Voyage to the "New World"

Christopher Columbus ◆ Prologue to the Logbook of the First Voyage (1492)   449

3. Columbus says of Hispaniola, "It is a land to be desired, and when seen, never to be left." What did he consider to be the attractions on Hispaniola? Did these portend future relationships between Europeans and the indigenous islanders?

4. At the end of his letter, Columbus made a direct appeal for more financial assistance from the Spanish monarchy. Might this request have affected the way in which he described his discoveries?

5. Columbus specifically noted two distinct future policies in the New World: the conversion of the indigenous peoples to Christianity and the pursuit of wealth from the accumulation of gold and other resources. Based on his own explanations, were these two goals compatible? Why or why not?

PROLOGUE TO THE LOGBOOK OF THE FIRST VOYAGE (1492)

Christopher Columbus

Most Christian and most exalted and most excellent and most mighty princes, King and Queen of the Spains* and of the islands of the sea, our sovereigns. . . . [In] this present year of 1492, your Highnesses concluded a [successful] end of the war with the Moors who reigned in Europe . . . and as Catholic Christians and as princes devoted to the holy Christian faith and its propagators, and enemies of the sect of Mahomet [Muhammad] and of all idolatries and heresies, took thought to send me, Christopher Columbus, to India, to see the princes and peoples and lands and . . . the manner which should be used to bring about their conversion to our Holy Faith. . . . I shall not go [to India] to the eastward, by which way it was the custom to go, but by way of the west, by which down to this day we do not know certainly that any one has passed. . . . [This voyage] has accorded me great rewards and ennobled me so that from that time henceforward I might style myself *Don*† and be high admiral of the Ocean Sea and [become] perpetual governor of the islands and [lands] which I should discover. . . . To this end, I thought to write all this journey very carefully . . . in which I will set all the seas and lands of the Ocean Sea in their true places. . . . And all these things will be a great enterprise.

Source: Christopher Columbus, *The Voyages of Christopher Columbus, Being the Journals of his First and Third, and the Letters Concerning his First and Last Voyages,* trans. and ed. Cecil Jane (London: Argonaut Press, 1930), 135–36.

*The marriage of King Fernando and Queen Ysabel united the formerly separate Spanish kingdoms of Aragon, Castile, and Leon.

†A title of nobility.

450   CHAPTER 15   ◆   Expanding Global Encounters in the Fourteenth through Sixteenth Centuries

LETTER DESCRIBING HIS FIRST VOYAGE
(1493)

Christopher Columbus

Since I know that you will be pleased at the great victory with which Our Lord has crowned my voyage, I write this to you, from which you will learn how in thirty-three days I passed from the Canary Islands to the Indies, with the fleet which the most illustrious king and queen, our sovereigns, gave to me. There I found very many islands, filled with people innumerable, and of them all I have taken possession for their Highnesses, by proclamation made and with the royal standard unfurled, and no opposition was offered to me.

To the first island which I found I gave the name "San Salvador," in remembrance of the blessed Savior, who had marvelously bestowed all this; the Indians call it "Guanahani." To the second island, I gave the name "Santa Maria de Concepcion" [Rum Cay]; to the third, "Fernandina"; to the fourth, "Isabella" . . . and so each island received a new name from me.*

When I came to Juana [Cuba], I followed its coast to the westward, and I found it to be so extensive that I thought that it must be the mainland, the province of Cathay [China]. And since there were neither towns nor villages on the seashore, but only small villages whose residents all fled immediately, I continued along the coast, thinking that I could not fail to find great cities and towns. At the end of many miles, seeing that there was no change . . . I retraced my path back to a remarkable harbor known to me. From that point, I sent two men inland to learn if there were a king or great cities. They traveled three days' journey, finding many small villages and numerous people, but nothing of importance, and so they returned.

I understood sufficiently from other Indians, whom I had previously seized there, that this land was nothing but an island, and I therefore followed its coast eastward for over three hundred miles to the point where it ended. From that point, I saw another island to the east, distant about fifty miles, and I gave it the name "Hispana" [Hispaniola].† I sailed there and followed its northern coast eastward for over five hundred miles.

This island and all the others are very fertile. . . . [Along the coast of Hispaniola] are many harbors, beyond comparison with others that I know in Christendom, and many rivers, good and large. Its lands are high, and there are many sierras and very lofty mountains. . . . [All the islands] are most beautiful, of a thousand shapes; all are accessible and are filled with trees of a thousand kinds, and so tall that they seem to touch the sky. I am told that they never lose their foliage, and this I can believe, for I saw them as green and lovely as they are in Spain in May, and some of them were

---

Source: Christopher Columbus, *The Voyages of Christopher Columbus, Being the Journals of his First and Third, and the Letters Concerning his First and Last Voyages,* trans. and ed. Cecil Jane (London: Argonaut Press, 1930), 259–64.

*All of these islands are part of the present-day Bahamas.

†The large island of Hispaniola is now divided between the nations of Haiti and the Dominican Republic. It is believed that Columbus's first voyage took him to the north coast of Haiti.

Christopher Columbus ◆ Letter Describing His First Voyage (1493)   451

flowering, some bearing fruit. . . . There are six or eight kinds of palm, which are a wonder to behold on account of their beautiful variety, but so are the other trees and fruits and plants. There are also marvelous pine groves, very wide and smiling plains, birds of many kinds, and fruits and honey in great diversity. In the interior, there are mines of metals, and the population is without number.

Hispana [Hispaniola] is a marvel. The sierras and the mountains, the plains, the arable and pasture lands, are so lovely and so rich for planting and sowing, for breeding cattle of every kind, and for building towns and villages. The harbors of the sea here are such as cannot be believed to exist unless they have been seen, and so with the rivers, many and great, and of good water, the majority of which contain gold. In the trees, fruits and plants, there is a great difference from those of Juana [Cuba]. In this island, there are many spices and great mines of gold and of other metals.

The people of this island, and of all the other islands which I have found and of which I have information, all go naked, men and women, as their mothers bore them, although some of the women cover a single place with the leaf of a plant or with a net of cotton which they make for the purpose. They have no iron or steel or weapons, nor are they inclined to use them. This is not because they are not well built and of handsome stature, but because they are very timid. They have no other arms than spears made of reeds, to which they fix a small sharpened stick. They do not dare to make use of these weapons against us, for many times it has happened that I have sent ashore two or three men to some town to have speech with them, and countless people have come out to them, and as soon as they have seen my men approaching, they have fled, a father not even waiting for his son. This is not because we have done them any harm; on the contrary, at every place where I have been and have been able to have speech with them, I have given gifts to them, such as cloth and many other things, receiving nothing in exchange. But they remain by nature incurably timid.

It is true that, once they have been reassured and have lost their fear of us, they are so innocent and so generous with all that they possess, that no one would believe it who has not seen it. They refuse nothing that they possess if it be asked of them. On the contrary, they invite any one to share it and display as much love as if they would give their hearts. They are content with whatever trifle or gift that is given to them, whether it be of value or valueless. I forbade that they should be given things so worthless as fragments of broken crockery, scraps of broken glass and ends of straps, although when they were able to get them, they fancied that they possessed the best jewel in the world. A sailor once received gold equal to the weight of two and a half coins for a little piece of strap, and others received much more for other things which were worth less. . . . They took even the pieces of the broken hoops of the wine barrels and, like savages, gave what they had, but this seemed to me to be wrong and I forbade it. I gave them a thousand handsome good things, which I had brought, in order that they might conceive affection for us and, more than that, might become Christians and be inclined to the love and service of your Highnesses and of the whole Spanish nation, and strive to aid us and to give us of the things which they have in abundance and which are necessary to us.

They do not hold any creed nor are they idolaters; they only believe that power and good are in the heavens. . . . This belief is not the result of ignorance, for they are actually of a very acute intelligence, they know how to navigate the seas, and it is

452   CHAPTER 15 ✦ Expanding Global Encounters in the Fourteenth through Sixteenth Centuries

amazing how good an account they give of everything. [Instead], this belief is because they have never seen people clothed or ships such as ours.

As soon as I arrived in the Indies, I took by force some natives at the first island that I found in order that they might give me information about these places. And so it was that they soon understood us, and we them, either by speech or signs, and they have been very helpful. I still have them with me, and they are always assured that I come from Heaven, despite all the discussions which they have had with me. They were the first to announce this wherever I went in the islands, and others went running from house to house, and to neighboring towns, crying loudly "Come! Come! See the men from Heaven!" So all, men and women alike, once their fear was set at rest, came out to welcome us, and they all brought something to eat and drink, which they gave with extraordinary affection and generosity.

In all the islands, they have very many canoes, which are like our rowboats, except they are not so broad, because they are made of a single log of wood. But a rowboat would not be able to keep up with them, since their speed is incredible. In these they navigate among all the islands, and carry their goods and conduct trade. In one of these canoes I have seen with seventy and eighty men, each one with his oar.

In all these islands, I saw no great diversity in the appearance of the people or in their manners and language. On the contrary, they all understand one another . . . and if their Highnesses assent, this will [assist] their conversion to our holy faith of Christ, to which they are very ready and favorably inclined.

I have already said how I went three hundred miles in a straight line from west to east along the seashore of the island of Juana [Cuba], and as a result of this voyage I can say that this island is larger than England and Scotland together. . . . There remains to the westward on this island two provinces to which I have not gone. One of these provinces they call "Avan," and I am told that the people here are born with tails. . . . The other island, Hispana [Hispaniola], has a circumference greater than all Spain. . . . It is a land to be desired and, when seen, never to be left. I have taken possession of this island and all others for their Highnesses so that they may dispose of them as they wish, and all are more richly endowed than I know how or am able to say. Hispana [Hispaniola] is the most conveniently located, and it has the greatest potential for gold mines and all other trade. I have taken possession of a large town, to which I gave the name "Villa de Navidad" [located on the north coast of Haiti], and in it I have made a fort, which by now will be entirely completed. At this fort, I have left enough men as seemed necessary, with arms and artillery and provisions for more than a year, as well as one of our ships and enough skilled men to build others. I also established great friendship with the king of that land, so much so that he was proud to call me "brother" and to treat me as such. And even were the king to change his attitude to one of hostility towards the men left behind, he does not have the power to hurt us. As I have already related, the natives go naked and they are the most timid people in the world, so that the few men whom I have left there alone could destroy them all. The island is without danger if our men follow the regulations and orders that we gave them.

In all these islands, it seems to me that each man is content with one wife, except the chiefs or kings who may have as many as twenty wives. It appears to me that the women work more than the men. I have not been able to learn if they hold private property, but it seemed to me that they all shared what they had, especially of eatable things. In these islands I have so far found no human monstrosities, as many expected . . . on the contrary, the whole population is very well formed. They are not black like the people in Guinea [West Africa], but their hair is flowing. . . .

And so I have found no monsters, nor have I heard of any, except on an island called Charis. . . . This island is inhabited by a people* who are regarded in all the islands as very fierce, and they are cannibals who eat human flesh. They have many canoes with which they range through all the islands of India and pillage and take whatever they can. They are no more malformed than are the others, except that they have the custom of wearing their hair long like women, and they use bows and arrows. . . . They are ferocious towards these other people who are excessively cowardly, but I regard them as no more fearsome than the others. . . . I have also been told of another island, which they assure me is larger than Hispana, where the people have no hair. In this place there is reportedly incalculable amounts of gold. . . .

To conclude this report . . . their Highnesses can see that I can supply them as much gold as they may need if their Highnesses will continue to assist [my voyages]. Moreover, I will provide them spices and cotton, as much as their Highnesses shall command; and mastic and aloe, as much as they shall order to be shipped; and slaves, as many as they shall order to be shipped and who will be from the idolaters. I believe also that I have found rhubarb and cinnamon, and I shall find a thousand other things of value. . . .

Our thanksgiving must be directed the most to the eternal God, Our Lord, Who gives to all those who walk in His way triumph over things which appear to be impossible, and this was one such glorious example. For although men have talked or have written of these distant lands, all was conjectural and without evidence. . . . It is our Redeemer who has given the victory to our most illustrious king and queen, and to their renowned kingdom . . . and all Christendom ought to feel delight and make great feasts and give solemn thanks to our Lord and Savior Jesus Christ, with many solemn prayers for the great exaltation which they shall have in the turning of so many pagan peoples to our Holy Faith, and afterwards for the temporal benefits, because not only Spain but all Christendom will have hence refreshment and gain.

These deeds that have been accomplished are thus briefly recorded while aboard ship, off the Canary Islands, on the fifteenth of February, in the year one thousand four hundred and ninety-three. I remain, at your orders and your service.

The Admiral

NOTES

1. Exploration and expansion have been constants in human history and can be seen in the early evolution of migration patterns, the creation of long-distance trade, and, in many cases, the formation of states and empires.

---

*Columbus is referring to the Caribs, from whom the "Caribbean" gets its name. Scholars believe the Caribs emigrated to the islands of the Caribbean from South America and took advantage of their warrior skills to raid and prey upon the indigenous peoples of the islands, the Arawaks.

454   CHAPTER 15   ◆   Expanding Global Encounters in the Fourteenth through Sixteenth Centuries

2. In some cases, such as the remote interior regions of Africa, these accounts are among the few written sources available for this time period.

3. The *hajj* is the annual pilgrimage to Mecca to worship and visit the holy sites of Islam. It is one of the five "Pillars of Faith," a duty that devout Muslims are expected to undertake once in their lifetimes, if possible. Some scholars have suggested that the ritual and celebration of the *hajj* has created a stimulus for travel that surpasses the rite of Christian pilgrimages during the Middle Ages.

4. In 1279, the Mongols had successfully invaded China and created their own dynasty (Yuan dynasty), the first instance when foreigners ruled over China. But the Mongols were mostly content to impose their rule only in the highest positions of authority, and they actually succeeded in linking China more closely with the outside world via Mongol-controlled overland trade networks in central Asia. Nonetheless, the rule of foreign "barbarians" over the illustrious "Middle Kingdom" proved intolerable to the Chinese, and in 1368, Chinese armies defeated the Mongols and reestablished their authority.

5. Some scholars suggest that the Confucian virtues of cultivating family and ancestral bonds were perceived by later Ming emperors to be in disharmony with the motives and actions inherent in exploration.

6. See the readings in chapter 14 that focus on cultural reactions to disease and bubonic plague.

7. Literally translates as the "Reconquest" and refers to the period of Christian holy war against Muslim control of Spain and Portugal that began as early as the tenth century but that culminated in the expulsion of Muslims (and Jews) from Spain in 1492.

8. The *Columbian Exchange* is a broad term used by historians to refer to the global spread of plants, animals, and diseases following the voyages of Christopher Columbus.

9. Mecca and Medina are both located in the mountainous regions along the Red Sea in the Arabian peninsula. Mecca was the birthplace of Muhammad, and it is the prime site for pilgrimages in Islam (the *hajj*). Medina was the city where Muhammad built a following, and it remains his burial place. Together, they represent two of the most holy sites in Islam.

10. Zhu Di, also known as the Yongle Emperor (1403–1424), was the third Ming emperor, whose great ambition was to rebuild Chinese power following the rule of the Mongols.

11. Scurvy is a painful and life-threatening disease caused by a deficiency in vitamin C (ascorbic acid). It was once a widespread malady among crewmen of sailing ships on long voyages due to the lack of fresh fruits and vegetables.

12. Beginning sometime in the ninth or tenth century, Muslim traders from Arabia moved to coastal towns in east Africa to facilitate their commercial activities. They frequently settled down and married African women, and their future progeny, language, and society became known as Swahili, a mixing of African and Arab bloodlines and cultures. By the time of da Gama's visit, generations of Swahili governed prosperous independent city-states along the coast from present-day Mozambique to Somalia.

CHAPTER 2

Cross-Cultural Perceptions in the New World

INTRODUCTION

On April 22, 1519, Hernan Cortés (1485–1547), captain of a Spanish armada, disembarked from his ship along the Yucatan coast, near the present-day city of Vera Cruz, Mexico. Because it was Good Friday, the day that Christians believe Jesus died on the cross, Cortés wore black. According to one of his men, Cortés's face "had little color and was inclined to be greyish. . . . His hair and beard were black and rather thin."[1] Unbeknownst to Cortés, it was also the year "One Reed" of the Aztec[2] calendar, and the day was a "9 Wind day," according to their recurring, 52-year dating system. It was part of the Aztec belief system that their Feathered Serpent god Quetzalcoatl would return on this date to reclaim his land from the Aztec emperors who were ruling in his absence. Moreover, Quetzalcoatl was to return from the direction the Spaniards had come, and he was thought to have light skin, a beard, and dark clothing. In other words, when Cortés stepped off his ship, he also stepped into the middle of the Aztec belief system.

The expedition led by Cortés consisted of 11 ships, 508 swordsmen, 32 crossbow men, 13 musketeers, 14 cannon, 16 horses, and several large war dogs. With this minuscule force, he set out to conquer an empire of some 25 million people.[3] He vowed to his emperor, Charles V of Spain, that he would go to Tenochtitlan, the capital of the Aztec emperor Mocteuzma II (commonly rendered Montezuma) and "have him prisoner or dead or subject to Your Majesty."[4] Although Cortés was motivated by rumors of Aztec treasure, his actions also demonstrated his belief that he was on a divinely sanctioned mission. As the first formal report of his expedition says, of one of his early clashes with a Mesoamerican army, "Surely this battle was won by the will of God rather than by our forces, for we were four hundred against forty thousand warriors."[5] No less than the Aztecs, the Spanish were equally motivated and influenced by their own fervently held belief system.

The Aztec–Spanish encounter is one of the most dramatic and tragic interactions in human history. Although much historical attention has focused on Cortés and Mocteuzma, the Spanish–Aztec conflict involved much more than the personal interactions between those two leaders. Rather, they embodied the values and visions of the civilizations that produced them, so that their dramatic encounter represents the coming together of two vividly different cultures, value systems, and understandings of the world. Hence, the Aztec–Spanish encounter allows us to explore deeply the workings of cross-cultural perceptions (and misperceptions). Furthermore, the historical recordings they have left behind both reflect and preserve these differential worldviews. As a result, by presenting two opposed interpretations of what actually occurred, the sources enable us to engage in one of the primary tasks of the historian: the critical analysis of sources and the evaluation of their accuracy and utility. The issues of cross-cultural perceptions and the critical skills necessary to assess them are the twin topics of this chapter.

In the historical encounter between the Spanish and the Aztecs, it was not just two civilizations that came into conflict, but two powerful, confident imperial structures that also clashed. It was only in 1492, the year of Columbus's first voyage, that the Spaniards had completed their centuries-long *reconquista* (reconquest) of the Iberian peninsula from the control of the Islamic Moors. The Spaniards' religion was a militant, aggressive Catholicism, forged in the long, hard centuries of their political and religious crusade against the Muslim Moors. By 1519, the Spanish had nearly thirty years of exploration and expansion in the Caribbean basin. They had conquered both Hispaniola[6] and Cuba, and they had established towns and estates on each island. Moreover, they had sent expeditions along the northern coast of South America, and Balboa had even crossed the isthmus of Panama to the Pacific. They had not, however, encountered any large, militarily powerful states until 1517, when the first of three exploratory expeditions westward from Cuba made contact with Mesoamerican civilization. Here they encountered sophisticated civilizations with large towns, thriving trade, and a seemingly ample supply of gold and precious stones. It was the wealth of the region that most impressed the Spaniards, and together with their religious fervor, it fueled their advance into the heartland of Mexico. As Cortés himself was to say to Mocteuzma, "We Spaniards have a disease of the heart that only gold can cure."[7]

The Aztecs, meanwhile, had themselves been relative latecomers to the central valley of Mexico and had experienced their own uphill climb to the summit of power. They had founded their capital Tenochtitlan in 1325 on an island in the swamps of the valley's main lake because all other land was already taken. From that modest beginning, their diligent efforts and fighting prowess had allowed them by 1428 to become the major power of the central valley. Like the Romans, the Aztecs conquered an area in which highly advanced agricultural civilization had already developed. In the case of the Aztecs, many of their social institutions and cultural traditions were adopted from earlier empires (the earlier Mayan and Teotihuacan, ca. 450–750, as well as Tula of the Toltecs, ca. 950–1150). Common cultural attributes, for example, included their maize-based agriculture, their writing and calendar systems, step pyramids, the ritual of human sacrifice, and the belief in a feathered serpent god.

One of the most striking features of Aztec culture was human sacrifice, which was deeply entwined in Mesoamerican cosmology.[8] As in many other cultures, ritual sacrifice was perceived as a means to propitiate the gods and to seek their continued blessings and good fortune. The Aztecs were particularly concerned with appeasing Huitzilopochtli (the god of war to whom they attributed their success and rise to power) with the ultimate sacrifice of human beings. But in their lore, the god Quetzalcoatl (the god of wind who brought rain clouds) had opposed human sacrifice and fought with Huitzulopochtli over the issue. Although Quetzalcoatl had lost and had been driven off, he promised one day to return and to reclaim his lands and his throne. The Aztec rulers believed themselves to be reigning in his absence.[9]

Hence the appearance of Cortés/Quetzalcoatl had enormous significance for the Aztec leaders and their people, and it profoundly shaped the character of Aztec–Spanish interactions. The Aztecs feared the arrival of Cortés/Quetzalcoatl but also remembered that the god had been banished once before and perhaps could be exiled again. How that would best be achieved—by bribes, by magic, or by force (if at all)—was the central focus of Aztec policy debates concerning the Spanish. In the eyes of the Spanish, human sacrifice was a shock and an abomination, contrary to all of their religious beliefs and values. Such views undoubtedly shaped their cross-cultural perceptions of the Aztecs and may help explain some of their subsequent actions and behaviors. We are fortunate to have two extraordinary written sources to use in evaluating the Aztec–Spanish encounter. After the conquest, the Spanish systematically destroyed much of Aztec history and culture, and as a result, the records we have of events from the Aztec perspective generally come to us through a Spanish filter. This is true even of the most comprehensive single account of Aztec culture and history at the time of the Conquest, *The General History of New Spain* (also known as the *Florentine Codex*),[10] written in 1575–1577. *The History of New Spain* was compiled under the supervision and at the behest of the Spanish Franciscan friar Bernardino de Sahagún, who had come to New Spain (Mexico) in 1529. Sahagún became deeply interested in the history and culture of the Aztecs, and he ultimately mastered the Nahuatl (Aztec) language. As a result, his encyclopedic account of Aztec society and daily life has a scope and rigor that other sources cannot approach.

The Spanish text we use was also prepared some time after the events. In Bernal Díaz del Castillo's work *The True History of the Conquest of New Spain*, we have a great rarity: the historical record of the views of an insider who had participated in one of history's momentous undertakings. He had been born in Spain in the fateful year of 1492. Like many young Spaniards, he journeyed to the New World to seek his fortune, and through relatives he was included in the expedition to Mexico. A common soldier, he nonetheless fought in many engagements as part of Cortés's forces. He composed the work in the 1560s, because he had read inaccurate accounts written by people who had no direct knowledge of the events. He was present at most of the events he discusses, and he describes what happened from a firsthand, eyewitness perspective. Although he was not a great writer, he writes with clarity. While Cortés himself wrote a series of dispatches to Emperor Charles V of Spain from Mexico, his reports have always been considered suspect, because they are thought by many to include a lot of special pleading by Cortés and therefore to be untrustworthy. This makes Díaz's record all the more valuable.

Three pictorial images of the conquest complete this chapter. Drawings, illustrations, paintings, and photographs can frequently serve as important historical documents. They recount events and people in a visual format, providing additional information to augment written sources. But images are also products of human culture, and they often express or reinforce political ideologies, social institutions, and cultural values. The three images included in this chapter help to illustrate these points. In the Tlaxcalan drawing, *Massacre at Cholula*, and in the Aztec *Massacre of the Mexican Nobility*, cross-cultural perceptions and power relations are powerfully expressed in an abstract and culturally defined manner. The final image, a European painting titled *Battle for Tenochtitlan*, portrays Cortés's final assault on the Aztec capital in a strikingly different manner. Comparing the stories told in these different images—as well as their unique styles of composition and expression—illustrates how visual images can be used to deepen our understanding of history.

The very complex cultural maps that both the Spanish and the Aztecs brought to their encounter make this an ideal instance for studying the way that cross-cultural perceptions are shaped by preexisting belief systems. Thus we can assess the degree to which, in cross-cultural interaction, it is not so much a matter of "seeing is believing" but rather that "believing is seeing." Moreover, the cultural backgrounds influenced the ways that these historic events were recorded, illustrated, and remembered by the two sides. Therefore, we have a "twice-told tale" that comes out very differently in the two narrations. Consequently, we can also perform the fundamental work of historical assessment by critiquing the sources and weighing their respective strengths, limitations, and inherent biases.

CHAPTER QUESTIONS

1. What were the most important factors shaping the vision that each side had of the other? How did this vision affect their behavior? Did the image that either side had of the other change over time? If so, why?

2. How do the pictorial images affect your understanding of this cross-cultural encounter? Do they impart information different from that in the texts?

3. These sources were produced specifically to explain or to represent this encounter from the point of view of one of the two groups. Can you identify instances in which the circumstances under which these sources were produced might have affected the way each side told the story?

4. Historians use primary sources to reconstruct the past. Using the sources provided here, what different stories can be told?

5. Human religious beliefs and rituals have meaning in terms of the cultural context that produced them. Should we then avoid all value judgments when studying other societies? Or are there some human behaviors—for example, the human sacrifice of the Aztecs or the convert-or-die practices of the Spanish—that ought to be condemned, even though they are highly valued in the societies that practice them?

40 CHAPTER 2 ◆ Cross-Cultural Perceptions in the New World

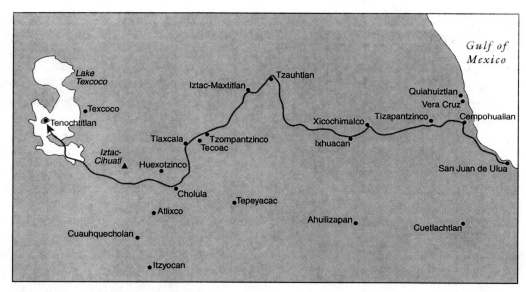

Map 2.1 Cortés's Route to Tenochtitlan

AN AZTEC ACCOUNT
OF THE CONQUEST OF MEXICO

The epic saga of the Spanish–Aztec encounter has been recounted elsewhere in sufficient detail, and only a brief account needs repeating here. Following the landing of Cortés and his forces in 1519, the first peoples they encountered were either unhappy subjects or outright enemies of the Aztec empire. Nonetheless, they opposed the Spanish in a number of military engagements. Although the native forces were more numerous and fought bravely, the Spanish overcame them, owing to the technological and psychological advantage of their weapons, especially their cavalry, which gave them an enormous advantage in speed and power. Those advantages were multiplied by the terror the horse and rider inspired, because the largest domesticated animal among the Mesoamericans was the dog.[11]

Once they were convinced that the Spanish could not be defeated, a number of these peoples allied themselves with Cortés against the Aztecs. The most significant allies were the Tlaxcalans, who provided soldiers to fight their longtime Aztec adversaries. Cortés also benefited from the assistance of a captive Aztec woman known to the Spanish as "Doña Marina." She informed Cortés about Mesoamerican and Aztec ways, and she helped the Spaniards more than once to escape ambush and other very dangerous situations.[12] By mid-October, the conquistadores were in Cholula, where they attacked and massacred a large number of warriors. The circumstances surrounding this event are unclear: According to Aztec sources, the massacre was a violent and unprovoked attack on unarmed men, whereas Spanish sources claim it was a necessary preemptive strike against Cholulans, who were planning their own massacre of the Spanish. Such discrepan-

An Aztec Account of the Conquest of Mexico   41

cies are not unusual and illustrate some of the difficulties faced by historians in the reconstruction of Mexican history.

By early November, the steady advance of the Spanish brought them to the outskirts of Tenochtitlan. The Aztec capital was built on an island in the middle of a lake, with three causeways leading to it and the massive temple complex in the middle. The city was densely populated, and its neighborhoods were connected by both streets and canals. The causeways were built of stone, but they had gaps in them that were bridged over with wooden constructions that could be removed in case of attack. They also had a vast number of war canoes that could attack a foe from the sides. It is difficult to estimate the population of the city, but it was at least 200,000, and perhaps much higher. It was greater than European cities of that era, and the Spanish were duly impressed.

Mocteuzma had been kept well informed on the advance of the foreigners, and he had sent numerous emissaries to present gifts and to gather information about the god's intentions. With his advisors divided on the best course of action, Mocteuzma personally greeted Cortés at his arrival, gave him numerous gifts, and housed him in a palace. Among other things, the Spaniards found a room filled with an incredible treasure of gold and jewelry, and Cortés dispatched survey parties to explore other sources of wealth. To ensure cooperation, Cortés placed Mocteuzma and other notables under his supervision and control in a form of house arrest. The situation remained tense but relatively peaceful until May 1520, when Cortés learned that a force of 1,300 men had been sent out by the governor of Cuba to arrest him and take over the expedition because of his failure to obey orders. Cortés had a great deal at stake. On the one hand, whoever won royal recognition would receive one-fifth of the treasure taken. On the other hand, if he did not win royal recognition, he could be arrested as a traitor and rebel. As it turned out, the leader of the second expedition was no match for Cortés, who boldly marched back to Vera Cruz, captured the other leader, won over his forces, and merged them with his own small force.

On arriving back in Tenochtitlan, Cortés found a much changed environment. The man he had left in charge in the capital, Pedro de Alvarado, had attacked and massacred a group of Aztec nobles, who were dancing unarmed in the plaza of the main temple in celebration of a major feast (this event is the subject of the Aztec painting included here as Figure 2.2 on page 67). After the massacre, the Spanish force had been attacked and cut off from almost all supplies. The city seethed with anger toward the Spanish, and fighting flared up again immediately after Cortés returned. It was at this point that Mocteuzma died. Once again, sources are not clear on the death of the Aztec leader. Some assert that he was struck down by a rock thrown by an Aztec warrior, others contend that he was killed by the Spanish, and still others maintain that he committed suicide. Whatever occurred, on June 30, 1520, Cortés led his forces out of the city in a desperate breakout that came to be known as the *Noche Triste*, or the "Night of Sorrows." Many Spaniards were killed or captured, and the captives were sacrificed. Others drowned in the canals surrounding the city, weighed down by gold and their greed.

When Cortés returned in January 1521, he brought an army of 500 Spaniards and tens of thousands of native allies, especially the Tlaxcalans. With the aid of

42   CHAPTER 2 ◆ Cross-Cultural Perceptions in the New World

Tlaxcalan laborers, they constructed thirteen sloops and mounted cannon on them, effectively cutting off both food and fresh water supplies to Tenochtitlan. Nonetheless, the city proved incredibly difficult to conquer, and the Spaniards suffered heavy losses. In addition, a smallpox epidemic broke out in October 1520 that lasted more than two months and claimed thousands of victims. Despite this, the Aztecs refused to surrender. On August 13, 1521, the last Aztec leader was captured, and the Tlaxcalan allies massacred many of the survivors in the city.

The first documents in this chapter contain descriptions of these monumental and agonizing events from the Aztec perspective. They were compiled at the behest and under the supervision of a Franciscan friar, Bernardino de Sahagún. Sahagún had arrived in New Spain, as the territory had been designated by Cortés, in 1529 at the age of thirty. He soon acquired a sophisticated mastery of Nahuatl, the Aztec language, and over the years he collected an invaluable mass of material relating to preconquest life of the native peoples. Beginning in 1547, the material was acquired by native Americans who were taught to write and who recorded the memories of elderly nobles who had witnessed the events. Later, Sahagún put the material together and edited it, finishing his *General History of New Spain* in 1577. Although the text was compiled under Spanish auspices and given final form by a Spanish Franciscan priest, it nonetheless imparts a sense of how the events of the conquest were perceived by the Aztecs themselves. In the view of most scholars, it remains the best and fullest native account of the conquest.

QUESTIONS TO CONSIDER

1. How did the Aztec belief system shape the Aztecs' perception of the Spanish and Cortés? What characteristics of the Spanish worked to reinforce Aztec perceptions?

2. How did the Spanish belief and value systems affect the Spaniards' perception of the Aztecs? How did subsequent Aztec and Spanish actions and reactions affect their mutual understanding?

3. Identify the different means which Mocteuzma sought to deal with Cortés and the Spanish. Does the text indicate that other Aztecs who shared his belief system might have reacted differently to the Spanish forces? If so, identify passages that give that impression.

4. Characterize the way the Spanish are depicted in this document. Based on what you know, is this an accurate portrayal of Cortés and his forces?

5. How might the circumstances in which the *Florentine Codex* was compiled have affected the interpretation of events presented in it? Would those circumstances make it more or less likely to present an accurate view of the Aztec understanding of the encounter?

Bernardino de Sahagún   ◆   *The General History of New Spain* (1577)   43

THE GENERAL HISTORY OF NEW SPAIN (1577)

Bernardino de Sahagún

The year 13-Rabbit* now approached its end. And when it was about to end, they [the Spaniards] appeared, they were seen again. The report of their coming was brought to Mocteuzma, who immediately sent out messengers. It was as if he thought the new arrival was our prince Quetzalcoatl.

This is what he felt in his heart: *He has appeared! He has come back! He will come here, to the place of his throne and canopy, for that is what was promised when he departed!*

Mocteuzma sent five messengers to greet the strangers and to bring them gifts. . . . He said to them: "Come forward, my Jaguar Knights, come forward. It is said that our lord has returned to this land. Go to meet him. Go to hear him. Listen well to what he tells you; listen and remember."

Mocteuzma also said to his messengers: "Here is what you are to bring our lord. This is the treasure of Quetzalcoatl." This treasure was the god's finery: a serpent mask inlaid with turquoise, a decoration for the breast made of quetzal feathers, a collar woven in the *ptatillo* style with a gold disk in the center, and a shield decorated with gold and mother-of-pearl and bordered with quetzal feathers with a pendant of the same feathers.

There was also a mirror like those which the ritual dancers wore. . . . The reverse of the mirror was a turquoise mosaic: it was encrusted and adorned with turquoise. And there was a spear-thrower inlaid with turquoise, a bracelet hung with little gold bells. . . .

Mocteuzma also gave them the finery of Tezcatlipoca[†] . . . : a helmet in the shape of a cone, yellow with gold and set with many stars, a number of earrings adorned with little gold bells. . . .

These were the many kinds of adornments that were known as "divine adornments." They were . . . to be taken as gifts of welcome along with many other objects. . . ."

Then Mocteuzma gave the messengers his final orders. He said to them: "Go now, without delay. Do reverence to our lord the god. Say to him: 'Your deputy, Mocteuzma, has sent us to you. Here are the presents with which he welcomes you home to Mexico.'" . . .

Source: Excerpted from *The Broken Spears: The Aztec Account of the Conquest of Mexico,* edited and with an introduction by Miguel Leon-Portilla (Boston: Beacon Press, 1962), 22–31, 33–35, 40–41, 51–52, 63–68. Copyright © 1962 Beacon Press. Reprinted by permission.

*The Aztecs had a repeating fifty-two-year calendar. The cycle was broken up into four signs (e.g., "Wind" and "Rabbit"), each with thirteen years. The Spanish arrived at the end of the thirteenth year designated by the sign of the Rabbit.

†The Aztec god of "Here and Now," who rules the everyday life of earth.

44   CHAPTER 2 ◆ Cross-Cultural Perceptions in the New World

One by one they did reverence to Cortés by touching the ground before him with their lips. They said to him: "If the god deign to hear us, your deputy Mocteuzma has sent us to render you homage. He has the City of Mexico in his care. He says: 'The god is weary.'"

Then they arrayed the Captain in the finery they had brought him as presents. . . . The Captain asked them: "And is this all? Is this your gift of welcome? Is this how you greet people?" . . .

Then the Captain gave orders, and the messengers were chained by the feet and by the neck. When this had been done, the great cannon was fired off. The messengers lost their senses and fainted away. They fell down side by side and lay where they had fallen. But the Spaniards quickly revived them: they lifted them up, gave them wine to drink and then offered food. . . .

While the messengers were away, Mocteuzma could neither sleep nor eat, and no one could speak with him. He thought that everything he did was in vain, and he sighed almost every moment. He was lost in despair, in the deepest gloom and sorrow. Nothing could comfort him, nothing could calm him, nothing could give him any pleasure.

He said: "What will happen to us? Who will outlive it? Ah, in other times I was contented, but now I have death in my heart! My heart burns and suffers, as if it were drowned in spices . . . ! But will our lord come here?"

[He was told] "The messengers have come back from the sea."

Then he . . . gave this order: "Two captives are to be painted with chalk."

The messengers went down to the House of the Serpent, and Mocteuzma arrived. The two captives were then sacrificed before his eyes: their breasts were torn open, and the messengers were sprinkled with their blood. This was done because the messengers had . . . seen the gods, their eyes had looked on their faces. They had even conversed with the gods!

When the sacrifice was finished, the messengers reported to the king. They told him how they had made the journey, and what they had seen and what food the strangers ate. Mocteuzma was astonished and terrified by their report, and the description of the strangers' food astonished him above all else.

He was also terrified to learn how the cannon roared, how its noise resounded, how it caused one to faint and grow deaf. The messengers told him: "A thing like a ball of stone comes out of its entrails: it comes out shooting sparks and raining fire. The smoke that comes out with it has a pestilent odor, like that of rotting mud. The odor penetrates to the brain and causes the greatest discomfort. If the cannon is aimed against a mountain, the mountain splits and cracks open. If it is aimed against a tree, it shatters the tree into splinters. This is a most unnatural sight, as if the tree had exploded from within."

The messengers also said: "Their trappings and arms are all made of iron. They dress in iron and wear iron casques on their heads. Their swords are iron; their bows are iron; their shields are iron; their spears are iron. Their deer carry them on their backs wherever they wish to go. The deer, our lord, are as tall as the roof of a house.

"The strangers' bodies are completely covered, so that only their faces can be seen. Their skin is white, as if it were made of lime. They have yellow hair, though

Bernardino de Sahagún ❖ *The General History of New Spain* (1577)   45

some of them have black. Their beards are long and yellow, and their mustaches are yellow. Their hair is curly, with very fine strands.

"As for their food, it is like human food. It is large and white, and not heavy. It is something like straw, but with the taste of a cornstalk, of the pith of a cornstalk. It is a little sweet, as if it were flavored with honey; it tastes of honey, it is sweet-tasting food.

"Their dogs are enormous, with flat ears and long dangling tongues. The color of their eyes is a burning yellow; their eyes flash fire and shoot off sparks. Their bellies are hollow, their flanks long and narrow. They are tireless and very powerful. They bound here and there, panting, with their tongues hanging out. And they are spotted like an ocelot."

When Mocteuzma heard this report, he was filled with terror. It was as if his heart had fainted, as if it had shriveled. It was as if he were conquered by despair. . . .

Mocteuzma sent out . . . his most gifted men, his prophets and wizards, as many as he could gather. He also sent out his noblest and bravest warriors. . . .

Mocteuzma also sent captives to be sacrificed, because the strangers might wish to drink their blood. The envoys sacrificed these captives in the presence of the strangers, but when the white men saw this done, they were filled with disgust and loathing. They spat on the ground, or wiped away their tears, or closed their eyes and shook their heads with abhorrence. They refused to eat the food that was sprinkled with blood, . . . it sickened them, as if the blood had rotted.

Mocteuzma ordered the sacrifice because he took the Spaniards to be gods; he believed in them and worshiped them as deities. That is why they were called "Gods who have come from heaven." . . .

Mocteuzma had sent the magicians to learn what sort of people the strangers might be, but they were also to see if they could work some charm against them, or do them some mischief. They might be able to direct a harmful wind against them, or cause them to break out in sores, or injure them in some way. Or they might be able to repeat some enchanted word, over and over, that would cause them to fall sick, or die, or return to their own land.

The magicians carried out their mission against the Spaniards, but they failed completely. They could not harm them in any way. . . .

When the Spaniards left their ships and began to march here . . . Mocteuzma was distraught and bewildered; he was filled with terror, not knowing what would happen to the city. The people were also terrified, debating the news among themselves. There were meetings and arguments and gossip in the street; there was weeping and lamenting. The people were downcast; they went about with their heads bowed down and greeted each other with tears.

At this time the Tlaxcaltecas* were enemies of Cholula. They feared the Cholultecas; they envied and cursed them; their souls burned with hatred for the people of

---

*The Tlaxcalans (called Tlaxcaltecas in the *Florentine Codex*) were enemies of the Aztecs. They had at first opposed Cortés, but, after they had lost a battle to the Spaniards, they became Cortés's most reliable allies.

46   CHAPTER 2   ◆   Cross-Cultural Perceptions in the New World

Cholula. This is why they brought certain rumors to Cortés, so that he would destroy them. They said to him: "Cholula is our enemy. It is an evil city. The people are as brave as the Aztecs and they are the Aztecs' friends."

When the Spaniards heard this, they marched against Cholula. . . . When they arrived, . . . an assembly was held in the courtyard of the god, but when they had all gathered together, the entrances were closed, so that there was no way of escaping.

Then the sudden slaughter began: knife strokes, and sword strokes, and death. The people of Cholula . . . had not suspected it. They faced the Spaniards without weapons, without their swords or their shields. The cause of the slaughter was treachery. They died blindly, without knowing why, because of the lies of the Tlaxcaltecas.

And when this had taken place, word of it was brought to Mocteuzma. . . . The common people were terrified by the news; they could do nothing but tremble with fright. It was as if the earth trembled beneath them, or as if the world were spinning before their eyes, as it spins during a fit of vertigo. . . .

When the massacre at Cholula was complete, the strangers set out again toward the City of Mexico. They came in battle array, as conquerors, and the dust rose in whirlwinds on the roads. Their spears glinted in the sun, and their pennons fluttered like bats. They made a loud clamor as they marched, for their coats of mail and their weapons clashed and rattled. Some of them were dressed in glistening iron from head to foot; they terrified everyone who saw them.

Their dogs came with them, running ahead of the column. They raised their muzzles high; they lifted their muzzles to the wind. They raced on before with saliva dripping from their jaws.

Then Mocteuzma dispatched various chiefs. . . . They gave the "gods" ensigns of gold, and ensigns of quetzal feathers, and golden necklaces. And when they were given these presents, the Spaniards burst into smiles; their eyes shone with pleasure; they were delighted by them. They picked up the gold and fingered it like monkeys; they seemed to be transported with joy, as if their hearts were illumined and made new.

The truth is that they longed and lusted for gold. Their bodies swelled with greed, and their hunger was ravenous; they hungered like pigs for gold. They snatched at the golden ensigns, waved them from side to side and examined every inch of them. They were like one who speaks a barbarous tongue; everything they said was in a barbarous tongue.

The Spaniards arrived. . . . Thus Mocteuzma went out to meet them. . . . He presented many gifts to the Captain and his commanders, those who had come to make war. He showered gifts upon them and hung flowers around their necks. . . . Then he hung the gold necklaces around their necks and gave them presents of every sort as gifts of welcome. . . .

And the king . . . stood up to welcome Cortés; he came forward, bowed his head low and addressed him in these words: "Our lord, you are weary. The journey has tired you, but now you have arrived on the earth. You have come to the city, Mexico. You have come here to sit on your throne, to sit under its canopy.

"The kings who have gone before, your representatives, guarded it and preserved it for your coming. The kings . . . ruled for you in the City of Mexico. The people were protected by their swords and sheltered by their shields." . . .

Bernardino de Sahagún ◆ *The General History of New Spain* (1577) **47**

"No, it is not a dream. I am not walking in my sleep. I am not seeing you in my dreams. I have seen you at last! I have met you face to face! I was in agony for five days, . . . and now you have come out of the clouds and mists to sit on your throne again.

"This was foretold by the kings who governed our city, and now it has taken place. You have come back to us; you have come down from the sky. Rest now, and take possession of your royal houses. Welcome to your lands, my lords!" . . .

Cortés replied in his strange and savage tongue, . . . "Tell, Mocteuzma that we are his friends. There is nothing to fear. We have wanted to see him for a long time, and now we have seen his face and heard his words. Tell him that we love him well and that our hearts are contented." . . .

[A]nd the Spaniards grasped Mocteuzma's hands and patted his back to show their affection for him. . . .

When the Spaniards entered the Royal House, they placed Mocteuzma under guard. . . . Then the Spaniards fired one of their cannons, and this caused great confusion in the city. The people scattered in every direction; they fled without rhyme or reason; they ran off as if they were being pursued. It was as if they had eaten the mushrooms that confuse the mind, or had seen some dreadful apparition. They were all overcome with terror, as if their hearts had fainted. And when night fell, the panic spread through the city and their fears would not let them sleep. . . .

When the Spaniards were installed in the palace, they asked Mocteuzma about the city's resources and reserves and about the warriors' ensigns and shields. They questioned him closely and then demanded gold.

Mocteuzma guided them to it. They surrounded him and crowded close with their weapons. He walked in the center, while they formed a circle around him.

When they arrived at the treasure house . . . , the riches of gold and feathers were brought out to them: ornaments made of quetzal feathers,* richly worked shields, disks of gold, the necklaces of the idols, gold nose plugs, gold greaves† and bracelets and crowns.

The Spaniards immediately stripped the feathers from the gold shields and ensigns. They gathered all the gold into a great mound and set fire to everything else, regardless of its value. Then they melted down the gold into ingots. As for the precious green stones, they took only the best of them; . . . The Spaniards searched through the whole treasure house, questioning and quarreling, and seized every object they thought was beautiful.

Next they went to Mocteuzma's storehouse, . . . where his personal treasures were kept. The Spaniards grinned like little beasts and patted each other with delight.

When they entered the hall of treasures, it was as if they had arrived in Paradise. They searched everywhere and coveted everything; they were slaves to their own greed. All of Mocteuzma's possessions were brought out: fine bracelets, necklaces with large stones, ankle rings with little gold bells, the royal crowns and all the royal

---

*Some of the Aztecs' most valued ornaments were feathers.

†A piece of armor that covered the shin.

finery—everything that belonged to the king and was reserved to him only. They seized these treasures as if they were their own, as if this plunder were merely a stroke of good luck.

A SPANISH ACCOUNT OF THE CONQUEST OF MEXICO

The best Spanish source on the Aztec–Spanish encounter was written by Bernal Díaz del Castillo, an old campaigner from Cortés's army. Born and raised in a poor family in Spain, Díaz began his military career as a common soldier. In 1514, he went to America to serve with the Spanish forces opening up the "New World," and he made two previous expeditions to the Yucatan prior to the one led by Hernando Cortés in 1519. According to his own accounts, he took part in over one hundred battles and was present at the surrender of Tenochtitlan in 1521. As a reward for services he received a commission as *regidor,* or governor, of Santiago de los Caballeros in Guatemala, where he was also awarded a minor, relatively unproductive grant of land and native labor (*encomienda*).[13] Unhappy with this grant, Díaz even traveled once to Spain to argue for a better reward for his services. Charles V and his government in Spain, who had no real appreciation for the caliber of foe that Cortés and company had bested, quickly grew weary of the conquistadores and their clamor for greater reward. After having read a published account of the conquest that he considered a distortion, Díaz set about writing his own account during the 1560s, when he was already an old man. He finished it when he was seventy-six years old. Though he had sent a copy to Spain, the work was not published until the next century, well after his long and eventful life had ended in 1581. The drama of the events and the intimacy and novelty of his observations make this a remarkable historical source.

Though many years had passed, Díaz seemed to have vivid memories of both the events and the personages he had witnessed. His memory for names failed him in only a few instances. For example, there was one native leader whose name he had forgotten, and whom he always referred to simply as "the fat lord." Such lapses are remarkably few and far between. Though he was not a polished writer, his style is clear and his voice confident, and he has left us an extraordinary and intimate recording of these epochal events from the Spanish point of view. The selections include Díaz's reconstruction of the events at Cholula, the Spaniards' entry into Tenochtitlan, the initial interactions between Cortés and Mocteuzma, and the Spanish decision to make the Aztec ruler a captive. These readings provide us with insights into the events that transpired, as well as giving us information on perceptions and attitudes of the participants.

Bernal Díaz del Castillo ◆ *The True History of the Conquest of New Spain* (1568)   49

1. Compare the Aztec explanation for the events at Cholula with explanations provided by Díaz. How do they differ? Whose version is more convincing to you? Why?

2. List the things about Aztec civilization that Díaz admires and then put them into categories (for example, technology, economics, culture, and so on).

3. What does Díaz reject about Aztec civilization? Categorize what he rejects and then compare that with what he admires. What general conclusions can you draw? How did the Spanish make value judgments?

4. How do the overall representations of the Spanish and the Aztecs provided by Díaz compare with the impressions that emerge from the *Florentine Codex*? How do you explain the differences?

5. How do the religious beliefs and practices of the Spanish and the Aztecs affect their behavior, as described by Díaz? Are any of their behaviors surprising?

THE TRUE HISTORY OF THE CONQUEST OF NEW SPAIN (1568)

Bernal Díaz del Castillo

[The excerpt begins with Díaz's account of the massacre at Cholula.]

After the people of Cholula had received us in the festive manner already described, and most certainly with [a show of] good will, it presently appeared that Mocteuzma sent orders to his ambassadors, who were still in our company, to negotiate with the Cholulans that an army of 20,000 men which Mocteuzma had sent and equipped, should on entering the city, join with them in attacking us by night or by day, get us into a hopeless plight, and bring all of us that they could [capture] bound to Mexico. And he sent grand promises together with many presents of jewels and cloths, also a golden drum, and he also sent word to the priests of the city that they were to retain twenty of us to sacrifice to their idols.

All was in readiness and the warriors whom Mocteuzma quickly sent were stationed in some ranchos and some rocky thickets about half a league from Cholula and some were already posted within the houses, and all had their arms ready for use, and had built up breastworks . . . and had dug holes and ditches in the streets so

Source: Bernal Díaz del Castillo, *The True History of the Conquest of New Spain*, vol. 1, Hakluyt Society, Second Series, XXIII (London, 1908), 132–35; vol. 2, Hakluyt Society, Second Series, XXIV (London, 1910), 4–18, 37–38, 39–40, 44, 55–58, 59–60, 69–79, 84–88. Some passages have been taken out of their original order without changing the sense. Díaz's spelling of two gods' names, Tescatepuca and Huichilobos, have been changed to their modern spellings—Tezcatlipoca and Huitzilopochtli, respectively—to avoid confusion.

50 CHAPTER 2 ◆ Cross-Cultural Perceptions in the New World

as to impede the horsemen, and they had already filled some houses with long poles and leather collars and cords with which they were to bind us and lead us to Mexico; but our Lord God so ordained that all their plots should be turned against them. . . .

[T]hey had taken us to our quarters, they fed us very well for the first two days, and although we saw them so peacefully inclined, we never gave up our good custom of keeping fully prepared, and on the third day they neither gave us anything to eat nor did any of the *Caciques** or priests make their appearance, and if any Indians came to look at us, they did not approach us, but remained some distance off, laughing at us as though mocking us. When our Captain saw this, he told our interpreters Doña Marina and Jeronimo de Aguilar to tell the Ambassadors of the Great Mocteuzma, who remained with us, to order the *Caciques* to bring some food, but all they brought was water and fire wood, and the old men who brought it said that there was no more maize.

That same day other Ambassadors arrived from Mocteuzma, and joined those who were already with us and they said to Cortés, very impudently, that their Prince had sent them to say that we were not to go to his city because he had nothing to give us to eat, and that they wished at once to return to Mexico with our reply. When Cortés saw that their speech was unfriendly, he replied to the Ambassadors in the blandest manner, that he marveled how such a great Prince as Mocteuzma should be so vacillating, and he begged them not to return to Mexico, for he wished to start himself on the next day, to see their Prince, and act according to his orders, and I believe that he gave the Ambassadors some strings of beads and they agreed to stay.

When this had been done, our Captain called us together, and said to us, "I see that these people are very much disturbed, and it behooves us to keep on the alert, in case some trouble is brewing among them," and he at once sent for the principal chief, whose name I now forget, telling him either to come himself or to send some other chieftains. The chief replied that he was ill and could not come.

When our Captain heard this, he ordered us to bring before him, with kindly persuasion, two of the numerous priests who were in the great Cue [step-pyramid temple] near our quarters. We brought two of them, without doing them any disrespect, and Cortés ordered each of them to be given a *chalchihuite*,[†] which are held by them to be as valuable as emeralds, and addressing them with friendly words he asked them what was the reason that the chief and chieftains and most of the priests were frightened, for he had sent to summon them and they did not want to come. It seems that one of these priests was a very important personage among them, who had charge of or command over all the Cues in the City, and was a sort of Bishop among the priests and was held in great respect. He replied that they, who were priests, had no fear of us, and if the chief and chieftain did not wish to come, he would go himself and summon them, and that if he spoke to them he believed they would do as he told them and would come.

Cortés at once told him to go, and that his companion should await his return. So the priests departed and summoned the chief and chieftains who returned in his com-

---

*Leaders or chiefs.

†Jade ornaments.

Bernal Díaz del Castillo ◆ *The True History of the Conquest of New Spain* (1568)   51

pany to Cortés' quarters. Cortés asked them, through our interpreters, what it was they were afraid of, and why they had not given us anything to eat, and said that if our presence in their city were an annoyance to them, we wished to leave the next day for Mexico to see and speak to the Lord Mocteuzma, and he asked them to provide carriers for the transport of the baggage and *tepusques* (which are the cannon) and to send us some food at once.

The chief was so embarrassed that he could hardly speak; he said that they would look for the food, but their Lord Mocteuzma had sent to tell them not to give us any, and was not willing that we should proceed any further.

While this conversation was taking place, three of our friends, the Cempoala Indians,* came in and said secretly to Cortés, that close by where we were quartered they had found holes dug in the streets, covered over with wood and earth, so that without careful examination one could not see them, that they had removed the earth from above one of the holes and found it full of sharp pointed stakes to kill the horses when they galloped, and that the *Azoteas*† had breastworks of adobes and were piled up with stones, and certainly this was not done with good intent for they also found barricades of thick timbers in another street. At this moment eight Tlaxcalans arrived, from the Indians whom we had left outside in the fields with orders that they were not to enter Cholula, and they said to Cortés, "Take heed, Malinche;‡ for this City is ill disposed, and we know that this night they have sacrificed to their Idol, which is the God of War, seven persons, five of them children, so that the God may give them victory over you, and we have further seen that they are moving all their baggage and women and children out of the city." When Cortés heard this, he immediately sent these Tlaxcalans back to their Captains, with orders to be fully prepared if we should send to summon them, and he turned to speak to the *Cacique,* priests and chieftains of Cholula and told them to have no fear and show no alarm, but to remember the obedience which they had promised to him, and not to swerve from it, lest he should have to chastise them. That he had already told them that we wished to set out on the morrow and that he had need of two thousand warriors from the city to accompany us, just as the Tlaxcalans had provided them, for they were necessary on the road. They replied that the men would be given, and asked leave to go at once to get them ready, and they went away very well contented, for they thought that between the warriors with whom they were to supply us, and the regiments sent by Mocteuzma, which were hidden in the rocky thickets and *barrancas* [canyons] we could not escape death or capture, for the horses would not be able to charge on account of certain breastworks and barricades which they immediately advised the troops to construct, so that only a narrow lane would be left through which it would be impossible for us to pass. They warned the Mexicans to be in readiness as we intended to

---

*The Cempoala were a coastal people held in tributary status by the Aztecs, and they were the first people Cortés's forces overcame and won as allies.

†A rooftop garden.

‡The name that the Aztecs applied to Cortés. The exact meaning of the name is open to debate. Bernal Díaz said that because Doña Marina was always with Cortés, he was called "Malinche,"which Díaz translated as "Marina's Captain." Others have defined "Malinche" as "Captain," and have interpreted "La Malinche" (or Doña Marina) as "the captain's woman."

52   CHAPTER 2   ◆   Cross-Cultural Perceptions in the New World

start on the next day and told them that they were going to give us two thousand warriors to accompany us, so that as we marched along, off our guard, between the two
forces our capture would be sure and they would be able to bind us, and this they
might look on as a certainty, for they [the Cholulans] had made sacrifices to their War
Idols who had promised them victory.

Let us cease speaking of this which they looked on as a sure thing and return to
our Captain who, as he wished to be more thoroughly informed about the plot and
all that was happening, told Doña Marina to take more *chalchihuites* to the two priests
who had been the first to speak, for they were not afraid, and to tell them with friendly
words that Malinche [Cortés] wished them to come back and speak to him, and to
bring them back with her. Doña Marina went and spoke to the priests in the manner
she knew so well how to use, and thanks to the presents they at once accompanied
her. Cortés addressed them and asked them to say truly what they knew, for they were
the priests of Idols and chieftains and ought not to lie, and that what they should say
would not be disclosed in any manner, for we were going to leave the next morning,
and he would give them a large quantity of cloth. They said the truth was that their
Lord Mocteuzma knew that we were coming to their city, and that every day he was
of many minds and could not come to any decision on the matter, that sometimes he
sent to order them to pay us much respect when we arrived and to guide us on the
way to his city, and at other times he would send word that it was not his wish that
we should go to Mexico, and now recently his [gods] Tezcatlipoca* and Huitzilopochtli, to whom he paid great devotion, had counseled him that we should either
be killed here in Cholula or should be sent, bound, to Mexico. That the day before he
had sent out twenty thousand warriors, and half of them were already within this city
and the other half were stationed nearby in some gullies, and that they already knew
that we were about to start tomorrow; they also told us about the barricades which
they had ordered to be made and the two thousand warriors that were to be given to
us, and how it had already been agreed that twenty of us were to be kept to be sacrificed to the Idols of Cholula.

Cortés ordered these men to be given a present of richly embroidered cloth, and
told them not to say anything [about the information they had given us] for, if they
disclosed it, on our return from Mexico we would kill them. He also told them that
we should start early the next morning and he asked them to summon all the *Caciques*
to come then so that he might speak to them.

That night Cortés took counsel of us as to what should be done, for he had very
able men with him whose advice was worth having, but as in such cases frequently
happens, some said that it would be advisable to change our course and go by Huex-
otzingo, others that we must manage to preserve the peace by every possible means
and that it would be better to return to Tlaxcala, others of us gave our opinion that if
we allowed such treachery to pass unpunished, wherever we went we should be
treated to worse [treachery], and that being there in the town, with ample provisions,
we ought to make an attack, for the Indians would feel the effect of it more in their
own homes than they would in the open, and that we should at once warn the Tlax-

---

*One of the Aztecs most powerful gods, associated with the sun and rebirth. Literally translated it
means "Smoking Mirror."

Bernal Díaz del Castillo ◆ *The True History of the Conquest of New Spain* (1568)   53

calans so that they might join in it. All thought well of this last advice. As Cortés had already told them that we were going to set out on the following day, for this reason we should make a show of tying together our baggage, which was little enough, and then in the large courts with high walls, where we were lodged, we should fall on the Indian warriors, who well deserved their fate. As regards the Ambassadors of Mocteuzma, we should dissemble and tell them that the evil-minded Cholulans had intended treachery and had attempted to put the blame for it on their Lord Mocteuzma, and on themselves as his Ambassadors, but we did not believe Mocteuzma had given any such orders, and we begged them to stay in their apartments and not have any further converse with the people of the city, so that we should not have reason to think they were in league with them in their treachery, and we asked them to go with us as our guides to Mexico.

They replied that neither they themselves nor their Lord Mocteuzma knew anything about that which we were telling them. Although they did not like it, we placed guards over the Ambassadors, so that they could not go out without our permission, and Mocteuzma should not come to know that we were well aware how it was he who had ordered it to be done.

All that night we were on the alert and under arms with the horses saddled and bridled, and with many sentinels and patrols, although indeed it was always our custom to keep a good watch, for we thought that for certain all the companies of the Mexicans as well as the Cholulans would attack us during the night.

There was an old Indian woman, the wife of a *Cacique,* who knew all about the plot and trap which had been arranged, and she had come secretly to Doña Marina our interpreter, having noticed that she was young and good looking and rich, and advised her, if she wanted to escape with her life, to come with her to her house, for it was certain that on that night or during the next day we were going to be killed, for the Great Mocteuzma had so arranged, and commanded that the Mexicans and the people of the city were to join forces, and not one of us was to be left alive, except those who would be carried bound to Mexico. Because she knew of this, and on account of the compassion she felt for Doña Marina, she had come to tell her that she had better get all her possessions together and come with her to her house, and she would there marry her to her son, the brother of a youth who was with another old woman who accompanied her.

When Doña Marina understood this (as she was always very shrewd) she said to her, "O mother, thank you much for this that you have told me, I would go with you at once but that I have no one here whom I can trust to carry my clothes and jewels of gold of which I have many, for goodness sake, mother, wait here a little while, you and your son, and tonight we will set out, for now, as you can see, the *Teules* [gods] are on the watch and will hear us."

The old woman believed what she said, and remained chatting with her, and Doña Marina asked her how they were going to kill us all, and how and when and where the plot was made. The old woman told her neither more nor less than what the two priests had already stated, and Doña Marina replied, "If this affair is such a secret, how is it that you came to know about it?" and the old woman replied that her husband had told her, for he was a captain of one of the parties in the city, and as captain he was now away with his warriors giving orders for them to join the squadrons of Mocteuzma in the *barrancas,* and she thought that they were already assembled waiting for us to set out, and that they would kill us there; as to the plot she had known about it for three days, for a gilded drum had been sent to her husband from Mexico, and rich cloaks and jewels of gold had been sent to three other captains to induce them to bring us bound to their Lord Mocteuzma.

When Doña Marina heard this she deceived the old woman and said, "How delighted I am to hear that your son to whom you wish to marry me is a man of distinction. We have already talked a good deal, and I do not want them to notice us, so Mother you wait here while I begin to bring my property, for I cannot bring it all at once, and you and your son, my brother, will take care of it, and then we shall be able to go." The old woman believed all that was told her, and she and her son sat down to rest. Then Doña Marina went swiftly to the Captain and told him all that had passed with the Indian woman. Cortés at once ordered her to be brought before him, and questioned her about these treasons and plots, and she told him neither more nor less than the priests had already said, so he placed a guard over the woman so that she could not escape.

When dawn broke, it was a sight to see the haste with which the *Caciques* and priests brought in the warriors, laughing and contented as though they had already caught us in their traps and nets, and they brought more Indian warriors than we had asked for, and large as they are (for they still stand as a memorial of the past) the courtyards would not hold them all.

Early as it was when the Cholulans arrived with the warriors, we were already quite prepared for what had to be done. The soldiers with swords and shields were stationed at the gate of the great court so as not to let a single armed Indian pass out. Our Captain was mounted on horseback with many soldiers round him, as a guard, and when he saw how very early the *Caciques* and priests and warriors had arrived, he said, "How these traitors long to see us among the *barrancas* so as to gorge on our flesh, but Our Lord will do better for us." Then he asked for the two priests who had let out the secret, and they told him that they were at the gate of the courtyard with the other *Caciques* who wished to come in, and he sent our interpreter, Aguilar, to tell them to go to their houses, for he had no need of their presence now. This was in order that, as they had done us a good turn, they should not suffer for it, and should not get killed. Cortés was on horseback and Doña Marina near to him, and he asked the *Caciques,* why was it, as we had done them no harm whatever, that they had wished to kill us on the previous night? and why should they turn traitors against us, when all we had said or done was to warn them against certain things of which we had already warned all the towns that we had passed through, namely, that they should not be wicked and sacrifice human beings, nor worship Idols, nor eat the flesh of their neighbors, nor commit unnatural crimes, but that they should live good lives; and to tell them about matters concerning our holy faith, and this without compulsion of any kind. To what purpose then had they quite recently prepared many long and strong poles with collars and cords and placed them in a house near to the Great Temple, and why for the last three days had they been building barricades and digging holes in the streets and raising breastworks on the roofs of the houses, and why had they removed their children and wives and property from the city? Their ill will

Bernal Díaz del Castillo • *The True History of the Conquest of New Spain* (1568)   55

however had been plainly shown, and they had not been able to hide their treason. They had not even given us food to eat, and as a mockery had brought us firewood and water, and said that there was no maize. He knew well that in the *barrancas* nearby, there were many companies of warriors and many other men ready for war who had joined the companies that night, laying in wait for us, ready to carry out their treacherous plans, thinking that we should pass along that road towards Mexico. So in return for our having come to treat them like brothers and to tell them what Our Lord God and the King have ordained, they wished to kill us and eat our flesh, and had already prepared the pots with salt and peppers and tomatoes. If this was what they wanted it would have been better for them to make war on us in the open field like good and valiant warriors, as did their neighbors the Tlaxcalans. He knew for certain all that had been planned in the city and that they had even promised to their Idol, the patron of warfare, that twenty of us should be sacrificed before it, and that three nights ago they had sacrificed seven Indians to it so as to ensure victory, which was promised them; but as the Idol was both evil and false, it neither had, nor would have power against us, and all these evil and traitorous designs which they had planned and put into effect were about to recoil on themselves. Doña Marina told all this to them and made them understand it very clearly, and when the priests, *Caciques,* and captains had heard it, they said that what had been stated was true but that they were not to blame for it, for the Ambassadors of Mocteuzma had ordered it at the command of their Prince.

Then Cortés told them that the royal laws decreed that such treasons as those should not remain unpunished and that for their crime they must die. Then he ordered a musket to be fired, which was the signal that we had agreed upon for that purpose, and a blow was given to them which they will remember for ever, for we killed many of them, so that they gained nothing from the promises of their false Idols.

Not two hours had passed before our allies, the Tlaxcalans, arrived, whom I have already said we had left out in the fields, and they had fought very fiercely in the streets where the Cholulans had posted other companies to defend the streets and prevent their being entered, but these were soon defeated. They [the Tlaxcalans] went about the city, plundering and making prisoners and we could not stop them, and the next day more companies from the Tlaxcalan towns arrived, and did great damage, for they were very hostile to the people of Cholula, and when we saw this, both Cortés and the captains and the soldiers, on account of the compassion that we had felt for them, restrained the Tlaxcalans from doing further damage, and Cortés ordered Cristobal de Olid to bring him all the Tlaxcalan captains together so that he could speak to them, and they did not delay in coming; then he ordered them to gather together all their men and go and camp in the fields and this they did, and only the men from Cempoala remained with us.

Just then certain *Caciques* and priests of Cholula who belonged to other districts of the town, and said that they were not concerned in the treasons against us (for it is a large city and they have parties and factions among themselves), asked Cortés and all of us to pardon the provocation of the treachery that had been plotted against us for the traitors had already paid with their lives. Then there came the two priests who were our friends and had disclosed the secret to us, and the old woman, the wife of

56   CHAPTER 2   ✦   Cross-Cultural Perceptions in the New World

the captain, who wanted to be the mother-in-law of Doña Marina, as I have already related, and all prayed Cortés for pardon.

When they spoke to him, Cortés made a show of great anger and ordered the Ambassadors of Mocteuzma, who were detained in our company, to be summoned. He then said that the whole city deserved to be destroyed, but that out of respect for their Lord Mocteuzma, whose vassals they were, he would pardon them, and that from now on they must be well behaved, and let them beware of such affairs as the last happening again, lest they should die for it.

Then, he ordered the Chiefs of Tlaxcala, who were in the fields, to be summoned, and told them to return the men and women whom they had taken prisoners, for the damage they had done was sufficient. Giving up the prisoners went against the grain with them [the Tlaxcalans], and they said that the Cholulans had deserved far greater punishment for the many treacheries they had constantly received at their hands. Nevertheless as Cortés ordered it, they gave back many persons, but they still remained rich, both in gold and mantles, cotton cloth, salt and slaves. Besides this Cortés made them and the people of Cholula friends, and, from what I have since seen and ascertained, that friendship has never been broken.

Furthermore Cortés ordered all the priests and *Caciques* to bring back the people to the city, and to hold their markets and fairs, and not to have any fear, for no harm would be done to them. They replied that within five days the city would be fully peopled again, for at that time nearly all the inhabitants were in hiding. They said it was necessary that Cortés should appoint a *Cacique* for them, for their ruler was one of those who had died in the Court, so he asked them to whom the office ought to go, and they said to the brother [of the late *Cacique*] so Cortés at once appointed him to be Governor, until he should receive other orders.

In addition to this, as soon as he saw the city was reinhabited, and their markets were carried on in safety, he ordered all the priests, captains and other chieftains of that city to assemble, and explained to them, very clearly the matters concerning our holy faith, and told them that they must cease worshiping idols, and must no longer sacrifice human beings or eat their flesh, nor rob one another, nor commit the offences which they were accustomed to commit, and that they could see how their Idols had deceived them, and were evil things not speaking the truth; let them remember the lies which they told only five days ago when seven persons had been sacrificed to them and they promised to give them victory, therefore all [that] they tell to the priests and to them is altogether evil, he begged them to destroy the Idols and break them in pieces. That if they did not wish to do it themselves we would do it for them. He also ordered them to whitewash a temple, so that we might set up a cross there.

They immediately did what we asked them in the matter of the cross, and they said that they would remove their Idols, but although they were many times ordered to do it, they delayed. Then the Padre de la Merced said to Cortés that it was going too far, in the beginning, to take away their Idols until they should understand things better, and should see how our expedition to Mexico would turn out and time would show us what we ought to do in the matter, that for the present the warnings we had given them were sufficient, together with the setting up of the Cross.

Bernal Díaz del Castillo   ◆   *The True History of the Conquest of New Spain* (1568)   57

[The Entry into Tenochtitlan, Description of the City and the Seizure of Mocteuzma]

The next day, in the morning, we arrived at a broad causeway,* and continued our march towards Iztapalapa, and when we saw so many cities and villages built in the water and other great towns on dry land and that straight and level causeway going towards Mexico, we were amazed and said that it was like the enchantments they tell of in the legend of Amadis,† on account of the great towers and cues and buildings rising from the water, and all built of masonry. And some of our soldiers even asked whether the things that we saw were not a dream? . . . And then when we entered that city of Iztapalapa, the appearance of the palaces in which they lodged us! How spacious and well built they were, of beautiful stone work and cedar wood, and the wood of other sweet scented trees, with great rooms and courts, wonderful to behold, covered with awnings of cotton cloth.

When we had looked well at all of this, we went to the orchard and garden, which was such a wonderful thing to see and walk in, that I was never tired of look-ing at the diversity of the trees, and noting the scent which each one had, and the paths full of roses, and the pond of fresh water. There was another thing to observe, that great canoes were able to pass into the garden from the lake through an opening that had been made so that there was no need for their occupants to land. And all was cemented and very splendid with many kinds of stone [monuments] with pic-tures on them, which gave much to think about. Then the birds of many kinds and breeds which came into the pond. I say again that I stood looking at it and thought that never in the world would there be discovered other lands such as these. . . . [Of all these wonders that I then beheld] today all is overthrown and lost, nothing left standing.

Early next day we . . . proceeded along the causeway which is here eight paces in width and runs so straight to the City of Mexico that it does not seem to turn either much or little, but, broad as it is, it was so crowded with people that . . . we were hardly able to pass . . . and the towers and cues were full of people as well as the canoes from all parts of the lake. It was not to be wondered at, for they had never before seen horses or men such as we are.

Gazing on such wonderful sights, we did not know what to say, or whether what appeared before us was real, for on one side on the land there were great cities, and in the lake ever so many more, and the lake itself was crowded with canoes, and in the causeway were many bridges at intervals and in front of us stood the great City of Mexico, and we, —we did not even number four hundred soldiers! . . .

The Great Mocteuzma who was approaching in a rich litter . . . got down from his litter and those great *Caciques* supported him with their arms beneath a mar-velously rich canopy of green colored feathers with much gold and silver embroidery and with pearls and *chalchihuites*, . . . which was wonderful to look at. . . . [T]here were many other Lords who walked before the Great Mocteuzma, sweeping the

---

*The Causeway of Cuitlahuac separating the lake of Chalco from the lake of Xochimilco.

†Amadis was a legendary knight in well-known Iberian tales. Cervantes parodies him in his famous work *Don Quixote*.

58   CHAPTER 2 ◆ Cross-Cultural Perceptions in the New World

ground where he would tread. . . . Not one of these chieftains dared even to think of looking him in the face, but kept their eyes lowered with great reverence. . . .

The Great Mocteuzma was about forty years old, of good height and well propor-tioned, slender, and spare of flesh, not very swarthy, but of the natural color and shade of an Indian. He did not wear his hair long, . . . his scanty black beard was well shaped and thin. His face was somewhat long, but cheerful, and he had good eyes and showed in his appearance and manner both tenderness and, when necessary, gravity. He was very neat and clean and bathed once every day in the afternoon. When Cortés was told that the Great Mocteuzma was approaching, . . . he dismounted and simultane-ously they paid great reverence to one another. Cortés thanked Mocteuzma through our interpreters, and Mocteuzma replied—"Malinche, you and your brethren are in your own house, rest awhile," and then he went to his palaces . . . not far away, and we divided our lodgings by companies, and placed the artillery pointing in a conven-ient direction, and the order which we had to keep was clearly explained to us, and that we were to be much on the alert, both the cavalry and all of us soldiers. A sump-tuous dinner was provided for us according to their use and custom, and we ate it at once. So this was our lucky and daring entry into the great city of Tenochtitlan Mexico on the 8ᵗʰ day of November the year of our Savior Jesus Christ 1519.

The next day Cortés decided to go to Mocteuzma's palace, . . . Cortés and he paid the greatest reverence to each other and then they took one another by the hand and Mocteuzma made him sit down on his couch on his right hand, and he also bade all of us to be seated. . . .

Then Cortés began to make an explanation through Doña Marina . . . (Doña Marina was a person of the greatest importance and was obeyed without question by the Indians throughout New Spain. . . . Doña Marina knew the language common to Mexico . . . without the help of Doña Marina we could not have understood the lan-guage of New Spain and Mexico. As Doña Marina proved herself such an excellent woman and good interpreter throughout the wars in New Spain, Cortés always took her with him.)* [Cortes] said . . . That in coming to see and converse with such a great Prince as he was, we had completed the journey and fulfilled the command which our great King and Prince had laid on us. But what he chiefly came to say on behalf of our Lord God had already been brought to his [Mocteuzma's] knowledge . . . that we were Christians and worshiped one true and only God, named Jesus Christ, who suffered death and passion to save us, and we told them that a cross . . . was a sign of the other Cross on which our Lord God was crucified for our salvation, and that the death and passion . . . was for the salvation of the whole human race, which was lost, and that this our God rose on the third day and is now in heaven, and it is He who made the heavens and earth, the sea and the sands, and created all the things there are in the world, and . . . nothing happens in the world without His holy will. That we believe in Him and worship Him, but that those whom they look upon as gods are not so, but are devils . . . and if their looks are bad their deeds are worse, and they could see that they were evil and of little worth, for where we had set up crosses . . .

---

*The excerpt in parentheses is inserted here from Bernal Díaz del Castillo, *The True History of the Conquest of New Spain, Vol. 1*, Hakluyt Society, Second Series, XXIII (London: Hakluyt Society, 1908), 132–35.

Bernal Díaz del Castillo ◆ *The True History of the Conquest of New Spain* (1568)   59

they dared not appear . . . through fear. . . .

The favor he now begged of him was his attention to the words . . . then he explained to him very clearly about the creation of the world, and how we are all brothers, sons of one father and one mother who were called Adam and Eve, and how such a brother as our great Emperor, grieving for the perdition of so many souls, such as those that their idols were leading to Hell, where they burn in living flames, had sent us, so that after what he [Mocteuzma] had now heard he would put a stop to it and they would no longer adore these Idols or sacrifice Indian men and women to them, for we were all brethren, nor should they commit sodomy or thefts. He also told them that, in course of time, our Lord and King would send some men who among us lead very holy lives, much better than we do, who will explain to them all about it, for at present we merely came to give them due warning, and so he prayed him to do what he was asked and carry it into effect. . . .

Mocteuzma replied, Senor Malinche, I have understood your words and arguments very well before now, from what you said to my servants at the sand dunes, this about three Gods and the Cross, and all those things that you have preached in the towns through which you have come. We have not made any answer to it because here throughout all time we have worshiped our own gods, and thought they were good, as no doubt yours are, so do not trouble to speak to us any more about them at present. Regarding the creation of the world, we have held the same belief for ages past, and for this reason we take it for certain that you are those whom our ancestors predicted would come from the direction of the sunrise. As for your great King, I feel that I am indebted to him, and I will give him of what I possess. . . .

While this conversation was going on Mocteuzma secretly sent a great *Cacique*, one of his nephews who was in his company, to order his stewards to bring certain pieces of gold, which it seems must have been put apart to give to Cortés, and ten loads of fine cloth, which he apportioned, the gold and mantels between Cortés and the four captains, and to each of us soldiers he gave two gold necklaces, each necklace being worth ten pesos, and two loads of mantles. The gold that he then gave us was worth in all more than a thousand pesos and he gave it all cheerfully and with the air of a great and valiant prince. As it was now past midday, so as not to appear importunate, Cortés said to him, "Senor Mocteuzma, you always have the habit of heaping load upon load in every day conferring favors on us, and it is already your dinner time." Mocteuzma replied that he thanked us for coming to see him, and then we took our leave with the greatest courtesy and we went to our lodgings.

And as we went along we spoke of the good manners and breeding which he showed in everything, and that we should show him in all ways the greatest respect, doffing our quilted caps when we passed before him, and this we always did, but let us leave this subject here, and pass on.

As we had already been four days in Mexico [City] and neither the Captain nor any of us had left our lodgings . . . , Cortés said to us that it would be well to go to the great Plaza and see the great Temple of Huitzilopochtli,* and that he wished to consult the Great Mocteuzma. . . . When we arrived at the great market place, called

---

*The Aztec god of war and their main deity.

Volume 2: 1500–

60   CHAPTER 2   ◆   Cross-Cultural Perceptions in the New World

Tlaltelolco, we were astounded at the number of people and the quantity of merchandise that it contained, and at the good order and control that was maintained, for we had never seen such a thing before. The chieftains who accompanied us acted as guides. Each kind of merchandise was kept by itself and its fixed place marked out . . . the dealers in gold, silver, and precious stones . . . , and embroidered goods. Then there were other wares consisting of Indian slaves both men and women: and I say that they bring as many of them to that great market for sale as the Portuguese bring negroes from Guinea; and they brought them along tied to long poles, with collars round their necks so that they could not escape, and others they left free. Next there were other traders who sold great pieces of cloth and cotton, and articles of twisted thread, and there were *cacahuateros* who sold cacao. In this way one could see every sort of merchandise that is to be found in the whole of New Spain, placed in arrangement in the same manner as they do in my own country . . . where they hold the fairs, where each line of booths has its particular kind of merchandise. . . . There were those who sold cloths . . . and ropes and the *cotaras** . . . and sweet cooked roots, and other tubers. . . . In another part of the market there were skins of tigers and lions, of otters and jackals, deer and other animals and badgers and mountain cats, and other classes of merchandise. . . .

[There were] those who sold beans and sage and other vegetables and herbs in another part, and those who sold fowls, cocks . . . rabbits, hares, deer, mallards, young dogs and other things of that sort in their part of the market, and . . . the fruiterers, and the women who sold cooked food . . . then every sort of pottery made in a thousand different forms from great water jars to little jugs, . . . then those who sold honey and honey paste and other dainties like nut paste, and those who sold lumber, boards, cradles, beams, blocks and benches . . . and the venders of *ocote*† . . . I must furthermore mention, asking your pardon, that they also sold many canoes full of human excrement, and these were kept in the creeks near the market, and this they use to make salt or for tanning skins, for without it they say that they cannot be well prepared. I know well that some gentlemen may laugh at this, but I say that it is so, and I may add that on all the roads it is a usual thing to have places made of reeds or straw or grass, so that they may be screened from the passers by, into these they retire when they wish to purge their bowels so that even that filth should not be lost. . . .

Now let us leave the great market place, and not look at it again, and arrive at the great courts and walls where the great Cue stands. Before reaching the great Cue there is a great enclosure of courts, it seems to me larger than the plaza of Salamanca, with two walls of masonry surrounding it and the court itself all paved with very smooth great white flagstones. And where there were not these stones it was cemented and burnished and all very clean, so that one could not find any dust or a straw in the whole place.

When we arrived near the great Cue and before we had ascended a single step of it, the Great Mocteuzma sent down from above, where he was making his sacrifices, six priests and two chieftains to accompany our Captain. On ascending the steps, which are one hundred and fourteen in number, they attempted to take him by the

---

*Sandals.

†Pine pitch for torches.

Bernal Díaz del Castillo ◆ *The True History of the Conquest of New Spain* (1568)   61

arms so as to help him ascend, (thinking that he would get tired) as they were accustomed to assist their lord Mocteuzma, but Cortés would not allow them to come near him. When we got to the top where there was a space like a platform and some large stones placed on it, on which they put the poor Indians for sacrifice, there was a bulky image like a dragon and other evil figures and much blood shed that very day.

When we arrived there Mocteuzma came out of an oratory where his cursed idols were, at the summit of the great Cue, and two priests came with him, and after paying great reverence to Cortés and to all of us he said, "You must be tired, Senor Malinche, from ascending this our great Cue," and Cortés replied through our interpreters who were with us that he and his companions were never tired by anything. Then Mocteuzma took him by the hand and told him to look at his great city and all the other cities that were standing in the water, and the many other towns on the land round the lake, and that if he had not seen the great market place well, that from where they were they could see it better.

So we stood looking about us, for that huge and cursed temple stood so high that from it one could see over everything very well, and we saw that the three causeways which led into Mexico, that is the causeway of Iztapalapa by which we had entered four days before, and that of Tacuba, along which later on we fled on the night of our great defeat, when Cuitlahuac the new prince drove us out of the city, as I shall tell later on, and that of Tepeaquilla, and we saw the fresh water that comes from Chapultepec which supplies the city, and we saw the bridges on the three causeways which were built at certain distances apart through which the water of the lake flowed in and out from one side to the other, and we beheld on that great lake a great multitude of canoes, some coming with supplies of food and others returning loaded with cargoes of merchandise; and we saw that from every house of that great city and of all the other cities that were built in the water it was impossible to pass from house to house, except by drawbridges which were made of wood or in canoes; and we saw in those cities Cues and oratories like towers and fortresses and all gleaming white, and it was a wonderful thing to behold; then the houses with flat roofs and on the causeways other small towers and oratories which were like fortresses.

After having examined and considered all that we had seen we turned to look at the great market place and the crowds of people that were in it, some buying and others selling, so that the murmur and hum of their voices and words that they used could be heard more than a league off. Some of the soldiers among us who had been in many parts of the world, in Constantinople, and all over Italy, and in Rome, said that so large a market place and so full of people, and so well regulated and arranged, they had never beheld before.

Let us leave this and return to our Captain, who said to Fray Bartolomé de Olmedo, who has often been mentioned by me, and who happened to be nearby him: "It seems to me, Senor Padre, that it would be a good thing to throw out a feeler to Mocteuzma, as to whether he would allow us to build our church here"; and the Padre replied that it would be a good thing if it were successful, but it seemed to him that it was not quite a suitable time to speak about it, for Mocteuzma did not appear to be inclined to do such a thing.

62   CHAPTER 2 ◆ Cross-Cultural Perceptions in the New World

Then our Cortés said to Mocteuzma through the interpreter Doña Marina, "Your Highness is indeed a very great prince and worthy of even greater things. We are rejoiced to see your cities, and as we are here in your temple, what I now beg as a favor is that you will show us your gods and idols." Mocteuzma replied that he must first speak with his high priests, and when he had spoken to them he said that we might enter into a small tower and apartment, a sort of hall, where there were two altars, with very richly carved boardings on the top of the roof. On each altar were two figures, like giants with very tall bodies and very fat, and the first which stood on the right hand they said was the figure of Huitzilopochtli their god of War; it had a very broad face and monstrous and terrible eyes, and whole of his body was covered with precious stones, and gold and pearls, and with seed pearls stuck on with a paste that they make in this country out of a sort of root, and all the body and head was covered with it, and the body was girdled by great snakes made of gold and precious stones, and in one hand he held a bow and in the other some arrows. And another small idol that stood by him, they said was his page, and he held a short lance and a shield richly decorated with gold and stones. Huitzilopochtli had round his neck some Indians' faces and other things like hearts of Indians, the former made of gold and the latter of silver, with many precious blue stones.

There were some braziers with incense which they call copal, and in them they were burning the hearts of the three Indians whom they had sacrificed that day, and they had made the sacrifice with smoke and copal. All the walls of the oratory were so splashed and encrusted with blood that they were black, the floor was the same and the whole place stank vilely. Then we saw on the other side on the left hand there stood the other great image the same height as Huitzilopochtli, and it had a face like a bear and eyes that shone, made of their mirrors which they call *Tezcat,* and the body plastered with precious stones like that of Huitzilopochtli, for they say that the two are brothers; and this Tezcatepuca* was the god of Hell and had charge of the souls of the Mexicans, and his body was girt with figures like little devils with snakes' tails. The walls were so clotted with blood and the soil so bathed with it that in the slaughter houses of Spain there is not such another stench.

They had offered to this Idol five hearts from that day's sacrifices. In the highest part of the Cue there was a recess of which the woodwork was very richly worked, and in it was another image half man and half lizard, with precious stones all over it, and half the body was covered with a mantle. They say that the body of this figure is full of all the seeds that there are in the world, and they say that it is the god of seed time and harvest, but I do not remember its name, and everything was covered with blood, both walls and altar, and the stench was such that we could hardly wait the moment to get out of it.

They had an exceedingly large drum there, and when they beat it the sound of it was so dismal and like, so to say, an instrument of infernal regions, that one could hear it a distance of two leagues, and they said that the skins it was covered with were those of great snakes. In that small place there were many diabolical things to be seen, bugles and trumpets and knives, and many hearts of Indians that they had

---

*Tezcatlipoca—"the Giver of Life."

Bernal Díaz del Castillo   ❖   *The True History of the Conquest of New Spain* (1568)   63

burned in fumigating their idols, and everything was so clotted with blood, and there was so much of it, that I curse the whole of it, and as it stank like a slaughter house we hastened to clear out of such a bad stench and worse sight. Our Captain said to Mocteuzma through our interpreter, half laughing, "Senor Mocteuzma, I do not understand how such a great Prince and wise man as you are has not come to the conclusion, in your mind, that these idols of yours are not gods, but evil things that are called devils, and so that you may know it and all your priests may see it clearly, do me the favor to approve of my placing a cross here on the top of this tower, and that in one part of these oratories where your Huitzilopochtli and Tezcatepuca stand we may divide off a space where we can set up an image of Our Lady (an image which Mocteuzma had already seen) and you will see by the fear in which these Idols hold it that they are deceiving you."

Mocteuzma replied half angrily, (and the two priests who were with him showed great annoyance,) and said: "Senor Malinche, if I had known that you would have said such defamatory things I would not have shown you my gods, we consider them to be very good, for they give us health and rains and good seed times and seasons and as many victories as we desire, and we are obliged to worship them and make sacrifices, and I pray you not to say another word to their dishonor."

When our Captain heard that and noted the angry looks he did not refer again to the subject, but said with a cheerful manner: "It is time for your Excellency and for us to return," and Mocteuzma replied that it was well, but that he had to pray and offer certain sacrifices on account of the great *tatacul,* that is to say sin, which he had committed in allowing us to ascend his great Cue, and being the cause of our being permitted to see his gods, and of our dishonoring them by speaking evil of them, so that before he left he must pray and worship. Then Cortés said "I ask your pardon if it be so," and then we went down the steps. . . .

When we were all assembled in those chambers, as it was our habit to inquire into and want to know everything, while we were looking for the best and most convenient site to place the altar, two of our soldiers, one of whom was a carpenter, named Alonzo Yañes, noticed on one of the walls marks showing that there had been a door there, and that it had been closed up and carefully plastered over and burnished. Now as there was a rumor and we had heard the story that Mocteuzma kept the treasure of his father Axayacatl in that building, it was suspected that it might be in this chamber which had been closed up and cemented only a few days before. Yañes spoke about it to Juan Velásquez de Leon and Francisco de Lugo, who were Captains and relations of mine, and Alonzo Yañes had attached himself to their company as a servant, and those Captains told the story to Cortés, and the door was secretly opened. When it was open and Cortés and some of his Captains went in first, and they saw such a number of jewels and slabs and plates of gold and *chalchihuites* and other great riches, that they were quite carried away and did not know what to say about such wealth. The news soon spread among all the other Captains and soldiers, and very secretly we went in to see it. When I saw it I marveled, and as at that time I was a youth and had never seen such riches in my life before, I took it for certain that there could not be another such store of wealth in the whole world. It was decided by all our captains and soldiers, that we should not dream of touching a

64   CHAPTER 2   ◆   Cross-Cultural Perceptions in the New World

particle of it, but that the stones should immediately be put back in the doorway and it should be sealed up and cemented just as we found it, and that it should not be spoken about, lest it should reach Mocteuzma's ears, until times should alter.

Let us leave this about the riches, and say that as we had such valiant captains and soldiers of good counsel and judgement, (and first of all we all believed for certain that our Lord Jesus Christ held his Divine hand over all our affairs,) four of our captains took Cortés aside in the church, with a dozen soldiers in whom he trusted and confided, and I was one of them, and we asked him to look at the net and trap in which we found ourselves, and to consider the great strength of that city, and observe the causeways and bridges, and to think over the words of warning that we had been given in all the towns we had passed through, that Mocteuzma had been advised by his Huitzilopochtli to allow us to enter into the city, and when we were there, to kill us. That he [Cortés] should remember that the hearts of men are very changeable, especially those of Indians, and he should not repose trust in the good will and affection that Mocteuzma was showing us, for at some time or other, when the wish occurred to him, he would order us to be attacked, and by the stoppage of our supplies of food or of water, or by the raising of any of the bridges, we should be rendered helpless. Then, considering the great multitude of Indian warriors that Mocteuzma had as his guard, what should we be able to do either in offence or defense? and as all the houses were built in the water, how could our friends the Tlaxcalans enter and come to our aid? He should think over all this that we had said, and if we wished to safeguard our lives, that we should at once, without further delay, seize Mocteuzma and should not wait until the next day to do it. He should also remember that the gold that Mocteuzma had given us and all that we had seen in the treasury of his father Axayaca, and all the food which we ate, all would be turned to arsenic poison in our bodies, for we could neither sleep by night nor day nor rest ourselves while these thoughts were in our minds, and that if any of our soldiers should give him other advice short of this, they would be senseless beasts who were dazed by the gold, incapable of looking death in the face.

When Cortés heard this he replied, "Don't you imagine, gentlemen, that I am asleep, or that I am free from the same anxiety, you must have felt that it is so with me; but what possibility is there of our doing a deed of such great daring as to seize such a great prince in his own palace, surrounded as he is by his own guards and warriors, by what scheme or artifice can we carry it out, so that he should not call on his warriors to attack us at once?" Our Captains replied, (that is Juan Velásquez de Leon and Diego de Ordás, Gonzalo de Sandoval and Pedro de Alvarado,) that with smooth speeches he should be got out of his halls and brought to our quarters, and should be told that he must remain a prisoner, and if he made a disturbance or cried out, that he would pay for it with his life; that if Cortés did not want to do this at once, he should give them permission to do it, as they were ready for the work, for, between the two great dangers in which we found ourselves, it was better and more to the purpose to seize Mocteuzma than to wait until he attacked us; for if he began the attack, what chance should we have? Some of us soldiers also told Cortés that it seemed to us that Mocteuzma's stewards, who were employed in providing us with food, were insolent and did not bring it courteously as during the first days. Also two of our Allies [from] the Tlaxcalan Indians said secretly to Jerónimo de Aguillar, our interpreter, that the Mexicans had not appeared to be well disposed towards us during the last two days. So we stayed a good hour discussing the question of whether or not we should take Mocteuzma prisoner, and how it was to be done, and to our Captain this last advice seemed opportune, that in any case we should take him prisoner, and we left it until the next day. All that night we were praying to God that our plan might tend to His Holy service.

The next morning after these consultations, there arrived, very secretly, two Tlaxcalan Indians with letters from Villa Rica and what they contained was the news that Juan de Escalante, who had remained there as Chief Alguacil, and six of our soldiers had been killed in a battle against the Mexicans, that his horse had also been slain, and many Totonacs who were in his company. Moreover, all the towns of the Sierra and Cempoala and its subject towns were in revolt, and refused to bring food or serve in the fort. They [the Spaniards] did not know what to do, for as formerly they had been taken to be Teules, that now after this disaster, both the Totonacs and Mexicans were like wild animals, and they could hold them to nothing, and did not know what steps to take.

When we heard this news, God knows what sorrow affected us all, for this was the first disaster we had suffered in New Spain. The interested reader may see how evil fortune came rolling on us. No one who had seen us enter into that city with such a solemn and triumphant reception, and had seen us in possession of riches which Mocteuzma gave every day both to our Captain and to us, and had seen the house that I have described full of gold, and how the people took us for *Teules*, that is for Idols, and that we were conquerors in all our battles, would have thought that now such a great disaster could have befallen us, namely that they no longer attributed to us our former repute, but looked upon us as men liable to be conquered, and that we should have to feel their growing insolence towards us.

As the upshot of much argument it was agreed that, by one means or another, we should seize Mocteuzma that very day, or we would all die in the attempt.

IMAGES OF THE CONQUEST

Pictorial images can greatly add to our understanding of history. As briefly discussed in the introduction, paintings, drawings, photographs, and other visual representations can augment historical texts, giving us a richer sense of time and place than can be achieved by the written word alone. Images not only provide us with additional information about "what happened," but they also have an immediate and powerful impact on our senses, emotions, and feelings.

When pictures are used in the reconstruction of history, they should be analyzed and appreciated on several different levels. The first thing to remember is that a picture is a form of storytelling, and that in any story, it is important to comprehend what is happening and who is involved. In this regard, it is frequently interesting to compare the stories told by visual images and written texts on the same subject. Second, images often provide glimpses into popular culture and details about everyday life in past societies. Pictures may provide important and interesting clues on manners of dress, types of food, important rituals, architectural

66 CHAPTER 2 ◆ Cross-Cultural Perceptions in the New World

Figure 2.1 *Massacre of Cholula*

styles, and so on. And lastly, images and pictures must be examined and understood as artistic human creations. The image maker has a story to tell, and he or she may use color, composition, and various cultural symbols to evoke specific responses on the part of the viewer. In other words, historical images are frequently a form of theater, consciously composed and represented to elicit a particular interpretation and reaction.[14]

The three images included in this section embody different interpretations of the conquest of Mexico. The first two images come from native sources depicting armed encounters with the Spanish. The last painting is a European interpretation of Cortés's final assault on Tenochtitlan in 1521. As you view these images, keep the following questions in mind.

QUESTIONS TO CONSIDER

1. What role does Doña Marina seem to play in the *Massacre of Cholula* (Figure 2.1)? Why might she be represented in this manner?

2. In *Massacre of the Mexica Nobility* (Figure 2.2), Alvarado was incensed by the Aztec dancing because it accompanied a festival that included human sacrifice. Does this information affect the way you interpret the painting?

3. What information is highlighted in the *Battle for Tenochtitlan* (Figure 2.3)? What historical data seem conspicuously absent? How might you account for this?

4. What cultural symbols can be found in each of these images? How important are they in understanding the meaning of the picture?

5. In what ways do these images contribute to your understanding of the conquest of Mexico? What are the limitations or problems associated with these images?

Images of the Conquest   67

Figure 2.2 *Massacre of the Mexica Nobility*

The image in Figure 2.1 shows Spanish soldiers and their Tlaxcalan allies attacking the Cholulans. Cortés claimed that the Cholulans had prepared a trap for the conquistadores and that they were warned in advance by Doña Marina (standing at the right). But Aztec sources claim that the attack was an unjustified slaughter of unarmed men, women, and children. There are several cultural symbols to note in this picture. The serpent at the top of the temple is likely a depiction of Huitzilopochtli (the god of war), and the Cholulan falling from the temple roof may represent a suicide. According to scholars, this picture is from a Tlaxcalan source.

The image in Figure 2.2 is an Aztec representation of the attack by Pedro de Alvarado on noble Aztecs who were dancing in the temple opposite the Spanish quarters in Tenochtitlan in connection with a religious celebration. Alvarado, always one of the most impetuous and headstrong of Cortés's captains, unleashed the attack on the unarmed dancers. This occurred while Cortés was marching back to Vera Cruz to defeat the second force sent by Velazquez to capture Cortés. After this, the Aztecs attacked the Spanish. When Cortés returned, he was allowed to enter the city, but then had to fight his way out on the so-called *Noche Triste,* or "Night of Sorrows."

Figure 2.3 shows a European painting that portrays Cortés's final assault on the Aztec capital in 1521. The Spanish attack included charges up the causeways leading to the island city, as well as the construction of thirteen sloops to fight the Aztec war canoes. The elevated structure at center is the main temple of Tenochtitlan. Note how the style, composition, and sentiments of this painting compare with the Tlaxcalan and Aztec images.

68   CHAPTER 2 ✦ Cross-Cultural Perceptions in the New World

Figure 2.3 *Battle for Tenochtitlan*

NOTES

1. Noted by Bernal Díaz and cited in Maurice Collis, *Cortés and Montezuma* (New York: Harcourt Brace, 1954), 34.

2. "Aztec" is really a misnomer. The people themselves was Nahua (speakers of the Nahuatl language), and the dominant group at the time of conquest was the Mexica. Aztlan referred to the territory, somewhere in the contemporary American southwest, from which the peoples had migrated to the central valley of Mexico.

3. Collis, 39, 60. Cortés first scuttled his ships so that his troops had no way to escape.

4. Harry Rosen, ed., *Conquest: Dispatches of Cortes from the New World* (New York: Grosset & Dunlap, 1962), 22.

5. Ibid., 12.

6. The name of the island now divided between Haiti and the Dominican Republic.

7. Cited in Stephen Greenblatt, *Marvellous Possessions: The Wonder of the New World* (Oxford, UK: Clarendon Press, 1991), 170, n.36.

8. A people's understanding of the universe and of their place in it. There is a current academic debate over Aztec mythology and the figure of Quetzalcoatl, but such issues lie outside of the main purposes of this chapter.

9. See the general discussion in Maurice Collis, *Cortés and Montezuma* (London: Faber, 1954).

Notes 69

10. *The General History* acquired the name the *Florentine Codex* because it was long stored in Florence, Italy.

11. Another reason for Spanish victories was that the Mesoamerican warrior sought first and foremost to capture, rather than to kill, an opponent. Senseless death in battle was seen as far less valuable than sacrificial death, which had religious and cosmic significance.

12. According to sources, Doña Marina was offered, along with twenty other slave girls, as a gift to Cortés. The Spanish baptized her "Marina" (she who came from the sea), but her people called her *"La Malinche,"* a term that has come to mean a traitor to his or her country or people. She ultimately played an important role in the conquest for Cortés, who took her as his interpreter, advisor, and lover. When she bore a child, she became, at least symbolically, the mother of the first Mexican, the first infant born of Indian and Spanish ancestry. Later, when Cortés brought his own wife from Spain to Mexico, Marina was married off to one of his soldiers, and she died in relative obscurity at the age of twenty-four.

13. An *encomienda* was a grant of land, together with authority over the native populations inhabiting that land. The natives were required to provide labor services to the holder of the *encomienda*. It guaranteed a supply of cheap labor to the Spanish overlords.

14. Ideally, the historian also seeks to investigate the artist in question and the circumstances behind this particular creation. At the same time, care must be taken when assigning "meaning" to images, for modern-day values and symbols may be quite different from those of the past or from different cultures.

CHAPTER 3

Perspectives on the Atlantic Slave Trade

INTRODUCTION

In the mid-fifteenth century, Europeans began to arrive along the shores of west Africa. Led by the Portuguese, their initial motive was trade, particularly in the valuable gold and ivory that came from the African interior. In return, African traders received brass, copper, liquor, manufactured goods, and cloth. In the Kongo kingdom of central Africa, the initial level of cross-cultural contact went much deeper. In the 1490s, Portuguese missionaries were invited to establish schools and churches in the kingdom, resulting in the conversion of the Kongo king to Catholicism and the establishment of diplomatic ties with Lisbon and the Vatican.

The rise of the Atlantic slave trade in the sixteenth through nineteenth centuries dramatically altered the character and impact of African–European encounters. For nearly three centuries, the Europeans' predominant interest in Africa centered on the enslavement and removal of its strongest and most productive people. Most historians estimate that between 10 and 12 million Africans were imported to the New World, in addition to the many more that died during capture and transport to the slave ships.[1] The Atlantic slave trade was the largest forced migration in world history, and for approximately 300 years, more Africans than Europeans crossed the Atlantic bound for the Americas. This chapter studies slavery and the slave trade from the differing perspectives of three participants—a slave trader, a slave, and a slave owner—to better understand the organization of the trade and the attitudes and behaviors that it inspired.

The main reason behind it all was sugar, a valuable but labor-intensive commodity. The planting and harvesting of vast acres of sugar cane, together with the processing of sugar juice into molasses and rum, required a large labor force engaged in difficult and tiring work. The use of slave labor on sugar plantations had proved so profitable in the Mediterranean as early as the thirteenth century that

Europeans were inclined to reestablish the same system on a much larger scale in the Americas. But whereas the soil and climate of Brazil and the islands of the Caribbean were ideal for the cultivation of sugar, labor supply was a problem. The indigenous Amerindians had been decimated by diseases, such as smallpox and measles, brought by the initial explorers; indentured servants were too few in number; and Europeans were generally reluctant to enslave other Europeans. Faced with these difficulties, Africans soon became the prime choice for slave labor. They had better immunity to tropical diseases than either Amerindians or Europeans, they were readily available and relatively inexpensive, and their cultural distinctiveness helped Europeans to contrive racial justifications for their enslavement.

For the most part, European slave merchants purchased their human cargoes from African chiefs or traders or from European middlemen residing in forts erected along the African coast. Africans had long practiced their own form of slavery, but in most societies, individuals who had lost their freedom as a result of crime, debt, or defeat in war had opportunities for assimilation and social advancement. Once the international trade in slaves began, however, the enslavement of people in Africa via warfare and kidnapping grew dramatically, and captives were increasingly perceived and treated as marketable commodities. In many parts of Africa, slaves were captured hundreds of miles from the coast and were brought to slave ships by long-distance traders. In exchange for their captives, African chiefs or traders bargained for and received metal bars, cloth, manufactured goods, liquor, and guns from European slave merchants.

Firearms played a particularly important and coercive role in the history of the slave trade. Some African leaders, such as the kings of Benin and Dahomey, eagerly sought commerce with European slave traders in order to obtain the new weapons that provided the military superiority to expand and protect their kingdoms, to gain new forms of wealth, and to produce even more slaves. Other African leaders who tried to resist the slave trade often found it impossible because of the new arms race. When the king of the Kongo initially refused to sell slaves, for example, Portuguese traders provided firearms to his rivals and enemies, forcing the king to either "slave or be enslaved." Ultimately, the Kongo kingdom was torn apart by civil war, and large numbers of war captives were sold into slavery in exchange for more guns, which perpetuated a cycle of violence and enslavement that continued for much of the sixteenth and seventeenth centuries.

Slave imports into the Americas peaked in the late eighteenth century, reaching approximately 80,000 a year in the 1780s. This great demand for slaves was partly due to the vast extension of the plantation system to tobacco, rice, sugar, and other commodities. But equally important, new slaves were needed to replace those that died so quickly. Approximately one-third of slaves perished within the first three years of captivity, and few survived beyond ten years. Such high mortality rates were most commonly the result of poor treatment and disease. Most slave owners found that it was more profitable to work their slaves to death and purchase fresh supplies from Africa than to provide them with the food, shelter, and rest required to promote longer, healthier lives. The tragic consequences can be

72   CHAPTER 3 ❖ Perspectives on the Atlantic Slave Trade

witnessed in demographic statistics from the British colony of Jamaica. Of the approximate 750,000 slaves imported to the small sugar island over the course of nearly two centuries, there remained only 350,000 Africans at the date of emancipation in 1808.

A year earlier, in 1807, Britain had become the first western nation to permanently terminate the African slave trade, followed by the United States in the following year.[2] The end of the legal importation of slaves from Africa, however, did not immediately end the practice of slavery itself. In the United States, slavery remained legal in many states until passage of the Thirteenth Amendment to the Constitution in 1865,[3] while in Brazil, slavery remained legal until 1888. But the enslavement of Africans was generally in decline in the nineteenth century, and historians have identified several factors crucial to the ultimate success of the abolitionist movement. Christian reformers, often assisted by former African slaves, successfully aroused public opinion in England and America by highlighting the apparent contradiction between Christian morality and slavery. In addition, the rise and spread of eighteenth-century Enlightenment ideas about the natural rights of people to life and liberty also played a role in changing attitudes about human bondage. But many historians also link the abolitionist movement to changing economic conditions in Europe and America. Beginning first in England, a new industrial class, with growing political power, was superseding the old planter aristocracy. In congruence with their own financial interests, they wished to keep Africans in Africa, producing the raw materials for their factories and purchasing the finished goods. But whereas Parliament formally ended slavery in the British Empire in 1833 and sent squadrons of the Royal Navy to west Africa to suppress the slave trade, smuggling and commerce by other nations continued well into the mid-nineteenth century.

The Atlantic slave trade had a tremendously important, yet often underappreciated, impact on world history. It helped to create a great circuit of international trade and commodity exchange that linked the agricultural exports of the Americas to the finished goods of Europe and the uprooted labor from Africa. Some historians believe that the profits derived from the sugar trade provided the much-needed capital to finance England's industrial revolution. Other historians have argued that the export of millions of African workers, together with the import of destructive guns, helped to lay the foundations for Africa's current state of underdevelopment. In the Americas, African slaves provided much of the agricultural skills and manual labor that significantly contributed to the prosperity of European settlers and their colonies. The slave trade also led to the creation of multicultural nations whose histories have long been marked by racial and ethnic disparities in wealth, opportunity, and power.

The three readings in this chapter provide deeper insights into the organization, ideas, and impact of the Atlantic slave trade. Each reading also provides a unique perspective from a firsthand participant in the trade. The first selection is from the journal of Jacques Barbot, a European maritime trader who recounted a slaving voyage to Africa and the West Indies in 1698–1699. His account describes the character of trade along the coast, his negotiations with African traders, and his advice concerning the "Middle Passage," or the long and perilous voyage from

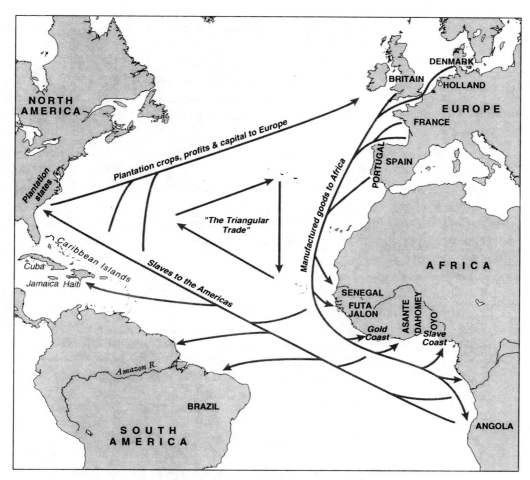

Map 3.1 General Patterns in Atlantic Slave Trade, Sixteenth through Eighteenth Centuries

Africa to America. The second selection is excerpts from the autobiography of Olaudah Equiano (1745–1797), an Igbo youth taken from his village in present-day Nigeria and sent to the West Indies and Virginia. Equiano's experience as a slave was exceptional, for with persistence and good fortune, he was able to obtain an education, convert to Christianity, and purchase his freedom, after which he became a prominent voice in the English abolitionist movement. His detailed and moving account provides rich information about the organization of the trade, the condition of slavery in the Caribbean, and cross-cultural attitudes. The final reading is from Thomas Jefferson (1743–1826), a leading American patriot, author of the Declaration of Independence, and third president of the United States (1801–1809). Jefferson was a proclaimer of the "natural rights" of mankind, an advocate of human liberty, and a slave owner. In the final reading, taken from his *Notes on the State of Virginia* (1781), Jefferson's ambiguous position on freedom and slavery becomes clearer, and it provides greater insights into his character, as well as the debate over slavery that troubled the American republic in its early history.

CHAPTER QUESTIONS

1. All three readings either directly or indirectly make an argument for or against slavery. How does each side use evidence and reasoning to support its case? What are the beliefs and assumptions inherent in each argument? What role do cultural perceptions play? When viewed in a comparative way, what insights or conclusions can be made?

2. Using the material in all three sources, trace the impact of slavery and the slave trade on the various parties directly affected. What different impacts can be identified? Despite the divergent perspectives of the sources, are there any commonalities in their assessments of impacts?

3. As described by Equiano, slavery in the Americas was brutal and violent. What can you find in each of the three readings that helps to explain the reasons why?

4. Jacques Barbot and Thomas Jefferson both assume the inherent inferiority of Africans. Imagine that they were able to meet Equiano at the time he wrote his memoirs. Do you think this meeting would change their opinions?

5. Using the readings as your sources of evidence, which factors (or combination of factors) most contributed to the slave trade? (a) European technological and military power, (b) economic incentives, (c) African cooperation, (d) racist attitudes.

THE PERSPECTIVE OF A SLAVE TRADER

Jacques Barbot (also known as James Barbot) was born around 1650 to a Protestant family in Saint-Martin on the Ile de Re, near the French seaport of La Rochelle. Little is known about his early life, but it is likely that he was engaged in commerce at an early age. The Barbot family had a long history in maritime trade, and Jacques' younger brother Jean (or John) became involved in slave trading at an early age, organizing voyages for the Royal Africa Company, one of the largest slave trading companies in Europe. In 1685, both Barbot brothers emigrated to England following the revocation of the Edict of Nantes, which had granted religious toleration of Protestantism in France. Once settled in England, they started their own commercial firm, assisted by additional investors and speculators.

Their first slaving expedition in 1697 ended in a disastrous shipwreck. The next year they tried again, purchasing the *Albion-Frigate* and refitting it for slaving operations. Jacques accompanied the *Albion-Frigate* on its maiden African

The Perspective of a Slave Trader   75

voyage to New Calabar, along what was then known as the "Slave Coast." The ship left England in 1698, carrying 24 guns, 60 men, and a cargo of manufactured goods worth 2,600 pounds sterling. In little more than three months' time they purchased 648 slaves and enough food and provisions for the "middle passage," or the trip across the Atlantic. The trip was not entirely successful: midway through the passage, the slaves found an opportunity to revolt, and in the ensuing fight three sailors and twenty-eight captives were killed before Europeans regained control. The *Albion* arrived safely in Barbados, but ill fortune continued to follow the Barbot family. In the following year, Jacques Barbot's son joined the family business and undertook his first slave voyage, but he contracted a fever and died en route to the West Indies.

Slave journals such as this were written primarily to instruct future travelers and traders about Africa, so they are a very useful historical source for understanding the organization and operation of the slave trade, although from one perspective. Barbot's journal reveals that slave trading was a dangerous but potentially very lucrative enterprise. Tropical fevers, competition from European rivals, profit-seeking African sellers, and the perilous "middle passage" made slave trading a risky business but one worth pursuing when one compares the purchase costs with the sale prices. It is also interesting to note the character of African–European relations as portrayed by Barbot and his attitudes concerning Africans and their culture. His account of African involvement in the trade, particularly the special role played by local leaders, also provides a glimpse into the impact of the slave trade on African society.

QUESTIONS TO CONSIDER

1. Examine the process and outcome of the negotiations between Barbot and the king of Bonny. What do they tell us about the organization of the trade? What do they say about cross-cultural relations?

2. In addition to slaves, what else is traded along the west African coast? Who benefits most from this trade? What impact might this have on African society?

3. In one instance, Barbot wishes that the king's brother, Pepprell, was "out of the way" in order to "facilitate trade." In Barbot's eyes, why was Pepprell an obstacle?

4. Examine the way the "slave mutiny" is portrayed by Barbot. What insights can be gained from his description of events and conditions?

5. What are Barbot's views about Africans? What are they based on? In what ways might they explain or justify his role in the slave trade?

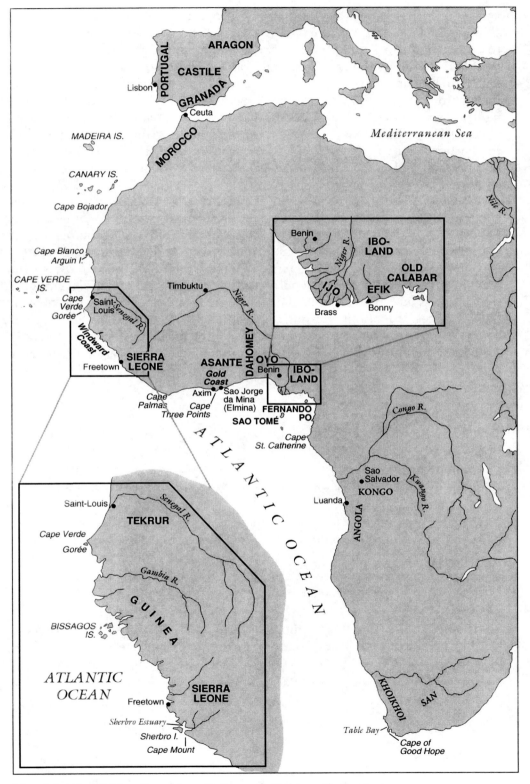

Map 3.2 West Africa, Seventeenth through Eighteenth Centuries

Jacques Barbot ◆ The Slaving Voyage of the *Albion-Frigate* (1698–1699)   **77**

THE SLAVING VOYAGE
OF THE *ALBION-FRIGATE* (1698–1699)

Jacques Barbot

This narrative of a voyage to New Calabar River, or Rio Real, on the Coast of Guinea,* is taken from the journal kept by Mr. Jacques Barbot, the supercargo, and part owner with other adventurers of London, in the *Albion-Frigate*, of 300 tons and 24 guns, a 10 percent ship.[†]

We sailed from the Downs,[‡] on the thirteenth of January, 1698–9, and arrived before Madeira island, the third of February, whence we proceeded immediately after we had got some wine and refreshments aboard. . . . On the 25th of February, we anchored before Sestro river where we stayed for nearly a month getting in wood, water, rice, fowls and other refreshments and provisions. King Peter[§] was still alive and well, but we got few elephant's teeth because they were held very dear.

On the 7th of April we came before Axim, the first Dutch fort on the Gold Coast and the next day anchored before the Prussian fort, Great Fredericksburgh, where the Prussian general received us very civilly, but told us he had no occasion for any of our goods. Trade everywhere on that coast was at a standstill by reason of the vast number of interlopers and other trading ships and also because of the wars among the natives. The fort was a very handsome fortress mounted with about forty guns. The general told me that six weeks before he had been assaulted by a pirate, who was forced to let him go, being too warmly received; and that there were two or three other pirates cruising about that Cape. . . . We had abundance of our men sick and several already dead, the weather being intolerably scorching hot, and we could get hardly any provisions save a few goats, very dear.

On the 17th of April, we were before Mina castle and found seven sail in the road, three or four of them tall ships, among which, two frigates, each of about thirty guns and a hundred and thirty men, cruisers at the coast, who had taken three

---

Source: Jacques Barbot's account has been preserved in his brother Jean Barbot's English account of his voyages, published in 1732. The selections in this reading come from P. E. H. Hair, Adam Jones, and Robin Law, eds., *Barbot on Guinea: The Writings of Jean Barbot on West Africa, 1678–1712, Vol. 2* (London: The Hakluyt Society, 1992), 681–98, and George Francis Dow, ed., *Slave Ships and Slaving* (Salem, MA: Marine Research Society, 1927), 73–87.

*"Guinea" was a generic term used to describe sub-Saharan Africa, particularly the coastal forest regions of west Africa.

[†]Following an act of 1698 that modified the commercial monopoly of the Royal Africa Company, independent traders could operate in west Africa as long as they paid a duty to the company of 10 percent of the value of their trade goods.

[‡]The Downs was an important anchorage and pilot station located off the East Kent coast. In the days of sail, ships would wait here for favorable winds before making their way out of the English Channel.

[§]It was common for European slave traders to give Africans western names, but it does not suggest these leaders were westernized or Christian. It is also nearly impossible to identify any of these chiefs by their African names.

interlopers of Zealand,* one of which carried thirty-six guns, who having made a brave resistance, the commander was to be tried for his life. One of the frigates having been already two years at the Coast, was ready to return home, with a thousand marks of gold. . . .

On the fifteenth, we arrived at Accra and anchored about a league and a half from shore. Here we stayed for eleven days, trading for gold, slaves and some few teeth; diverting ourselves by turns, with the English, Dutch and Danish commanders of the forts, but more intimately with Mr. Trawne, the Danish chief, who had his lady with him. On making sail, as we worked our small bower aboard, both cable and buoy-rope breaking, we were forced to sail, leaving the anchor behind, which was hitched among the rocks at the bottom. We had purchased sixty-five slaves along the Gold Coast, besides gold and elephants' teeth and after saluting the three European forts, each with nine guns, we steered for New Calabar to buy more slaves, being followed by our small sloop under sail. . . .

At last, at three o'clock in the afternoon of the 17th of June, we came to an anchor off New Calabar river, on five and a half fathom muddy sand, by guess north and south of Foko point, and the next morning, by day-break, we sent our longboat with three men to sail to land for intelligence and to bring some black to pilot us into Calabar, together with samples of some merchandise. We spied a ship lying in Bandy [Bonny] river, as much as we could see it, and the next day sent one of the pilots in the pinnace to sound the bar. He returned at seven at night, with much trouble, the wind and sea being so high. Our long-boat not returning, as expected, by the 22d we began to be much concerned. The weather all the while was very cold and it blowing very hard from south-south-west.

At eleven o'clock on the morning of the 23d, we spied a boat near the bar [and] found it was a great canoe with nine black rowers, besides other blacks, and the master of our long-boat. . . . The King of Bandy [Bonny], William, had sent us two or three of his pilots, in the canoe, with certificates of several English masters of ships they had piloted formerly safe in, some of them drawing thirteen foot of water. Our frigate then drew fourteen foot and a half water.

Our man reported that the ship we could see within the river was English, commanded by Captain Edwards, who had got his complement of slaves, being five hundred, in three weeks time, and was ready to sail for the West Indies. He also reported, that as soon as the blacks could see our ship off at sea, they immediately went up the river to buy slaves, besides a hundred and fifty that were in the town when he left it; and that King William had assured him, he would engage to furnish five hundred slaves for our loading, all lusty and young. Upon which we consulted aboard with the officers and unanimously agreed to carry up the ship, if possible, for the greater expedition. . . .

The next morning we saluted the black king of Great Bandy, with seven guns; and soon after fired as many for Captain Edwards, when he got aboard, to give us the most necessary advice concerning the trade we designed to drive there. At ten he returned ashore, being again saluted with seven guns. We also went ashore to compliment the King and make him overtures of trade, but he gave us to understand that he

---

*The "interlopers of Zealand" were private Dutch traders encroaching upon the monopoly of the Dutch West India Company.

Jacques Barbot ◆ The Slaving Voyage of the *Albion-Frigate* (1698–1699)   79

Figure 3.1 Barbot Presents Himself to the King of Sestro, 1681

expected one bar of iron for each slave, more than Edwards had paid for his; and he also objected much against our basins, tankards, yellow beads, and some other merchandise, as being of little or no demand there at that time.

On the 26th we had a conference with the King and principal natives of the country, about trade, which lasted from three o'clock till night, without any result, they insisting to have thirteen bars of iron for a male and ten for a female slave; objecting that they were now scarce, because of the many ships that had exported vast quantities of late. The King treated us at supper and we took leave of him. The next morning he sent for a barrel of brandy, at two bars of iron per gallon and at ten o'clock we went ashore and renewed our conference but concluded nothing. Four days later we had a new conference at which the King's brother made us a discourse, saying he was sorry we would not accept his proposals; that it was not his fault, he having a great esteem and regard for the whites, who had much enriched him by trade; that what he so earnestly insisted on, thirteen bars for males, and ten for female slaves, came from the country people holding up the price of slaves at the inland markets, seeing so many large ships resort to Bandy for them; but to moderate matters and encourage trading with us, he would be content with thirteen bars for males and nine bars and two brass rings for females, and the next day the trade was concluded on these terms and the King promised to come aboard and be paid his duties.

There was a heavy rain all the morning, the next day, and at two o'clock in the afternoon, we fetched the King from the shore. He came with all of his attendants and officers, in three large canoes, and was saluted with seven guns. He had on an old-fashioned scarlet coat, laced with gold and silver, very rusty, with a fine hat on his head, but was bare-footed. His brother, Pepprell, came with him and was a sharp blade and a mighty talking black, always making sly objections against something or other, and teasing us for this or that present, as well as for something to drink. It were to be wished that such a one as he were out of the way, to facilitate trade.

We filled them with drinks of brandy and bowls of punch, till night, at such a rate that they all being about fourteen, with the King, had such loud clamorous tattling and discourses among themselves, as were hardly to be endured. With much patience, however, all our matters were at last adjusted indifferently, after their way, who are not very scrupulous to find excuses or objections for not keeping literally to any verbal contract, for they have not the art of reading and writing, and therefore we are forced to stand to their agreement, which often is no longer than they think fit to hold it themselves. The King ordered the public crier to proclaim permission of trade with us, with the noise of his trumpets, made of elephant's teeth, we paying sixteen brass rings to the fellow for his fee. The blacks objected much against our wrought pewter and tankards, green beads, and other goods, which they would not accept.

We gave the usual presents to the King and his officers. To the King, we gave a hat, a firelock [musket], and nine bunches of beads; to his officers, we gave two firelocks, eight hats and nine narrow Guinea stuffs.* We also advanced to the King, by way of loan, the value of 150 bars of iron, in sundry goods, in order to repair forthwith to the inland markets to buy yams.

All the regulations having been agreed upon, supper was served, and it was comical, as well as shocking, to observe the behavior of the blacks, both King and subjects making a confused noise, and all of them talking together and emptying the dishes as soon as set down; everyone filling his pockets with meat as well as his belly, especially of hams and neat's tongues;† falling on all together, without regard to rank or manners, as they could lay their hands on food, and having drank and eaten till they were ready to burst, they returned ashore receiving a salute of seven guns as they went.

Two days afterwards the King sent aboard thirty slaves, men and women, out of which we picked nineteen and returned him the rest, and so from day to day, either by means of our armed sloop making voyages to New Calabar town or by our contract with the King, by degrees we had aboard 648 slaves of all sexes and ages, including the sixty-five we purchased at the Gold Coast, all very fresh and sound, very few exceeding forty years of age. The King supplied us with yams and bananas, and plantains, which are a sort of banana dried, yet somewhat green, a food well liked by the natives. . . .

The town of Great Bandy [Bonny] is built on a little island much as that of Calabar, it being marshy, swampy ground, and somewhat larger, but like it in buildings, and its people employ themselves in trade, and some at fishing, by means of long and large canoes, some of them sixty foot long and seven broad, rowed by sixteen, eighteen or twenty paddlers, carrying European goods and fish to the upland blacks and bringing back to the coast, by way of exchange, a vast number of slaves and some

---

*Lengths of cotton cloth.

†Pickled ox tongue.

Jacques Barbot   ◆   The Slaving Voyage of the *Albion-Frigate* (1698–1699)   81

large elephant's teeth. The principal thing that passes as current money among the natives is brass rings, for the arms and legs, which they call *bochie;* and they are so particular in the choice of them that they will often turn over a whole cask before they find two to please their fancy.

The English and Dutch also trade a great deal of copper in small bars, about three feet long and weighing about a pound and a quarter each, which the blacks of Calabar work with much art, splitting the bar into three parts, which they polish as fine as gold and twist the three pieces together very ingeniously, like cords, to make into arm rings. But the most current goods for trade are iron bars, striped Guinea clouts of many colors, horse-bells, hawks-bells, rangoes, pewter basins of one, two, three and four pounds weight, tankards of pewter, small glazed beads, yellow, green, purple and blue, and copper armlets or arm rings, of Angola make, the latter being peculiar to the Portuguese.

Their large canoes are made of the trunks of big trees and framed much like the canoes at the Gold Coast, but much longer, sometimes being seventy feet in length. They are very sharp pointed at each end and are fitted with benches, for the convenience of the paddlers who sit as near the sides of the canoes as possible. They commonly hang at the head of the canoe two shields and along the sides, bundles of spears. Every canoe also has a hearth in the head of it, on which they dress their victuals and they also have a contrivance by which they can set up an awning made of mats. Some have a sort of quarter-deck made of strong reeds, but the slaves, when they carry any, lie exposed to all weathers. Such canoes are navigated with eighteen to twenty hands and when armed for war commonly carry seventy or eighty men, with all necessary provisions, generally yams, bananas, chickens, hogs, goats or sheep and palm wine and palm oil. . . .

It is customary here for the king of Bandy to treat the officers of every trading ship, at their first arrival, and the officers return the treat to the king, some days before they have their compliment of slaves and yams aboard. Accordingly, on the twelfth of August we treated the king and his principal officers, with a goat, a hog, and a barrel of punch; and that is an advertisement to the Blacks ashore, to pay in to us what they owe us, or to furnish with all speed, what slaves and yams they have contracted to supply us with, else the king compels them to it. At that time also such of the natives as have received from us a present, use to present us, each with a boy or girl slave in requital. According to this custom we treated the Blacks ashore on the fifteenth of August . . . as also the Black ladies; the king lending us his music, to the noise of which we had a long diversion of dances and sports of both sexes, some not unpleasing to behold.

On the 22d of August, 1699, we let fly our colors and fired a gun, for a signal to the blacks of our being near ready to sail and to hasten aboard with the rest of the slaves and the yams contracted for. . . . As to the management of the slaves aboard, we lodged the two sexes apart, by means of a strong partition at the main-mast. The fore part was set apart for the men and behind the mast for the women. In large ships, carrying five or six hundred slaves, the deck ought to be at least five and a half or six foot high, making it the more airy and convenient and consequently far more healthy for them. We built a sort of half deck along the sides, with deals and spars brought from England, which extended no farther than the side of our scuttles, and so the slaves lay in two rows, one above the other, and as close together as they could be crowded. . . .

82   CHAPTER 3   ◆   Perspectives on the Atlantic Slave Trade

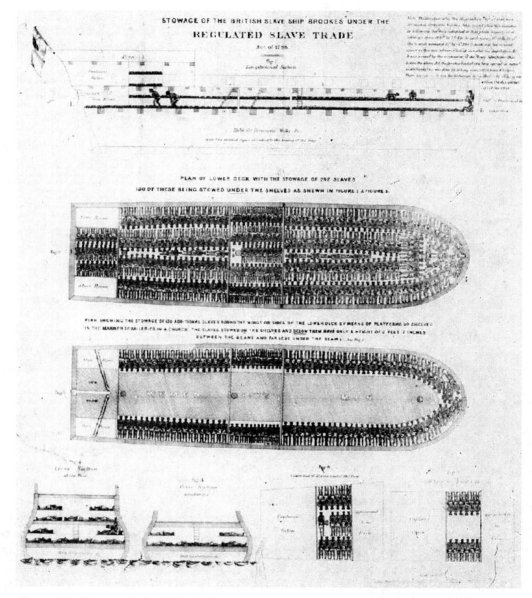

Figure 3.2 Diagram of a Slave Ship

We were very nice in keeping the places where the slaves lay clean and neat, appointing some of the ship's crew to do that office constantly and several of the slaves themselves to be assistants to them and thrice a week we perfumed between decks with a quantity of good vinegar in pails, and red-hot iron bullets in them, to expel the bad air, after the place had been well washed and scrubbed with brooms; after which the deck was cleaned with cold vinegar, and in the daytime, in good weather, we left the scuttles open and shut them again at night.

It has been observed that some slaves fancy they are being carried away to be eaten, which makes them desperate, and others are so on account of their captivity,

Jacques Barbot ◆ The Slaving Voyage of the *Albion-Frigate* (1698–1699)   83

so that if care be not taken, they will mutiny and destroy the ship's crew in hopes to get away. One day, about one in the afternoon, after dinner, according to custom we caused them, one by one, to go down between decks, to have each his pint of water. Most of them were yet above deck and many of them were provided with knives which we had indiscreetly given them two or three days before, not suspecting the least attempt of this nature from them. It afterwards appeared that others had pieces of iron which they had torn off the forecastle door, having premeditated this revolt. They had also broken off the shackles from the legs of several of their companions, which also served them. Thus armed they suddenly fell upon our men and stabbed one of the stoutest, who received fourteen or fifteen wounds from their knives so that he expired shortly. Next they assaulted our boatswain and cut one of his legs so round the bone that he could not move, the nerves being cut through.

Others cut the cook's throat to the windpipe and yet others wounded three of the sailors and threw one of them overboard from the fore-castle, who, however, by good providence, got hold of the bowline of the foresail and saved himself, along the lower wale of the quarter-deck, where we stood in arms, firing on the revolted slaves, of whom we killed some and wounded many, which so terrified the rest that they gave way and dispersed themselves. Many of the most mutinous leaped overboard and drowned themselves with much resolution, showing no manner of concern for life. Thus we lost twenty-eight slaves and having mastered them, caused all to go between decks, giving them good words. The next day however we had them all again upon deck and caused about thirty of the ringleaders to be severely whipped by all our men.

To prevent a recurrence of such misfortune we used to visit them daily, narrowly searching every corner between decks, and taking care not to leave any tools or nails or other things in the way, which, however, cannot always be so exactly observed, where so many people are in the narrow compass of a ship. We had as many of our men as convenient to lie in the quarter-deck, and gun-room, and our principal officers in the great cabin, where we kept all our small-arms in readiness with sentinels constantly at the door and avenues to it, being thus ready to disappoint any further attempts our slaves might make on a sudden. These precautions contributed much to keep them in awe and if all those who carry slaves duly observed them, we should not hear of so many revolts as have happened.

It is true, we allowed them much more liberty and used them with more tenderness than most other Europeans would think prudent, as we had them all on deck, every day in good weather. . . . We took care they did wash from time to time, to prevent vermin, which they are subject to. Towards evening the blacks would divert themselves on the deck, as they thought fit; some conversing together, others dancing, singing or sporting after their manner, which often made us pastime, especially the females, who, being apart from the males and on the quarter deck and many of them young sprightly maidens, full of jollity and good humor, afforded us abundance of recreation. . . .

As for the sick and wounded, our surgeons, in their daily visits between decks, finding any indisposed, caused them to be carried to a room reserved for a sort of hospital, where proper remedies could be applied. This could not leisurely be done between decks because of the great heat that is there continually, which is sometimes so excessive that the surgeons would faint away and the candles would not burn, and besides, in such a crowd of brutish people there are many so greedy that they will snatch from the sick the fresh meat or liquor that is given them. Nor is it advisable to put sick slaves into the long-boat upon deck for being thus exposed in the open air and lying there in the cool of the nights after coming out of the excessively hot hold, they are soon taken with violent cholics and bloody fluxes and die in a few days time. . . .

The slaves of New Calabar are a strange sort of brutish creatures, very weak and slothful, but cruel and bloody in their temper, always quarreling, biting and fighting and sometimes choking and murdering one another without mercy, and whoever carries such slaves to the West Indies, has need to pray for a quick passage, that they may arrive there alive and in health. . . .

As soon as a slave ship arrives at port in the West Indies, the planters and other inhabitants flock aboard to buy as many slaves as they have occasion for. The price being agreed upon, they search every slave, limb by limb, to see whether they are sound and strong and it is diverting enough to see the examining even of those parts which are not to be named. This done, every buyer carries away his slaves and provides them with nourishment, clothing and health. We sold off all our slaves briskly at about seven thousand pounds weight of brown sugar, a piece, the Indian pieces, as they term it there, and set sail on our return voyage deeply laden with sugar, cotton and other goods. The frigate was very leaky but we continued our voyage without any remarkable accident, only our leaks increased very much so that we had much toil to keep up the ship to the end of our voyage, our two pumps going without intermission day and night, which extremely fatigued our crew, though numerous, and made us all very uneasy.

At length, by God's providence, we spied land to leeward of us, being part of the English coast near Dartmouth and four days later we came to an anchor in the river Thames and so ended our voyage.

THE PERSPECTIVE OF A SLAVE

In 1789, Olaudah Equiano published his autobiography, titled *The Interesting Narrative of the Life of Olaudah Equiano, or Gustavus Vassa the African, written by himself.* The title is most appropriate, for there is little doubt that he did indeed live a very interesting and exceptional life. Born around 1745 in what is now southeastern Nigeria, he was only eleven years old when he and his sister were kidnapped by African slave traders, brought to the coast, and sold to a European slave merchant. He was then shipped across the Atlantic to the West Indies, enduring and surviving a horrific experience during the "middle passage." He was subsequently sent to a plantation in Virginia, where he was purchased by Captain Michael Pascal, an officer in the Royal British Navy. Equiano served Pascal well for several years, acting as a shipboard powder boy during several campaigns of the Seven Years' War. While living in England, he was able to receive some schooling, and he converted to Christianity.

His next master, a Philadelphia businessman named Robert King, returned Equiano to the West Indies and employed him as a shipping clerk. Equiano took advantage of his tolerant Quaker master and his commercial travels to engage in some petty trading of his own, and he eventually saved enough to purchase his freedom in 1766. He continued his maritime voyages as a free man for several years, joining expeditions to the Mediterranean, Central America, and a near-fatal exploratory voyage to the Arctic. He later joined the British abolitionist movement and became a popular speaker against slavery and the slave trade in England. In 1787, he was briefly involved with an ill-fated project to repatriate free blacks to Sierra Leone,[4] but he was forced to resign after he complained about corruption and mismanagement within the organization. He returned to his speaking tours across England and wrote his autobiography, which sold very well in Great Britain and the United States. By most accounts, he died in 1797, his final wish to return to Africa as a missionary unfulfilled.

The reading is excerpts taken from Equiano's autobiography. Although originally written to promote the abolitionist cause, his accounts of his experiences seem mostly accurate. His story begins with his description of village life in Africa prior to his capture. Here he acknowledges that Africans had their own institution of slavery, but he strives to make a clear distinction between it and the slavery that he experienced and witnessed in the Caribbean. He then recounts the manner in which he was captured, brought to the coast, and transported to the West Indies. His detailed and moving description clearly conveys the shock and subsequent demoralization that accompanied the loss of freedom and removal from one's ancestral home. It is also interesting to compare his story with the account found in Jacques Barbot's journal and to identify, analyze, and explain the ways in which they are similar and different. The next section focuses on Equiano's experiences in the Caribbean, his views on African–European relations, and his unceasing efforts to win his freedom. Through his own example, he illustrates the behaviors and attitudes required for slaves to make the most of their situation. The reading ends with his final plea for abolition, in which he crafts an argument that blends both moral and economic factors in support of ending the trade in slaves.

QUESTIONS TO CONSIDER

1. According to Equiano, how were most slaves obtained? What goods did Africans receive in exchange for slaves? Is there a connection between the two that helps explain why Africans may have participated in the slave trade?

2. How does Equiano distinguish between African slavery and the slavery practiced in the West Indies? Why do you think he felt it so important to include this in his autobiography?

3. In what ways does Equiano's description of the "middle passage" differ from the account of Jacques Barbot? How do they differ on the depiction of slave suicides?

4. What are the moral and economic arguments proposed by Equiano to arouse public opinion against the slave trade? How would he view the ideal relationship between Africa and England?

86   CHAPTER 3   ◆   Perspectives on the Atlantic Slave Trade

Figure 3.3 Olaudah Equiano

5. Despite his condition, Equiano was a confident individual who never lost sight of his goal to win his freedom. Identify the behaviors and attitudes that Equiano found necessary to achieve his goal. What do these tell you about the nature of African–European relations during this era?

THE INTERESTING NARRATIVE OF THE LIFE OF OLAUDAH EQUIANO (1789)

Olaudah Equiano

Life in Africa

That part of Africa known by the name of Guinea to which the trade for slaves is carried on extends along the coast about 3,400 miles, from the Senegal to Angola, and includes a variety of kingdoms. Of these the most considerable is the kingdom of Benin, both as to extent and wealth, the richness and cultivation of the soil, the power of its king, and the number and warlike disposition of the inhabitants. It is situated nearly under the line and extends along the coast about 70 miles, but runs back into

Source: Olaudah Equiano, *The Interesting Narrative of the Life of Olaudah Equiano, or Gustavus Vassa the African, written by himself,* in *Equiano's Travels,* ed. Paul Edwards (Oxford: Heinemann Press, 1996), 1–3, 6–9, 13–14, 22–28, 57–67, 143–46. Copyright © 1996 Heinemann Publishers. Reprinted with permission.

Olaudah Equiano ◆ *The Interesting Narrative of the Life of Olaudah Equiano* (1789)   87

the interior part of Africa to a distance hitherto I believe unexplored by any traveler, and seems only terminated at length by the empire of Abyssinia, near 1,500 miles from its beginning. This kingdom is divided into many provinces or districts, in one of the most remote and fertile of which, called Eboe, I was born in the year 1745, situated in a charming fruitful vale, named Essaka.* The distance of this province from the capital of Benin and the sea coast must be very considerable, for I had never heard of white men or Europeans, nor of the sea. . . .

As we live in a country where nature is prodigal of her favors, our wants are few and easily supplied; of course, we have few manufactures. They consist for the most part of calico cloth, earthenware, ornaments, and instruments of war and husbandry. . . . We have also markets, at which I have been frequently with my mother. These are sometimes visited by stout mahogany-colored men from the south-west of us: we call them *Oye-Eboe,* which term signifies red men living at a distance. They generally bring us fire-arms, gunpowder, hats, beads, and dried fish. The last we esteemed a great rarity as our waters were only brooks and springs. These articles they barter with us for odoriferous woods and earth, and our salt of wood ashes. They always carry slaves through our land, but the strictest account is exacted of their manner of procuring them before they are suffered to pass. Sometimes indeed we sold slaves to them, but they were only prisoners of war, or such among us as had been convicted of kidnaping, or adultery, and some other crimes which we esteemed heinous. This practice of kidnaping induces me to think that, notwithstanding all our strictness, their principal business among us was to entrap our people. I remember too they carried great sacks along with them, which not long after I had an opportunity of fatally seeing applied to that infamous purpose.

Our land is uncommonly rich and fruitful, and produces all kinds of vegetables in great abundance. We have plenty of Indian corn, and vast quantities of cotton and tobacco. . . . All our industry is exerted to improve those blessings of nature. Agriculture is our chief employment, and everyone, even the children and women, are engaged in it. Thus we are all habituated to labor from our earliest years. Everyone contributes something to the common stock, and as we are unacquainted with idleness we have no beggars.

Our tillage is exercised in a large plain or common, some hours walk from our dwellings, and the neighbors resort thither in a body. . . . This common is often the theater of war and therefore when our people go out to till their land they not only go in a body, but generally take their arms with them for fear of a surprise, and when they apprehend an invasion they guard the avenues to their dwellings by driving sticks into the ground, which are so sharp at one end as to pierce the foot and are generally dipped in poison. From what I can recollect of these battles, they appear to have been irruptions of one little state or district on the other to obtain prisoners or booty. Perhaps they were incited to this by those traders who brought the European goods I mentioned amongst us. Such a mode of obtaining slaves in Africa is common, and I believe more are procured this way and by kidnaping than any other. When a trader wants slaves he applies to a chief for them and tempts him with his wares. It is not extraordinary if on this occasion he yields to the temptation with as little firmness, and accepts the price of his fellow creature's liberty with as little reluctance as the enlightened

---

*Located in present-day Nigeria.

88   CHAPTER 3   ◆   Perspectives on the Atlantic Slave Trade

merchant. Accordingly he falls on his neighbors and a desperate battle ensues. If he prevails and takes prisoners he gratifies his avarice by selling them, but if his party be vanquisher and he falls into the hands of the enemy, he is put to death: for as he has been known to foment their quarrels it is thought dangerous to let him survive, and no ransom can save him, though all other prisoners may be redeemed. We have firearms, bows and arrows, broad two-edged swords and javelins: we have shields also which cover a man from head to foot. All are taught the use of these weapons; even our women are warriors and march boldly out to fight along with the men. . . . Those prisoners which were not sold or redeemed we kept as slaves: but how different was their condition from that of the slaves in the West Indies! With us they do no more work than other members of the community, even their master; their food, clothing and lodging were nearly the same as theirs, (except that they were not permitted to eat with those who were freeborn), and there was scarce any other difference between them than a superior degree of importance which the head of a family possesses in our state, and that authority which, as such, he exercises over every part of his household. Some of these slaves have slaves under them as their own property and for their own use.

Captured

My father, besides many slaves, had a numerous family of which seven lived to grow up, including myself and a sister who was the only daughter. As I was the youngest of the sons I became, of course, the greatest favorite with my mother and was always with her; and she used to take particular pains to form my mind. I was trained up from my earliest years in the art of war, my daily exercise was shooting and throwing javelins, and my mother adorned me with emblems after the manner of our greatest warriors. In this way I grew up until I turned the age of eleven, when an end was put to my happiness in the following manner. Generally when the grown people in the neighborhood were gone far in the fields to labor, the children assembled together in some of the neighbors' premises to play, and commonly some of us used to get up a tree to look out for any assailant or kidnapper that might come upon us, for they sometimes took those opportunities of our parents' absence to attack and carry off as many as they could seize. One day, as I was watching at the top of a tree in our yard, I saw one of those people come into the yard of our next neighbor to kidnap a child, there being many stout young people in it. Immediately I gave the alarm, and the rogue was surrounded by the stoutest of the youth, who entangled him with cords so that he could not escape till some of the grown people came and secured him. But alas! Before long it was my fate to be thus attacked and to be carried off when none of the grown people were nigh.

One day, when all our people were gone out to their works as usual and only I and my dear sister were left to mind the house, two men and a woman got over our walls, and in a moment seized us both, and without giving us time to cry out, or make resistance, they stopped our mouths and ran off with us into the nearest wood. Here they tied our hands and continued to carry us as far as they could till night came on, when we reached a small house where the robbers halted for refreshment and spent the night. We were then unbound but were unable to take any food, and being quite overpowered by fatigue and grief, our only relief was some sleep, which allayed our misfortune for a short time. The next morning we left the house and continued traveling all the day. For a long time we kept to the woods, but at last we came into a road

Olaudah Equiano ◈ *The Interesting Narrative of the Life of Olaudah Equiano* (1789)   **89**

which I believed I knew. I had now some hopes of being delivered, for we had advanced but a little way before I discovered some people at a distance, on which I began to cry out for their assistance: but my cries had no other effect than to make them tie me faster and stop my mouth, and then they put me into a large sack. They also stopped my sister's mouth and tied her hands and in this manner we proceeded till we were out of the sight of these people. When we went to rest the following night they offered us some food, but we refused it, and the only comfort we had was in being in one another's arms all that night and bathing each other with our tears. But alas! We were soon deprived of even the small comfort of weeping together. The next day proved a day of greater sorrow than I had yet experienced, for my sister and I were then separated while we lay clasped in each other's arms. It was in vain that we besought them not to part us; she was torn from me and immediately carried away, while I was left in a state of distraction not to be described. I cried and grieved continually, and for several days I did not eat anything but what they forced into my mouth. . . .

The Middle Passage

The first object which saluted my eyes when I arrived on the coast, was the sea, and a slave ship, which was then riding at anchor, and waiting for its cargo. These filled me with astonishment, which was soon converted into terror, when I was carried on board. I was immediately handled, and tossed up to see if I were sound, by some of the crew; and I was now persuaded that I had gotten into a world of bad spirits, and that they were going to kill me. Their complexions, too, differing so much from ours, their long hair, and the language they spoke, (which was very different from any I had ever heard) united to confirm me in this belief. Indeed, such were the horrors of my views and fears at the moment, that, if ten thousand worlds had been my own, I would have freely parted with them all to have exchanged my condition with that of the meanest slave in my own country. When I looked round the ship too, and saw a large furnace of copper boiling, and a multitude of black people of every description chained together, every one of their countenances expressing dejection and sorrow, I no longer doubted of my fate; and, quite overpowered with horror and anguish, I fell motionless on the deck and fainted. When I recovered a little, I found some black people about me, who I believed were some of those who had brought me on board, and had been receiving their pay; they talked to me in order to cheer me, but all in vain. I asked them if we were not to be eaten by those white men with horrible looks, red faces, and long hair. They told me I was not: and one of the crew brought me a small portion of spirituous liquor in a wine glass, but, being afraid of him, I would not take it out of his hand. One of the blacks, therefore, took it from him and gave it to me, and I took a little down my palate, which, instead of reviving me, as they thought it would, threw me into the greatest consternation at the strange feeling it produced, having never tasted any such liquor before. Soon after this, the blacks who brought me on board went off, and left me abandoned to despair.

I was not long suffered to indulge my grief; I was soon put down under the decks, and there I received such a salutation in my nostrils as I had never experienced in my life: so that, with the loathsomeness of the stench, and crying together, I became so sick and low that I was not able to eat, nor had I the least desire to taste any thing. I now wished for the last friend, death, to relieve me; but soon, to my grief, two of the

90   CHAPTER 3   ◆   Perspectives on the Atlantic Slave Trade

white men offered me eatables; and, on my refusing to eat, one of them held me fast by the hands, and laid me across, I think the windlass, and tied my feet, while the other flogged me severely. I had never experienced any thing of this kind before, and although not being used to the water, I naturally feared that element the first time I saw it, yet, nevertheless, could I have got over the nettings, I would have jumped over the side, but I could not; and besides, the crew used to watch us very closely who were not chained down to the decks, lest we should leap into the water; and I have seen some of these poor African prisoners most severely cut, for attempting to do so, and hourly whipped for not eating. This indeed was often the case with myself. In a little time after, amongst the poor chained men, I found some of my own nation, which in a small degree gave ease to my mind. I inquired of these what was to be done with us? They gave me to understand, we were to be carried to these white people's country to work for them. I then was a little revived, and thought, if it were no worse than working, my situation was not so desperate; but still I feared I should be put to death, the white people looked and acted, as I thought, in so savage a manner; for I had never seen among any people such instances of brutal cruelty; and this not only shown towards us blacks, but also to some of the whites themselves. One white man in particular I saw, when we were permitted to be on deck, flogged so unmercifully with a large rope near the foremast, that he died in consequence of it; and they tossed him over the side as they would have done a brute. This made me fear these people the more; and I expected nothing less than to be treated in the same manner. . . .

At last, we came in sight of the island of Barbados, at which the whites on board gave a great shout, and made many signs of joy to us. We did not know what to think of this; but as the vessel drew nearer, we plainly saw the harbor, and other ships of different kinds and sizes, and we soon anchored amongst them, off Bridgetown. Many merchants and planters now came on board, though it was in the evening. They put us in separate parcels, and examined us attentively. They also made us jump, and pointed to the land, signifying we were to go there. We thought by this, we should be eaten by these ugly men, as they appeared to us; and, when soon after we were all put down under the deck again, there was much dread and trembling among us, and nothing but bitter cries to be heard all the night from these apprehensions, insomuch, that at last the white people got some old slaves from the land to pacify us. They told us we were not to be eaten, but to work, and were soon to go on land, where we should see many of our country people. This report eased us much. And sure enough, soon after we were landed, there came to us Africans of all languages.

We were conducted immediately to the merchant's yard, where we were all pent up together, like so many sheep in a fold, without regard to sex or age. . . . We were not many days in the merchant's custody, before we were sold after their usual manner, which is this: On a signal given, (as the beat of a drum) the buyers rush at once into the yard where the slaves are confined, and make choice of that parcel they like best. The noise and clamor with which this is attended, and the eagerness visible in the countenances of the buyers, serve not a little to increase the apprehension of terrified Africans, who may well be supposed to consider them as the ministers of that destruction to which they think themselves devoted. In this manner, without scruple, are relations and friends separated, most of them never to see each other again. I remember, in the vessel in which I was brought over, in the men's apartment, there were

Olaudah Equiano ✻ *The Interesting Narrative of the Life of Olaudah Equiano* (1789)   91

several brothers, who, in the sale, were sold in different lots; and it was very moving on this occasion, to see and hear their cries at parting. O, ye nominal Christians! might not an African ask you, "Learned you this from your God, who says unto you, 'Do unto all men as you would men should do unto you?' Is it not enough that we are torn from our country and friends, to toil for your luxury and lust of gain? Must every tender feeling be likewise sacrificed to your avarice? Are the dearest friends and relations, now rendered more dear by their separation from their kindred, still to be parted from each other, and thus prevented from cheering the gloom of slavery, with the small comfort of being together; and mingling their sufferings and sorrows? Why are parents to lose their children, brothers their sisters, husbands their wives?" Surely, this is a new refinement in cruelty, which, while it has no advantage to atone for it, thus aggravates distress; and adds fresh horrors even to the wretchedness of slavery.

[After a short stay in Barbados and then in Virginia, Equiano was sold to a British seaman, who took him back to England. Seizing every opportunity to improve his condition, he learned to read and write, and converted to Christianity and was baptized Gustavus Vassa (a name given to him by his owner). But although Equiano continued to serve his master well at home and at sea (where he served as a powder boy during naval engagements with the French in the Seven Years' War), he was eventually sold to another master named Mr. King, and taken back to the Caribbean.]

Life as a Slave

Mr King dealt in all manner of merchandise and kept from one to six clerks. He loaded many vessels in a year, particularly to Philadelphia, where he was born and was connected with a great mercantile house in that city. He had besides many vessels of different sizes which used to go about the island and others, to collect rum, sugar, and other goods. I understood pulling and managing these boats very well, and this hard work, which was the first that he set me to, in the sugar season used to be my constant employment. . . . I had the good fortune to please my master in every department in which he employed me, and there was scarcely any part of his business or household affairs in which I was not occasionally engaged. I often supplied the place of a clerk in receiving the delivering cargoes to the ships, in tending stores, and delivering goods: and besides this I used to shave and dress my master when convenient, and take care of his horse, and when it was necessary, which was very often, I worked likewise on board of different vessels of his. By these means I became very useful to my master, and saved him, as he used to acknowledge, above a hundred pounds a year. Nor did he scruple to say I was of more advantage to him than any of his clerks, though their usual wages in the West Indies are from sixty to a hundred pounds current a year. . . .

I have sometimes heard it asserted that a negro cannot earn his master the first cost, but nothing can be further from the truth. I suppose nine-tenths of the mechanics throughout the West Indies are negro slaves, and I well know the coopers among them earn two dollars a day, the carpenters the same and oftentimes more, as also the masons, smiths, and fishermen, etc. and I have known many slaves whose masters would not take a thousand pounds current for them. But surely this assertion refutes itself, for if it be true, why do the planters and merchants pay such a price for slaves? And, above all, why do those who make this assertion exclaim the most loudly against

92   CHAPTER 3 ◆ Perspectives on the Atlantic Slave Trade

the abolition of the slave trade? So much are men blinded, and to such inconsistent arguments are they driven by mistaken interest! I grant, indeed, that slaves are sometimes, by half-feeding, half-clothing, over-working and stripes, reduced so low that they are turned out as unfit for service and left to perish in the woods or expire on a dunghill. . . .

It was very common in several of the islands, particularly at St. Kitt's, for the slaves to be branded with the initial letters of their master's name; and a load of heavy iron hooks hung about their necks. Indeed, on the most trifling occasions, they were loaded with chains; and often instruments of torture were added. The iron muzzle, thumb-screws, etc., are so well known, as not to need a description, and were sometimes applied for the slightest faults. I have seen a negro beaten till some of his bones were broken, for only letting a pot boil over. Is it surprising that usage like this should drive the poor creatures to despair, and make them seek a refuge in death from those evils which render their lives intolerable. . . . They frequently do [commit suicide]. A negro man, on board a vessel of my master, while I belonged to her, having been put in irons for some trifling misdemeanor, and kept in that state for some days, being weary of life, took an opportunity of jumping overboard into the sea; however, he was picked up without being drowned. Another, whose life was also a burden to him, resolved to starve himself to death, and refused to eat any victuals. This procured him a severe flogging; and he also, on the first occasion which offered, jumped overboard at Charleston, but was saved.

Nor is there any greater regard shown to the little property [of slaves], than there is to the persons and lives of the negroes. I have already related an instance or two of particular oppression out of many which I have witnessed; but the following is frequent in all the islands. The wretched field-slaves, after toiling all the day for an unfeeling owner, who gives them but little food, steal sometimes a few moments from rest or refreshment to gather some small portion of grass, according as their time will admit. This they commonly tie up in a parcel; either a bit's worth (sixpence) or half a bit's worth, and bring it to town, or to the market, to sell. Nothing is more common than for the white people on this occasion to take the grass from them without paying for it. . . . Other [whites] have committed acts of violence on the poor, wretched, and helpless females, whom I have seen for hours stand crying to no purpose, and get no redress or pay of any kind. . . .

The small account in which the life of a negro is held in the West Indies, is so universally known, that it might seem impertinent to quote the following extract, if some people had not been hardy enough of late to assert that negroes are on the same footing in that respect as Europeans. By the [laws] of the Assembly of Barbados, it is enacted "That if any negro, or other slave, under punishment by his master, or his order, for running away, or any other crime or misdemeanor towards his said master, unfortunately shall suffer in life or member, no person whatsoever shall be liable to a fine; but if any person shall, out of wantonness, or only of bloody-mindedness, or cruel intention, wilfully kill a negro, or other slave, of his own, he shall pay into the public treasury fifteen pounds sterling." And it is the same in most, if not all, of the West India islands. . . .

I have often seen slaves, particularly those who were meager, in different islands, put into scales and weighed, and then sold from three pence to six pence or nine

Olaudah Equiano ◆ *The Interesting Narrative of the Life of Olaudah Equiano* (1789)   93

pence a pound. My master, however, whose humanity was shocked at this mode, used to sell such by the lumps. And after a sale, it was not uncommon to see negroes taken from their wives, wives taken from their husbands, and children from their parents, and sent off to other islands, and wherever else their merciless lords choose; and probably never more during life see each other! Oftentimes my heart has bled at these partings, when the friends of the departed have been at the water side, and with sighs and tears, have kept their eyes fixed on the vessel, till it went out of sight. . . .

Nor was such usage as this confined to particular places or individuals; for, in all the different islands in which I have been, (and I have visited no less than fifteen,) the treatment of the slaves was nearly the same; so nearly, indeed, that the history of an island, or even a plantation, with a few such exceptions as I have mentioned, might serve for a history of the whole. Such a tendency has the slave trade to debauch men's minds, and harden them to every feeling of humanity! For I will not suppose that the dealers in slaves are born worse than other men—No; it is the fatality of this mistaken avarice,* that it corrupts the milk of human kindness and turns it into gall. And, had the pursuits of those men been different, they might have been as generous, as tender-hearted and just, as they are unfeeling, rapacious, and cruel. Surely this traffic cannot be good, which spreads like a pestilence, and taints what it touches! [It] violates that first natural right of mankind, equality and freedom, and gives one man a dominion over his fellows which God could never intend! For it raises the owner to a state as far above man as it depresses the slave below it; and, with all the presumption of human pride, sets a distinction between them, immeasurable in extent, and endless in duration!

Yet how mistaken is the avarice even of the planters. Are slaves more useful by being thus humbled to the condition of brutes, than they would be if suffered to enjoy the privileges of men? The freedom which diffuses health and prosperity throughout Britain answers "No." When you make men slaves, you deprive them of half their virtue, you set them, in your own conduct, an example of fraud, rapine, and cruelty, and compel them to live with you in a state of war; and yet you complain that they are not honest or faithful! You stupify them with whippings and brandings, and think it necessary to keep them in a state of ignorance. And yet you assert that they are incapable of learning; that their minds are such a barren soil or moor, that culture would be lost on them; and that they come from a climate, where nature, though prodigal of her bounties in a degree unknown to yourselves, has left man alone scant and unfinished, and incapable of enjoying the treasures she has poured out for him! An assertion at once impious and absurd. Why do you use those instruments of torture? Are they fit to be applied by one rational being to another? And are you not struck with shame and mortification, to see the partakers of your nature reduced so low? But, above all, are there no dangers attending this mode of treatment? Are you not hourly in dread of an insurrection? But by changing your conduct, and treating your slaves as men, every cause of fear would be banished. They would be faithful, honest, intelligent, and vigorous; and peace, prosperity, and happiness would attend you.

---

*Greed.

Plea to End Slavery

Such were the various scenes which I was a witness to and the fortune I experienced until the year 1777. Since that period my life has been more uniform and the incidents of it fewer than in any other equal number of years preceding; I therefore hasten to the conclusion of a narrative, which I fear the reader may think already sufficiently tedious.

I hope to have the satisfaction of seeing the renovation of liberty and justice resting on the British government, to vindicate the honor of our common nature. . . . It is upon these grounds that I hope and expect the attention of gentlemen in power. These are designs consonant to the elevation of their rank and the dignity of their stations: they are ends suitable to the nature of a free and generous government; and, connected with views of empire and dominion, suited to the benevolence and solid merit of the legislature. . . . May Heaven make the British senators the givers of light, liberty, and science, to the uttermost parts of the earth: then will be glory to God on the highest, on earth peace, and goodwill to men. . . . May the blessings of the Lord be upon the heads of all those who commiserated the cases of the oppressed negroes, and the fear of God prolong their days; and may their expectations be filled with gladness. . . !

As the inhuman traffic of slavery is to be taken into the consideration of the British legislature, I doubt not, if a system of commerce was established in Africa, the demand for manufactures would most rapidly augment, as the native inhabitants will insensibly adopt the British fashions, manners, customs, etc. In proportion to the civilization, so will be the consumption of British manufactures. . . . A commercial intercourse with Africa opens an inexhaustible source of wealth to the manufacturing interests of Great Britain, and to all which the slave trade is an objection. . . .

If I am not misinformed, the manufacturing interest is equal, if not superior, to the landed interest, as to the value, for reasons which will soon appear. The abolition of slavery, so diabolical, will give a most rapid extension of manufactures, which is totally and diametrically opposite to what some interested people assert. . . . [Similarly], the manufactures of [England] must and will, in the nature and reason of things, have a full and constant employ by supplying the African markets. . . .

[The] population [and resources] of Africa abound in valuable and useful returns; the hidden treasures of centuries will be brought to light and into circulation. Industry, enterprise, and mining, will have their full scope, proportionably as they civilize. In a word, it lays open an endless field of commerce to the British manufacturer and merchant adventurer. The manufacturing interest and the general interests are synonymous. The abolition of slavery would be in reality a universal good. Tortures, murder, and every other imaginable barbarity and iniquity, are practiced upon the poor slaves with impunity. I hope the slave trade will be abolished. I pray it may be an event at hand. The great body of manufacturers, uniting in the cause, will considerably facilitate and expedite it; and as I have already stated, it is most substantially their interest and advantage, and as such the nation's at large, (except those persons concerned in the manufacturing of neck-yokes, collars, chains, handcuffs, leg bolts, thumb-screws, iron muzzles . . . and other instruments of torture used in the slave trade). In a short time one sentiment alone will prevail, from motives of interest as well as justice and humanity. Europe contains one hundred and twenty millions of inhabitants. Query: how many millions does Africa contain? . . . If the blacks were permitted to remain in their own country, they would double themselves every fifteen years. In proportion to such increase, will be the demand for manufactures. Cotton and indigo grow spontaneously in most parts of Africa; thus a consideration this of no small consequence to the manufacturing towns of Great Britain. It opens a most immense, glorious, and happy prospect—the clothing, etc. of a continent ten thousand miles in circumference, and immensely rich in productions of every denomination in return for manufactures.

I have only therefore to request the reader's indulgence and conclude. I am far from the vanity of thinking there is any merit in this narrative: I hope censure will be suspended when it is considered that it was written by one who was as unwilling as unable to adorn the plainness of truth by the coloring of imagination. My life and fortune have been extremely checkered and my adventures various. Even those I have related are considerably abridged. If any incident in this little work should appear uninteresting and trifling to most readers, I can only say as my excuse, for mentioning it that almost every event of my life made an impression on my mind and influenced my conduct. I early accustomed myself to look for the hand of God in the minutest occurrence and to learn from it a lesson of morality and religion, and in this light every circumstance I have related was to me of importance. After all, what makes any event important, unless by its observation we become better and wiser, and learn 'to do justly, to love mercy, and to walk humbly before God'? To those who are possessed of this spirit there is scarcely any book of incident so trifling that does not afford some profit, while to others the experiences seem of no use; and even to pour out to them the treasures of wisdom is throwing the jewels of instruction away.

THE PERSPECTIVE OF A SLAVE OWNER

In 1781, while recovering from a fall from his horse, Thomas Jefferson (1743–1826) penned his *Notes on the State of Virginia*, a wide-ranging critical assessment of conditions in his home state in the successful aftermath of the American victory at Yorktown. At age thirty-eight, he already had a distinguished career, having served as a colonial legislator, a member of Virginia's House of Delegates, and governor of Virginia. He was also widely known and respected for the drafting of the Declaration of Independence in 1776 (see chapter 6). In this document, Jefferson clearly expressed the Enlightenment era's concern for the natural rights of mankind, which Jefferson identified as the rights of life, liberty, and happiness for all. But in his *Notes on the State of Virginia*, Jefferson's views on Africans and slavery seem to conflict with his earlier stated beliefs. This is more understandable when one considers the ambiguities and contradictions within Jefferson's own life. Although he drafted legislation to end the slave trade in Virginia in 1778, Jefferson remained a slave owner until the day he died.[5] And although he clearly regarded Africans as an inferior people, there is widespread evidence that he had an amorous affair with Sally Hemings, one of his slaves.

Such contradictions were not unique in American history, for slavery set American ideals of liberty and equality in direct conflict with American racial prejudices. Nor was the contradiction ever resolved for Jefferson. In 1789, Jefferson entered national politics once again, serving as George Washington's secretary of state, John Adams's vice president, and finally as president from 1801 to 1809. As a national leader, Jefferson did little to resolve the issue of slavery or the slave trade. Although he recognized the immorality of slavery, he was unable to envision a workable remedy. As Jefferson explained the dilemma in 1820, "We have the wolf by the ears; and we can neither hold him, nor safely let him go. Justice is in one scale, and self-preservation in the other."

The following excerpts from Jefferson's *Notes on the State of Virginia* center on his arguments against the abolition of slavery. As a man of the Enlightenment era, he endeavored to present a rational argument, based on compelling logic and specific evidence that focus on racial differences. As you read his account, examine carefully his use of logic, data, and historical comparisons. Jefferson concludes his remarks with a consideration of the moral impact of slavery. Do these remarks conflict with his earlier conclusions? How do they compare with Equiano's discussion on the impact of slavery?

QUESTIONS TO CONSIDER

1. In what ways does Jefferson assert that whites are superior to blacks? What is his evidence and reasoning? What assumptions are implicit in his judgments?

2. In his efforts to explain why Africans are inferior, Jefferson argues that it cannot merely be attributed to the conditions in which slaves live. How does he attempt to use history to prove his point? What are the flaws in his argument? Why do you think Jefferson seemed to ignore individuals like Olaudah Equiano in his assessments and conclusions?

3. In Jefferson's view, the United States could never become a successful, peaceful multiracial nation. Why? What solution does Jefferson suggest? What might be some of the obstacles in his ideal plan?

4. Compare and contrast Jefferson's depiction of African society and culture with the description provided by Equiano. What are the implications of the differing accounts?

5. At the end of his essay, Jefferson concedes that slavery is immoral and an evil to all associated with it. What evils concern him the most? What issues does he ignore?

NOTES ON THE STATE OF VIRGINIA (1781)

Thomas Jefferson

It will probably be asked [by those who support abolition], "Why not retain and incorporate the blacks into the state, and thus save the expense of supplying, by im-

---

Thomas Jefferson ◆ *Notes on the State of Virginia* (1781)   97

portation of white settlers, the vacancies they will leave?" Deep rooted prejudices entertained by the whites; ten thousand recollections, by the blacks, of the injuries they have sustained; new provocations; the real distinctions which nature has made; and many other circumstances, will divide us into parties, and produce convulsions, which will probably never end but in the extermination of the one or the other race.

To these objections, which are political, may be added others, which are physical and moral. The first difference which strikes us is that of color. Whether the black of the negro resides in the membrane between the skin, . . . or the color of the blood, the color of the bile, or from that of some other secretion, the difference is fixed in nature, and is as real as if its seat and cause were better known to us. And is this difference of no importance? Is it not the foundation of a greater or less share of beauty in the two races? Are not the fine mixtures of red and white, the expressions of every passion by greater or less suffusions of color in the one, preferable to that eternal monotony, which reigns in the countenances, that immovable veil of black which covers all the emotions of the other race? Add to these, flowing hair, a more elegant symmetry of form. . . . The circumstance of superior beauty, is thought worthy of attention in the propagation of our horses, dogs, and other domestic animals; why not in that of man? Besides those of color, figure, and hair, there are other physical distinctions proving a difference of race. They have less hair on the face and body. They secrete less by the kidneys, and more by the glands of the skin, which gives them a very strong and disagreeable odor. This greater degree of transpiration renders them more tolerant of heat, and less so of cold than the whites. . . . They seem to require less sleep. A black after hard labor through the day, will be induced by the slightest amusements to sit up till midnight, or later, though knowing he must be out with the first dawn of the morning. They are at least as brave, and more adventuresome. But this may perhaps proceed from a want of forethought, which prevents their seeing a danger till it be present. . . .

[African slaves] are more ardent after their female: but love seems with them to be more an eager desire, than a tender delicate mixture of sentiment and sensation. Their griefs are transient. Those numberless afflictions . . . are less felt, and sooner forgotten with them. In general, their existence appears to participate more of sensation than reflection. To this must be ascribed their disposition to sleep when abstracted from their diversions, and unemployed in labor. An animal whose body is at rest, and who does not reflect, must be disposed to sleep of course. Comparing them by their faculties of memory, reason, and imagination, it appears to me that in memory they are equal to the whites; in reason much inferior, as I think one could scarcely be found capable of tracing and comprehending the investigations of Euclid;* and that in imagination they are dull, tasteless, and anomalous. It would be unfair to follow them to Africa for this investigation.

We will consider them here, on the same stage with the whites, and where the facts are not apocryphal on which a judgement is to be formed. It will be right to make great allowances for the difference of condition, of education, of conversation, of the sphere in which they move. Many millions of them have been brought to, and

---

*Euclid was a classical Greek geometer who established a mathematical school at Alexandria around 300 BCE.

born in America. Most of them indeed have been confined to tillage, to their own homes, and their own society: yet many have been so situated, that they might have availed themselves of the conversation of their masters; many have been brought up to the handicraft arts, and from that circumstance have always been associated with the whites. Some have been liberally educated, and all have lived in countries where the arts and sciences are cultivated to a considerable degree, and have had before their eyes samples of the best works from abroad.

The Indians, with no advantages of this kind, will often carve figures on their pipes not destitute of design and merit. They will crayon out an animal, a plant, or a country, so as to prove the existence of a germ in their minds which only wants cultivation. They astonish you with strokes of the most sublime oratory; such as prove their reason and sentiment strong, their imagination glowing and elevated. But never yet could I find that a black had uttered a thought above the level of plain narration; never saw even an elementary trait of painting or sculpture. In music they are more generally gifted than the whites with accurate ears for tune and time, and they have been found capable of imagining a small catch [melody].* Whether they will be equal to the composition of a more extensive run of melody, or of complicated harmony, is yet to be proved. . . .

The improvement of the blacks in body and mind, in the first instance of their mixture with the whites, has been observed by every one, and proves that their inferiority is not the effect merely of their condition of life. We know that among the Romans, about the Augustan age especially, the condition of their slaves was much more deplorable than that of the blacks on the continent of America. . . . Yet notwithstanding these and other discouraging circumstances among the Romans, their slaves were often their rarest artists. They excelled too in science, insomuch as to be usually employed as tutors to their masters' children. Epictetus, Terence, and Phaedrus, were slaves.† But they were of the race of whites. It is not their condition then, but nature, which has produced the distinction. Whether further observation will or will not verify the conjecture, that nature has been less bountiful to them in the endowments of the head, I believe that in those of the heart she will be found to have done them justice. That disposition to theft with which they have been branded, must be ascribed to their situation, and not to any depravity of the moral sense. The man, in whose favor no laws of property exist, probably feels himself less bound to respect those made in favor of others. . . .

The opinion, that they are inferior in the faculties of reason and imagination, must be hazarded with great diffidence. To justify a general conclusion, requires many observations, even where the subject may be submitted to the anatomical knife, to optical classes, to analysis by fire, or by solvents. How much more then where it is a faculty, not a substance, we are examining; where it eludes the research of all the Senses; where the conditions of its existence are various and variously combined; where the effects of those which are present or absent bid defiance to calculation; let

---

*Note by Jefferson: "The instrument proper to them is the Banjar [banjo], which they brought hither from Africa, and which is the original of the guitar. . . ."

†Epictetus was a famous Roman teacher and philosopher; Terence was a major playwright; and Phaedrus penned a collection of popular fables and short stories.

Thomas Jefferson ◆ *Notes on the State of Virginia* (1781)   99

me add too, as a circumstance of great tenderness, where our conclusion would degrade a whole race of men from the rank in the scale of beings which their Creator may perhaps have given them. To our reproach it must be said, that though for a century and a half we have had under our eyes the races of black and of red men, they have never yet been viewed by us as subjects of natural history. I advance it therefore as a suspicion only, that the blacks, whether originally a distinct race, or made distinct by time and circumstances, are inferior to the whites in the endowments both of body and mind. It is not against experience to suppose, that different species of the same genus, or varieties of the same species, may possess different qualifications. Will not a lover of natural history then, one who views the gradations in all the races of animals with the eye of philosophy, excuse an effort to keep those in the department of man as distinct as nature has formed them?

This unfortunate difference of color, and perhaps of faculty, is a powerful obstacle to the emancipation of these people. Many of their advocates, while they wish to vindicate the liberty of human nature are anxious also to preserve its dignity and beauty. Some of these, embarrassed by the question "What further is to be done with them?" join themselves in opposition with those who are actuated by sordid avarice only. Among the Romans emancipation required but one effort. The slave, when made free, might mix with, without staining the blood of his master. But with us a second is necessary, unknown to history. When freed, he is to be removed beyond the reach of mixture.

. . . There must doubtless be an unhappy influence on the manners of our people produced by the existence of slavery among us. The whole commerce between master and slave is a perpetual exercise of the most boisterous passions, the most unremitting despotism on the one part, and degrading submissions on the other. Our children see this, and learn to imitate it; for man is an imitative animal. This quality is the germ of all education in him. From his cradle to his grave he is learning to do what he sees others do. If a parent could find no motive either in his philanthropy or his self love, for restraining the intemperance of passion towards his slave, it should always be a sufficient one that his child is present. But generally it is not sufficient. The parent storms, the child looks on, catches the lineaments of wrath, puts on the same airs in the circle of smaller slaves, gives a loose to the worst of passions, and thus nursed, educated, and daily exercised in tyranny, cannot but be stamped by it with odious peculiarities. The man must be a prodigy who can retain his manners and morals undepraved by such circumstances. And with what denunciations should the statesman receive, who, permitting one half the citizens thus to trample on the rights of the other, transforms those into despots, and these into enemies, destroys the morals of the one part, and the love of country of the other? For if a slave can have a country in this world, it must be any other in preference to that in which he is born to live and labor for another; in which he must lock up the faculties of his nature, contribute as far as depends on his individual endeavors to the disappearance of the human race, or entail his own miserable condition on the endless generations proceeding from him. With the morals of the people, their industry also is destroyed. For in a warm climate, no man will labor for himself who can make another labor for him. This is so true, that of the proprietors of slaves a very small proportion indeed are ever seen to labor.

100   CHAPTER 3 ◆ Perspectives on the Atlantic Slave Trade

And can the liberties of a nation be thought secure when we have removed their only firm basis, a conviction in the minds of the people that these liberties are of the gift of God? That they are not to be violated but with his wrath? Indeed I tremble for my country when I reflect that God is just: that his justice cannot sleep forever: that considering numbers, nature and natural means only, a revolution of the wheel of fortune, an exchange of situation is among possible events: that it may become probable by supernatural interference! The Almighty has no attribute which can take side with us in such a contest. But it is impossible to be temperate and to pursue this subject through the various considerations of policy, of morals, of history natural and civil. We must be contented to hope they will force their way into every one's mind. I think a change already perceptible, since the origin of the present revolution. The spirit of the master is abating, that of the slave rising from the dust, his condition mollifying, the way I hope preparing, under the auspices of heaven, for a total emancipation, and that this is disposed, in the order of events, to be with the consent of the masters, rather than by their extirpation.

NOTES

1. Slave trade statistics from David Eltis, Stephen D. Behrendt, David Richardson, and Herbert S. Klein, *The Trans-Atlantic Slave Trade: A Database on CD-ROM* (Cambridge and New York: Cambridge University Press, 1999).

2. During the French Revolution, radical reformers in 1794 were the first Europeans to abolish slavery in their colonial possessions until slavery was reinstated by Napoleon from 1802 to 1815. (See the readings on Haiti in chapter 6.)

3. President Lincoln's Emancipation Proclamation (1863) was a war measure that did not free slaves in the border states or in areas of the Confederacy already under Union occupation and control.

4. Sierra Leone was a slave trading outpost until the late eighteenth century, when it became a new homeland for freed slaves. Between 1790 and 1800, approximately 1,500 freedmen, under the leadership of British abolitionists, were returned to Africa to establish the settlement of Freetown. The new colony was controlled by the Sierra Leone Company, which forcefully held off resistance from local inhabitants while the settlers supported themselves by farming. After Britain outlawed the slave trade in 1808, it took over from the financially troubled company, using it as a naval base for antislavery patrols. Between 1808 and 1864, an additional 50,000 liberated slaves settled at Freetown, and their descendants, known as Creoles, became active as Christian missionaries and traders along the coast of west Africa, as well as the ruling elites of the region.

5. Because of his poor business practices and money problems, Jefferson was unable to free his slaves upon his death. Instead, they were sold off to new masters to pay off the debt.

CHAPTER 6

Liberty and Revolution in the Atlantic World, 1776–1850

INTRODUCTION

For much of human history, mankind has lived under various forms of authoritarian political regimes. Possessing magnificent wealth and great power, leaders have frequently ruled over their people with an absolute authority that was sanctioned and justified not by popular assent but by divine will. In most societies, there was very little opportunity for the average person to make his or her voice heard or opinion count at the highest level of decision making. A momentous change occurred during the European Enlightenment of the seventeenth and eighteenth centuries, when political absolutism was challenged by the concept of a government "for the people, by the people." Starting with the premise that people possess basic human rights and liberties, Enlightenment philosophers crafted a new theory called "liberalism"[1] that placed sovereignty in the hands of the people. The consequences have changed world history. Reformers and revolutionaries from around the world have embraced the ideals of liberalism to rebel against unjust authority and to provide a blueprint for their new secular governments and national identities.

The historical documents in this chapter explore the origins, character, and meaning of liberalism within the setting of early revolutionary movements in the Atlantic world during the late eighteenth and early nineteenth centuries. The readings illustrate how liberal ideas served to inspire, motivate, and justify popular rebellions in the United States, France, and South America against authoritarian rule. Yet the readings also highlight the important and complex encounter between theoretical ideals and historical realities, for within each of the revolutionary settings under study, specific events, cultural conditions, and personal perspectives served to redefine and reshape the liberal ideals of liberty, equality, and freedom.

Historians typically trace the roots of modern liberal philosophy to the great political thinkers of the European Enlightenment.[2] One of the most important and influential was John Locke (1632–1704), whose faith in human logic and historical progress was examined in chapter 4. In his *Two Treatises of Government* (1690), Locke postulated that people formed communities and governments to protect their God-given natural rights of life, liberty, and property. If a government attempted to rule absolutely and violate the natural rights of individuals, it reneged on its "contract" and lost legitimacy, freeing the community to form a new government. Another major theorist was Jean-Jacques Rousseau (1712–1778), who agreed with Locke that people enter into a contract with their government to protect liberties. But in *The Social Contract* (1762), Rousseau further argued for a direct democracy, believing that authority could be expressed only in the "general will" of the people, which would serve and promote the common good of the community. In their attack on absolutism, both Locke and Rousseau offered a radical reassessment of human rights and social institutions, and their ideas had a profound influence on the reformers of the French Revolution and the Founding Fathers of the United States.

The American Revolution (1776–1789) began as a rebellion against British colonial rule and evolved into one of the most enduring and influential liberal revolutions. Historians typically view the revolution in two distinct phases: the war for independence (1776–1783) and the crafting of a new government (1783–1789). In the first phase, tensions over British policies toward its American colonies escalated in the mid-eighteenth century, leading to armed skirmishes at Lexington and Concord in 1775 and increased demands for independence. The revolution officially began when the Second Continental Congress adopted the Declaration of Independence (1776), a document written primarily by Thomas Jefferson (1743–1826). A well-read man and avid admirer of Enlightenment philosophy, Jefferson proposed a model of governance that freely borrowed from the work of John Locke. But in the context of revolutionary action, the ideals and principles expressed in the Declaration of Independence have also come to reflect and shape American self-identity. As Jefferson himself explained, the Declaration was "neither aiming at originality of principle or sentiment, nor copied from any particular and previous writing," but was intended to be "an expression of the American mind."

At the successful conclusion of the war in 1783, the newly independent states faced the challenge of establishing a new federal government. Their first attempt, the Articles of Confederation (1781–1787), proved too weak and ineffective for the nation's needs, and in 1787, Congress called for a Constitutional Convention to debate and draft a new national charter. One of the most influential leaders in these debates was James Madison (1751–1836), a 36-year-old delegate from Virginia who advocated a strong national government. In order to sway Congress and public opinion to his model of governance, Madison penned a series of essays known as *The Federalist Papers*[3] that carefully outlined his ideas and proposals. In Federalist Paper No. 10, Madison discussed the issue of "factions," or special interest groups that might infringe upon the rights of others and disregard the public good. Madison's solution was ultimately enshrined in the United States Constitution: a system of political representation to ensure stability by imposing limitations on popular sovereignty.

Introduction   157

In 1828, the election of Andrew Jackson from Tennessee as the seventh president (and the first from west of the Appalachian mountains) marked the beginnings of a significant shift in American politics. Campaigning as the candidate of the "common man," Jackson tapped into widespread public discontent with governmental policies that were seen as favoring the plantation elite of the south and the commercial elite of the north. With more citizens and frontiersmen championing the "will of the people," pressure mounted to reform and democratize America's political process. One of the most articulate spokesmen of these changes was George Bancroft (1800–1891), an eminent scholar, ardent Jacksonian democrat, and future founder of the United States Naval Academy. In a speech titled "The Office of the People in Art, Government, and Religion" (1835), Bancroft challenged the views of Madison by advocating an extension of democratic values and institutions in America. "The duty of America," he explained, "is to secure the culture and happiness of the masses by reliance on themselves."

Although the Jacksonian era has been called the age of the "common man," such democratic tendencies clearly had distinct limitations. By law, the "common man" generally referred only to adult white males. Women, minorities, and slaves were denied political power and full citizenship, and to many of them, the promises embedded in Jefferson's Declaration of Independence rang hollow.[4] One of the most vocal and articulate critics was Frederick Douglass, a former slave who had escaped his bondage, bought his freedom, and became one of America's leading abolitionist leaders. In an Independence Day oration titled "What to the Slave Is the 4th of July?" (1852), Douglass condemned American hypocrisy for the glaring contradiction between its ideals of liberty and its continuing practice of slavery. His essay offers an important perspective on the limitations and meaning of liberalism within the context of American history.

The success of the American Revolution excited and inspired liberal thinkers in Europe and especially in France, which was still governed by an absolute monarchy. In 1789, King Louis XVI was forced to convene a rare meeting of the Estates General, France's traditional assembly, to deal with a financial crisis that threatened to bankrupt the state. But the meeting had unintended consequences, as liberal reformers seized the opportunity to dismantle the laws and institutions of the "Old Regime" altogether. Under their leadership, the Estates General was transformed into a National Assembly, which produced a new vision for France in the Declaration of the Rights of Man and Citizen (1789). Insisting that "men are born free and equal," the Declaration attacked the foundations of absolutism and asserted that sovereignty rested on the will of the people.

Although the monarchy and many members of the nobility believed that the liberal reformers had gone too far, there were others who believed the reforms had not gone far enough. Among these were revolutionary women, who sought to extend the principles of liberty and equality to all citizens, regardless of gender. One of the most famous of these early feminists was the writer and activist Olympe de Gouges, who penned the Declaration of the Rights of Women in 1791. Blaming both male chauvinism and female complicity for the inferior status and subjugation of women in France, de Gouges demanded equal participation in the new social order and full rights for women as equal contributors to society. Although

158   CHAPTER 6   ✦   Liberty and Revolution in the Atlantic World, 1776–1850

her uncompromising stand on controversial issues ultimately led her to the guillo-tine in 1793, Olympe de Gouges is revered as one of the French Revolution's most dedicated proponents of human rights and a pioneer of the modern feminist movement.

Another group who felt that the revolution had not gone far enough were the Jacobins, a radical political organization led by the dynamic and idealistic Maximi-lien Robespierre. The Jacobins went beyond the moderate liberals by advocating an end to the monarchy, the extension of political rights beyond the propertied classes, and the abolition of slavery in the French colonies. In the fall of 1792, with the revolution threatened by foreign invasions and domestic plots in support of the monarchy, the Jacobins were able to gain control of the National Assembly and domestic policy. Under the leadership of Robespierre and his Committee of Public Safety, the French Revolution now entered its "radical phase," in which terror and violence were used as instruments of the state. In an address on "The Moral and Political Principles of Domestic Policy" (1794), Robespierre described his utopian revolutionary ideals and justified his use of terror and the guillotine. But the radi-cals' search for enemies of the revolution became relentless, until at last even the leaders, including Robespierre himself, were sentenced to death. As one enemy of Robespierre gleefully pointed out, the revolution "devoured its own children."

Across the Atlantic, in the European colonies of the Caribbean and South America, discontent with colonial rule, commercial restrictions, and social in-equities also grew in the eighteenth century. Inspired by the ideals and successes of the liberal revolutions in the United States and France, some colonial settlers imitated their North American counterparts by demanding political independence. But the situation in the Caribbean and South America was made much more com-plex by competing national allegiances and racial identities, which imparted unique definitions of "freedom" and "equality."

The first major revolution occurred in Saint-Domingue (now known as Haiti), France's most important and prosperous sugar-producing colony. The Haitian Revolution began in 1789, when white colonists demanded more self-government, better trade policies, and judicial reform consistent with the Declara-tion of Rights of Man and Citizen. But the ultimate outcome of the Haitian Revolution was not to be decided by whites alone, for in 1791, the slaves of the island (who were not included in the granting of new liberties) revolted against their masters. The slaves were organized and led by Toussaint L'Ouverture, a former slave and skilled politician who successfully battled French, Spanish, and British forces to retain the freedom of blacks. In a series of letters to French authorities, Toussaint explained his goals and strategies using the ideals and rhetoric of liberal-ism in his defense. But the French were not swayed by his sentiments, and in 1802, he was treacherously seized and deported to France, where he was confined until his death the following year. Facing continued resistance by L'Ouverture's follow-ers, French forces finally withdrew in 1803, and Haiti followed the United States as the second independent colony in the New World.

In the Spanish possessions of South America, colonists fumed under tight im-perial control and policies that favored those born in Spain over the *Creoles*, or American-born descendants of Spanish families. Inspired by events in the United

States, the Creoles launched their own independence movement in 1807. Central to their success was Simón Bolívar, proclaimed the "Liberator" by his contemporaries and widely recognized as the hero of South American independence. From 1807 to 1825, he led numerous military expeditions against Spanish rule from Colombia to Peru and later served as the president of Gran Colombia (Colombia, Venezuela, and Equador) and Peru. But although dedicated to the independence of the Spanish colonies, he was not ready or willing to grant full political rights to the people. As he explained in "The Jamaican Letter" of 1815, he believed that South Americans lacked the unity and "virtue" required for such liberal reforms, and he instead advocated a kind of authoritarian republicanism, consisting of a strong central executive and a hereditary legislature. As a consequence, his political philosophy has had the unique legacy of advancing and justifying the competing claims of both democrats and dictators in South America's political history.

The liberty revolutions of the Atlantic world have had profound influence on human history. Many historians conclude that they have provided the model for the modern nation-state, one based on liberal principles, secular authority, and rational institutions. Others claim that they represent the first truly ideological revolutions, for they embraced radically new ideas about human rights and social progress. But the readings in this chapter also reveal significant variances in the definitions of "liberty," "equality," and "freedom," and many of these differences continue to fuel political debates today.

CHAPTER QUESTIONS

1. Among the numerous authors in this chapter, who are the proponents of democracy? How do they defend their views? Who are the opponents of democracy and what is their argument? What factors might account for the different perspectives on democracy? Which perspective do you find the most persuasive?

2. Olympe de Gouges and Frederick Douglass are two individuals who found fault with the limitations of early liberalism. What are the similarities in their complaints and demands? How might liberal political leaders respond to these complaints?

3. Some revolutionaries, such as Robespierre and Toussaint L'Ouverture, employed extreme, antiliberal measures in their attempt to safeguard hard-won liberties. How would you assess their actions? Was their extremism a fundamental betrayal of their liberal ideals? Or is extremism in defense of liberty justified under certain conditions?

4. Many historians contend that there is a close link between the rise of political liberalism and the development of modern nationalism. In what ways might the two forces be related? Did liberals use feelings of nationalism and patriotism to achieve their political reforms? In what ways might patriotism work against liberal goals and values? Does national/group identity threaten individual identity and power?

160   CHAPTER 6 ❖ Liberty and Revolution in the Atlantic World, 1776–1850

5. In your perception, how has the definition of liberalism changed since the days of James Madison? In what ways has the philosophy of liberalism remained consistent?

THE AMERICAN REVOLUTION
The Revolutionary Ideals of Jefferson

On July 4, 1826, on the fiftieth anniversary of the Declaration of Independence, Thomas Jefferson died at the age of eighty-three at his home at Monticello, Virginia. On his tombstone, he had engraved the three major achievements for which he wanted to be remembered: "Author of the Declaration of American Independence, of the Statute of Virginia for religious freedom,[5] and Father of the University of Virginia." These three accomplishments share the common ideal of freedom: freedom from colonial rule, freedom of religious belief, and freedom of rational thought and inquiry. Indeed, through much of his life as a public servant—and despite his seemingly contradictory practice of owning slaves[6]—Jefferson remained steadfastly devoted to the Enlightenment ideals of individual liberty that he expressed so eloquently in the Declaration of Independence.

Jefferson was born to a distinguished and wealthy family in Albemarle County, Virginia, in 1743. After attending the College of William and Mary and studying law, he served six years as a representative in Virginia's colonial House of Burgesses before his election to the Second Continental Congress in 1776. After passage of the Declaration of Independence, he returned to Virginia, and as a member of the state legislature, he introduced the statute for religious toleration and other liberal measures. After a brief term as governor of Virginia (1779–1781), he returned to national politics in 1783 and served as a member of Congress, minister to France, and secretary of state in the first Washington administration. After a brief retirement at Monticello, he became the presidential candidate of the Democratic-Republican party in 1796. Jefferson narrowly lost the election to the Federalist candidate John Adams, but under the Constitutional provisions then in effect, he became vice president. In 1800, Jefferson again ran for president and was elected third president of the United States. As president, Jefferson reduced the power of the military and federal government, but he also doubled the size of the nation with the Louisiana Purchase (1803). After completion of his second term in 1809, Jefferson devoted most of the remaining seventeen years of his life to the founding of the University of Virginia.

The Declaration of Independence has three basic sections. It begins with a statement of political ideals, followed by a list of specific grievances against British colonial policies and a concluding final proclamation of independence. In defining the proper relationship between government and the people in the first section, Jefferson borrowed key concepts from the political theories of John Locke and other Enlightenment thinkers. But in his affirmation of political ideals, Jefferson was also creating a much broader definition of what it meant to be American. This is what gives the Declaration of Independence its special place in American his-

Thomas Jefferson ◆ Declaration of Independence (1776)   161

tory: It is a clear statement of values, a blueprint for governmental institutions and laws, and a bond of unity through a common sense of national identity.

QUESTIONS TO CONSIDER

1. According to Jefferson, what is the purpose of government? Under what circumstances is it justifiable to abolish government? If people are given the right to rebel, why does Jefferson not fear frequent revolutions?

2. Jefferson's theory of government is founded on his belief in human rights and "the laws of nature." What are these rights and laws? In what ways are these beliefs so crucial to his political philosophy?

3. On what occasions does Jefferson make reference to God in this address? How do such references influence his message? Do they seem to reinforce or conflict with his political views?

4. Jefferson states that the Declaration was written out of "decent respect to the opinions of mankind. . . ." Given the contents of the document, might there be other motives as well?

5. Some historians claim that the Declaration of Independence is one of the best expressions of American national identity. What ideas do you believe have been the most significant in shaping American identity? In what areas has American identity most strayed from the ideals of the Declaration?

DECLARATION OF INDEPENDENCE (1776)

Thomas Jefferson

When in the course of human events, it becomes necessary for one people to dissolve the political bands which have connected them with another, and to assume among the powers of the earth, the separate and equal station to which the laws of nature and of nature's God entitle them, a decent respect to the opinions of mankind requires that they should declare the causes which impel them to the separation.

We hold these truths to be self-evident: That all men are created equal; that they are endowed by their Creator with certain unalienable rights; that among these are life, liberty, and the pursuit of happiness; that, to secure these rights, governments are instituted among men, deriving their just powers from the consent of the governed; that whenever any form of government becomes destructive of these ends, it is the right of the people to alter or to abolish it, and to institute new government, laying its foundation on such principles, and organizing its powers in such form, as to them shall seem most likely to effect their safety and happiness. Prudence, indeed, will dictate

Source: The Declaration of Independence is in the public domain.

162   CHAPTER 6   ◆   Liberty and Revolution in the Atlantic World, 1776–1850

that governments long established should not be changed for light and transient causes; and accordingly all experience hath shown that mankind are more disposed to suffer, while evils are sufferable than to right themselves by abolishing the forms to which they are accustomed. But when a long train of abuses and usurpations, pursuing invariably the same object, evinces a design to reduce them under absolute despotism, it is their right, it is their duty, to throw off such government, and to provide new guards for their future security. Such has been the patient sufferance of these colonies; and such is now the necessity which constrains them to alter their former systems of government. The history of the present King of Great Britain is a history of repeated injuries and usurpations, all having in direct object the establishment of an absolute tyranny over these states. To prove this, let facts be submitted to a candid world. . . .

[A detailed list of grievances follows]

In every stage of these oppressions we have petitioned for redress in the most humble terms; our repeated petitions have been answered only by repeated injury. A prince, whose character is thus marked by every act which may define a tyrant, is unfit to be the ruler of a free people.

Nor have we been wanting in our attentions to our British brethren. We have warned them, from time to time, of attempts by their legislature to extend an unwarrantable jurisdiction over us. We have reminded them of the circumstances of our emigration and settlement here. We have appealed to their native justice and magnanimity; and we have conjured them, by the ties of our common kindred, to disavow these usurpations which would inevitably interrupt our connections and correspondence. They too, have been deaf to the voice of justice and of consanguinity. We must, therefore, acquiesce in the necessity which denounces our separation, and hold them as we hold the rest of mankind, enemies in war, in peace friends.

We, therefore, the representatives of the United States of America, in General Congress assembled, appealing to the Supreme Judge of the world for the rectitude of our intentions, do, in the name and by the authority of the good people of these colonies solemnly publish and declare, That these United Colonies are, and of right ought to be, *FREE AND INDEPENDENT STATES*; that they are absolved from all allegiance to the British crown and that all political connection between them and the state of Great Britain is, and ought to be, totally dissolved; and that, as free and independent states, they have full power to levy war, conclude peace, contract alliances, establish commerce, and do all other acts and things which independent states may of right do. And for the support of this declaration, with a firm reliance on the protection of Divine Providence, we mutually pledge to each other our lives, our fortunes, and our sacred honor.

The Fears of the Founding Fathers

James Madison (1751–1836) was one of Virginia's leading patriots during the Revolutionary War, was elected fourth president of United States, and led the nation during the War of 1812 with Britain. But he is probably most remembered for his pivotal role in the crafting and ratification of the United States Constitution (ratified in 1789) and its first ten amendments, more commonly known as the Bill of Rights (1791). Known and respected among his contemporaries for his skilled writing and argumentation, Madison was one of the most influential of the Founding Fathers.

Madison was born at Port Conway, Virginia, in 1751, the oldest child of an affluent, plantation-owning family. After studying law and government at the College of New Jersey (Princeton University), he returned to the family estate of Montpelier in Virginia and took up the cause of the American Revolution. Although he served in the Virginia colonial government, he was barred from military service in the Continental Army because of poor health. Chosen by Virginia's governor to represent the state in the Continental Congress from 1780 to 1789, Madison earned fame for crafting a model of government that became the blueprint of the Constitution. Madison believed in the value of a strong federal government whose power was divided among three branches and monitored through a system of "checks and balances." To promote its ratification by the states, Madison joined Alexander Hamilton of New York in penning *The Federalist Papers,* a collection of essays that were intended to explain and justify features of the new government. Following the ratification of the Constitution in 1789, Madison was elected to the new House of Representatives and sponsored the adoption of the Bill of Rights. After serving as secretary of state during the Jefferson administrations (1801–1809), Madison was elected to his own two terms as president from 1809 to 1817. Following his presidency, he retired to his plantation at Montpelier, and he remained interested and engaged in politics until his death in 1836.

The Federalist Papers are considered one of the most significant collection of documents in American political thought. Written primarily by Madison and Hamilton in 1787–1788 under the pseudonym *Publius,*[7] the eighty-five essays promoted the provisions and philosophy of the proposed new Constitution. In Federalist Paper No. 10, Madison discussed the threat of "factions" that could undermine the basic rights and liberties of citizens. Distrustful of democracy, he advocated a representative government made up of wise and propertied male citizens who might better discern "the true interests" of the country. Although some critics have charged that Madison and the other Founding Fathers were more concerned with protecting property than they were with liberty or equality, others credit Madison for establishing a stable and responsive government that has survived the test of time.

QUESTIONS TO CONSIDER

1. How does Madison define factions? Why does he consider them a "mortal disease of popular governments"?
2. According to Madison, what are the primary causes of factions? What role does property play in their formation? Do you agree with his assessment that factions are "sown into the nature of man"?

164   CHAPTER 6 ◆ Liberty and Revolution in the Atlantic World, 1776–1850

3. Madison asserts that "democracy offers no cure for the mischiefs of factions." Why? What advantages does he find in a republic?

4. What can be inferred from Federalist Paper No. 10 about Madison's views on human nature and social hierarchy? How central are these views in shaping his political philosophy?

5. Some scholars believe that Madison linked liberty more with property than with democracy. Do you agree? In your assessment, does Madison's anti-democratic sentiment betray the ideals and vision outlined in Jefferson's Declaration of Independence? Why or why not?

FEDERALIST NO. 10 (THE UNION AS A SAFEGUARD AGAINST DOMESTIC FACTION AND INSURRECTION) (1787)

James Madison

Among the numerous advantages promised by a well-constructed Union, none deserves to be more accurately developed than its tendency to break and control the violence of faction. The friend of popular governments never finds himself so much alarmed for their character and fate, as when he contemplates their propensity to this dangerous vice. . . . The instability, injustice, and confusion introduced into the public councils, have, in truth, been the mortal diseases under which popular governments have everywhere perished; as they continue to be the favorite and fruitful topics from which the adversaries to liberty derive their most specious declamations. The valuable improvements made by the American constitutions* on the popular models, both ancient and modern, cannot certainly be too much admired; but it would be an unwarrantable partiality, to contend that they have as effectually obviated the danger on this side, as was wished and expected. Complaints are everywhere heard from our most considerate and virtuous citizens, equally the friends of public and private faith, and of public and personal liberty, that our governments are too unstable, that the public good is disregarded in the conflicts of rival parties, and that measures are too often decided, not according to the rules of justice and the rights of the minor party, but by the superior force of an interested and overbearing majority. . . .

By a faction, I understand a number of citizens, whether amounting to a majority or a minority of the whole, who are united and actuated by some common impulse

---

Source: From *The Federalist, A Commentary on the Constitution of the United States, Being a Collection of Essays Written in Support of the Constitution Agreed upon September 17, 1787, by the Federal Convention.* From the original text of Alexander Hamilton, John Jay, and James Madison. With an introduction by Edward Mead Earle. (New York: The Modern Library), 53–62.

*Referring chiefly to the state governments and to the Articles of Confederation, which provided the separate states some central authority during and immediately after the Revolutionary War from 1781 to 1789.

James Madison ◈ Federalist No. 10 (1787)   **165**

of passion, or of interest, adverse to the rights of other citizens, or to the permanent and aggregate interests of the community.

There are two methods of curing the mischiefs of faction: the one, by removing its causes; the other, by controlling its effects. There are again two methods of removing the causes of faction: the one, by destroying the liberty which is essential to its existence; the other, by giving to every citizen the same opinions, the same passions, and the same interests.

It could never be more truly said than of the first remedy, that it was worse than the disease. Liberty is to faction what air is to fire, an aliment without which it instantly expires. But it could not be less folly to abolish liberty, which is essential to political life, because it nourishes faction, than it would be to wish the annihilation of air, which is essential to animal life, because it imparts to fire its destructive agency.

The second expedient is as impracticable as the first would be unwise. As long as the reason of man continues fallible, and he is at liberty to exercise it, different opinions will be formed. As long as the connection subsists between his reason and his self-love, his opinions and his passions will have a reciprocal influence on each other; and the former will be objects to which the latter will attach themselves. The diversity in the faculties of men, from which the rights of property originate, is not less an insuperable obstacle to a uniformity of interests. The protection of these faculties is the first object of government. From the protection of different and unequal faculties of acquiring property, the possession of different degrees and kinds of property immediately results; and from the influence of these on the sentiments and views of the respective proprietors, ensues a division of the society into different interests and parties.

The latent causes of faction are thus sown in the nature of man; and we see them everywhere brought into different degrees of activity, according to the different circumstances of civil society. A zeal for different opinions concerning religion, concerning government, and . . . an attachment to different leaders ambitiously contending for pre-eminence and power . . . have, in turn, divided mankind into parties, inflamed them with mutual animosity, and rendered them much more disposed to vex and oppress each other than to co-operate for their common good. So strong is this propensity of mankind to fall into mutual animosities, that where no substantial occasion presents itself, the most frivolous and fanciful distinctions have been sufficient to kindle their unfriendly passions and excite their most violent conflicts. But the most common and durable source of factions has been the various and unequal distribution of property. Those who hold and those who are without property have ever formed distinct interests in society. Those who are creditors, and those who are debtors, fall under a like discrimination. A landed interest, a manufacturing interest, a mercantile interest, a moneyed interest, with many lesser interests, grow up of necessity in civilized nations, and divide them into different classes, actuated by different sentiments and views. . . .

The inference to which we are brought is, that the CAUSES of faction cannot be removed, and that relief is only to be sought in the means of controlling its EFFECTS.

If a faction consists of less than a majority, relief is supplied by the republican principle, which enables the majority to defeat its sinister views by regular vote. It may clog the administration, it may convulse the society; but it will be unable to execute and mask its violence under the forms of the Constitution. When a majority is

166   CHAPTER 6   ◆   Liberty and Revolution in the Atlantic World, 1776–1850

included in a faction, the form of popular government, on the other hand, enables it to sacrifice to its ruling passion or interest both the public good and the rights of other citizens. . . .

From this view of the subject it may be concluded that a pure democracy, by which I mean a society consisting of a small number of citizens, who assemble and administer the government in person, can admit of no cure for the mischiefs of faction. A common passion or interest will, in almost every case, be felt by a majority of the whole; a communication and concert result from the form of government itself; and there is nothing to check the inducements to sacrifice the weaker party or an obnoxious individual. Hence it is that such democracies have ever been spectacles of turbulence and contention; have ever been found incompatible with personal security or the rights of property; and have in general been as short in their lives as they have been violent in their deaths. Theoretic politicians, who have patronized this species of government, have erroneously supposed that by reducing mankind to a perfect equality in their political rights, they would, at the same time, be perfectly equalized and assimilated in their possessions, their opinions, and their passions.

A republic, by which I mean a government in which the scheme of representation takes place, opens a different prospect, and promises the cure for which we are seeking. Let us examine the points in which it varies from pure democracy, and we shall comprehend both the nature of the cure and the efficacy which it must derive from the Union.

The two great points of difference between a democracy and a republic are: first, the delegation of the government, in the latter, to a small number of citizens elected by the rest; secondly, the greater number of citizens, and greater sphere of country, over which the latter may be extended.

The effect of the first difference is, on the one hand, to refine and enlarge the public views, by passing them through the medium of a chosen body of citizens, whose wisdom may best discern the true interest of their country, and whose patriotism and love of justice will be least likely to sacrifice it to temporary or partial considerations. Under such a regulation, it may well happen that the public voice, pronounced by the representatives of the people, will be more consonant to the public good than if pronounced by the people themselves, convened for the purpose. On the other hand, the effect may be inverted. Men of factious tempers, of local prejudices, or of sinister designs, may, by intrigue, by corruption, or by other means, first obtain the suffrages, and then betray the interests, of the people. The question resulting is, whether small or extensive republics are more favorable to the election of proper guardians of the public weal [well-being]; and it is clearly decided in favor of the latter by two obvious considerations:

In the first place, it is to be remarked that, however small the republic may be, the representatives must be raised to a certain number, in order to guard against the cabals* of a few; and that, however large it may be, they must be limited to a certain number, in order to guard against the confusion of a multitude. Hence, the number of representatives in the two cases not being in proportion to that of the two constituents, and being proportionally greater in the small republic, it follows that, if the propor-

---

*A group of persons secretly united to overturn or usurp an established authority.

James Madison ✦ Federalist No. 10 (1787)   **167**

tion of fit characters be not less in the large than in the small republic, the former will present a greater option, and consequently a greater probability of a fit choice.

In the next place, as each representative will be chosen by a greater number of citizens in the large than in the small republic, it will be more difficult for unworthy candidates to practice with success the vicious arts by which elections are too often carried; and the suffrages of the people being more free, will be more likely to centre in men who possess the most attractive merit and the most diffusive and established characters.

It must be confessed that in this, as in most other cases, there is a mean, on both sides of which inconveniences will be found to lie. By enlarging too much the number of electors, you render the representatives too little acquainted with all their local circumstances and lesser interests; as by reducing it too much, you render him unduly attached to these, and too little fit to comprehend and pursue great and national objects. The federal Constitution forms a happy combination in this respect; the great and aggregate interests being referred to the national, the local and particular to the State legislatures.

The other point of difference is, the greater number of citizens and extent of territory which may be brought within the compass of republican than of democratic government; and it is this circumstance principally which renders factious combinations less to be dreaded in the former than in the latter. The smaller the society, the fewer probably will be the distinct parties and interests composing it; the fewer the distinct parties and interests, the more frequently will a majority be found of the same party; and the smaller the number of individuals composing a majority, and the smaller the compass within which they are placed, the more easily will they concert and execute their plans of oppression. Extend the sphere, and you take in a greater variety of parties and interests; you make it less probable that a majority of the whole will have a common motive to invade the rights of other citizens; or if such a common motive exists, it will be more difficult for all who feel it to discover their own strength, and to act in unison with each other. Besides other impediments, it may be remarked that, where there is a consciousness of unjust or dishonorable purposes, communication is always checked by distrust in proportion to the number whose concurrence is necessary.

Hence, it clearly appears, that the same advantage which a republic has over a democracy, in controlling the effects of faction, is enjoyed by a large over a small republic—is enjoyed by the Union over the States composing it. . . .

In the extent and proper structure of the Union, therefore, we behold a republican remedy for the diseases most incident to republican government. And according to the degree of pleasure and pride we feel in being republicans, ought to be our zeal in cherishing the spirit and supporting the character of Federalists.

PUBLIUS.

An Argument for Democratic Reform

George Bancroft (1800–1891) was one of the more important, if less famous, political voices in America during the nineteenth century. He was also the nation's

168   CHAPTER 6 ◆ Liberty and Revolution in the Atlantic World, 1776–1850

leading historian, producing a ten-volume *History of the United States* that took nearly forty years to complete. Both in his scholarly writings and during his career in public service, Bancroft challenged the assumptions of Madison and the Founding Fathers by advocating an extension of democratic values and institutions in America.

Born in 1800 in Worcester, Massachusetts, Bancroft initially seemed destined for a life in academia. Graduating from Harvard University, he founded the innovative Round Hill School for boys and began work on his monumental *History of the United States*. But he also became increasingly devoted to the cause of democratic reform, and his published essays attacking the Bank of the United States and political elites thrilled Jacksonian Democrats. At their urging, he left the Round Hill School in 1831, entered party politics in Massachusetts, lost a race for governor in 1844, but was appointed secretary of the navy a year later by President James Polk, a fellow Democrat. As secretary of the navy (1845–46), Bancroft founded the United States Naval Academy in Annapolis, Maryland, and he helped design military strategy for the Mexican War (1846–47). In the mid-1850s, Bancroft broke with the Democrats over their continued support of slavery and shifted his allegiance to the newly formed Republican Party. He supported Abraham Lincoln in the 1860 election and believed that the Civil War was necessary to preserve the Union.[8] Following the war, Bancroft served as ambassador to Prussia and to the German Empire (1867–74), after which the elderly historian and diplomat retired to work on further editions of his beloved *History* before his death in Washington, D.C., in 1891.

"The Office of the People" was a speech given by Bancroft at Willamstown College (now Williams College) in Massachusetts in August 1835. His oration reflects two significant trends in early-nineteenth-century American history. The first is his high regard for democracy and his assertion that "the best government rests on the people and not on the few." The second trend is Bancroft's spiritualism, a reflection of New England's transcendental movement most frequently associated with Ralph Waldo Emerson.[9] In both regards, Bancroft's reasoning and political philosophy are quite distinct from the logic and perspective of James Madison, and a close comparison of the two provides a fascinating glimpse into American historical and cultural change.

QUESTIONS TO CONSIDER

1. Bancroft believes that all men are imbued with "spirit." How does he conceptualize this "spirit" and why does he view it as so important?

2. Bancroft states that "men cannot agree in an absurdity; neither can they agree in a falsehood." How did he come to this conclusion, and how does it relate to his definition of "truth"? Is his argument convincing? What are the implications, especially to individuals who hold views that conflict with majority opinion?

George Bancroft ◆ "The Office of the People in Art, Government, and Religion" (1835)   169

3. Madison asserted that the election of wise representatives would serve to temper the passions of the masses; in contrast, Bancroft argues that "the people collectively are wiser than the most gifted individual." Which argument do you find more convincing? Why?

4. Bancroft's political philosophy is highly influenced by his religious views. In your assessment, do his spiritual views undermine his political argument? Does it violate the separation of church and state in America?

5. Bancroft argues that the mark of a great civilization is not its might or wealth, but the degree to which it puts its faith "in the intelligence of the common man." Do you agree? If so, what might be the implications to present-day American government organization or domestic policy?

"THE OFFICE OF THE PEOPLE IN ART, GOVERNMENT, AND RELIGION" (1835)

George Bancroft

The material world does not change in its masses or in its powers. The stars shine with no more lustre than when they first sang together in the glory of their birth. The flowers that gemmed the fields and the forests, before America was discovered, now bloom around us in their season. . . . The earth turns on its axis and perfects its revolutions and renews its seasons without increase or advancement.

But a like passive destiny does not attach to the inhabitants of the earth. For them the expectations of social improvement are no delusion; the hopes of philanthropy are more than a dream. The five senses do not constitute the whole inventory of our sources of knowledge. They are the organs by which thought connects itself with the external universe; but the power of thought is not merged in the exercise of its instruments. We have functions which connect us with heaven, as well as organs which set us in relation with earth. We have not merely the senses opening to us the external world, but an internal sense, which places us in connection with the world of intelligence and the decrees of God.

There is *spirit in man*—not in the privileged few; not in those of us only who by the favor of Providence have been nursed in public schools. *It is in man;* it is the attribute of the race. The Spirit, which is the guide to truth, is the gracious gift to each member of the human family.

Reason exists within every breast. I mean not that faculty which deduces inferences from the experiences of the senses, but that higher faculty which from the

Source: From George Bancroft, *Literary and Historical Miscellanies* (New York: Harper & Brothers, 1857), 408–35.

infinite treasures of its own consciousness originates truth and assents to it by the force of intuitive evidence; that faculty which raises us beyond the control of time and space, and gives us faith in things eternal and invisible. There is not the difference between one mind and another which the pride of philosophers might conceive. . . .

If it be true that the gifts of mind and heart are universally diffused, if the sentiment of truth, justice, love, and beauty exists in every one then it follows, as a necessary consequence, that the common judgment in taste, politics, and religion is the highest authority on earth and the nearest possible approach to an infallible decision. . . .

If reason is a universal faculty, the universal decision is the nearest criterion of truth. The common mind winnows opinions; it is the sieve which separates error from certainty. The exercise by many of the same faculty on the same subject would naturally lead to the same conclusions. But if not, the very differences of opinion that arise prove the supreme judgment of the general mind. Truth is one. It never contradicts itself: One truth cannot contradict another truth. Hence truth is a bond of union. But error not only contradicts truth, but may contradict itself; so that there may be many errors, and each at variance with the rest. Truth is therefore of necessity an element of harmony; error as necessarily an element of discord. Thus there can be no continuing universal judgment but a right one. Men cannot agree in an absurdity; neither can they agree in a falsehood.

If wrong opinions have often been cherished by the masses, the cause always lies in the complexity of the ideas presented. Error finds its way into the soul of a nation only through the channel of truth. It is to a truth that men listen; and if they accept error also, it is only because the error is for the time so closely interwoven with the truth that the one cannot readily be separated from the other. . . .

In like manner the best government rests on the people and not on the few, on persons and not on property, on the free development of public opinion and not on authority; because the munificent Author of our being has conferred the gifts of mind upon every member of the human race without distinction of outward circumstances. . . .

The public happiness is the true object of legislation, and can be secured only by the masses of mankind themselves awakening to the knowledge and the care of their own interests. Our free institutions have reversed the false and ignoble distinctions between men; and refusing to gratify the pride of caste, have acknowledged the common mind to be the true material for a commonwealth. . . . The world can advance only through the culture of the moral and intellectual powers of the people. To accomplish this end by means of the people themselves is the highest purpose of government. If it be the duty of the individual to strive after a perfection like the perfection of God, how much more ought a nation to be the image of Deity. . . . The duty of America is to secure the culture and the happiness of the masses by their reliance on themselves.

. . . There may be those who scoff at the suggestion that the decision of the whole is to be preferred to the judgment of the enlightened few. They say in their hearts that the masses are ignorant; that farmers know nothing of legislation; that mechanics

George Bancroft ◆ "The Office of the People in Art, Government, and Religion" (1835)   **171**

should not quit their workshops to join in forming public opinion. But true political science does indeed venerate the masses. It maintains, not as has been perversely asserted, that "the people can make right," but that the people can discern right. Individuals are but shadows, too often engrossed by the pursuit of shadows; the race is immortal. Individuals are of limited sagacity; the common mind is infinite in its experience. . . . Individuals may be false; the masses are ingenuous and sincere. Individuals claim the divine sanction of truth for the deceitful conceptions of their own fancies; the Spirit of God breathes through the combined intelligence of the people. . . .

Thus the opinion which we respect is, indeed, not the opinion of one or of a few, but the sagacity of the many. It is hard for the pride of cultivated philosophy to put its ear to the ground and listen reverently to the voice of lowly humanity; yet the people collectively are wiser than the most gifted individual, for all his wisdom constitutes but a part of theirs. . . .

It is not by vast armies, by immense natural resources, by accumulations of treasure, that the greatest results in modern civilization have been accomplished. . . . The exact measure of the progress of civilization is the degree in which the intelligence of the common mind has prevailed over wealth and brute force; in other words, the measure of the progress of civilization is the progress of the people. . . .

A Critique of American Liberty from a Former Slave

Frederick Douglass (1817–1895) was one of the most exceptional human rights leaders in American history. His fiery speeches and eloquent writing made him an important leader of the nineteenth-century abolitionist movement, and his autobiography, *The Narrative of the Life of Frederick Douglass* (1845), is considered a classic in American history and literature. Douglass devoted his life foremost to the issues of freedom and equality, and his powerful words on these subjects provide another important perspective on the meaning and the limitations of the American Revolution.

Born the son of an unknown white planter and a black slave mother in 1818, Douglass toiled as a slave on a Maryland plantation until he was sent to Baltimore to train as a house servant. But when his new master discovered that Douglass was learning to read and write (with the assistance of the master's wife), he was sent back to the plantation to be "rebroken" through hard work and discipline. When Douglass resisted, he was regularly beaten. Shortly thereafter, at the age of twenty, Douglass fled Maryland and headed north, where he eventually settled in Massachusetts, changed his name,[10] and found part-time work as a laborer.

In 1841, Douglass attended an antislavery meeting, where he was invited to come from the audience to recount his experiences as a slave. His story was so powerful and moving that he was immediately recruited as a speaker by the Massachusetts Anti-Slavery Society. But after the publication of his *Narrative* unmasked his identity and location, he had to flee to Europe to avoid recapture by his former owner. After a two-year speaking tour in Britain, Douglass returned to

Massachusetts in 1847 with enough earnings to purchase his freedom and to establish *The North Star,* a newspaper expressly for blacks. Throughout the next decade, Douglass continued to campaign for abolition, and when the Civil War began in 1861, he advised President Lincoln to make slavery the central moral issue in the war. During Reconstruction, Douglass accepted several governmental posts, including U.S. minister to Haiti (1889–1891), but he continued to work for full civil rights for blacks and for women until his death in 1895.

One of the most vexing challenges faced by Douglass during his long career was public skepticism about his slave background. Many whites in both the north and the south doubted that such an articulate and intelligent man as Douglass could ever have been a lowly and ignorant slave, which in itself reveals much about prevailing racial attitudes and assumptions in America at that time. This skepticism compelled him not only to write his *Narrative* but also to address and challenge white misconceptions in all of his speeches and writings. One of Douglass's most critical speeches occurred on July 5, 1852, at a meeting of the Rochester (N.Y.) Ladies' Anti-Slavery Society. In his address, "What to the Slave Is the 4th of July?" Douglass used "scorching irony" to denounce American slavery, which he claimed showed a shocking disregard for both the Constitution and the Bible. He concluded that Independence Day was a holiday only for whites; for blacks and slaves, it was only a bitter reminder of the fact that they had no freedom or liberty to celebrate.

QUESTIONS TO CONSIDER

1. What are Douglass's main criticisms of America? How does his image of America compare with the values advanced by Jefferson in the Declaration of Independence?

2. Douglass's speech contains an excerpt from one of the biblical Psalms. How is this passage related to his speech? To whom does he compare the plight of the black slaves in America? What might be his purpose in drawing such an analogy?

3. According to Douglass, the question "Is the slave a man?" was already answered satisfactorily. How does Douglass present this issue? Why might this be a crucial issue in the abolitionist debate?

4. In the abolitionist struggle, Douglass claimed that what was needed was "not light but fire." What might this suggest? Do you think he believed that the contradiction between slavery and freedom in America must inevitably lead to conflict?

5. Douglass notes that he and his fellow abolitionists were frequently criticized as having been too radical, militant, and harsh in their denunciations of America. How does Douglass respond to that charge? In your view, was Douglass's "scorching irony" excessively inflammatory?

Frederick Douglass ✦ "What to the Slave Is the 4th of July?" (1852)   **173**

"WHAT TO THE SLAVE IS THE 4th OF JULY?"
(1852)

Frederick Douglass

Fellow-Citizens-pardon me, and allow me to ask, why am I called upon to speak here today? What have I, or those I represent, to do with your national independence? Are the great principles of political freedom and of natural justice, embodied in that Declaration of Independence, extended to us? And am I, therefore, called upon to bring our humble offering to the national altar, and to confess the benefits, and express devout gratitude for the blessings, resulting from your independence to us?

Would to God, both for your sakes and ours, that an affirmative answer could be truthfully returned to these questions! Then would my task be light, and my burden easy and delightful. . . .

But, such is not the state of the case. I say it with a sad sense of the disparity between us. I am not included within the pale of this glorious anniversary. Your high independence only reveals the immeasurable distance between us. The blessings in which you this day rejoice, are not enjoyed in common. The rich inheritance of justice, liberty, prosperity, and independence, bequeathed by your fathers, is shared by you, not by me. The sunlight that brought life and healing to you, has brought stripes and death to me. This Fourth of July is *yours,* not *mine. You* may rejoice, I must mourn. To drag a man in fetters into the grand illuminated temple of liberty, and call upon him to join you in joyous anthems, were inhuman mockery and sacrilegious irony. Do you mean, citizens, to mock me, by asking me to speak today? If so, there is a parallel to your conduct. And let me warn you that it is dangerous to copy the example of a nation whose crimes, towering up to heaven, were thrown down by the breath of the Almighty, burying that nation in irrecoverable ruin! I can today take up the plaintive lament of a peeled and woe-smitten people.

"By the rivers of Babylon, there we sat down. Yea! we wept when we remembered Zion. We hanged our harps upon the willows in the midst thereof. For there, they that carried us away captive, required of us a song; and they who wasted us required of us mirth, saying, Sing us one of the songs of Zion. How can we sing the Lord's song in a strange land? If I forget thee, O Jerusalem, let my right hand forget her cunning. If I do not remember thee, let my tongue cleave to the roof of my mouth."*

Fellow-citizens, above your national, tumultuous joy, I hear the mournful wail of millions, whose chains, heavy and grievous yesterday, are today rendered more

---

Source: Frederick Douglass, "What to the Slave Is the 4th of July?" in *Narrative of the Life of Frederick Douglass,* David Blight, ed., 141–45. Copyright © 1993 Bedford Books. Reprinted by permission of Bedford/St. Martin's Press. This shortened version of the speech is the one Douglass reprinted in his autobiography, *My Bondage and My Freedom* (1855). The complete speech can be found in John W. Blassingame, ed., *The Frederick Douglass Papers,* series 1, vol. 2 (New Haven: Yale University Press, 1982): 359–88.

*The biblical quote is from Psalms 137:1–6.

174   CHAPTER 6 ◆ Liberty and Revolution in the Atlantic World, 1776–1850

intolerable by the jubilant shouts that reach them. If I do forget, if I do not faithfully remember those bleeding children of sorrow this day, "may my right hand forget her cunning, and may my tongue cleave to the roof of my mouth!" To forget them, to pass lightly over their wrongs, and to chime in with the popular theme, would be treason most scandalous and shocking, and would make me a reproach before God and the world. My subject then, fellow-citizens, is AMERICAN SLAVERY. I shall see this day and its popular characteristics from the slave's point of view. Standing there, identified with the American bondman, making his wrongs mine, I do not hesitate to declare, with all my soul, that the character and conduct of this nation never looked blacker to me than on this Fourth of July. Whether we turn to the declarations of the past, or to the professions of the present, the conduct of the nation seems equally hideous and revolting. America is false to the past, false to the present, and solemnly binds herself to be false to the future. Standing with God and the crushed and bleeding slave on this occasion, I will, in the name of humanity which is outraged, in the name of liberty which is fettered, in the name of the Constitution and the Bible, which are disregarded and trampled upon, dare to call in question and to denounce, with all the emphasis I can command, everything that serves to perpetuate slavery—the great sin and shame of America! I will not equivocate; I will not excuse; I will use the severest language I can command; and yet not one word shall escape me that any man, whose judgment is not blinded by prejudice, or who is not at heart a slaveholder, shall not confess to be right and just.

But I fancy I hear some one of my audience say, it is just in this circumstance that you and your brother abolitionists fail to make a favorable impression on the public mind. Would you argue more, and denounce less, would you persuade more and rebuke less, your cause would be much more likely to succeed. But, I submit, where all is plain there is nothing to be argued. What point in the anti-slavery creed would you have me argue? On what branch of the subject do the people of this country need light? Must I undertake to prove that the slave is a man? That point is conceded already. Nobody doubts it. The slave-holders themselves acknowledge it in the enactment of laws for their government. They acknowledge it when they punish disobedience on the part of the slave. There are seventy-two crimes in the state of Virginia, which, if committed by a black man, (no matter how ignorant he be,) subject him to the punishment of death; while only two of these same crimes will subject a white man to the like punishment. What is this but the acknowledgment that the slave is a moral, intellectual, and responsible being. The manhood of the slave is conceded. It is admitted in the fact that southern statute books are covered with enactments forbidding, under severe fines and penalties, the teaching of the slave to read or write. When you can point to any such laws, in reference to the beasts of the field, then I may consent to argue the manhood of the slave. When the dogs in your streets, when the fowls of the air, when the cattle on your hills, when the fish of the sea, and the reptiles that crawl, shall be unable to distinguish the slave from a brute, then will I argue with you that the slave is a man!

For the present, it is enough to affirm the equal manhood of the negro race. Is it not astonishing that, while we are plowing, planting, and reaping, using all kinds of mechanical tools, erecting houses, constructing bridges, building ships, working in metals of brass, iron, copper, silver, and gold; that, while we are reading, writing, and

Frederick Douglass ◆ "What to the Slave Is the 4th of July?" (1852)   175

ciphering, acting as clerks, merchants, and secretaries, having among us lawyers, doctors, ministers, poets, authors, editors, orators, and teachers; that, while we are engaged in all manner of enterprises common to other men—digging gold in California, capturing the whale in the Pacific, feeding sheep and cattle on the hillside, living, moving, acting, thinking, planning, living in families as husbands, wives, and children, and, above all, confessing and worshiping the Christian's God, and looking hopefully for life and immortality beyond the grave—we are called upon to prove that we are men!

Would you have me argue that man is entitled to liberty? That he is the rightful owner of his own body? You have already declared it. Must I argue the wrongfulness of slavery? Is that a question for republicans? Is it to be settled by the rules of logic and argumentation, as a matter beset with great difficulty, involving a doubtful application of the principle of justice, hard to be understood? How should I look today in the presence of Americans, dividing and subdividing a discourse, to show that men have a natural right to freedom, speaking of it relatively and positively, negatively and affirmatively? To do so, would be to make myself ridiculous, and to offer an insult to your understanding. There is not a man beneath the canopy of heaven that does not know that slavery is wrong for him.

What! Am I to argue that it is wrong to make men brutes, to rob them of their liberty, to work them without wages, to keep them ignorant of their relations to their fellow-men, to beat them with sticks, to flay their flesh with the lash, to load their limbs with irons, to hunt them with dogs, to sell them at auction, to sunder their families, to knock out their teeth, to burn their flesh, to starve them into obedience and submission to their masters? Must I argue that a system, thus marked with blood and stained with pollution, is wrong? No; I will not. I have better employment for my time and strength than such arguments would imply.

What, then, remains to be argued? Is it that slavery is not divine; that God did not establish it; that our doctors of divinity are mistaken? There is blasphemy in the thought. That which is inhuman cannot be divine. Who can reason on such a proposition! They that can, may; I cannot. The time for such argument is past.

At a time like this, scorching irony, not convincing argument, is needed. Oh! Had I the ability, and could I reach the nation's ear, I would today pour out a fiery stream of biting ridicule, blasting reproach, withering sarcasm, and stern rebuke. For it is not light that is needed, but fire; it is not the gentle shower, but thunder. We need the storm, the whirlwind and the earthquake.

The feeling of the nation must be quickened; the conscience of the nation must be roused; the propriety of the nation must be startled; the hypocrisy of the nation must be exposed; and its crimes against God and man must be proclaimed and denounced.

What to the American slave is your Fourth of July? I answer, a day that reveals to him, more than all other days in the year, the gross injustice and cruelty to which he is the constant victim. To him, your celebration is a sham; your boasted liberty, an unholy license; your national greatness, swelling vanity; your sounds of rejoicing are empty and heartless; your denunciations of tyrants, brass-fronted impudence; your shouts of liberty and equality, hollow mockery; your prayers and hymns, your sermons and thanksgivings, with all your religious parade and solemnity, are to him mere

Volume 2: 1500–

176   CHAPTER 6 ◆ Liberty and Revolution in the Atlantic World, 1776–1850

bombast, fraud, deception, impiety, and hypocrisy—a thin veil to cover up crimes which would disgrace a nation of savages. There is not a nation on the earth guilty of practices more shocking and bloody, than are the people of these United States, at this very hour.

Go where you may, search where you will, roam through all the monarchies and despotisms of the old world, travel through South America, search out every abuse, and when you have found the last, lay your facts by the side of the every-day practices of this nation, and you will say with me, that, for revolting barbarity and shameless hypocrisy, America reigns without a rival.

THE FRENCH REVOLUTION
A Declaration of the Rights of Man

In August 1789, the French National Assembly adopted the Declaration of the Rights of Man and Citizen. Together with Locke's Second Treatise on Government (1690) and the American Declaration of Independence (1776) and the United States Constitution (1789), the Declaration of the Rights of Man and Citizen is considered one of the pivotal documents in the development of political liberalism. In its concise seventeen points, the Declaration of the Rights of Man and Citizen espouses the Enlightenment ideals of human equality, natural rights, and a government that emanates from the will of the people.

The Declaration was also a reaction against royal absolutism and the huge disparities of wealth, status, and power that defined and characterized the three main social classes or "estates" of the Old Regime. The first and second estates, comprising the clergy and nobility, made up less than 10 percent of the population and controlled most of the nation's wealth but were exempt from paying taxes. Consequently, the financial and labor burden of France was borne chiefly by the third estate, a disparate group made up of the professional middle classes[11] (doctors, lawyers, merchants, and so on), the rural peasants, and the urban working class. Political rights were also uneven. Power rested in the person of the king, who ruled in an absolute manner, sanctioned by divine right. But the royal bureaucracy was so intrusive, corrupt, and inefficient that all social classes dreamed of a change.

Consequently, the financial crisis of 1789 that initiated the convening of the Estates General reflected, in large part, the inefficiency and inequities of French society. The representatives from the middle class seized the opportunity to push for liberal reforms and declared their intention to write a constitution for France that would limit the power and privilege of the monarchy, the nobility, and the clergy. Their efforts received crucial support from the urban workers, who stormed and seized the weapons at the Bastille when King Louis XVI tried to quash the revolution. With the king under arrest and the power of the monarchy temporarily checked, the new National Assembly adopted the Declaration of the Rights of Man and Citizen on August 26, 1789, which marked the beginning of the end of the Old Regime.

Declaration of the Rights of Man and Citizen (1789)   **177**

1. How would you summarize the major principles of the Declaration of the Rights of Man and Citizen? In what ways can the document be seen as a triumph of liberalism?

2. Article 3 states, "The principle of all sovereignty resides essentially in the nation. No body nor individual may exercise any authority which does not proceed directly from the nation." What does this mean? What are the possible implications of this statement?

3. Historians commonly assert that the Declaration of the Rights of Man effectively marked the end of the Old Regime. How does the Declaration fundamentally challenge the foundations of absolutism?

4. In your assessment, who were the winners and the losers in the first phase of the French Revolution?

5. Identify the similarities and differences between the Declaration of the Rights of Man and the American Declaration of Independence.

DECLARATION OF THE RIGHTS OF MAN AND CITIZEN (1789)

The representatives of the French people, organized as a National Assembly, believing that the ignorance, neglect, or contempt of the rights of man are the sole cause of public calamities and of the corruption of governments, have determined to set forth in a solemn declaration the natural, unalienable, and sacred rights of man, in order that this declaration, being constantly before all the members of the Social body, shall remind them continually of their rights and duties; in order that the acts of the legislative power, as well as those of the executive power, may be compared at any moment with the objects and purposes of all political institutions and may thus be more respected, and, lastly, in order that the grievances of the citizens, based hereafter upon simple and incontestable principles, shall tend to the maintenance of the constitution and redound to the happiness of all. Therefore the National Assembly recognizes and proclaims, in the presence and under the auspices of the Supreme Being, the following rights of man and of the citizen:

1. Men are born and remain free and equal in rights. Social distinctions may be founded only upon the general good.

2. The aim of all political association is the preservation of the natural and imprescriptible rights of man. These rights are liberty, property, security, and resistance to oppression.

Source: From James H. Robinson and Charles A. Beard, eds., *Readings in Modern European History,* Vol. 1 (Boston: Ginn and Co., 1908), 260–62.

3. The principle of all sovereignty resides essentially in the nation. No body nor individual may exercise any authority which does not proceed directly from the nation.

4. Liberty consists in the freedom to do everything which injures no one else; hence the exercise of the natural rights of each man has no limits except those which assure to the other members of the society the enjoyment of the same rights. These limits can only be determined by law.

5. Law can only prohibit such actions as are hurtful to society. Nothing may be prevented which is not forbidden by law, and no one may be forced to do anything not provided for by law.

6. Law is the expression of the general will. Every citizen has a right to participate personally, or through his representative, in its foundation. It must be the same for all, whether it protects or punishes. All citizens, being equal in the eyes of the law, are equally eligible to all dignities and to all public positions and occupations, according to their abilities, and without distinction except that of their virtues and talents.

7. No person shall be accused, arrested, or imprisoned except in the cases and according to the forms prescribed by law. Any one soliciting, transmitting, executing, or causing to be executed, any arbitrary order, shall be punished. But any citizen summoned or arrested in virtue of the law shall submit without delay, as resistance constitutes an offense.

8. The law shall provide for such punishments only as are strictly and obviously necessary, and no one shall suffer punishment except it be legally inflicted in virtue of a law passed and promulgated before the commission of the offense.

9. As all persons are held innocent until they shall have been declared guilty, if arrest shall be deemed indispensable, all harshness not essential to the securing of the prisoner's person shall be severely repressed by law.

10. No one shall be disquieted on account of his opinions, including his religious views, provided their manifestation does not disturb the public order established by law.

11. The free communication of ideas and opinions is one of the most precious of the rights of man. Every citizen may, accordingly, speak, write, and print with freedom, but shall be responsible for such abuses of this freedom as shall be defined by law.

12. The security of the rights of man and of the citizen requires public military forces. These forces are, therefore, established for the good of all and not for the personal advantage of those to whom they shall be entrusted.

13. A common contribution is essential for the maintenance of the public forces and for the cost of administration. This should be equitably distributed among all the citizens in proportion to their means.

14. All the citizens have a right to decide, either personally or by their representatives, as to the necessity of the public contribution; to grant this freely; to know to what uses it is put; and to fix the proportion, the mode of assessment and of collection and the duration of the taxes.

15. Society has the right to require of every public agent an account of his administration.

16. A society in which the observance of the law is not assured, nor the separation of powers defined, has no constitution at all.

17. Since property is an inviolable and sacred right, no one shall be deprived thereof except where public necessity, legally determined, shall clearly demand it, and then only on condition that the owner shall have been previously and equitably indemnified.

A Feminist Perspective on the Revolution, 1791

Olympe de Gouges (1745–1793) was the outspoken and unyielding feminist leader of the French Revolution who demanded that the revolutionary liberal reforms be extended to include gender equality in all aspects of public and private life. Born to a modest working-class family in 1745, de Gouges at the age of sixteen married a wealthier older man who died shortly after the birth of their only son. Vowing never to remarry, she moved to Paris in 1788, and with the funds bequeathed to her by her husband, she decided to become a writer. When the revolution broke out the following year, she immediately embraced the ideals and goals of the liberals but was disappointed when the French Assembly failed to expand the new rights and liberties to women. She became a more ardent feminist and a vocal critic of the liberals, but her ideas on gender equality were considered radical and were never fully accepted by any group. When she dared to criticize the centralization of power under the rule of Robespierre and the Jacobins, she was branded a counterrevolutionary and guillotined in 1793.

A prolific writer, de Gouges produced more than thirty political pamphlets during the French Revolution, championing such diverse causes as the abolition of slavery, the creation of a national theater, and the extension of paved roads. But her primary passion was equal rights for women. In the Declaration of the Rights of Women and the Female Citizen (1791), de Gouges provided an interesting view of the role and status of women in France in late-eighteenth-century France. Taking the Declaration of the Rights of Man and Citizen as her inspiration, she wrote a strongly worded counterdeclaration that blamed gender inequality on both male chauvinism and female complicity. Although her efforts to promote women's rights were largely unsuccessful, her admonition to women that "it is in your power to free yourselves" has been heralded as one of the defining moments in feminist history.

QUESTIONS TO CONSIDER

1. Olympe de Gouges asserts that gender inequality is not "natural." What is the basis for her argument? What is the importance of this argument? How does it fit with the philosophy of the Enlightenment?

2. Compare the articles in the Declaration of the Rights of Women with those in the Rights of Man. What are the commonalities? What are the differences? In your view, is de Gouges arguing for equal rights or for special rights for women?

3. Olympe de Gouges claims that the initial stage of the French Revolution produced a "more pronounced scorn, a more marked disdain" for women. Why might this be true?

4. According to de Gouges, women have done "more harm than good" in reinforcing their inferior position. How does she explain this? How do you assess her argument?

5. Using her "Form for a Social Contract between Men and Women" as a guide, how would you infer the status and position of most married women? How does her form attempt to correct these problems? Would you accept this kind of contract in your own marriage relationship?

DECLARATION OF THE RIGHTS OF WOMAN AND THE FEMALE CITIZEN (1791)

Olympe de Gouges

Man, are you capable of being just? It is a woman who poses the question; you will not deprive her of that right at least. Tell me, what gives you sovereign empire to oppress my sex? Your strength? Your talents? Observe the Creator in his wisdom; survey in all her grandeur that nature with whom you seem to want to be in harmony, and give me, if you dare, an example of this tyrannical empire. Go back to animals, consult the elements, study plants, finally glance at all the modifications of organic matter, and surrender to the evidence when I offer you the means; search, probe, and distinguish, if you can, the sexes in the administration of nature. Everywhere you will find them mingled; everywhere they cooperate in harmonious togetherness in this immortal masterpiece.

Man alone has raised his exceptional circumstances to a principle. Bizarre, blind, bloated with science and degenerated—in a century of enlightenment and wisdom—into the crassest ignorance, he wants to command as a despot a sex which is in full possession of its intellectual faculties; he pretends to enjoy the Revolution and to claim his rights to equality in order to say nothing more about it.

Mothers, daughters, sisters [and] representatives of the nation demand to be constituted into a national assembly. Believing that ignorance, omission, or scorn for the rights of woman are the only causes of public misfortunes and of the corruption of

Olympe de Gouges ◆ Declaration of the Rights of Woman and the Female Citizen (1791)   **181**

governments, [the women] have resolved to set forth in a solemn declaration the natural, inalienable, and sacred rights of woman in order that this declaration, constantly exposed before all the members of the society, will ceaselessly remind them of their rights and duties. . . .

Consequently, the sex that is as superior in beauty as it is in courage during the suffering of maternity recognizes and declares in the presence and under the auspices of the Supreme Being, the following Rights of Woman and of Female Citizens.

1. Woman is born free and lives equal to man in her rights. Social distinctions can be based only on the common utility.

2. The purpose of any political association is the conservation of the natural rights of woman and man; these rights are liberty, property, security, and especially resistance to oppression.

3. The principle of all sovereignty rests essentially with the nation, which is nothing but the union of woman and man; no body and no individual can exercise any authority which does not come expressly from it [the nation].

4. Liberty and justice consist of restoring all that belongs to others; thus, the only limits on the exercise of the natural rights of woman are perpetual male tyranny; these limits are to be reformed by the laws of nature and reason.

. . .

6. The laws must be the expression of the general will; all female and male citizens must contribute either personally or through their representatives to its formation; it must be the same for all: male and female citizens, being equal in the eyes of the law, must be equally admitted to all honors, positions, and public employment according to their capacity and without other distinctions besides those of their virtues and talents.

7. No woman is an exception: she is accused, arrested, and detained in cases determined by law. Women, like men, obey this rigorous law. . . .

. . .

17. Property belongs to both sexes whether united or separate; for each it is an inviolable and sacred right; no one can be deprived of it, since it is the true patrimony of nature, unless the legally determined public need obviously dictates it, and then only with a just and prior indemnity.

Woman, wake up; the tocsin* of reason is being heard throughout the whole universe; discover your rights. The powerful empire of nature is no longer surrounded by prejudice, fanaticism, superstition, and lies. The flame of truth has dispersed all the clouds of folly and usurpation. Enslaved man has multiplied his strength and needs recourse to yours to break his chains. Having become free, he has become unjust to his companion. Oh, women, women! When will you cease to be blind? What advantage have you received from the Revolution? A more pronounced scorn, a more marked disdain. . . . [C]ourageously oppose the force of reason to the empty

---

*An alarm bell; a warning signal.

182 CHAPTER 6 ◆ Liberty and Revolution in the Atlantic World, 1776–1850

pretensions of superiority; unite yourselves beneath the standards of philosophy; deploy all the energy of your character, and you will soon see these haughty men, not groveling at your feet as servile adorers, but proud to share with you the treasures of the Supreme Being. Regardless of what barriers confront you, it is in your power to free yourselves; you have only to want to. . . .

Women have done more harm than good. Constraint and dissimulation have been their lot. What force has robbed them of, ruse returned to them; they had recourse to all the resources of their charms, and the most irreproachable persons did not resist them. Poison and the sword were both subject to them . . . anything which characterizes the folly of men, profane and sacred, all have been subject to the cupidity and ambition of this sex, formerly contemptible and respected, and since the revolution, respectable and scorned.

. . . Under the Old Regime, all was vicious, all was guilty. . . . A woman only had to be beautiful or amiable; when she possessed these two advantages, she saw a hundred fortunes at her feet. If she did not profit from them, she had a bizarre character or a rare philosophy which made her scorn wealth; then she was deemed to be like a crazy woman; the most indecent made herself respected with gold. . . . [A]nd at an age when the slave has lost all her charms, what will become of this unfortunate woman? The victim of scorn, even the doors of charity are closed to her; she is poor and old, they say; why did she not know how to make her fortune.

Reason finds other examples that are even more touching. A young, inexperienced woman, seduced by a man whom she loves, will abandon her parents to follow him; the ingrate will leave her after a few years, and the older she has become with him, the more inhuman is his inconstancy; if she has children, he will likewise abandon them. If he is rich, he will consider himself excused from sharing his fortune with his noble victims. . . .

. . . Marriage is the tomb of trust and love. The married woman can with impunity give bastards to her husband, and also give them the wealth which does not belong to them. The woman who is unmarried has only one feeble right; ancient and inhuman laws refuse to her for her children the right to the name and the wealth of their father; no new laws have been made in this matter. . . .

[De Gouges proposes a new marriage contract between man and woman]

We, [name of man] and [name of woman], moved by our own will, unite ourselves for the duration of our lives, and for the duration of our mutual inclinations, under the following conditions: We intend and wish to make our wealth communal, meanwhile reserving to ourselves the right to divide it in favor of our children and of those toward whom we might have a particular inclination, mutually recognizing that our property belongs directly to our children, from whatever bed they come, and that all of them without distinction have the right to bear the name of the fathers and mothers who have acknowledged them, and we are charged to subscribe to the law which punished the renunciation of one's own blood. We likewise obligate ourselves, in case of separation, to divide our wealth and to set aside in advance the portion the law indicates for our children, and in the event of a perfect union, the one who dies will divest himself of half his property in his children's favor, and if one dies childless,

Olympe de Gouges ✦ Declaration of the Rights of Woman and the Female Citizen (1791)   183

the survivor will inherit by right, unless the dying person has disposed of half the common property in favor of one who he judged deserving. That is approximately the formula for the marriage act I propose for execution. . . .

I offer a foolproof way to elevate the soul of women; it is to join them to all the activities of man; if man persists in finding this way impractical, let him share his fortune with woman, not at his caprice, but by the wisdom of laws. Prejudice falls, morals are purified, and nature regains all her rights. Add to this the marriage of priests and the strengthening of the king on his throne, and the French government cannot fail.

Terror in Defense of Liberty

Maximilien Robespierre (1758–1794), known to his contemporaries as "the Incorruptible," remains one of the most controversial figures of the French Revolution. To his enemies, he was viewed as the Devil incarnate; to the Parisian masses of 1793, he was seen as the unwavering champion of freedom and equality. Under his leadership, the French Revolution entered its so-called radical phase (1792–1794), when as many as 40,000 people were guillotined in order to complete what he viewed as "the war of liberty against tyranny."

Robespierre was born to a poor family in the French town of Arras in 1758. With the aid of a scholarship, he studied law in Paris and became enamored with the ideas of Rousseau, especially his concept of the ultimate and infallible "general will" of the people. After practicing law for several years, Robespierre was elected to the Estates General in 1789, where he joined the more radical, prodemocratic Jacobin party. He was an energetic and uncompromising advocate of democratic reforms, and he won the admiration and support of the Parisian working classes as he rose to leadership within the Jacobins. In 1793, he was elected to the twelve-member Committee of Public Safety, where he continued to consolidate his power. Robespierre believed that he understood the needs and aspirations of the people, as well as the cunning treacheries of their enemies, and he was willing to adopt extreme measures in order to protect and preserve his vision of the revolution. In early 1794, he arrested and executed some of his former political allies, but by midyear, his own position was growing precarious within a divided Committee of Public Safety. In July, his enemies issued an arrest warrant and Robespierre was tried and guillotined the following day.

Six months prior to his death, when he was at the height of his power, Robespierre gave a speech on "The Moral and Political Principles of Domestic Policy" (February 1794). By this time, the revolutionary armies of France had succeeded in repelling the foreign invaders, but Robespierre still worried about domestic counterrevolutionaries and spies at home. His speech offers a fascinating insight into Robespierre's vision of the revolution, as well as his justification for the use of terror. It also raises some interesting questions about the meaning of the French Revolution, the use of extremism in defense of liberty, and the relationship between democracy, nationalism, and "virtue."

QUESTIONS TO CONSIDER

1. What kind of society did Robespierre wish to create in France? How did his vision compare with the one implied in the Declaration of the Rights of Man and Citizen? What is significant about the differences?

2. Robespierre claimed that democracy was sustained by "virtue." What does he mean by virtue? Do you agree with his assessment? Why or why not?

3. In order to finish the "war of liberty against tyranny," Robespierre said that one must "lead the people by reason, and the people's enemies by terror." How did he define "terror" and justify its usage? In your view, does the use of terror betray or defend the ideals of the revolution?

4. In the immediate aftermath of the French Revolution, Robespierre was remembered as an evil and radical zealot. From today's perspective, how radical were his ideas and methods? Was he evil?

5. Contrary to Robespierre's assessment, some historians have concluded that the ideals of liberalism/democracy and nationalism are actually in opposition to each other. Using Robespierre's speech and life as evidence, how might you explain the relationship between democracy and nationalism?

"THE MORAL AND POLITICAL PRINCIPLES OF DOMESTIC POLICY" (1794)

Maximilien Robespierre

Some time ago we set forth the principles of our foreign policy; today we come to expound the principles of our internal policy.

After having proceeded haphazardly for a long time, swept along by the movement of opposing factions, the representatives of the French people have finally demonstrated a character and a government. . . . But, up to the very moment when I am speaking, it must be agreed that we have been guided, amid such stormy circumstances, by the love of good and by the awareness of our country's needs rather than by an exact theory and by precise rules of conduct, which we did not have even leisure enough to lay out. . . .

What is the goal toward which we are heading? The peaceful enjoyment of liberty and equality; the reign of that eternal justice whose laws have been inscribed, not in marble and stone, but in the hearts of all men, even in that of the slave who forgets them and in that of the tyrant who denies them.

We seek an order of things in which all the base and cruel passions are enchained, all the beneficent and generous passions are awakened by the laws; where ambition becomes the desire to merit glory and to serve our country; where distinc-

Maximilien Robespierre ◆ "The Moral and Political Principles of Domestic Policy" (1794)   185

tions are born only of equality itself; where the citizen is subject to the magistrate, the magistrate to the people, and the people to justice; where our country assures the well-being of each individual, and where each individual proudly enjoys our country's prosperity and glory; where every soul grows greater through the continual flow of republican sentiments, and by the need of deserving the esteem of a great people; where the arts are the adornments of the liberty which ennobles them and commerce the source of public wealth rather than solely the monstrous opulence of a few families.

In our land we want to substitute morality for egotism, integrity for formal codes of honor, principles for customs, a sense of duty for one of mere propriety, the rule of reason for the tyranny of fashion, scorn of vice for scorn of the unlucky; self-respect for insolence, grandeur of soul for vanity, love of glory for the love of money, good people in place of good society . . . which is to say, all the virtues and all the miracles of the republic in place of all the vices of the monarchy. . . .

What kind of government can realize these wonders? Only a democratic or republican government. . . . Democracy is not a state in which the people, continually meeting, regulate for themselves all public affairs, still less is it a state in which a tiny fraction of the people, acting by isolated, hasty, and contradictory measures, decide the fate of the whole society. . . . Democracy is a state in which the sovereign people, guided by laws which are of their own making, do for themselves all that they can do well, and by their delegates do all that they cannot do for themselves. . . .

But, in order to lay the foundations of democracy among us and to consolidate it, in order to arrive at the peaceful reign of constitutional laws, we must finish the war of liberty against tyranny and safely cross through the storms of the revolution: that is the goal of the revolutionary system which you have put in order. . . .

Now, what is the fundamental principle of popular or democratic government, that is to say, the essential mainspring which sustains it and makes it move? It is virtue. I speak of the public virtue which worked so many wonders in Greece and Rome and which ought to produce even more astonishing things in republican France—that virtue which is nothing other than the love of the nation and its laws. . . .

Since the soul of the Republic is virtue . . . it follows that the first rule of your political conduct ought to be to relate all your efforts to maintaining equality and developing virtue. . . . Thus everything that tends to excite love of country, to purify morals, to elevate souls, to direct the passions of the human heart toward the public interest ought to be adopted or established by you. Everything which tends to concentrate them in the abjection of selfishness, to awaken enjoyment for petty things and scorn for great ones, ought to be rejected or curbed by you. Within the scheme of the French revolution, that which is immoral is impolitic, that which is corrupting is counterrevolutionary. . . .

This great purity of the French Revolution's fundamental elements . . . is precisely what creates our strength and our weakness: our strength, because it gives us the victory of truth over deception and the rights of public interest over private interests; our weakness, because it rallies against us all men who are vicious, all those who in their hearts plan to despoil the people. . . . We must smother the internal and external enemies of the Republic or perish, [and] in these circumstances, the first maxim of our policy ought to be to lead the people by reason and the people's enemies by terror.

If the mainspring of popular government in peacetime is virtue, amid revolution it is at the same time [both] virtue and terror: virtue, without which terror is fatal; terror, without which virtue is impotent. Terror is nothing but prompt, severe, inflexible justice; it is therefore an emanation of virtue. . . . It has been said that terror was the mainspring of despotic government. Does our government, then, resemble a despotism? Yes! . . . Subdue liberty's enemies by terror, and you will be right, as founders of the Republic. The government of the revolution is the despotism of liberty against tyranny. . . .

Some people would like to govern revolutions by the quibbles of the law courts and treat conspiracies against the Republic like legal proceedings against private persons. Tyranny kills; liberty argues. And the code made by the conspirators themselves is the law by which they are judged.

REVOLUTIONS IN THE CARIBBEAN AND LATIN AMERICA
The Haitian Revolution

Toussaint L'Ouverture was the founder of the second independent nation in the New World and the leader of the most successful slave revolt in western history. He was born on a plantation in the French colony of Saint-Domingue (now Haiti) and lived his first thirty-four years as a slave. His experience in bondage was less brutal and more fortunate than that of most slaves in Haiti, and in 1777 he was granted his freedom. When the slave revolt broke out in 1791, Toussaint first helped his former master to escape before he joined the attacks on other plantations. He soon emerged as a principal leader among the former slaves and was determined to preserve their liberty from slavery.

When France and Spain went to war in 1793, Toussaint and his fighters initially sided with the Spaniards of Santo Domingo (now the Dominican Republic), and they scored several victories against their former masters. But a year later, Toussaint shifted his allegiances back to France after the Jacobin-controlled government had abolished slavery. In return for his assistance, the French government named him lieutenant governor of the colony. Toussaint proved himself a skilled diplomat and master politician who eventually dismissed the island's governor and placed himself in command. But when Napoleon seized power in France, the government announced its decision to restore Saint-Domingue as a profitable colony, which also meant a restoration of slavery on the island. In 1802, French forces invaded Haiti, and after first declaring their willingness to negotiate, they secretly arrested Toussaint and sent him to life confinement in France, where he died in 1803. In that same year, after continued bloody resistance, French forces quit Saint-Domingue, and Haiti won its liberty and independence.

The readings from the Haitian Revolution cover a seven-year time span that highlights the tension between Toussaint's idealistic principles and the pragmatic policies he felt compelled to adopt. In the short Proclamation of 29 August 1793, Toussaint makes clear his goals and attempts to encourage others to join him. In his letter to the French Minister of Marine (13 April 1799), Toussaint further explains his goals and actions to the French government now controlled by the more conservative Directory, which viewed Toussaint with suspicion and disfavor. In a similar letter to the Directory (28 October 1797), Toussaint attempted to

Toussaint L'Ouverture ◆ Speeches and Letters on the Haitian Revolution (1793–1800)   **187**

reaffirm his commitment to the ideals of liberty while also exposing the double standards by which colonial nations have condemned the actions of the colonized. The last document, the Forced Labor Decree of 1800, contains the essence of Toussaint's social and economic policy, which was centered on the militarization of Haitian society. Although Toussaint's forced-labor policy did help restore the economy of the island, it was perceived by many to contradict his stance on liberty, and it significantly weakened his support among the black working classes. Consequently, when French forces invaded in 1802, Toussaint was unable to rally sufficient support, and he was arrested and sent into exile. But although Haitians were unhappy with Toussaint, they were not willing to lose their liberty to the French. Fighting soon resumed, and when the French recognized the futility of their efforts and withdrew their forces, Haiti proclaimed its independence in 1803.

QUESTIONS TO CONSIDER

1. How does Toussaint explain the origins of the slave uprising in the letter to the Minister of Marine? Toussaint further explains his failure to maintain alliance between blacks and "men of color." What caused this failure, and why is it significant? What might it tell us about identities on Haiti?

2. In the letter to the Directory, how does Toussaint refute the charge that the "gross negroes" of Haiti are "incapable of distinguishing between unrestrained license and austere liberty"? Why does he suggest that the French are hypocritical in their assessments? What impact does this have?

3. Why does Toussaint wish to militarize agricultural society? How do his actions and explanations compare with Robespierre's justification for terror?

4. The revolution in Haiti was clearly made more complex because of race perceptions. How does Toussaint see the issue of race? How does he view whites? How does he view blacks?

5. In your assessment, was Toussaint a man guided more by principle or by pragmatic expediency? Be sure to reinforce your conclusions with evidence.

SPEECHES AND LETTERS ON THE HAITIAN REVOLUTION (1793–1800)

Toussaint L'Ouverture

Proclamation of 29 August 1793

Brothers and Friends:

I am Toussaint L'Ouverture. My name is perhaps known to you. I have undertaken to avenge you. I want liberty and equality to reign throughout St. Domingue. I am working toward that end. Come and join me, brothers, and combat by our side for the same cause.

Letter to the Minister of Marine, 13 April 1799

The first successes obtained in Europe by the partisans of liberty over the agents of despotism were not slow to ignite the sacred fire of patriotism in the souls of all Frenchmen in St. Domingue. At that time, men's hopes turned to France, whose first steps toward her regeneration promised them a happier future. . . . [The whites in St. Domingue] wanted to escape from their arbitrary government, but they did not intend the revolution to destroy either the prejudices that debased the men of color* or the slavery of the blacks, whom they held in dependency by the strongest law. In their opinion, the benefits of the French regeneration were only for them. They proved it by their obstinate refusal to allow the people of color to enjoy their political rights and the slaves to enjoy the liberty that they claimed. Thus, while whites were erecting another form of government upon the rubble of despotism, the men of color and the blacks united themselves in order to claim their political existence; the resistance of the former having become stronger, it was necessary for the latter to rise up in order to obtain [political recognition] by force of arms. The whites, fearing that this legitimate resistance would bring general liberty to St. Domingue, sought to separate the men of color from the cause of the blacks in accordance with Machiavelli's principle of divide and rule. Renouncing their claims over the men of color, they accepted the April Decree [1792].† As they had anticipated, the men of color, many of whom are slave holders, had only been using the blacks to gain on political commands. Fearing the enfranchisement of the blacks, the men of color deserted their comrades in arms, their companions in misfortune, and aligned themselves with the whites to subdue them.

Treacherously abandoned, the blacks fought for some time against the reunited whites and the men of color; but, pressed on all sides, losing hope, they accepted the offers of the Spanish king, who, having at that time declared war on France, offered freedom to those blacks of St. Domingue who would join his armies. Indeed, the silence of pre-Republican France on the long-standing claims for their natural rights made by the most interested, the noblest, the most useful portion of the population of St. Domingue . . . extinguished all glimmer of hope in the hearts of the black slaves and forced them, in spite of themselves, to throw themselves into the arms of a protective power that offered the only benefit for which they would fight. More unfortunate than guilty, they turned their arms against their fatherland. . . .

Such with the crimes of these blacks, which have earned them to this day the insulting titles of brigands, insurgents, rebels. . . . At that time, I was one of the leaders of these auxiliary troops, and I can say without fear of contradiction that I owed my

---

*By "men of color" Toussaint refers to the mulattos, or people of mixed racial ancestry. In Haiti, their status and position in society was barely above that of blacks.

†In the April Decree of 1792, the French Assembly, now dominated by liberals from the business and commercial classes, issued a law that gave full citizenship to people of color but not to blacks or slaves. Some historians contend that this measure was intended to weaken Toussaint's forces and allow white plantation owners to retake control of the island.

Toussaint L'Ouverture ◆ Speeches and Letters on the Haitian Revolution (1793–1800)   189

elevation in these circumstances only to the confidence that I had inspired in my brothers by the virtues for which I am still honored today. . . .

Letter to the Directory, 28 October 1797

Second Assertion [made by a critic in the French Assembly]: "Everyone is agreed in portraying the Colony in the most shocking state of disorder and groaning under the military government. And what a military government! In whose hands is it confined? In that of ignorant and gross negroes, incapable of distinguishing between unrestrained license and austere liberty."

This shocking disorder in which the Commission* found St. Domingue was not the consequence of the liberty given to the blacks, but the result of the uprising of thirty Ventose [mulattos],[†] for prior to this period, order and harmony reigned in all Republican territory as far as the absence of laws would allow. All citizens blindly obeyed the orders of General Laveaux; his will was the national will for them, and they submitted to him as a man invested with the authority emanating from the generous nation that had shattered their chains.

If, upon the arrival of the Commission, St. Domingue groaned under a military government, this power was not in the hands of the blacks; they were subordinate to it, and they only executed the orders of General Laveaux. These were the blacks who, when France was threatened with the loss of this Colony, employed their arms and their weapons to conserve it, to reconquer the greatest part of its territory that treason had handed over to the Spanish and English. . . . These were the blacks who . . . flew to the rescue of General Laveaux . . . and who, by repressing the audacious rebels who wished to destroy the national representation, restored it to its rightful depository.

Such was the conduct of those blacks in whose hands . . . the military government of St. Domingue found itself, such are those negroes accused of being ignorant and gross; undoubtedly they are, because without education there can only be ignorance and grossness. But must one impute to them the crime of this educational deficiency or, more correctly, accuse those who prevented them by the most atrocious punishments from obtaining it? And are only civilized people capable of distinguishing between good and evil, of having notions of charity and justice? The men of St. Domingue have been deprived of an education; but even so, they no longer remain in a state of nature, and because they haven't arrived at the degree of perfection that education bestows, they do not merit being classed apart from the rest of mankind, being confused with animals. . . .

Undoubtedly, one can reproach the inhabitants of St. Domingue, including the blacks, for many faults, even terrible crimes. But even in France, where the limits of sociability are clearly drawn, doesn't one see its inhabitants, in the struggle between

---

*In 1796, a group of civil commissioners arrived from France, instructed by the Directory to ascertain the situation and to begin to reestablish full French authority over the island. By this time, Toussaint had privately come to the conclusion that the liberty of blacks could be guaranteed only under an independent black government.

†Refers to an attempted coup in 1796 by the mulattos against French Governor Laveaux. The plotters were thwarted by Toussaint and his army, and a grateful (and militarily weak) Governor Laveaux rewarded Toussaint by naming him lieutenant governor.

190   CHAPTER 6 ◆ Liberty and Revolution in the Atlantic World, 1776–1850

despotism and liberty, going to all the excesses for which the blacks are reproached by their enemies? The fury of the two parties has been equal in St. Domingue; and if the excesses of the blacks in these critical moments haven't exceeded those committed in Europe, must not an impartial judge pronounce in favor of the former? Since it is our enemies themselves who present us as ignorant and gross, aren't we more excusable than those who, unlike us, were not deprived of the advantages of education and civilization?

Forced Labor Decree, 12 October 1800

Citizens,

After putting an end to the war in the South, our first duty has been to return thanks to the Almighty; which we have done with the zeal becoming so great a blessing: Now, Citizens, it is necessary to consecrate all our moments to the prosperity of St. Domingo, to the public tranquility, and consequently, to the welfare of our fellow citizens.

But, to attain this end in an effectual manner, all the civil and military officers must make it their business, everyone in their respective department, to perform the duties of their offices with devotion and attachment to the public welfare.

You will easily conceive, Citizens, that Agriculture is the support of Government; since it is the foundation of Commerce and Wealth, the source of Arts and Industry, it keeps everybody employed, as being the mechanism of all Trades. And, from the moment that every individual becomes useful, it creates public tranquility; disturbances disappear together with idleness, by which they are commonly generated, and everyone peaceably enjoys the fruits of his industry. Officers civil and military, this is what you must aim at; such is the plan to be adopted, which I prescribe to you; and I declare in the most peremptory manner, that it shall be enforced: My country demands this salutary step; I am bound to it by my office, and the security of our liberties demands it imperiously. But in order to secure our liberties, which are indispensable to our happiness, every individual must be usefully employed, so as to contribute to the public good, and the general tranquility.

Considering that the soldier, who has sacred duties to perform, as being the safeguard of the people . . . is strictly subordinate to his superior officers: It is of great importance that overseers, drivers and field-negroes, who in like manner have their superiors, should conduct themselves as officers . . . and soldiers in whatever may concern them.

Considering that when an officer . . . or a soldier deviates from his duty he is delivered over to a court-martial to be tried and punished according to the laws of the Republic, for in military service no rank is to be favoured when guilty: The overseers, drivers and field-negroes, as subject to constant labour, and equally subordinate to their superiors, shall be punished in like manner, in case of failure in their respective duties.

Whereas a soldier cannot leave his company, his battalion, or half-brigade, and enter into another, without the severest punishment, unless provided with a commission in due form from his Chief; field-negroes are forbidden to quit their respective plantations without a lawful permission. This is by no means attended to, since they change their place of labour as they please, go to and fro, and pay not the least attention to agriculture, though the only means of furnishing sustenance to the military,

Toussaint L'Ouverture ✦ Speeches and Letters on the Haitian Revolution (1793–1800)   191

their protectors. They even conceal themselves in towns, in villages, and mountains, where . . . they live by plunder, and in a state of open hostility to society. . . .

The Liberator of South America, 1815

Simón Bolívar (1783–1830), known as "the Liberator" of South America from Spanish colonial rule, hardly fits the stereotypical image of a revolutionary. Born to an aristocratic Venezuelan Creole family that owned plantations worked by slave labor, Bolívar seemed destined for a life of wealth and privilege. But after he was orphaned at the age of nine, he was raised and educated by private tutors who inspired in him an admiration for the ideals of the Enlightenment. After a period of study in Europe during the height of Napoleon's career, he returned to South America at the age of twenty-four committed to the cause of independence. Venezuela was already in ferment, and when the colony declared its independence from Spanish rule in 1811, Bolívar joined the army of the young republic and soon gained command. After several years of inconclusive military victories and defeats in Venezuela and elsewhere, Bolívar launched a brilliant surprise attack across the Andes that defeated the Spanish in Colombia. Thereafter, Bolívar's forces gained unstoppable momentum and successively liberated Venezuela (1821), Ecuador (1822), Peru (1824), and Bolívia (1825), the latter named in his honor. Following the wars of independence, Bolívar played a pivotal role in the formation of new republican governments, and he dreamed of creating a league of Hispanic American states that would unite much of South America. But both tasks were undermined by regional disputes and factional infighting, and several new republics fell into civil war. In his effort to maintain the unity of Gran Colombia (comprising the modern nations of Colombia, Venezuela, and Ecuador), Bolívar assumed dictatorial powers in 1828 but was unable to prevent the secession of Venezuela a year later. Feeling embittered and betrayed by self-serving political opportunists posing as liberal reformers, Bolívar retired from public life in 1829, and he died of tuberculosis the following year.

"The Jamaican Letter" (1815) is one of Bolívar's earliest and most important political essays on the course of South American independence. It was written during his self-imposed exile on Jamaica (then a British colony) after a major military defeat in Venezuela. Historians are uncertain to whom the letter was addressed, but they speculate that the recipient was the English governor of the island. The letter affirms Bolívar's unfailing dedication to the cause of independence and the ideals of liberty and freedom. But in his ruminations on the future, Bolívar also reveals his antiliberal, authoritarian leanings. Believing that the masses lacked the experience and "virtue" for a democracy, Bolívar advocated an oligarchic government with power concentrated in the hands of a strong, paternal executive and a hereditary legislature. His political philosophy is an interesting mixture of liberal and authoritarian ideas, and it is still frequently reflected in current political debate in much of South America. As you read the following letter, also keep in mind how Bolívar's ideas compare with those of Madison and Robespierre.

QUESTIONS TO CONSIDER

1. According to Bolívar, what are the unique challenges of ethnicity and identity faced by the leaders of the revolution? How does this affect his political ideas? What role does he envision for indigenous Indians and imported black slaves in the new nations?

2. Bolívar laments the fact that Spanish America was denied "active and effective tyranny." What does he mean by this? Why does he think it is significant?

3. According to Bolívar, what stands in the way of liberal and republican governments? Why can't South America follow the model of the United States? What kind of governmental system does Bolívar favor?

4. Some historians claim that Bolívar's political philosophy was based on liberal principles tempered by a realistic assessment of the current situation. Others claim that his authoritarianism stems from a deep distrust of the masses. In your view, which assessment is more correct?

5. How might future leaders in South America use Bolívar's letter to press for more liberal reforms? How might others use his writing to justify the curtailment of freedoms?

"THE JAMAICAN LETTER" (1815)

Simón Bolívar

Kingston, Jamaica, September 6 1815

My dear Sir . . .

With what a feeling of gratitude I read that passage in your letter in which you say to me: "I hope that the success which then followed Spanish arms may now turn in favor of their adversaries, the badly oppressed people of South America." I take this hope as a prediction, if it is justice that determines man's contests. Success will crown our efforts, because the destiny of America has been irrevocably decided; the tie that bound her to Spain has been severed. . . . At present . . . we are threatened with the fear of death, dishonor, and every harm; there is nothing we have not suffered at the hands of that unnatural stepmother—Spain. The veil has been torn asunder. We have already seen the light, and it is not our desire to be thrust back into darkness. The chains have been broken; we have been freed, and now our enemies seek to enslave us anew. For this reason America fights desperately, and seldom has desperation failed to achieve victory. . . .

Source: Simón Bolívar, "Reply of a South American to a Gentleman of this Island [Jamaica]," in *Selected Writings of Bolívar, Vol. 1 (1810–1822)*, ed. Harold Bierck; compiled by Vincente Lecuna; transl. Lewis Bertrand (New York: Colonial Press, 1951), 103–22.

Simón Bolívar ◆ "The Jamaican Letter" (1815)   193

It is even more difficult to foresee the future fate of the New World, to set down its political principles, or to prophesy what manner of government it will adopt. . . . We are young in the ways of almost all the arts and sciences, although, in a certain manner, we are old in the ways of civilized society. I look upon the present state of America as similar to that of Rome after its fall. Each part of Rome adopted a political system conforming to its interest and situation or was led by the individual ambitions of certain chiefs, dynasties, or associations. But this important difference exists: those dispersed parts later reestablished their ancient nations, subject to the changes imposed by circumstances or events. But we scarcely retain a vestige of what once was; we are, moreover, neither Indian nor European, but a species midway between the legitimate proprietors of this country and the Spanish usurpers. In short, though Americans by birth we derive our rights from Europe, and we have to assert these rights against the rights of the natives, and at the same time we must defend ourselves against the invaders. This places us in a most extraordinary and involved situation. Notwithstanding that it is a type of divination to predict the result of the political course which America is pursuing, I shall venture some conjectures which, of course, are colored by my enthusiasm and dictated by rational desires rather than by reasoned calculations.

The role of the inhabitants of the American hemisphere has for centuries been purely passive. Politically they were nonexistent. We are still in a position lower than slavery, and therefore it is more difficult for us to rise to the enjoyment of freedom. Permit me these transgressions in order to establish the issue. States are slaves because of either the nature or the misuse of their constitutions; a people is therefore enslaved when the government, by its nature or its vices, infringes on and usurps the rights of the citizen or subject. Applying these principles, we find that America was denied not only its freedom but even an active and effective tyranny. . . .

We have been harassed by a conduct which has not only deprived us of our rights but has kept us in a sort of permanent infancy with regard to public affairs. If we could at least have managed our domestic affairs and our internal administration, we could have acquainted ourselves with the processes and mechanics of public affairs. We should also have enjoyed a personal consideration, thereby commanding a certain unconscious respect from the people, which is so necessary to preserve amidst revolutions. That is why I say we have even been deprived of an active tyranny, since we have not been permitted to exercise its functions. . . .

The Americans have risen rapidly without previous knowledge of, and, what is more regrettable, without previous experience in public affairs, to enact upon the world stage the eminent roles of legislator, magistrate, minister of the treasury, diplomat, general, and every position of authority, supreme or subordinate, that comprises the hierarchy of a fully organized state. . . .

. . . Uncertain of our destiny, and facing anarchy for want of a legitimate, just, and liberal government, we threw ourselves headlong into the chaos of revolution. Attention was first given to obtaining domestic security against enemies within our midst, and then it was extended to the procuring of external security. Authorities were set up to replace those we had deposed, empowered to direct the course of our revolution and to take full advantage of the fortunate turn of events; thus we were able to found a constitutional government worthy of our century and adequate to our situation.

194   CHAPTER 6   ◆   Liberty and Revolution in the Atlantic World, 1776–1850

The first steps of all the new governments are marked by the establishment of *juntas** of the people. These *juntas* speedily draft rules for the calling of congresses, which produce great changes. Venezuela erected a democratic and federal government, after declaring for the rights of man. A system of checks and balances was established, and general laws were passed granting civil liberties, such as freedom of the press and others. In short, an independent government was created. New Granada uniformly followed the political institutions and reforms introduced by Venezuela, taking as the fundamental basis of her constitution the most elaborate federal system ever to be brought into existence. Recently the powers of the chief executive have been increased, and he has been given all the powers that are properly his. . . .

[However] events in Costa Firme [Venezuela] have proved that institutions which are wholly representative are not suited to our character, customs, and present knowledge. In Caracas [Venezuela], party spirit arose in the societies, assemblies, and popular elections; these parties led us back into slavery.[†] Thus, while Venezuela has been the American republic with the most advanced political institutions, she has also been the clearest example of the inefficacy of the democratic and federal system for our new-born states. In New Granada, the large number of excess powers held by the provincial governments and the lack of centralization in the general government have reduced that fair country to her present state. For this reason her foes, though weak, have been able to hold out against all odds. As long as our countrymen do not acquire the abilities and political virtues that distinguish our brothers of the north [the United States], wholly popular systems, far from working to our advantage, will, I greatly fear, bring about our downfall. Unfortunately, these traits, to the degree in which they are required, do not appear to be within our reach. On the contrary, we are dominated by the vices that one learns under the rule of a nation like Spain, which has only distinguished itself in ferocity, ambition, vindictiveness, and greed.

It is harder, Montesquieu[‡] has written, to release a nation from servitude than to enslave a free nation. This truth is proven by the annals of all times, which reveal that most free nations have been put under the yoke, but very few enslaved nations have recovered their liberty. Despite the convictions of history, South Americans have made efforts to obtain liberal, even perfect, institutions, doubtless out of that instinct to aspire to the greatest possible happiness, which, common to all men, is bound to follow in civil societies founded on the principles of justice, liberty, and equality. But are we capable of maintaining in proper balance the difficult charge of a republic? Is it conceivable that a newly emancipated people can soar to the heights of liberty, and, unlike Icarus, neither have its wings melt nor fall into an abyss? Such a marvel is inconceivable and without precedent. There is no reasonable probability to bolster our hopes. . . .

Among the popular and representative systems, I do not favor the federal system. It is over-perfect, and it demands political virtues and talents far superior to our own. For the same reason I reject a monarchy that is part aristocracy and part democracy, although with such a government England has achieved much fortune and splendor.

---

*A group or committee that takes governmental power, often in the aftermath of a revolution.

[†]Bolívar refers to an incident in 1811, when treasonable action by a local faction opened the fortress at Caracas to Spanish forces.

[‡]The baron de Montesquieu (1689–1755) was a prominent political philosopher of the Enlightenment.

Simón Bolívar ◆ "The Jamaican Letter" (1815)   **195**

Since it is not possible for us to select the most perfect and complete form of government, let us avoid falling into demagogic anarchy or monocratic tyranny. These opposite extremes would only wreck us on similar reefs of misfortune and dishonor; hence, we must seek a mean between them. I say: Do not adopt the best system of government, but the one that is most likely to succeed.

By the nature of their geographic location, wealth, population, and character, I expect that the Mexicans, at the outset, intend to establish a representative republic in which the executive will have great powers. These will be concentrated in one person, who, if he discharges his duties with wisdom and justice, should almost certainly maintain his authority for life. . . .

New Granada will unite with Venezuela, if they can agree to the establishment of a central republic. . . . The Indians living there can be civilized, and our territorial possessions could be increased. . . . This nation should be called Colombia as a just and grateful tribute to the discoverer of our hemisphere. Its government might follow the English pattern, except that in place of a king there will be an executive who will be elected for life, but his office will never be hereditary, if a republic is desired. There will be a hereditary legislative chamber or senate. This body can interpose itself between the violent demands of the people and the great powers of the government during periods of political unrest. . . .

Surely unity is what we need to complete our work of regeneration. The division among us, nevertheless, is nothing extraordinary, for it is characteristic of civil wars to form two parties, conservatives and reformers. The former are commonly the more numerous, because the weight of habit induces obedience to established powers; the latter are always fewer in number although more vocal and learned. Thus, the physical mass of the one is counterbalanced by the moral force of the other; the contest is prolonged, and the results are uncertain. Fortunately, in our case, the mass has followed the learned.

I shall tell you with what we must provide ourselves in order to expel the Spaniards and to found a free government. It is *union,* obviously; but such union will come about through sensible planning and well-directed actions rather than by divine magic. America stands together because it is abandoned by all other nations. It is isolated in the center of the world. It has no diplomatic relations, nor does it receive any military assistance; instead, America is attacked by Spain, which has more military supplies than any we can possibly acquire through furtive means.

When success is not assured, when the state is weak, and when results are distantly seen, all men hesitate; opinion is divided, passions rage, and the enemy fans these passions in order to win an easy victory because of them. As soon as we are strong and under the guidance of a liberal nation which will lend us her protection, we will achieve accord in cultivating the virtues and talents that lead to glory. Then will we march majestically toward that great prosperity for which South America is destined. Then will those sciences and arts which, born in the East, have enlightened Europe, wing their way to a free Colombia, which will cordially bid them welcome.

I am, Sir, etc., etc.

Simón Bolívar

196   CHAPTER 6   ◆   Liberty and Revolution in the Atlantic World, 1776–1850

NOTES

1. Liberalism (derived from the Latin *liber,* or "free") has been defined in many different ways, and its meaning has changed over time. In its original, classic definition, it meant a political philosophy that favored the maximum individual freedom possible, the protection of political and civil liberties, and a limited government based on the consent of the people.

2. Historians also attribute the rise of liberal philosophy to changes associated with European economic expansion overseas and the pressures for reform that accompanied the widening of trade and increased prosperity. These changes and their impact are further discussed in chapter 7.

3. *The Federalist Papers* also contain essays written by Madison's key political allies, Alexander Hamilton and John Jay, both of New York. They were published between 1787 and 1788.

4. See chapter 3 for Jefferson's views on slavery.

5. Jefferson's bill provided for complete religious liberty and was one of the first of its kind in America.

6. As expressed in his *Notes on the State of Virginia* (see chapter 3), Jefferson agonized over the morality of slavery but was able to rationalize it on the basis of perceived racial differences. In his original draft of the Declaration of Independence, Jefferson included a clause that criticized Britain for introducing slavery to North America, but this was deleted by the Continental Congress prior to its adoption in 1776.

7. Some scholars contend that Madison and Hamilton employed the pseudonym *Publius* (Latin for "the public") to highlight their admiration for the Roman Republic.

8. When Lincoln was assassinated in 1865, Bancroft was chosen to write and deliver the official eulogy at the funeral.

9. The transcendental movement of the early nineteenth century was part of the larger Romantic movement in the United States, which, in turn, was a reaction against the impersonal and overly rational philosophy of the Enlightenment. As expressed by Emerson, all people could experience a higher morality and closer union with God through the love and contemplation of nature.

10. Douglass was born Frederick Augustus Washington Bailey, but adopted the surname "Douglass" to elude slave hunters.

11. The definition of "middle class" has changed considerably since the French Revolution. At that time, "middle class" generally designated a career choice, either in commercial activities (from banker to shopkeeper) or in professional trades (lawyers, doctors, etc.).

CPSIA information can be obtained
at www.ICGtesting.com
Printed in the USA
FFOW01n1841310815
16371FF

* M G H 0 0 0 0 0 5 3 1 0 1 *